D1569594

Proclaim Liberty Throughout the Land
The Hebrew Bible in the United States:
A Sourcebook

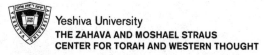

Yeshiva University
THE ZAHAVA AND MOSHAEL STRAUS
CENTER FOR TORAH AND WESTERN THOUGHT

PROCLAIM LIBERTY
THROUGHOUT THE LAND
★ ★ ★ ★ ★ ★ ★ ★ ★ ★ ★ ★ ★ ★
THE HEBREW BIBLE IN THE UNITED STATES:
A SOURCEBOOK

Editors

Meir Y. Soloveichik
Matthew Holbreich
Jonathan Silver
Stuart W. Halpern

Straus Center for Torah and Western Thought
The Toby Press

Proclaim Liberty Throughout the Land
The Hebrew Bible in the United States: A Sourcebook

First Edition, 2019

The Toby Press LLC
POB 8531, New Milford, CT 06776–8531, USA
& POB 2455, London W1A 5WY, England
www.tobypress.com

Cover images: iStock.com/kreicher
iStock.com/juliaf

ISBN 978-1-59264-465-0, *hardcover*

A cip catalogue record for this title is available from the British Library

Printed and bound in the United States

To Rob and Ellen Kapito,
lovers of American Jewish history and devoted friends of
the Zahava and Moshael Straus Center
for Torah and Western Thought
of Yeshiva University,
with profound gratitude

"We Americans are driven to a rejection of the maxims of the past, seeing that, ere long, the van of nations must, of right, belong to ourselves…. Escaped from the house of bondage, Israel of old did not follow after the ways of the Egyptians. To her was given an express dispensation; to her were given new things under the sun. And we Americans are the peculiar, chosen people – the Israel of our time; we bear the ark of the liberties of the world."

Herman Melville, *White Jacket, or, The World in a Man-of-War* (1850)

"Proclaim liberty throughout the land and to all the inhabitants thereof."

Leviticus 25:10

Contents

PART TWO: REVOLUTIONARY AMERICA

PART FOUR: SLAVERY, ABOLITIONISM,
AND THE CIVIL WAR

Preface

Ift was on the immortal date of July 4, 1776, that the Continental
Congress voted not only to declare independence, but also to create a
symbol of the nascent nation: "Resolved, That Dr. Franklin, Mr. J. Adams
and Mr. Jefferson, be a committee, to bring in a device for a seal for the
United States of America." Two members of the committee drew directly
on the Hebrew Bible in putting forward their proposals. Thomas Jefferson chose an image to which he would return in his second inaugural
address: "The Children of Israel in the Wilderness, led by a Cloud by
day, and Pillar of Fire by night." Benjamin Franklin's proposal was even
more striking: Moses at the Red Sea raising his staff, "thereby causing
the same to overwhelm Pharaoh who is sitting in an open Chariot, a
Crown on his Head and a Sword in Hand. Rays from a Pillar of Fire in
the Clouds reaching to Moses, to express that he acts by Command of
the Deity." Franklin further suggested that this picture be joined with
the following motto: "Rebellion to Tyrants is obedience to God." That
these scenes from the book of Exodus loomed so large even in the minds
of the men who were the most secular of the American founders is the
ultimate indication that the imagery of the Hebrew Bible so dramatically
impacted the thinking and language of America's statesmen. The events

of July 4 testify not only to the miracle of the American founding, but also to the extraordinary impact that the Jews had on the development of the West.

It is for the study of this impact that I first proposed the founding of what became Yeshiva University's Straus Center for Torah and Western Thought. Months later, in a conversation about the mission of the Straus Center, Dr. Matthew Holbreich first made the brilliant suggestion that the Straus Center produce a volume illustrating how the Bible inspired some of the most important documents in the history of the United States. Dr. Holbreich and our colleague Dr. Jonathan Silver deserve the lion's share of the credit for this volume, as it is they who tirelessly shepherded this project from its infancy to its glorious conclusion. I express my thanks as well as to Dr. Stuart W. Halpern, who has been so integral to all that takes place at the Straus Center, including the production of this book. Dr. Yael Hungerford, Rabbi Daniel Tabak, and Moshe Halbertal each read the manuscript with great care and attention, and it is was much improved by their comments and suggestions. As always, I express profound gratitude to Zahava and Moshael Straus, our partners in every single success achieved by the Straus Center. I also thank our partners at The Toby Press, especially Matthew Miller, Reuven Ziegler, Ita Olesker, Tomi Mager, and Tani Bayer.

Eight decades after America's founding, with the United States on the brink of war, Abraham Lincoln visited Independence Hall in Philadelphia before his inauguration. In emphasizing the sanctity of America's founding principles, Lincoln turned to the imagery and language of the Hebrew Bible. "All my political warfare," Lincoln said, "has been in favor of the teachings that come forth from these sacred walls. May my right hand forget its cunning, and my tongue cleave to the roof of my mouth, if ever I prove false to these teachings" (cf. Ps. 137:5–6). We offer this book as testimony to the Hebraic roots of the American founding, so that loyalty to its principles may be inspired for generations to come.

Meir Y. Soloveichik

Introduction

On August 10, 1774, John Adams left Boston dressed in a new red coat, in full view of the British, on his way to Philadelphia for the First Continental Congress.[1] In response to the Boston Tea Party, the British Parliament had passed the Coercive Acts, stripping Massachusetts of its ability to govern itself. With Massachusetts in near open revolt, the colonies called a Continental Congress to discuss a coordinated response. Along the post road from Boston to Philadelphia, the Massachusetts delegates were celebrated, church bells rang, and prayers were offered. Congress convened. At the opening, the delegates wondered whether a prayer should be said, and if so, by which Protestant denomination's minister. The room was filled with Quakers and Presbyterians and Anabaptists and Congregationalists. Would not a prayer be inherently sectarian, dividing the delegates before they were ever united? The great revolutionary Samuel Adams rose and said that he would hear a prayer from any

---

1. See the account of this episode in David McCullough, *John Adams* (New York: Simon and Schuster, 2002), 41.

pious man, as he was no bigot. The next day Reverend Jacob Duché read Psalm 35, which begins:

> Plead my cause, O Lord, with those who strive with me;
> Fight against those who fight against me.
> Take hold of shield and buckler,
> ·And stand up for my help.
> Also draw out the spear,
> And stop those who pursue me.
> Say to my soul,
> I am your salvation.

The American Republic was born to the music of the Hebrew Bible. The men of the First Continental Congress, despite their religious diversity, were united by a shared heritage rooted in the text of the Hebrew Bible, stretching back to their Puritan forefathers who founded the Bay Colony more than one hundred years earlier. John Adams, who recorded that significant moment of American history, thought the Bible "the best book in the world."[2]

Turning to the Hebrew Bible for inspiration, solidarity, comfort, and purpose, as the men of the First Continental Congress did, is a common theme in American history. Three years later, when Benjamin Franklin, Thomas Jefferson, and John Adams were asked to design the new great seal of the United States, both Franklin and Jefferson chose a theme from Exodus. For both, the Israelites coming out of Egyptian bondage would be the emblem of the new country's freedom. The Israelites' story was the American story. The Bible, and especially the Hebrew Bible, was the single most cited book during the Revolutionary era – more than the French political philosopher Montesquieu and the Roman statesmen Cato and Plutarch.[3]

---

2. Adams to Jefferson, Dec. 25, 1813. L. J. Capon, ed., *The Adams-Jefferson Letters* (Chapel Hill: University of North Carolina Press, 1959), 2:412.
3. Donald Lutz, "The Relative Influence of European Writers on Late Eighteenth-Century American Political Thought," *American Political Science Review* 78 (1984): 189–97.

In nineteenth-century America, clubs existed whose sole purpose was to put a Bible into the hands of every American.[4] During the last few months of the Civil War, Lincoln turned to the Hebrew Bible for inspiration when writing his second inaugural address. Two hundred and sixteen years after that prayer in the Continental Congress, President Bill Clinton gave voice to his vision of a revitalized United States with the hope of establishing a "New Covenant," the Hebraic term for a binding compact across generations.[5] From the Puritan fathers to the American Framers, from slavery to abolition, from the Liberty Bell to America's celebration of national Thanksgiving, the Hebrew Bible is one of America's formative books, reflecting in the new continent, in the new nation, in America's rebirth of freedom, the moral and narrative inspiration of ancient Israel.

The premise of this reader is that the Hebrew Bible is a foundational text in the American tradition. Its influence exists alongside *Cato's Letters*, the philosophy of John Locke, and Plutarch's exemplars of civic leadership and moral purpose.[6] It is a foundational text in the American literary canon. One cannot understand the American political tradition and its articulations through time without understanding America's relationship with the Hebrew Bible. This sourcebook contributes to such an understanding. Its purpose is to assemble the primary sources of American public history and allow the reader to hear the Hebraic echoes that have been particularly influential.

We employ the term "Hebraic" to describe the influence of the Hebrew Bible as opposed to the New Testament. The "Hebrew Bible" refers to the Pentateuch, the Prophets, and the Writings. This anthology is the story of the Jewish Bible, or the Christian Old Testament, and its

4. Mark A. Noll, "The United States as a Biblical Nation," *The Bible in America: Essays in Cultural History*, eds. Nathan O. Hatch and Mark A. Noll (Oxford: Oxford University Press, 1982), 40.
5. Clinton used the term in a series of speeches at Georgetown University at the start of his campaign for president and in his acceptance speech to the Democratic National Convention in 1992.
6. See Wilson Carey McWilliams, "The Bible in the American Political Tradition," in *Redeeming Democracy in America*, ed. Patrick Deneen (Lawrence: University Press of Kansas, 2011), 29–54.

power in American history. It is not a volume about the Jewish experience in America. For most of American history there were few Jews in America. Moreover, Jewish thought encompasses a wider spectrum, that while rooted in the Hebrew Bible, extends outward into talmudic debates, legal norms, philosophy, poetry, and the history and culture of the Jewish people. Much of Jewish thought is dedicated to religious jurisprudence and is framed by the religious debates of the Talmud. For the most part, the mainstream of the American public had little access to, and little interest in, post-biblical Jewish thought. The traditional American passion for the Hebrew Bible is distinct from the Jewish religion and the history of Jewish law and letters. We therefore also use the term "Hebraic" to crystallize the distinction between the Hebrew Bible and Jewish thought and history.

We further use "Hebraic" to distinguish the subject of this volume from Christianity. The use of the Hebrew Bible in America is bound up with Christian theology and doctrine, more so than with Judaism, especially in the early Puritan colonies and during the religious awakenings of the nineteenth century. But the metaphors, images, and narrative arcs that Americans have taken from the Hebrew Bible to describe their own experience are distinct from, and cannot be fully encompassed or captured by, Christian theology.

The influence of the Hebrew Bible can be understood in at least four ways.

First, the Hebrew Bible is a source for, and an element of, collective identity and self-identification. One way to gain access to how people think about themselves is to notice the names they give to places that surround them, to cities and rivers and valleys and colleges. The American countryside is filled with names of biblical places such as "Zion," "Canaan," "Shiloh," and "Salem."[7] Many American colleges, such as Yale and Dartmouth, were founded as seminaries with broader purposes, and chose Hebrew mottos to encapsulate their mission. Harvard College required its students to study Hebrew. As late as 1817 orations at Harvard were occasionally delivered in Hebrew.

---

7. Robert Alter, *Pen of Iron: American Prose and the King James Bible* (Princeton: Princeton University Press, 2010), prelude.

Political assemblies in America often open with prayers, and on great national occasions, presidents often turn to the Bible as America's unifying text. The national government has declared days of thanksgiving and repentance. When Revolutionary pastors read of the Persian court in the book of Esther they thought of Britain; when they preached about the depredations of British tyranny, they explained themselves in the language of Ahasuerus and Haman.[8] When Thomas Paine wanted to make a case to the colonies that monarchy was a primitive, outdated, and illegitimate form of government, he cited the book of Samuel. Washington was compared to Moses and to Gideon.[9] When Washington died, most houses of religious worship eulogized him with words from the Hebrew Bible.

From the colonial period to the Civil Rights movement, ministers and preachers were some of the most important figures in American political life, and Hebraic themes were brought into public discourse through them. During the Revolutionary War, biblical themes were used to cast aspersions on perceived enemies. Colonists who were not quick enough to come to the aid of their brethren were said to have suffered from the curse of Meroz (see Judg. 5:23).[10] Later, some of the largest reform movements in American history, including the movement for prohibition, took their inspiration from religious movements that were themselves but applications and interpretations of the Hebrew Bible. Its story has reflected Americans to themselves and endowed the people of the United States with an identity set apart from that of the other nations.

Second, the Hebrew Bible has been a source of political and cultural vocabulary. That is, the Hebrew Bible provided a series of narratives and themes that were powerful in the minds of the Puritan settlers, revolutionaries, African slaves, leaders of the Civil Rights movement, and the broader population.[11] To notice this is to already see that the

---

8. Eran Shalev, *American Zion: The Old Testament as Political Text from the Revolution to the Civil War* (New Haven: Yale University Press, 2014), 26–28.

9. See Timothy Dwight, *The Conquest of Canaan* (Hartford: Elisha Babcock, 1785).

10. For more on the curse of Meroz, see Noll, "United States," 42, and Shalev, 34–38.

11. Noll, "United States," commenting on this phenomenon, notes that "much more frequently, however, the Bible was not so much the truth above all truth as it was the story above all stories. On public occasions Scripture appeared regularly as the

Hebrew Bible is not just a source of private contemplation. It is a public book that has been felt in public debates and public social movements. The biblical vocabulary has taught Americans to speak and think about chosenness, exodus, and covenant. For Americans the Bible is, as Mark Noll puts it, "the story of all stories," containing a "storehouse of types" that they have grafted onto their collective life.[12] These big ideas have had different uses and have held different meanings, expressing aspiration and aspersion, collective longing and individual disappointment. But regardless of the sentiments expressed or the hopes shared, it was biblical vocabulary that Americans have been impelled to use.

These narrative themes are perhaps the most powerful and enduring cultural resonances of the Hebrew Bible in America. It is worth going through each briefly. "Chosenness" is the idea that God selected a people for a special mission to advance His ultimate plan. The Protestant Reformation and Calvinism placed "election," another word for chosenness, at the center of Protestant theology, which migrated north to Amsterdam and west to the New World.[13] The Puritan settlers conceived of themselves as a "New Israel," chosen by God to plant a vine in the wilderness; the Mormons, on their long march to the West, also thought they were a latter-day chosen people heading toward a new Zion; and the United States as a whole saw itself as a chosen nation.

Chosenness is not a singular concept. Rather, it oscillates in American history between two different modes. On the one hand the rhetoric of chosenness sanctifies the present, providing it with divine sanction. This variation allies with a form of American nationalism in which the current national form and its current projects are identified with God's ultimate plan. Josiah Strong's writings on Manifest Destiny exemplify this nationalist triumphalism. The notion of "the chosen nation" is also, on the other hand, a way to critique the present generation for not living up to the divine mission for which they were elected.

typical narrative imparting significance to the antitypical events, people, and situations of United States history" (43).

12. Noll, "United States," 43.
13. Gordon Schochet, "Introduction: Hebraic Roots, Calvinist Plantings, American Branches," *Hebraic Political Studies* 4:2 (Spring 2009): 99–103.

This latter interpretation divorces or puts distance between any given national project and divine intent.

These divergent postures prompt two different cultural moods: one of triumphalism and one of aspirationalism. Each cultural mood has its own specific form of rhetoric. In the case of triumphalism there is bombast, a feature that is readily seen when the United States interpreted chosenness as a justification of imperialism. The other rhetorical mood associated with aspirational critique tends toward the form of the jeremiad. The jeremiad is a rhetorical critique rooted in a shared aspiration to achieve a common goal that the community has failed to attain. It chastens the community for its failures, reminds them that divine judgment will be visited upon the people for failing to live up to their covenantal promise, and recalls their purpose to them, giving them renewed confidence that redemption is possible through rededication and sacrifice.[14] The jeremiad is the form of rhetoric adopted by Jonathan Edwards and by Abraham Lincoln in his second inaugural address, for example.

The narrative of Exodus is another central element of the American political vocabulary. The book of Exodus recounts the journey of the Hebrew people into Egyptian bondage and their miraculous liberation from it. The American people have used the Exodus narrative in identifying tyranny, expressing the longing for freedom, and describing the journey out of enslavement and the jubilation of liberation. To the Puritans, England was Egypt, the house of bondage, and their voyage across the Atlantic was their exodus, their parting of the seas. For the enslaved population, the North was Zion, and their songs and hymns reverberated with some of the greatest melodies of collective longings for freedom in the American tradition, with such songs as "Go Down Moses" and "Didn't Ol' Pharaoh Get Lost." Washington and Lincoln were both called Moses. In fact, Washington was compared to Jacob

---

14. Andrew Murphy, *Prodigal Nation* (Oxford: Oxford University Press, 2009). See also idem, "New Israel in New England: The American Jeremiad and the Hebrew Scriptures," *Hebraic Political Studies* 4:2 (Spring 2009): 128–56.

and Joshua, Samuel and Elijah, David and Daniel.[15] Finally, to speak of Exodus is also to speak of Egypt, of Pharaoh, of plagues, and of judgment. It was used to brand the English and the Southern slave owners as the tyrants who would meet with divine wrath. Lincoln, perhaps the single greatest employer of Hebraic tropes in American history, warned that if America became Egypt and did not redeem itself, it would meet with the same fate.

Another element in the American Hebraic vocabulary is "covenant." A covenant is different from a contract. A contract entails rights of voluntary exit and is premised on the joining together for mutual self-interest. A covenant, on the other hand, is an intergenerational commitment to a higher cause that transcends the individual and to which the individual dedicates himself. Both are very much present in the American tradition. The Declaration of Independence is an example. It is on the one hand an expression of classic liberal Enlightenment social contract theory. The individual, who is morally prior to the state and who is endowed with natural rights, voluntarily circumscribes his natural rights to enter into a mutually convenient compact with others to form a limited government. When government is destructive of those rights, then the people can form a new government based on new principles. But conjoined with the contractarianism of the Declaration are the mutual pledges of the delegates, as representatives of the people of the colonies, of their lives, property, and sacred honor, for the cause that temporally transcends their lives, property, and sacred honor. This mutual binding that combines contract and covenant also characterizes the Mayflower Compact. A contract is not automatically self-enforcing; it requires sacrifice and dedication, the words that resonate most strongly in Abraham Lincoln's Gettysburg Address.

A third way that the Hebrew Bible has influenced American public life is seen by looking at rhetorical tools employed in cultural and political debates. Beyond providing a common language in which debates could be expressed, key Hebraic references became actual authorities,

---

15. Noll, "United States," 44. See also Michael Walzer, *Exodus and Revolution* (New York: Basic Books, 1986).

on whose merit audiences were more likely to be persuaded. Thomas Paine's *Common Sense* is an example of relying on the Hebrew Bible as a source of rhetorical authority. Paine argues, based on the book of Samuel, that the Bible is anti-monarchical and thus provides a justification for a break with England. Whatever the intrinsic merits of the argument, Paine understood that appealing to the Bible as a source of authority would resonate with his biblically literate audience.

Moreover, because the Hebrew Bible has been a rhetorical authority, it is often found on multiple sides of American debates. The fact that orators and writers employed the Bible in polemics does not necessarily mar the book. Rather, it indicates just how exalted a status it had in American public life. An argument that was based on the Hebrew Bible, they believed, would confer unique authority on their views. So there have been arguments for both republicanism and monarchy, for and against revolution, and for and against the Articles of Confederation and the Constitution – all with the Hebrew Bible serving as a proof text. It was used to denounce slavery, and it was used to justify slavery. But both parties to a debate thought it necessary to demonstrate that the Hebrew Bible was on their side.

It is important to distinguish between the way the Americans used the Hebrew Bible in political debates and the Bible's own teaching about politics. Exploring the Hebraic teaching on politics (one should probably say biblical *teachings* in the plural) is a rich exegetical enterprise.[16] The Hebrew Bible is filled with stories that are open to multiple interpretations. There are stories of the founding of cities and of their destruction, the rise and fall of kings and of political institutions. The

---

16. For a larger discussion of the political teaching of the Hebrew Bible, see Michael Walzer, *Exodus and Revolution,* and idem, *In God's Shadow: Politics in the Hebrew Bible* (New Haven: Yale University Press, 2012); Yoram Hazony, *The Philosophy of Hebrew Scripture* (Cambridge: Cambridge University Press, 2012); Leon Kass, *The Beginning of Wisdom* (Chicago: University of Chicago Press, 2006); Daniel Elazar, *The Covenant Tradition in Politics,* 4 vols. (New Brunswick: Transaction Publishers, 1994–1998); Joshua Berman, *Created Equal: How the Bible Broke with Ancient Political Thought* (Oxford: Oxford University Press, 2011); and Eric Nelson, *The Hebrew Republic: Jewish Sources and The Transformation of European Political Thought* (Cambridge: Harvard University Press, 2011).

Hebrew Bible is a story of the creation of the universe, the origins of human society, the rise of a family into a clan and nation in exile, the return of the nation to its ancestral homeland, and its political and military rise and fall. The book of Samuel alone, for instance, offers a complex interplay of secular and divine power: the emergence of the political out of the shadow of divine exclusivity and the negotiation of the relationship of political to priestly power. The political lessons in the Bible are also tightly bound to the complex psychologies of individuals like Samuel, Saul, David, and Jonathan, which take on heightened importance in dynastic successions. One should resist the temptation to conclude that the Hebrew Bible has a single political teaching. One should also resist thinking that its teaching neatly overlaps with the commitments of our early Republic or the liberal democracy we have become. While Americans have often enlisted the Bible as proof and guarantor of their political views, the biblical text resists any single authoritative interpretation.

A fourth way that the Hebrew Bible has influenced America is through the powerful and eloquent language of the King James Bible. It influenced American novelists such as Nathaniel Hawthorne, Herman Melville, and William Faulkner, and statesmen like Presidents Lincoln, Theodore Roosevelt, and Woodrow Wilson. In fact, in the nineteenth century there was an entire genre of writing that mimicked the Bible.[17] The way a nation writes is the product of, and influences, the way a nation thinks about itself. Noted biblical scholar and translator Robert Alter remarked that "style is not merely a constellation of aesthetic properties but is the vehicle of a particular vision of reality."[18] To hear the resonant and powerful words of Lincoln's second inaugural address without reference to the moral world of the Hebrew Bible is to truncate the text and excise worlds of meaning.

The Hebraic worldview, which runs deeper than language and cultural conversation, articulates a vision of human life that is redemptive, endowed with sacred meaning, and which seeks to combine righteousness and freedom. It is this worldview that has contributed to the

17. Shalev, 1–14.
18. Alter, 4.

American moral language of liberty.[19] Throughout history, Americans saw their own lives through Hebraic stories and took moral meaning from their reenactment of biblical episodes. Puritans, American slaves, and Civil Rights leaders understood their suffering and struggle through a Hebraic lens. They believed their suffering had meaning in light of their final objectives, that their struggles were not their struggles alone but were part of a longer story stretching back to the enslavement and exodus from Egypt, and that their trials would not only redeem themselves but an entire nation. America is not a purely secular regime founded on purely secular principles.

As this anthology demonstrates, the influence of the Hebrew Bible is not uniform across American time and space. The early Puritan colonies were more devout than were those founded in Virginia, which were dedicated to more pecuniary speculation. There are periods in American history, such as those of the early Puritan colonies and the Great Awakenings, where fervor for the Bible was at a high pitch. And there are other points, especially in the late twentieth century, when large segments of the population did not see the Bible as a moral authority or its narrative as inspirational. Regions and subgroups in America differed in devotional intensity. The Bible of the slave taught freedom, the Bible of the slave master, obedience. Presidents, congressional orators, and American public figures also differ in their relation to the Bible. Some, like Washington, Adams, and Lincoln, incorporated Hebraic language to a far greater degree than did others, like Madison and Jefferson. The Hebrew Bible is a part of the American tapestry, though its color and place change over time.

While scholars of American political institutions disagree about the historical and intellectual inspirations that underpin America, this book shows that the Hebrew Bible has played an integral role in the American past, alongside Roman republicanism, the English Common Law tradition, and the political doctrines of John Locke, Cato, and Montesquieu. Some authors did turn to the *respublicum hebraeorum*

---

19. Shalev, 1–14. See also Michael Novak, *On Two Wings: Humble Faith and Common Sense at the American Founding* (New York: Encounter Books, 2003).

for a constitutional model for the new American regime.[20] And even if the institutions of the American government differ from those of the ancient Israelites, we should resist the temptation to fetishize political institutions and identify America with its government. Our political institutions give American politics their form, but they do not provide the essence. Republican government is designed for a free people – free in the classical understanding as capable of self-rule. A self-ruling citizenry requires a moral character, and for most of American history it was thought that moral character of any stripe would have to be inculcated, at least to some extent, by religious practice. That practice was not primarily to be the end of government, or at least the federal government. But just because there was to be no establishment of religion – that is, no national church – and a guarantee of the free exercise of religion, does not mean the founders or later statesmen thought religion unimportant. Moreover, some of the moral energy that prompts political reform and legal change in American history, especially in the nineteenth century, grew out of cultural practices in the bosom of American society that were influenced by religious revivals. America's grand social movements, from abolition to prohibition to Civil Rights, were infused with the urgency and passion of religious mission. That mission was one of freedom and renewal, and was expressed in what became the particularly American lexicon of promised lands, chosen peoples, exile and return to Zion, sin and redemption. Figures such as Abraham Lincoln and Martin Luther King Jr. employed these uniquely Hebraic tropes to express something deep in the American psyche, something that involves free and equal participation in public life, but goes much beyond it. If Thomas Jefferson could explain the Declaration of Independence as an expression of the common American mind,[21] President Lincoln and Reverend King gave voice to the common American heart.

We also believe the Hebrew Bible should remain an integral component of the American future. National continuity entails that change take place within the framework of a national tradition. That tradition

---

20. See Shalev, 50–82.
21. Letter from Thomas Jefferson to Henry Lee, May 8, 1825. Available at https://founders.archives.gov/documents/Jefferson/98-01-02-5212.

is, of course, flexible. America is a nation that cares about equality and freedom, for instance, but what equality and freedom mean may change over time. However, it is our commitment to those concepts that provides the framework in which debate and change can take place. So too the Hebrew Bible. It provides a part of the framework in which we understand and debate our national destiny, our place in world history, and our understanding of our own past. The American story integrates Hebraic insights, and this volume hopes to make it easier to uncover a fuller and more accurate version of the American past, and therewith, the American prospect.

Note on the Hebraic sources: Following many of the primary sources of American history, the relevant citations from the Hebrew Bible have been provided, along with the King James translation commonly used during that era. In some instances, additional verses have been added for further context. On occasion, rabbinic sources have been provided as well. Due to space considerations, not all biblical citations mentioned in the American sources are provided. When the American sources cite extensively from the Hebrew Bible, a separate biblical companion text is not provided, as additional context was not deemed necessary. When there is a discrepancy between the Jewish and Christian textual traditions, the Jewish chapter and verses are added in brackets. The reader is encouraged to study the wider context of the Hebraic works in their original language, or in translation, for enhanced understanding of the passages in which the citations originally appear, and for a fuller appreciation of how they are echoed in the American sources.

Part One

The Puritans to the Revolution

Introduction

The story of America begins long before the United States. Beginnings are always more than just beginnings. Their influence is always felt, more or less so, like tributaries flowing into the great body of a larger culture. The United States, declaring independence from its motherland in 1776 and gaining it in 1783, has in effect two distinct foundings and two sets of Founding Fathers. On the one hand there was Benjamin Franklin, George Washington, Thomas Jefferson, James Madison, and John Adams. But before them there was John Winthrop, Cotton Mather, and Jonathan Edwards. To understand their world, the culture of early America, one must plumb the recesses of an even earlier age: the Protestant Reformation and the political and theological reactions it provoked.

Gripped by an awareness of man's sinfulness and God's grace, leading reformation thinkers Martin Luther and John Calvin gave their followers a new theology and proposed new ways of life. Scripture taught them the importance of being vigilant against mankind's natural propensity to pride and sin. The depravities that lurk in man's soul could never be fully ameliorated, but reformed thinkers developed strategies to minimize the harm they might cause. The first strategy was to elaborate a theology that privileged the virtues of humility and self-government. For, if man can never fully rid himself of his sinfulness, then it should at least be muted. The second strategy was to remind adherents of the ancient truth of man's social nature. Human shortcomings show our limits, and our limits help us to see our dependence on one another. Through our dependence we come to develop feelings of attachment and loyalty. The community is stitched together, first by the necessities of individual insufficiency, then over time by fellowship and love.

The religious and social ideas of the reformers spawned a great war in England. Reformers sought to rid the Church of England of supposed Popist vanity and extravagance and reclaim what they thought was their faith's original and austere purity. A sect of the reformers in England were called the Puritans. They were literalists, believing that one should precisely follow biblical prescriptions. Persecuted, fearful for their communal safety, and eventually expelled from England, the Puritans fled first to Holland. They then decided to purchase land in the New World, to incorporate in a distant land where their religious life could flourish unmolested.

The Puritans thought about themselves in Hebraic terms. They understood their communal history as a reenactment of the biblical drama of slavery and persecution, followed by exodus and wandering, leading to covenant and redemption. To the Puritan mind, their collective similarity to the Israelites of antiquity was not a metaphor. It was an actual sign that they were furthering God's plan for the world just as God's earlier elect did so many years before. They saw that history is not a random succession of events. It has direction and divine purpose, and the Puritans, as the Israelites, were chosen to play a special role in that history.

Also like the ancient Israelites, the Puritans sealed their divine election with a covenant. Puritan covenanting predates the Lockean social contract that so powerfully inspired America's political founders. The difference between a "contract" and a "covenant" is subtle but profound. A social contract describes an arrangement in which members of society give away aspects of their freedom in order to gain something else for themselves. In a covenant, the two parties come together to achieve what neither can achieve alone, a destiny. In the words of H. Richard Niebuhr, a covenant is the "binding together in one body politic of persons who assume through unlimited promise responsibility to and for each other, and for the common laws, under God."[1] Notice how John Winthrop describes human relations in "A Model of Christian Charity," below. Is he describing a relationship based on interest or love? Is it more like a contract, or more like a covenant?

But if the Puritans were enthusiastic about the Hebrew Bible, even inspiring the rediscovery of the Hebrew language in early America (notice, for example, the insignia of Yale College), they were also conflicted. The reformed tradition appropriated much from the Hebrew Bible, though their own theological tradition was different from and at times forthrightly critical of it.

The story of the covenant, for example, is reinterpreted in Christian theology. In the Jewish theology of the Hebrew Bible, God chose the ancient Israelites and their descendants in a particularistic covenant. But in the Christian theology of the New Testament, God's national covenant is superseded by a universal one, signified in the world-historical meaning of Jesus. The Christian God teaches universal, not particular, love. Reformed Protestant theology expresses the expansion of God's love in three covenants: the covenant of works (with Adam, that obedience brings life and disobedience death), the covenant of redemption (that God would sacrifice Jesus, and by means of belief in him mankind would be redeemed), and the covenant of grace (that one is given eternal life and forgiveness of sin through belief in Jesus). The theological shift raises interesting questions of comparative theology: How do the three Puritan covenants relate to the Noachide, Abrahamic, Mosaic, and Davidic covenants? Are these covenants unconditional or conditional, universal or particular? How is covenant reconciled with predestination and grace, and is that a Hebraic theological problem or one that is specific to Calvinist theology? These difficult theological quandaries play themselves out in disagreements between Massachusetts religious leader Cotton Mather and Roger Williams, the founder of Rhode Island; and

---

1. See H. Richard Niebuhr, "The Idea of Covenant and American Democracy," *Church History* 23:2 (June 1954): 126–35. See also Jonathan Sacks, *The Home We Build Together* (New York and London: Bloomsbury Academic, 2009). On the Puritans' influence on American identity, see George McKenna, *The Puritan Origins of American Patriotism* (New Haven: Yale University Press, 2009).

between the Puritans and Anne Hutchinson, whom they exiled for her antinomian beliefs.

The Puritans and their distinctly Hebraic beliefs have remained in various ways and in varying magnitudes a part of American culture. Like the architects of many state constitutions and the American Constitution, the Puritans were strong believers in written documents that outlined the rights and responsibilities of individuals to each other. The most famous of these documents was the Mayflower Compact. More than a contract that outlines the rights of the counterparties, the document is a covenant that ties successive generations to a divine mission. Covenantal ideas are found in the Declaration of Independence and numerous inaugural addresses by American presidents. Connected to the Hebraic and Puritan idea that a community was shaped by the mold of its covenant, the Puritans also believed that they were like the ancient Israelites, chosen by God for a special destiny, an "errand into the wilderness," as they called it. This belief has morphed over time into what we now call American exceptionalism, or the idea that America has a special role to play in the world. The Puritans also had a strong commitment to participatory democracy and self-government, though it was, admittedly, in a limited sense. One could vote in public life only if one was a member of the Church, which had stringent membership requirements that included proving personal experience of God's grace. Nevertheless, their communal New England spirit was to inspire successive generations of democratic reformers.

There are, however, other elements of Puritan life that are no longer in sync with mainstream America. Religion for them encompassed all aspects of life. The law compelled all healthy-bodied people to attend church. The center of Puritan life was worship at weekly Church meetings where psalms were recited (not sung, for music was then thought a ritual of Catholic profanity), and the center of worship was the sermon. An average New Englander who lived a full life would hear over two thousand sermons, each sermon spanning two hours. The life of the average American today – even among religious Americans – rarely includes exposure to four thousand hours of preaching.

Despite the fact that we live in a world very different from that of the Puritans, their story has become part of American mythology.

Some of this mythology was self-created. Descendants of the Puritan founders knew their ancestors did something special and they wanted to tell their own version of it. That is not to say that their histories are not to be trusted – far from it. It is to say that we should pay special attention to how they told the stories of themselves. Notice, for instance, how Cotton Mather, below, tells the story of John Winthrop as a latter-day Moses. And notice also the difference between the way the Puritans thought of themselves and the way we think of the Puritans. Today, they are depicted in the American imagination as stern men, dressed in black, taciturn, religiously inspired, and bigoted perhaps, even to the point of being violent. The word "puritanical" came to signify "repressive." Just look at George Boughton's famous painting *Puritans Going to Church* (1867), depicting hardened men on a snowy winter's day, weapons in hand. That caricature has some truth, but it is of course not fully true. Inspired by the gravity of their mission, the Puritans were also a happy lot, rejoicing in the great grace of God, living a life free from foreign interference, with a magnificent awareness of their own destiny and significance. They saw their mission taking place in a world entirely new, ready to be remade by their hands. They thought they were living epic lives, fulfilling their destiny, founding something that would last unto the thirtieth generation – that they were men living in extraordinary times, doing extraordinary things.

MAYFLOWER COMPACT (1620)

There were 102 passengers aboard the Mayflower. *They were a motley crew. Only about half of them were the religious Protestant dissenters we now call the Pilgrims. The rest were tradesmen and workers. The* Mayflower's *arduous journey across the Atlantic took two months, as was told by William Bradford, a Pilgrim aboard and leader of the first colony. Bradford makes for good reading. Though they intended to sail for Virginia, the ship reached the New World around Cape Cod in winter. The journey to and settlement of the eastern seaboard was a dangerous, difficult undertaking. Half of the original settlers in Plymouth died in the first winter.*

Bradford's book is more than a tale of adventure. It is in his mind a sacred story, the recounting of an exodus. At the end of chapter 9, before the Pilgrims set foot ashore on November 11, Bradford offered a benediction of sorts: *"Our Fathers were Englishmen which came over this ocean, and were ready to perish in this wilderness; but they cried unto the Lord, and He heard their voice, and looked on their adversity, &c. Let them therefore praise the Lord, because He is good, and His mercies endure forever. Yea, let them which have been redeemed of the Lord, shew how He hath delivered them from the hand of the oppressor. When they wandered in the desert wilderness out of the way, and found no city to dwell in, both hungry and thirsty and their soul was overwhelmed in them. Let them confess before the Lord His loving kindness, and His wonderful works before the sons of men."*

Bradford then related the origins of the Mayflower Compact: *"I shall a little return back, and begin with a combination made by them before they came ashore; being the first foundation of their government in this place. Occasioned partly by the discontented and mutinous speeches that some of the strangers amongst them had let fall from them in the ship: That when they came ashore they would use their own liberty, for none had power to command them, the patent they had being for Virginia and not for New England, which belonged to another government, with which the Virginia Company had nothing to do. And partly that such an act by them done, this their condition considered, might be as firm as any patent and in some respects more sure."* The Mayflower Compact was thus intended to cure immediate legal problems as well as put an end to mutiny and dissent. But it turned into the first and singularly important "American" document.

Agreement between the Settlers at New Plymouth

IN THE NAME OF GOD, AMEN. We, whose names are underwritten, the Loyal Subjects of our dread Sovereign Lord King James, by the Grace of God, of Great Britain, France, and Ireland, King, Defender of the Faith, &c. Having undertaken for the Glory of God, and Advancement of the Christian Faith, and the Honour of our King and Country, a Voyage to plant the first Colony in the northern Parts of Virginia; Do by these Presents, solemnly and mutually, in the Presence of God and one another, covenant and combine ourselves together into a civil Body Politick, for our better Ordering and Preservation, and Furtherance of the Ends aforesaid: And by Virtue hereof do enact, constitute, and frame, such just and equal Laws, Ordinances, Acts, Constitutions, and Officers, from time to time, as shall be thought most meet and convenient for the general Good of the Colony; unto which we promise all due Submission and Obedience. IN WITNESS whereof we have hereunto subscribed our names at Cape-Cod the eleventh of November, in the Reign of our Sovereign Lord King James, of England, France, and Ireland, the eighteenth, and of Scotland the fifty-fourth, Anno Domini; 1620.

JOHN WINTHROP (1587–1649)

Although the early American population was small, its experiences were well-chronicled because of the prolific writing of a few early settlers and preachers. One of the more important among them was John Winthrop. Born in England in 1587 to a wealthy family, John Winthrop was educated at Trinity Council and became a lawyer. A devout man, Winthrop kept a journal in which he chronicled his inner life. His first wife died early and his second wife died in childbirth. He married for a third time in 1618. After the ascension of Charles I and the return of Catholicism to the throne, the Puritans were increasingly persecuted. The Pilgrims first settled in Plymouth in 1620. In 1628 a group of Puritans purchased a controlling interest in a trading company, set it up as a profit venture, and then reorganized it for colonization in the New World. Winthrop became involved in this later settlement attempt – what was to become the Massachusetts Bay Colony. In 1630, aboard the Arbella, Winthrop delivered the following speech, either during or right before the crossing.

A Model of Christian Charity (1630)

God almighty in His most holy and wise providence hath so disposed of the condition of mankind, as in all times some must be rich, some poor, some high and eminent in power and dignity, others mean and in subjection.

Reason: First, to hold conformity with the rest of His works, being delighted to show forth the glory of His wisdom in the variety and difference of the creatures and the glory of His power, in ordering all these differences for the preservation and good of the whole.

Reason: Secondly, that He might have the more occasion to manifest the work of His spirit. First, upon the wicked in moderating and restraining them, so that the rich and mighty should not eat up the poor, nor the poor and despised rise up against their superiors and shake off their yoke. Secondly, in the regenerate, in exercising His graces in them, as in the great ones, their love, mercy, gentleness, temperance, etc., in the poor and inferior sort, their faith, patience, obedience, etc.

Reason: Thirdly, that every man might have need of others, and from hence they might all be knit more nearly together in the bond of brotherly affection. From hence it appears plainly that no man is made more honorable than another, or more wealthy, etc., out of any particular and singular respect to himself, but for the glory of his Creator and the common good of the creature, man....

Thus stands the cause between God and us. We are entered into covenant with Him for this work, we have taken out a commission, the Lord hath given us leave to draw our own articles. We have professed to enterprise these actions upon these and these ends, we have hereupon besought Him of favor and blessing. Now if the Lord shall please to hear us, and bring us in peace to the place we desire, then hath He ratified this covenant and sealed our commission, [and] will expect a strict performance of the articles contained in it; but if we shall neglect the observations of these articles which are the ends we have propounded, and dissembling with our God, shall fall to embrace this present world and prosecute our carnal intentions, seeking great things for ourselves and our posterity, the Lord will surely break out in wrath against us, be revenged of such a perjured people, and make us know the price of the breach of such a covenant.

Now the only way to avoid this shipwreck and to provide for our posterity is to follow the counsel of Micah, to do justly, to love mercy, to walk humbly with our God. For this end we must be knit together in this work as one man, we must entertain each other in brotherly affection, we must be willing to abridge ourselves of our superfluities for the supply of others' necessities. We must uphold a familiar commerce together in all meekness, gentleness, patience, and liberality, we must delight in each other, make others' conditions our own, rejoice together, mourn together, labor and suffer together, always having before our eyes our commission and community in the work, our community as members of the same body. So shall we keep the unity of the spirit in the bond of peace. The Lord will be our God and delight in all our ways, so that we shall see much more of His wisdom, power, goodness, and truth than formerly we have been acquainted with. We shall find that the God of Israel is among us, when ten of us shall be able to resist a thousand of our enemies, when He shall make us a praise and glory, that men shall say of succeeding plantations, the Lord make it like that of New England. For we must consider that we shall be as a city upon a hill, the eyes of all people are upon us. So that if we shall deal falsely with our God in this work we have undertaken and so cause Him to withdraw His present help from us, we shall be made a story and byword throughout the world, we shall open the mouths of enemies to speak evil of the ways of God and all professors for God's sake, we shall shame the faces of many of God's worthy servants, and cause their prayers to be turned into curses upon us till we be consumed out of the good land whither we are going.

And to shut up this discourse with that exhortation of Moses, that faithful servant of the Lord in his last farewell to Israel, Deut. 30. Beloved there is now set before us life and good, death and evil, in that we are commanded this day to love the Lord our God, and to love one another, to walk in His ways and to keep His commandments and His ordinance, and His laws, and the articles of our covenant with Him that we may live and be multiplied, and that the Lord our God may bless us in the land whither we go to possess it. But if our hearts shall turn away so that we will not obey, but shall be seduced and worship other Gods, our pleasures, our profits, and serve them, it is propounded unto us this day we shall surely perish out of the good land whither we pass over this vast sea to possess it. Therefore let us choose life, that we, and our seed, may live, by obeying His voice, and cleaving to Him, for He is our life and our prosperity.

Hebraic Sources

Winthrop looked to Micah and the covenant between God and the Israelites in the Hebrew Bible as a model of political community.

Micah 6

(ח) הִגִּיד לְךָ אָדָם מַה טּוֹב וּמָה ה' דּוֹרֵשׁ מִמְּךָ כִּי אִם עֲשׂוֹת מִשְׁפָּט
וְאַהֲבַת חֶסֶד וְהַצְנֵעַ לֶכֶת עִם אֱ-לֹהֶיךָ.

⁸ It hath been told thee, O man, what is good, and what the Lord doth require of thee: only to do justly, and to love mercy, and to walk humbly with thy God.

Leviticus 26

(ג) אִם־בְּחֻקֹּתַי תֵּלֵכוּ וְאֶת־מִצְוֹתַי תִּשְׁמְרוּ וַעֲשִׂיתֶם אֹתָם.

(ד) וְנָתַתִּי גִשְׁמֵיכֶם בְּעִתָּם וְנָתְנָה הָאָרֶץ יְבוּלָהּ וְעֵץ הַשָּׂדֶה יִתֵּן פִּרְיוֹ.

(ה) וְהִשִּׂיג לָכֶם דַּיִשׁ אֶת־בָּצִיר וּבָצִיר יַשִּׂיג אֶת־זָרַע וַאֲכַלְתֶּם לַחְמְכֶם לָשֹׂבַע וִישַׁבְתֶּם לָבֶטַח בְּאַרְצְכֶם.

(ו) וְנָתַתִּי שָׁלוֹם בָּאָרֶץ וּשְׁכַבְתֶּם וְאֵין מַחֲרִיד וְהִשְׁבַּתִּי חַיָּה רָעָה מִן־הָאָרֶץ וְחֶרֶב לֹא־תַעֲבֹר בְּאַרְצְכֶם.

(ז) וּרְדַפְתֶּם אֶת־אֹיְבֵיכֶם וְנָפְלוּ לִפְנֵיכֶם לֶחָרֶב.

(ח) וְרָדְפוּ מִכֶּם חֲמִשָּׁה מֵאָה וּמֵאָה מִכֶּם רְבָבָה יִרְדֹּפוּ וְנָפְלוּ אֹיְבֵיכֶם לִפְנֵיכֶם לֶחָרֶב.

(ט) וּפָנִיתִי אֲלֵיכֶם וְהִפְרֵיתִי אֶתְכֶם וְהִרְבֵּיתִי אֶתְכֶם וַהֲקִימֹתִי אֶת־בְּרִיתִי אִתְּכֶם.

(י) וַאֲכַלְתֶּם יָשָׁן נוֹשָׁן וְיָשָׁן מִפְּנֵי חָדָשׁ תּוֹצִיאוּ.

(יא) וְנָתַתִּי מִשְׁכָּנִי בְּתוֹכְכֶם וְלֹא־תִגְעַל נַפְשִׁי אֶתְכֶם.

(יב) וְהִתְהַלַּכְתִּי בְּתוֹכְכֶם וְהָיִיתִי לָכֶם לֵא-לֹהִים וְאַתֶּם תִּהְיוּ־לִי לְעָם.

(יג) אֲנִי ה' אֱ-לֹהֵיכֶם אֲשֶׁר הוֹצֵאתִי אֶתְכֶם מֵאֶרֶץ מִצְרַיִם מִהְיֹת לָהֶם עֲבָדִים וָאֶשְׁבֹּר מֹטֹת עֻלְּכֶם וָאוֹלֵךְ אֶתְכֶם קוֹמְמִיּוּת.

(יד) וְאִם־לֹא תִשְׁמְעוּ לִי וְלֹא תַעֲשׂוּ אֵת כָּל־הַמִּצְוֹת הָאֵלֶּה.

(טו) וְאִם־בְּחֻקֹּתַי תִּמְאָסוּ וְאִם אֶת־מִשְׁפָּטַי תִּגְעַל נַפְשְׁכֶם לְבִלְתִּי עֲשׂוֹת אֶת־כָּל־מִצְוֹתַי לְהַפְרְכֶם אֶת־בְּרִיתִי.

(טז) אַף־אֲנִי אֶעֱשֶׂה־זֹּאת לָכֶם וְהִפְקַדְתִּי עֲלֵיכֶם בֶּהָלָה אֶת־הַשַּׁחֶפֶת וְאֶת־הַקַּדַּחַת מְכַלּוֹת עֵינַיִם וּמְדִיבֹת נָפֶשׁ וּזְרַעְתֶּם לָרִיק זַרְעֲכֶם וַאֲכָלֻהוּ אֹיְבֵיכֶם.

(יז) וְנָתַתִּי פָנַי בָּכֶם וְנִגַּפְתֶּם לִפְנֵי אֹיְבֵיכֶם וְרָדוּ בָכֶם שֹׂנְאֵיכֶם וְנַסְתֶּם וְאֵין־רֹדֵף אֶתְכֶם.

³ If ye walk in My statutes, and keep My commandments, and do them;
⁴ then I will give your rains in their season, and the land shall yield her produce, and the trees of the field shall yield their fruit.
⁵ And your threshing shall reach unto the vintage, and the vintage shall reach unto the sowing time; and ye shall eat your bread until ye have enough, and dwell in your land safely.
⁶ And I will give peace in the land, and ye shall lie down, and none shall make you afraid; and I will cause evil beasts to cease out of the land, neither shall the sword go through your land.
⁷ And ye shall chase your enemies, and they shall fall before you by the sword.
⁸ And five of you shall chase a hundred, and a hundred of you shall chase ten thousand; and your enemies shall fall before you by the sword.

⁹ And I will have respect unto you, and make you fruitful, and multiply you; and will establish My covenant with you.

¹⁰ And ye shall eat old store long kept, and ye shall bring forth the old from before the new.

¹¹ And I will set My tabernacle among you, and My soul shall not abhor you.

¹² And I will walk among you, and will be your God, and ye shall be My people.

¹³ I am the Lord your God, who brought you forth out of the land of Egypt, that ye should not be their bondmen; and I have broken the bars of your yoke, and made you go upright.

¹⁴ But if ye will not hearken unto Me, and will not do all these commandments;

¹⁵ and if ye shall reject My statutes, and if your soul abhor Mine ordinances, so that ye will not do all My commandments, but break My covenant;

¹⁶ I also will do this unto you: I will appoint terror over you, even consumption and fever, that shall make the eyes to fail, and the soul to languish; and ye shall sow your seed in vain, for your enemies shall eat it.

¹⁷ And I will set My face against you, and ye shall be smitten before your enemies; they that hate you shall rule over you; and ye shall flee when none pursueth you.

Deuteronomy 28

(א) וְהָיָה אִם שָׁמוֹעַ תִּשְׁמַע בְּקוֹל ה' אֱ-לֹהֶיךָ לִשְׁמֹר לַעֲשׂוֹת אֶת כָּל מִצְוֹתָיו אֲשֶׁר אָנֹכִי מְצַוְּךָ הַיּוֹם וּנְתָנְךָ ה' אֱ-לֹהֶיךָ עֶלְיוֹן עַל כָּל גּוֹיֵי הָאָרֶץ.

(ב) וּבָאוּ עָלֶיךָ כָּל הַבְּרָכוֹת הָאֵלֶּה וְהִשִּׂיגֻךָ כִּי תִשְׁמַע בְּקוֹל ה' אֱ-לֹהֶיךָ.

(ג) בָּרוּךְ אַתָּה בָּעִיר וּבָרוּךְ אַתָּה בַּשָּׂדֶה.

(ד) בָּרוּךְ פְּרִי בִטְנְךָ וּפְרִי אַדְמָתְךָ וּפְרִי בְהֶמְתֶּךָ שְׁגַר אֲלָפֶיךָ וְעַשְׁתְּרוֹת צֹאנֶךָ.

(ה) בָּרוּךְ טַנְאֲךָ וּמִשְׁאַרְתֶּךָ.

(ו) בָּרוּךְ אַתָּה בְּבֹאֶךָ וּבָרוּךְ אַתָּה בְּצֵאתֶךָ.

(ז) יִתֵּן ה' אֶת אֹיְבֶיךָ הַקָּמִים עָלֶיךָ נִגָּפִים לְפָנֶיךָ בְּדֶרֶךְ אֶחָד יֵצְאוּ אֵלֶיךָ וּבְשִׁבְעָה דְרָכִים יָנוּסוּ לְפָנֶיךָ.

(ח) יְצַו ה' אִתְּךָ אֶת הַבְּרָכָה בַּאֲסָמֶיךָ וּבְכֹל מִשְׁלַח יָדֶךָ וּבֵרַכְךָ בָּאָרֶץ אֲשֶׁר ה' אֱ-לֹהֶיךָ נֹתֵן לָךְ.

(ט) יְקִימְךָ ה' לוֹ לְעַם קָדוֹשׁ כַּאֲשֶׁר נִשְׁבַּע לָךְ כִּי תִשְׁמֹר אֶת מִצְוֹת ה' אֱ-לֹהֶיךָ וְהָלַכְתָּ בִּדְרָכָיו.

(י) וְרָאוּ כָּל עַמֵּי הָאָרֶץ כִּי שֵׁם ה' נִקְרָא עָלֶיךָ וְיָרְאוּ מִמֶּךָּ.

(יא) וְהוֹתִרְךָ ה' לְטוֹבָה בִּפְרִי בִטְנְךָ וּבִפְרִי בְהֶמְתְּךָ וּבִפְרִי אַדְמָתֶךָ עַל הָאֲדָמָה אֲשֶׁר נִשְׁבַּע ה' לַאֲבֹתֶיךָ לָתֶת לָךְ.

(יב) יִפְתַּח ה' לְךָ אֶת אוֹצָרוֹ הַטּוֹב אֶת הַשָּׁמַיִם לָתֵת מְטַר אַרְצְךָ בְּעִתּוֹ וּלְבָרֵךְ אֵת כָּל מַעֲשֵׂה יָדֶךָ וְהִלְוִיתָ גּוֹיִם רַבִּים וְאַתָּה לֹא תִלְוֶה.

(יג) וּנְתָנְךָ ה' לְרֹאשׁ וְלֹא לְזָנָב וְהָיִיתָ רַק לְמַעְלָה וְלֹא תִהְיֶה לְמָטָּה כִּי תִשְׁמַע אֶל מִצְוֹת ה' אֱ-לֹהֶיךָ אֲשֶׁר אָנֹכִי מְצַוְּךָ הַיּוֹם לִשְׁמֹר וְלַעֲשׂוֹת.

(יד) וְלֹא תָסוּר מִכָּל הַדְּבָרִים אֲשֶׁר אָנֹכִי מְצַוֶּה אֶתְכֶם הַיּוֹם יָמִין וּשְׂמֹאול לָלֶכֶת אַחֲרֵי אֱלֹהִים אֲחֵרִים לְעָבְדָם.
(טו) וְהָיָה אִם לֹא תִשְׁמַע בְּקוֹל ה' אֱ־לֹהֶיךָ לִשְׁמֹר לַעֲשׂוֹת אֶת כָּל מִצְוֹתָיו וְחֻקֹּתָיו אֲשֶׁר אָנֹכִי מְצַוְּךָ הַיּוֹם וּבָאוּ עָלֶיךָ כָּל הַקְּלָלוֹת הָאֵלֶּה וְהִשִּׂיגוּךָ.
(טז) אָרוּר אַתָּה בָּעִיר וְאָרוּר אַתָּה בַּשָּׂדֶה.
(יז) אָרוּר טַנְאֲךָ וּמִשְׁאַרְתֶּךָ.
(יח) אָרוּר פְּרִי בִטְנְךָ וּפְרִי אַדְמָתֶךָ שְׁגַר אֲלָפֶיךָ וְעַשְׁתְּרֹת צֹאנֶךָ.
(יט) אָרוּר אַתָּה בְּבֹאֶךָ וְאָרוּר אַתָּה בְּצֵאתֶךָ.
(כ) יְשַׁלַּח ה' בְּךָ אֶת הַמְּאֵרָה אֶת הַמְּהוּמָה וְאֶת הַמִּגְעֶרֶת בְּכָל מִשְׁלַח יָדְךָ אֲשֶׁר תַּעֲשֶׂה עַד הִשָּׁמֶדְךָ וְעַד אֲבָדְךָ מַהֵר מִפְּנֵי רֹעַ מַעֲלָלֶיךָ אֲשֶׁר עֲזַבְתָּנִי.

[1] And it shall come to pass, if thou shalt hearken diligently unto the voice of the Lord thy God, to observe to do all His commandments which I command thee this day, that the Lord thy God will set thee on high above all the nations of the earth.
[2] And all these blessings shall come upon thee, and overtake thee, if thou shalt hearken unto the voice of the Lord thy God.
[3] Blessed shalt thou be in the city, and blessed shalt thou be in the field.
[4] Blessed shall be the fruit of thy body, and the fruit of thy land, and the fruit of thy cattle, the increase of thy kine, and the young of thy flock.
[5] Blessed shall be thy basket and thy kneading-trough.
[6] Blessed shalt thou be when thou comest in, and blessed shalt thou be when thou goest out.
[7] The Lord will cause thine enemies that rise up against thee to be smitten before thee; they shall come out against thee one way, and shall flee before thee seven ways.
[8] The Lord will command the blessing with thee in thy barns, and in all that thou puttest thy hand unto; and He will bless thee in the land which the Lord thy God giveth thee.
[9] The Lord will establish thee for a holy people unto Himself, as He hath sworn unto thee; if thou shalt keep the commandments of the Lord thy God, and walk in His ways.
[10] And all the peoples of the earth shall see that the name of the Lord is called upon thee; and they shall be afraid of thee.
[11] And the Lord will make thee over-abundant for good, in the fruit of thy body, and in the fruit of thy cattle, and in the fruit of thy land, in the land which the Lord swore unto thy fathers to give thee.
[12] The Lord will open unto thee His good treasure the heaven to give the rain of thy land in its season, and to bless all the work of thy hand; and thou shalt lend unto many nations, but thou shalt not borrow.
[13] And the Lord will make thee the head, and not the tail; and thou shalt be above only, and thou shalt not be beneath; if thou shalt hearken unto the commandments of the Lord thy God, which I command thee this day, to observe and to do them;
[14] and shalt not turn aside from any of the words which I command you this day, to the right hand, or to the left, to go after other gods to serve them.

¹⁵ But it shall come to pass, if thou wilt not hearken unto the voice of the Lord thy God, to observe to do all His commandments and His statutes which I command thee this day; that all these curses shall come upon thee, and overtake thee.

¹⁶ Cursed shalt thou be in the city, and cursed shalt thou be in the field.

¹⁷ Cursed shall be thy basket and thy kneading-trough.

¹⁸ Cursed shall be the fruit of thy body, and the fruit of thy land, the increase of thy kine, and the young of thy flock.

¹⁹ Cursed shalt thou be when thou comest in, and cursed shalt thou be when thou goest out.

²⁰ The Lord will send upon thee cursing, discomfiture, and rebuke, in all that thou puttest thy hand unto to do, until thou be destroyed, and until thou perish quickly; because of the evil of thy doings, whereby thou hast forsaken Me.

Deuteronomy 30

(טו) רְאֵה נָתַתִּי לְפָנֶיךָ הַיּוֹם אֶת הַחַיִּים וְאֶת הַטּוֹב וְאֶת הַמָּוֶת וְאֶת הָרָע.

(טז) אֲשֶׁר אָנֹכִי מְצַוְּךָ הַיּוֹם לְאַהֲבָה אֶת ה' אֱ-לֹהֶיךָ לָלֶכֶת בִּדְרָכָיו וְלִשְׁמֹר מִצְוֹתָיו וְחֻקֹּתָיו וּמִשְׁפָּטָיו וְחָיִיתָ וְרָבִיתָ וּבֵרַכְךָ ה' אֱ-לֹהֶיךָ בָּאָרֶץ אֲשֶׁר אַתָּה בָא שָׁמָּה לְרִשְׁתָּהּ.

(יז) וְאִם יִפְנֶה לְבָבְךָ וְלֹא תִשְׁמָע וְנִדַּחְתָּ וְהִשְׁתַּחֲוִיתָ לֵאלֹהִים אֲחֵרִים וַעֲבַדְתָּם.

(יח) הִגַּדְתִּי לָכֶם הַיּוֹם כִּי אָבֹד תֹּאבֵדוּן לֹא תַאֲרִיכֻן יָמִים עַל הָאֲדָמָה אֲשֶׁר אַתָּה עֹבֵר אֶת הַיַּרְדֵּן לָבוֹא שָׁמָּה לְרִשְׁתָּהּ.

(יט) הַעִדֹתִי בָכֶם הַיּוֹם אֶת הַשָּׁמַיִם וְאֶת הָאָרֶץ הַחַיִּים וְהַמָּוֶת נָתַתִּי לְפָנֶיךָ הַבְּרָכָה וְהַקְּלָלָה וּבָחַרְתָּ בַּחַיִּים לְמַעַן תִּחְיֶה אַתָּה וְזַרְעֶךָ.

(כ) לְאַהֲבָה אֶת ה' אֱ-לֹהֶיךָ לִשְׁמֹעַ בְּקֹלוֹ וּלְדָבְקָה בוֹ כִּי הוּא חַיֶּיךָ וְאֹרֶךְ יָמֶיךָ לָשֶׁבֶת עַל הָאֲדָמָה אֲשֶׁר נִשְׁבַּע ה' לַאֲבֹתֶיךָ לְאַבְרָהָם לְיִצְחָק וּלְיַעֲקֹב לָתֵת לָהֶם.

¹⁵ See, I have set before thee this day life and good, and death and evil,

¹⁶ in that I command thee this day to love the Lord thy God, to walk in His ways, and to keep His commandments and His statutes and His ordinances; then thou shalt live and multiply, and the Lord thy God shall bless thee in the land whither thou goest in to possess it.

¹⁷ But if thy heart turn away, and thou wilt not hear, but shalt be drawn away, and worship other gods, and serve them;

¹⁸ I declare unto you this day, that ye shall surely perish; ye shall not prolong your days upon the land, whither thou passest over the Jordan to go in to possess it.

¹⁹ I call heaven and earth to witness against you this day, that I have set before thee life and death, the blessing and the curse; therefore choose life, that thou mayest live, thou and thy seed;

²⁰ to love the Lord thy God, to hearken to His voice, and to cleave unto Him; for that is thy life, and the length of thy days; that thou mayest dwell in the land which the Lord swore unto thy fathers, to Abraham, to Isaac, and to Jacob, to give them.

COTTON MATHER (1663–1728)

*Cotton Mather was an influential American Puritan minister and pamphle-
teer. He wrote 469 separate books, which prompted renowned religious historian Mark Noll to quip that "he never had a thought he felt was unworthy
of publication." He might be best known today, in infamy, for his influence
on the Salem witch trials. The Salem trials took place in an intense period
of colonial history. The colonists were at war with Native American tribes;
in such a climate people are prone to hysteria, and none more than a people
disposed to thinking God and sin are at work in their deliverance or perdi-
tion. The Salem trials of 1692–1693 resulted in the death of more than a
dozen young women who were convicted of being witches. Hundreds of others
were accused of or jailed for witchcraft. The juxtaposition of Mather's literary output and Hebraic metaphor reminds us that the Bible can be used in
both salutary and nefarious ways, of the connection between seeing oneself
as divinely elected and infallible, and acting self-righteously.*

*An important part of the Puritan legacy is the way in which they told
their story. The words, metaphors, and symbols by which one writes about
oneself and others are windows into a historical world and mind. Cotton
Mather's* "Nehemias Americanus [American Nehemia]. The Life of John
Winthrop, Esq., Governor of the Massachuset (sic) Colony" *in* Magnalia
Christi Americana (or, The Great Works of Christ in America), *is a masterpiece of self-created mythology. He wrote a history of the United States
as if he were the author of the Pentateuch writing the history of the Hebrew
nation. In this way American history became a self-consciously sacred reenactment of the biblical drama. The book outlined the development of religion
in North America from 1620 to the end of the seventeenth century. In book 2,
chapter 4, Mather described John Winthrop in decidedly Hebraic terms. He
is compared to Hebraic prophets throughout the work.*[2]

Magnalia Christi Americana (1702)

Nehemias Americanus – "The Life of John Winthrop, Esq., Governor
of the Massachusetts Colony" (*Magnalia*, book 2, chapter 4)

2. *Magnalia Christi Americana, Books I and II*, ed. Kenneth B. Murdock (Cambridge: Harvard University Press, 1977), 213–28.

Comparisons to Nehemiah and Joseph
(Section 6, l. 41; Section 6, l. 66)

But whilst he thus did, as our New-English *Nehemiah*, the part of a *ruler* in managing the public affairs of our American Jerusalem, when there were Tobijahs and Sanballats enough to vex him, and give him the experiment of Luther's observation, *Omnis qui regit est tanquam signum, in quod omnia jacula, Satan et Mundus dirigunt* [Those in authority are a target, at whom Satan and the world launch all their arrows]; he made himself still an exacter *parallel* unto that governour of Israel, by doing the part of a neighbour among the distressed people of the new plantation. To teach them the frugality necessary for those times, he abridged himself of a thousand comfortable things, which he had allowed himself elsewhere: his *habit* was not that *soft raiment*, which would have been disagreeable to a wilderness; his table was not covered with the superfluities that would have invited unto sensualities: water was commonly his own drink, though he gave wine to others. But at the same time his liberality unto the needy was even beyond measure generous; and therein he was continually causing "the blessing of him that was ready to perish to come upon him, and the heart of the widow and the orphan to sing for joy" [Job 29:13]: but none more than those of deceased Ministers, whom he always treated with a very singular compassion; among the instances whereof we still enjoy with us the worthy and now aged son of that reverend Higginson, whose death left his family in a wide world soon after his arrival here, publickly acknowledging the charitable Winthrop for his *foster-father*. It was oftentimes no small trial unto his faith, to think how a table for the people should be furnished when they first came into the wilderness! and for very many of the people his own good works were needful, and accordingly employed for the answering of his faith. Indeed, for a while the governour was the *Joseph*, unto whom the whole body of the people repaired when their corn failed them; and he continued relieving of them with his open-handed bounties, as long as he had any stock to do it with; and a lively *faith* to *see* the return of the "bread after many days" [Eccl. 11:1], and not starve in the days that were to pass till that return should be seen, carried him cheerfully through those expences....

...The words of Josephus about *Nehemiah*, the governour of Israel, we will now use upon this governour of New-England, as his EPITAPH.

VIR FUIT INDOLE BONUS, AC JUSTUS:
ET POPULARIUM GLORIAE AMANTISSIMUS:
QUIBUS ETERNUM RELIQUIT MONUMENTUM,
NOVANGLORUM MOENIA

[He was by nature a man, at once benevolent and just:
most zealous for the honour of his countrymen;
and to them he left an imperishable monument –
the walls of Jerusalem.
(The Latin paraphrase substitutes New England for Jerusalem.)]

Comparison to Moses (Section 4, ll. 4–5)
Accordingly when the noble design of carrying a colony of chosen people into an American wilderness, was by some eminent persons undertaken, *this* eminent person was, by the consent of all, chosen for the *Moses*, who must be the leader of so great an undertaking: and indeed nothing but a *Mosaic spirit* could have carried him through the temptations, to which either his farewel to his own land, or his travel in a strange land, must needs expose a gentleman of his education. Wherefore having sold a fair estate of six or seven hundred a year, he transported himself with the effects of it into New-England in the year 1630, where he spent it upon the service of a famous plantation, founded and formed for the seat of the most *reformed Christianity*: and continued there, conflicting with temptations of all sorts, as many years as the *nodes* of the *moon* take to dispatch a revolution. Those persons were never concerned in a new plantation, who know not that the unavoidable difficulties of such a thing will call for all the prudence and patience of a mortal man to encounter therewithal; and they must be very insensible of the influence, which the *just wrath* of Heaven has permitted the *devils* to have upon this world, if they do not think that the difficulties of a new plantation, devoted unto the evangelical worship of our Lord Jesus Christ, must be yet more than ordinary. How prudently, how patiently, and with how much resignation to our Lord Jesus Christ, our brave Winthrop waded through these difficulties, let posterity consider with admiration. And know, that as the picture of this their governour was, after his death, hung up with honour in the state-house of his country, so the wisdom,

courage, and holy zeal of his life, were an example well-worthy to be copied by all that shall succeed him in government.

Comparison to David and Jacob (Section 12, l. 90, Section 12, l. 91)
But it was not long before those clouds were dispelled, and he enjoyed in his holy soul the great consolations of God! While he thus lay ripening for heaven, he did out of obedience unto the *ordinance* of our Lord, send for the elders of the church to pray with him; yea, they and the whole church *fasted* as well as *prayed* for him; and in that *fast* the venerable Cotton preached on Psal. xxxv. 13, 14: "When they were sick, I humbled my self with fasting; I behaved my self as though he had been my friend or brother; I bowed down heavily as one that mourned for his mother": from whence I find him raising that observation, "The sickness of one that is to us as a friend, a brother, a mother, is a just occasion of deep humbling our souls with fasting and prayer"; and making this application.

> Upon this occasion we are now to attend this duty for a governour, who has been to us as a friend in his *counsel* for all things, and help for our bodies by *physick*, for our estates by *law*, and of whom there was no fear of his becoming an *enemy*, like the friends of *David*: a governour who has been unto us as a brother; not usurping authority over the church; often speaking his advice, and often contradicted, even by young men, and some of low degree; yet not replying, but offering satisfaction also when any supposed offences have arisen; a governour who has been unto us as a mother, parent like distributing his goods to brethren and neighbours at his first coming; and *gently* bearing our infirmities without taking notice of them.

Such a governour, after he had been more than ten several times by the people chosen their governour, was New-England now to lose; who having, like *Jacob*, first left his council and blessing with his children gathered about his bed-side; and, like *David*, "served his generation by the will of God," he "gave up the ghost," and fell asleep on March 26, 1649. Having, like the dying Emperour Valentinian, this above all his other *victories* for his triumphs, *His overcoming of himself.*

ABSTRACT OF THE LAWS OF NEW ENGLAND
AND NEW HAVEN LEGAL CODE

*When Alexis de Tocqueville came to the United States from France in the
1830s, he was struck by the combination of religious and political freedom
that existed there. He was one of the first thinkers to posit what might be
called the "two founding" thesis, that is, that the United States was first
founded by the Puritans and then later by the people we traditionally call
"the founders" during the time of the Revolution. When writing about early
Puritan laws, he says:*

The legislators of Connecticut begin with the penal laws, and, strange
to say, they borrow their provisions from the text of Holy Writ. "Whosoever shall worship any other God than the Lord," says the preamble
of the Code, "shall surely be put to death." This is followed by ten or
twelve enactments of the same kind, copied verbatim from the books
of Exodus, Leviticus, and Deuteronomy – Blasphemy, sorcery, adultery, and rape were punished with death; an outrage offered by a son
to his parents was to be expiated by the same penalty. The legislation
of a rude and half-civilized people was thus applied to an enlightened
and moral community. The consequence was, that the punishment of
death was never more frequently prescribed by statute, and never more
rarely enforced. The chief care of the legislators in this body of penal
laws was the maintenance of orderly conduct and good morals in the
community; thus they constantly invaded the domain of conscience,
and there was scarcely a sin which was not subject to magisterial cen-
sure. The reader is aware of the rigor with which these laws punished
rape and adultery; intercourse between unmarried persons was likewise
severely repressed. The judge was empowered to inflict either a pecuniary penalty, a whipping, or marriage on the misdemeanants, and if
the records of the old courts of New Haven may be believed, prosecu-
tions of this kind were not infrequent. We find a sentence, bearing the
date of May 1, 1660, inflicting a fine and reprimand on a young woman
who was accused of using improper language and of allowing herself
to be kissed. The Code of 1650 abounds in preventive measures. It
punishes idleness and drunkenness with severity. Innkeepers were

forbidden to furnish more than a certain quantity of liquor to each consumer; and simple lying, whenever it may be injurious, is checked by a fine or a flogging. In other places the legislator, entirely forgetting the great principles of religious toleration that he had himself demanded in Europe, makes attendance on divine service compulsory, and goes so far as to visit with severe punishment, and even with death, Christians who chose to worship God according to a ritual differing from his own. Sometimes, indeed, the zeal for regulation induces him to descend to the most frivolous particulars: thus a law is to be found in the same code which prohibits the use of tobacco. It must not be forgotten that these fantastic and oppressive laws were not imposed by authority, but that they were freely voted by all the persons interested in them, and that the customs of the community were even more austere and puritanical than the laws. In 1649 a solemn association was formed in Boston to check the worldly luxury of long hair.[3]

The legal code originally entitled "Abstract of the Laws of New England" was written by John Cotton (1585–1682); John Winthrop called it "Moses His Judicials." It was divided into ten sections and covered all aspects of law: inheritance, trespass, criminal, including law on witchcraft and the Sabbath. Below the opening and some of the laws of Connecticut are excerpted.

Opening of "Moses His Judicials" (1641)

I take the question thus, whether we as Xtians [Christians] or as people of god, are not bound to establish the Lawes & penalties set down in the scripture as they were given to the Jewes & no other but they; Q. 2 th. open : 1. w' I meane by Lawes? A [Of] the Lawes given to Jewes in scripture, some were Temporary. & only bound them during the time of the old Testament, 2 the rest were [perpetual] & bind [them] for ever ; / The temporary Lawes are 1. all such as had any refer. to X? & state of ye gospell ; as a shadow & rudiment : 2 any that had any speciall respect & p'tic: [particularly] appropriated to the land of Canaan, or to the Jewes yr dwellinge.

---

3. Alexis de Tocqueville, *Democracy in America*, vol. 1, ch. 2.

The [perpetual] Lawes are 1 : the 10 Command. as deliv"1 on M: Sinay : 2 all such as have grounds 1 ends or effects [that] are [perpetual]. & of these Lawes some are mixt ; [they] have some branches or circumstances temporary & yet the Law p'petuall ; or wc have some branches & reasons [perpetual]. & yet law temporary, & so far as these Lawes [there] is any [thing] morall or [perpetual], so far it binds ; / Q. 2. [what is meant] by no other but these : A : by this I meane not only those wc are literally expressed ; but also all such necessary consequences or diducts, [that] may be justly drawn from them. Resp. [response] all these [perpetual] Lawes bind us ;

Resp. all these [perpetual] Lawes bind us ; Reas : 1. [because] god who was y" bound up in covenant [with them] to be [their] god ; hath put us in [their] stead & is become or god as well as [theirs] & [hence] we are as [much] bound to there Lawes as well as [them"]: / Reas. 2. if god hath given us no other for the governing of the commonwealth y" we either may be Lawlesse ; & have w' Lawes we please or else be bound to these ; but god hath giuen us no other nor are we Lawless, for we are under the law to god & to [Christ] ; / Reas. 3. if otherwise ; we can make no use of those lawes & penal ties but they are as antiquated then we are bound to observe them Reas : 4 : / If the Jewes be now still under the bond of them & so to observe them [when] they are an established commonwealth ; then we are bound to observe [them] ; at : ergo : / bec.[ause] [there] is no other reuel \ that they shall be other Lawes ;

New Haven Legal Code based on "Moses His Judicials" (1656)
That for felonies of Goods, or cattle stolen, the Thief not to suffer death, but to make restitution, according to Gods law, as the case shall be, and be bounden to serve in case he cannot satsfie. Prov. 6.30.31, Exo. 22.1.4.7, Job. 20.15.18, 2 Sam. 12.6, Luk. 19.8

That no man be convicted in any case Capital, but by the Testimony of two witnesses at least. Deut. 17.6, 2 Corinthians 13.1, Heb. 10.28, Numb. 35.30

All estates of inheritance, are to be Estates in Fee simple, and no Intails upon the Heirs Males. Numb. 27.7.8, I Tim. 5.8, Gen. 23.11, 17.20

Schooles of learning are to be maintained, and godly learned men to be countenanced and encouraged. Acts 19.9, 1 Kings 18.4, 1 Sam. 19.20

That there be Juricatories, and Courts established in every Citie and County, where the Judges may sit constantly in open places to hear, and determine all controversies. Exod. 18.13.25.26, Deut. 21.19, Prov. 31.23 and 25.7 [25:8], Ruth 4.1.2.9 ...

Hebraic Sources

The New Haven Legal Code drew on the legal standards of the Hebrew Bible in shaping its own laws, as well as on its narrative and ethical sections.

<u>Punishment for Stealing</u>
Proverbs 6

(ל) לֹא יָבוּזוּ לַגַּנָּב כִּי יִגְנוֹב לְמַלֵּא נַפְשׁוֹ כִּי יִרְעָב.
(לא) וְנִמְצָא יְשַׁלֵּם שִׁבְעָתָיִם אֶת כָּל הוֹן בֵּיתוֹ יִתֵּן.

[30] Men do not despise a thief, if he steal to satisfy his soul when he is hungry;
[31] But if he be found, he must restore sevenfold; he shall give all the substance of his house.

Exodus 22

(לז) כִּי יִגְנֹב אִישׁ שׁוֹר אוֹ שֶׂה וּטְבָחוֹ אוֹ מְכָרוֹ חֲמִשָּׁה בָקָר יְשַׁלֵּם תַּחַת הַשּׁוֹר וְאַרְבַּע צֹאן תַּחַת הַשֶּׂה.
(ג) אִם הִמָּצֵא תִמָּצֵא בְיָדוֹ הַגְּנֵבָה מִשּׁוֹר עַד חֲמוֹר עַד שֶׂה חַיִּים שְׁנַיִם יְשַׁלֵּם.
(ו) כִּי יִתֵּן אִישׁ אֶל רֵעֵהוּ כֶּסֶף אוֹ כֵלִים לִשְׁמֹר וְגֻנַּב מִבֵּית הָאִישׁ אִם יִמָּצֵא הַגַּנָּב יְשַׁלֵּם שְׁנָיִם.

[1] [21:37] If a man steal an ox, or a sheep, and kill it, or sell it, he shall restore five oxen for an ox, and four sheep for a sheep.
[4] [22:3] If the theft be found in his hand alive, whether it be ox, or ass, or sheep, he shall restore double.
[7] [22:6] If a man shall deliver unto his neighbor money or stuff to keep, and it be stolen out of the man's house; if the thief be found, let him pay double.

Job 20

(טו) חַיִל בָּלַע וַיְקִאֶנּוּ מִבִּטְנוֹ יֹרִשֶׁנּוּ אֵ־ל.

(יח) מֵשִׁיב יָגָע וְלֹא יִבְלָע כְּחֵיל תְּמוּרָתוֹ וְלֹא יַעֲלֹס.

[15] He hath swallowed down riches, and he shall vomit them up again: God shall cast them out of his belly.

[18] That which he laboured for shall he restore, and shall not swallow it down: according to his substance shall the restitution be, and he shall not rejoice therein.

II Samuel 12

(ו) וְאֶת הַכִּבְשָׂה יְשַׁלֵּם אַרְבַּעְתָּיִם עֵקֶב אֲשֶׁר עָשָׂה אֶת הַדָּבָר הַזֶּה וְעַל אֲשֶׁר
לֹא חָמָל.

[6] And he shall restore the lamb fourfold, because he did this thing, and because he had no pity.

Conviction in a Capital Case
Deuteronomy 17

(ו) עַל פִּי שְׁנַיִם עֵדִים אוֹ שְׁלֹשָׁה עֵדִים יוּמַת הַמֵּת לֹא יוּמַת עַל פִּי עֵד אֶחָד.

[6] At the mouth of two witnesses, or three witnesses, shall he that is worthy of death be put to death; but at the mouth of one witness he shall not be put to death.

Numbers 35

(ל) כָּל מַכֵּה נֶפֶשׁ לְפִי עֵדִים יִרְצַח אֶת הָרֹצֵחַ וְעֵד אֶחָד לֹא יַעֲנֶה בְנֶפֶשׁ לָמוּת.

[30] Whoso killeth any person, the murderer shall be put to death by the mouth of witnesses; but one witness shall not testify against any person to cause him he die.

Inheritance and Estates
Numbers 27

(ז) כֵּן בְּנוֹת צְלָפְחָד דֹּבְרֹת נָתֹן תִּתֵּן לָהֶם אֲחֻזַּת נַחֲלָה בְּתוֹךְ אֲחֵי אֲבִיהֶם וְהַעֲבַרְתָּ
אֶת נַחֲלַת אֲבִיהֶן לָהֶן.

(ח) וְאֶל בְּנֵי יִשְׂרָאֵל תְּדַבֵּר לֵאמֹר אִישׁ כִּי יָמוּת וּבֵן אֵין לוֹ וְהַעֲבַרְתֶּם אֶת
נַחֲלָתוֹ לְבִתּוֹ.

(ט) וְאִם אֵין לוֹ בַּת וּנְתַתֶּם אֶת נַחֲלָתוֹ לְאֶחָיו.

(י) וְאִם אֵין לוֹ אַחִים וּנְתַתֶּם אֶת נַחֲלָתוֹ לַאֲחֵי אָבִיו.
(יא) וְאִם אֵין אַחִים לְאָבִיו וּנְתַתֶּם אֶת נַחֲלָתוֹ לִשְׁאֵרוֹ הַקָּרֹב אֵלָיו מִמִּשְׁפַּחְתּוֹ
וְיָרַשׁ אֹתָהּ וְהָיְתָה לִבְנֵי יִשְׂרָאֵל לְחֻקַּת מִשְׁפָּט כַּאֲשֶׁר צִוָּה ה' אֶת מֹשֶׁה.

[7] The daughters of Zelophehad speak right: thou shalt surely give them a possession of an inheritance among their father's brethren; and thou shalt cause the inheritance of their father to pass unto them.
[8] And thou shalt speak unto the children of Israel, saying: If a man die, and have no son, then ye shall cause his inheritance to pass unto his daughter.
[9] And if he have no daughter, then ye shall give his inheritance unto his brethren.
[10] And if he have no brethren, then ye shall give his inheritance unto his father's brethren.
[11] And if his father have no brethren, then ye shall give his inheritance unto his kinsman that is next to him of his family, and he shall possess it. And it shall be unto the children of Israel a statute of judgment, as the Lord commanded Moses.

Genesis 23

(יא) לֹא אֲדֹנִי שְׁמָעֵנִי הַשָּׂדֶה נָתַתִּי לָךְ וְהַמְּעָרָה אֲשֶׁר בּוֹ לְךָ נְתַתִּיהָ לְעֵינֵי בְנֵי
עַמִּי נְתַתִּיהָ לָּךְ קְבֹר מֵתֶךָ.
(יז) וַיָּקָם שְׂדֵה עֶפְרוֹן אֲשֶׁר בַּמַּכְפֵּלָה אֲשֶׁר לִפְנֵי מַמְרֵא הַשָּׂדֶה וְהַמְּעָרָה אֲשֶׁר
בּוֹ וְכָל הָעֵץ אֲשֶׁר בַּשָּׂדֶה אֲשֶׁר בְּכָל גְּבֻלוֹ סָבִיב.
(כ) וַיָּקָם הַשָּׂדֶה וְהַמְּעָרָה אֲשֶׁר בּוֹ לְאַבְרָהָם לַאֲחֻזַּת קָבֶר מֵאֵת בְּנֵי חֵת.

[11] Nay, my lord, hear me: the field give I thee, and the cave that is therein, I give it thee; in the presence of the sons of my people give I it thee: bury thy dead.
[17] And the field of Ephron, which was in Machpelah, which was before Mamre, the field, and the cave which was therein, and all the trees that were in the field, that were in all the borders round about, were made sure
[20] And the field, and the cave that is therein, were made sure unto Abraham for a possession of a buryingplace by the sons of Heth.

Supporting the Devout
I Kings 18

(ד) וַיְהִי בְּהַכְרִית אִיזֶבֶל אֵת נְבִיאֵי ה' וַיִּקַּח עֹבַדְיָהוּ מֵאָה נְבִיאִים וַיַּחְבִּיאֵם
חֲמִשִּׁים אִישׁ בַּמְּעָרָה וְכִלְכְּלָם לֶחֶם וָמָיִם.

[4] For it was so, when Jezebel cut off the prophets of the Lord, that Obadiah took an hundred prophets, and hid them by fifty in a cave, and fed them with bread and water.

I Samuel 19

(כ) וַיִּשְׁלַח שָׁאוּל מַלְאָכִים לָקַחַת אֶת דָּוִד וַיַּרְא אֶת לַהֲקַת הַנְּבִיאִים נִבְּאִים וּשְׁמוּאֵל עֹמֵד נִצָּב עֲלֵיהֶם וַתְּהִי עַל מַלְאֲכֵי שָׁאוּל רוּחַ אֱ־לֹהִים וַיִּתְנַבְּאוּ גַּם הֵמָּה.

(כא) וַיַּגִּדוּ לְשָׁאוּל וַיִּשְׁלַח מַלְאָכִים אֲחֵרִים וַיִּתְנַבְּאוּ גַם הֵמָּה וַיֹּסֶף שָׁאוּל וַיִּשְׁלַח מַלְאָכִים שְׁלִשִׁים וַיִּתְנַבְּאוּ גַּם הֵמָּה.

(כב) וַיֵּלֶךְ גַּם הוּא הָרָמָתָה וַיָּבֹא עַד בּוֹר הַגָּדוֹל אֲשֶׁר בַּשֶּׂכוּ וַיִּשְׁאַל וַיֹּאמֶר אֵיפֹה שְׁמוּאֵל וְדָוִד וַיֹּאמֶר הִנֵּה בנוית [בְּנָיוֹת] בָּרָמָה.

(כג) וַיֵּלֶךְ שָׁם אֶל נוית [נָיוֹת] בָּרָמָה וַתְּהִי עָלָיו גַּם הוּא רוּחַ אֱ־לֹהִים וַיֵּלֶךְ הָלוֹךְ וַיִּתְנַבֵּא עַד בֹּאוֹ בנוית [בְּנָיוֹת] בָּרָמָה.

(כד) וַיִּפְשַׁט גַּם הוּא בְּגָדָיו וַיִּתְנַבֵּא גַם הוּא לִפְנֵי שְׁמוּאֵל וַיִּפֹּל עָרֹם כָּל הַיּוֹם הַהוּא וְכָל הַלָּיְלָה עַל כֵּן יֹאמְרוּ הֲגַם שָׁאוּל בַּנְּבִיאִם.

[20] And Saul sent messengers to take David: and when they saw the company of the prophets prophesying, and Samuel standing as appointed over them, the Spirit of God was upon the messengers of Saul, and they also prophesied.

[21] And when it was told Saul, he sent other messengers, and they prophesied likewise. And Saul sent messengers again the third time, and they prophesied also.

[22] Then went he also to Ramah, and came to a great well that is in Sechu: and he asked and said, Where are Samuel and David? And one said, Behold, they be at Naioth in Ramah.

[23] And he went thither to Naioth in Ramah: and the Spirit of God was upon him also, and he went on, and prophesied, until he came to Naioth in Ramah.

[24] And he stripped off his clothes also, and prophesied before Samuel in like manner, and lay down naked all that day and all that night. Wherefore they say, Is Saul also among the prophets?

Judicial System
Exodus 18

(יג) וַיְהִי מִמָּחֳרָת וַיֵּשֶׁב מֹשֶׁה לִשְׁפֹּט אֶת הָעָם וַיַּעֲמֹד הָעָם עַל מֹשֶׁה מִן הַבֹּקֶר עַד הָעָרֶב.

(יד) וַיַּרְא חֹתֵן מֹשֶׁה אֵת כָּל אֲשֶׁר הוּא עֹשֶׂה לָעָם וַיֹּאמֶר מָה הַדָּבָר הַזֶּה אֲשֶׁר אַתָּה עֹשֶׂה לָעָם מַדּוּעַ אַתָּה יוֹשֵׁב לְבַדֶּךָ וְכָל הָעָם נִצָּב עָלֶיךָ מִן בֹּקֶר עַד עָרֶב.

(יט) עַתָּה שְׁמַע בְּקֹלִי אִיעָצְךָ וִיהִי אֱ־לֹהִים עִמָּךְ הֱיֵה אַתָּה לָעָם מוּל הָאֱ־לֹהִים וְהֵבֵאתָ אַתָּה אֶת הַדְּבָרִים אֶל הָאֱ־לֹהִים.

(כ) וְהִזְהַרְתָּה אֶתְהֶם אֶת הַחֻקִּים וְאֶת הַתּוֹרֹת וְהוֹדַעְתָּ לָהֶם אֶת הַדֶּרֶךְ יֵלְכוּ בָהּ וְאֶת הַמַּעֲשֶׂה אֲשֶׁר יַעֲשׂוּן.

(כא) וְאַתָּה תֶחֱזֶה מִכָּל הָעָם אַנְשֵׁי חַיִל יִרְאֵי אֱ־לֹהִים אַנְשֵׁי אֱמֶת שֹׂנְאֵי בָצַע וְשַׂמְתָּ עֲלֵהֶם שָׂרֵי אֲלָפִים שָׂרֵי מֵאוֹת שָׂרֵי חֲמִשִּׁים וְשָׂרֵי עֲשָׂרֹת.

(כב) וְשָׁפְטוּ אֶת הָעָם בְּכָל עֵת וְהָיָה כָּל הַדָּבָר הַגָּדֹל יָבִיאוּ אֵלֶיךָ וְכָל הַדָּבָר הַקָּטֹן יִשְׁפְּטוּ הֵם וְהָקֵל מֵעָלֶיךָ וְנָשְׂאוּ אִתָּךְ.

(כג) אִם אֶת הַדָּבָר הַזֶּה תַּעֲשֶׂה וְצִוְּךָ אֱ־לֹהִים וְיָכָלְתָּ עֲמֹד וְגַם כָּל הָעָם הַזֶּה עַל מְקֹמוֹ יָבֹא בְשָׁלוֹם.

(כד) וַיִּשְׁמַע מֹשֶׁה לְקוֹל חֹתְנוֹ וַיַּעַשׂ כֹּל אֲשֶׁר אָמָר.

(כה) וַיִּבְחַר מֹשֶׁה אַנְשֵׁי חַיִל מִכָּל יִשְׂרָאֵל וַיִּתֵּן אֹתָם רָאשִׁים עַל הָעָם שָׂרֵי אֲלָפִים שָׂרֵי מֵאוֹת שָׂרֵי חֲמִשִּׁים וְשָׂרֵי עֲשָׂרֹת.

(כו) וְשָׁפְטוּ אֶת הָעָם בְּכָל עֵת אֶת הַדָּבָר הַקָּשֶׁה יְבִיאוּן אֶל מֹשֶׁה וְכָל הַדָּבָר הַקָּטֹן יִשְׁפּוּטוּ הֵם.

[13] And it came to pass on the morrow, that Moses sat to judge the people; and the people stood about Moses from the morning unto the evening.

[14] And when Moses' father-in-law saw all that he did to the people, he said: What is this thing that thou doest to the people? Why sittest thou thyself alone, and all the people stand about thee from morning unto even?

[19] Hearken now unto my voice, I will give thee counsel, and God be with thee: be thou for the people before God, and bring thou the causes unto God.

[20] And thou shalt teach them the statutes and the laws, and shalt show them the way wherein they must walk, and the work that they must do.

[21] Moreover thou shalt provide out of all the people able men, such as fear God, men of truth, hating unjust gain; and place such over them, to be rulers of thousands, rulers of hundreds, rulers of fifties, and rulers of tens.

[22] And let them judge the people at all seasons; and it shall be, that every great matter they shall bring unto thee, but every small matter they shall judge themselves; so shall they make it easier for thee and bear the burden with thee.

[23] If thou shalt do this thing, and God command thee so, then thou shalt be able to endure, and all this people also shall go to their place in peace.

[24] So Moses hearkened to the voice of his father-in-law, and did all that he had said.

[25] And Moses chose able men out of all Israel, and made them heads over the people, rulers of thousands, rulers of hundreds, rulers of fifties, and rulers of tens.

[26] And they judged the people at all seasons: the hard causes they brought unto Moses, but every small matter they judged themselves.

Deuteronomy 16

Although the following three verses were not cited in the above excerpt, they informed the codifiers' worldview.

(יח) שֹׁפְטִים וְשֹׁטְרִים תִּתֶּן לְךָ בְּכָל שְׁעָרֶיךָ אֲשֶׁר ה' אֱ־לֹהֶיךָ נֹתֵן לְךָ לִשְׁבָטֶיךָ וְשָׁפְטוּ אֶת הָעָם מִשְׁפַּט צֶדֶק.

(יט) לֹא תַטֶּה מִשְׁפָּט לֹא תַכִּיר פָּנִים וְלֹא תִקַּח שֹׁחַד כִּי הַשֹּׁחַד יְעַוֵּר עֵינֵי חֲכָמִים וִיסַלֵּף דִּבְרֵי צַדִּיקִם.

(כ) צֶדֶק צֶדֶק תִּרְדֹּף לְמַעַן תִּחְיֶה וְיָרַשְׁתָּ אֶת הָאָרֶץ אֲשֶׁר ה' אֱ-לֹהֶיךָ נֹתֵן לָךְ.

[18] Judges and officers shalt thou make thee in all thy gates, which the Lord thy God giveth thee, tribe by tribe; and they shall judge the people with righteous judgment.
[19] Thou shalt not wrest judgment; thou shalt not respect persons; neither shalt thou take a gift; for a gift doth blind the eyes of the wise, and pervert the words of the righteous.
[20] Justice, justice shalt thou follow, that thou mayest live, and inherit the land which the Lord thy God giveth thee.

Deuteronomy 21

(יח) כִּי יִהְיֶה לְאִישׁ בֵּן סוֹרֵר וּמוֹרֶה אֵינֶנּוּ שֹׁמֵעַ בְּקוֹל אָבִיו וּבְקוֹל אִמּוֹ וְיִסְּרוּ אֹתוֹ וְלֹא יִשְׁמַע אֲלֵיהֶם.

(יט) וְתָפְשׂוּ בוֹ אָבִיו וְאִמּוֹ וְהוֹצִיאוּ אֹתוֹ אֶל זִקְנֵי עִירוֹ וְאֶל שַׁעַר מְקֹמוֹ.

[18] If a man have a stubborn and rebellious son, which will not obey the voice of his father, or the voice of his mother, and that, when they have chastened him, will not hearken unto them:
[19] Then shall his father and his mother lay hold on him, and bring him out unto the elders of his city, and unto the gate of his place;

Proverbs 25

(ח) אַל תֵּצֵא לָרִב מַהֵר פֶּן מַה תַּעֲשֶׂה בְּאַחֲרִיתָהּ בְּהַכְלִים אֹתְךָ רֵעֶךָ.

[8] Go not forth hastily to strive, lest thou know not what to do in the end thereof, when thy neighbour hath put thee to shame.

Proverbs 31

(כג) נוֹדָע בַּשְּׁעָרִים בַּעְלָהּ בְּשִׁבְתּוֹ עִם זִקְנֵי אָרֶץ.

[23] Her husband is known in the gates, when he sitteth among the elders of the land.

Ruth 4

(א) וּבֹעַז עָלָה הַשַּׁעַר וַיֵּשֶׁב שָׁם וְהִנֵּה הַגֹּאֵל עֹבֵר אֲשֶׁר דִּבֶּר בֹּעַז וַיֹּאמֶר סוּרָה שְׁבָה פֹּה פְּלֹנִי אַלְמֹנִי וַיָּסַר וַיֵּשֵׁב.

(ב) וַיִּקַּח עֲשָׂרָה אֲנָשִׁים מִזִּקְנֵי הָעִיר וַיֹּאמֶר שְׁבוּ פֹה וַיֵּשֵׁבוּ.

(ט) וַיֹּאמֶר בֹּעַז לַזְּקֵנִים וְכָל הָעָם עֵדִים אַתֶּם הַיּוֹם כִּי קָנִיתִי אֶת כָּל אֲשֶׁר לֶאֱלִימֶלֶךְ וְאֵת כָּל אֲשֶׁר לְכִלְיוֹן וּמַחְלוֹן מִיַּד נָעֳמִי.

[1] Then went Boaz up to the gate, and sat him down there: and, behold, the kinsman of whom Boaz spake came by; unto whom he said, Ho, such a one! turn aside, sit down here. And he turned aside, and sat down.

[2] And he took ten men of the elders of the city, and said, Sit ye down here. And they sat down.

[9] And Boaz said unto the elders, and unto all the people, Ye are witnesses this day, that I have bought all that was Elimelech's, and all that was Chilion's and Mahlon's, of the hand of Naomi.

SAMUEL DANFORTH (1626–1674)

The Puritans were a people of preachers, and preachers give speeches. It is not surprising, therefore, that the Puritan legacy extends to American rhetoric. Below is an excerpt from a well-known speech by Samuel Danforth, a preacher in Massachusetts (and also an astronomer who wrote a pamphlet entitled "An Astronomical Description of the Late Comet"). This speech is an example of what is known as a jeremiad. It derives eponymously from Jeremiah, who warned the Israelites about the coming downfall if they did not repent. A jeremiad can be a book or poem – it is often a speech in the American tradition – in which the speaker reveals the audience's sins, warns that their sins will lead to their punishment or even destruction, but admonishes that such destruction can be averted if they understand their wayward ways and repent. A jeremiad thus combines a lament over present failings and sin with an optimistic call to redemption and change. Sin is often understood both as a theological concept and as a departure from the ways of the fathers, envisioning thereby that the first generations were purer and heartier and the current ones loose and corrupt, and that the future redemption is also a return to the original purity of the fathers. Redemption is a return to the ancient ways. The jeremiad form has been used throughout American history, most notably by Abraham Lincoln, Frederick Douglass, and Martin Luther King Jr.

A Brief Recognition of New-England's Errand into the Wilderness (March 11, 1670)[4]

Doct. Such as have sometime left their pleasant Cities and Habitations to enjoy the pure Worship of God in a Wilderness, are apt in time to abate

---

4. McKenna, 39.

and cool in their affection thereunto: but then the Lord calls upon them seriously and thoroughly to examine themselves, what it was that drew them into the Wilderness, and to consider that it was not the expectation of ludicrous levity, nor of Courtly pomp and delicacy, but of the free and clear dispensation of the Gospel and Kingdome of God. This Doctrine consists of two distinct Branches; let me open them severally.

Branch I. Such as have sometime left their pleasant Cities and Habitations, to enjoy the pure Worship of God in a Wilderness, are apt in time to abate and cool in their affection thereunto. To what purpose did the Children of Israel leave their Cities and Houses in Egypt, and go forth into the Wilderness? was it not to hold a feast to the Lord, and to sacrifice to the God of their fathers? That was the onely reason, which they gave of their motion to Pharaoh, Exod. 5. 1, 3. but how soon did they forget their Errand into the Wilderness, and corrupt themselves in their own Inventions? within a few months after their coming out of Egypt, they make a Calf in Horeb, and worship the molten Image, and change their glory into the similitude of an Ox that eateth grass, Psal. 106. 19, 20. Exod. 32. 7, 8. yea for the space of forty years in the Wilderness, while they pretended to Sacrifice to the Lord, they indeed worshipped the Stars and the Host of Heaven, and together with the Lords Tabernacle, carried about with them the Tabernacle of Moloch, Amos 5. 25, 26. Acts 7. 42, 43. And how did they spend their time in the Wilderness, but in tempting God, and in murmuring against their godly and faithful Teachers and Rulers, Moses and Aaron; Psal. 95.8. To what purpose did the Children of the Captivity upon Cyrus his Proclamation, leave their Houses which they had built, and their Vineyards and Oliveyards which they had planted in the Province of Babylon, and return to Judea and Jerusalem, which were now become a Wilderness? was it not that they might build the House of God at Jerusalem, and set up the Temple-worship? But how shamefully did they neglect that great and honourable Work for the space of above forty years? They pretended that Gods time was not come to build his House, because of the rubs and obstructions which they met with; whereas all their difficulties and discouragements hindred not their building of stately houses for themselves, Hag. 1. 2, 3, 4. To what purpose did Jerusalem & all Judea, & all the region round about Jordan, leave their several Cities and Habitations, and flock into the Wilderness of Judea? was it not to see that burning and shining light, which God had raised up? To hear his heavenly Doctrine, and partake of that new Sacrament, which he administred? O how they were affected with his rare and excellent gifts! with his clear, lively and powerful Ministry! The Kingdome of Heaven pressed in upon them with a holy violence, and the violent, the zealous and affectionate hearers of the Gospel, took it by force, Mat. 11. 12. Luk. 16. 16. They leapt over all discouragements and impediments, whether outward, as Legal Rites and Ceremonies, or inward, the sense of their own sin and unworthiness, and pressed into the Kingdome of God, as men rush into a Theatre to see a pleasant Sight, or as Souldiers run into a besieged City, to take the Spoil thereof: but their hot fit is soon over, their affection lasted but for an hour, i.e. a short season, Joh. 5. 35.

Reas. 1. Because the affection of many to the Ministry of the Gospel and the pure Worship of God, is built upon temporary and transitory grounds, as the novelty and strangeness of the matter, the rareness and excellency of Ministerial Gifts, the voice of the people, the countenance of great men, and the hope of worldly advantage. The Jews had lien in ignorance and darkness a long time, being trained up under the superstitious observances of their old Traditions, which were vain, empty and unprofitable Customes, and the Church wanted the gift of Prophecy about four hundred years, and therefore when John the Baptist arose like a bright and burning light, shining amongst them with admirable gifts of the Spirit, and extraordinary severity and gravity of manners, proclaiming the Coming and Kingdom of the Messias (which had been oft promised and long expected) and pressing the people to Repentance and good works; O how they admire and reverence him? especially, when grown popular, and countenanced by Herod the Tetrarch. What sweet affections are kindled! what great expectations are raised! what ravishing joy is conceived! Hoping (as its probable) to make use of his Authority to cast off the Roman yoke, and recover their Civil Liberties, Riches and Honours. But after a little acquaintance with John (for he was a publick Preacher but a year and half) his Doctrine, Administrations and Prophetical Gifts, grew common and stale things, and of little esteem with them; especially, when they saw their carnal hopes frustrated, the Rulers disaffected, and Herods countenance and carriage toward him changed.

Reas. 2. Because Prejudices and Offences are apt to arise in the hearts of many against the faithful Dispensers of the Gospel. The Pharisees and Lawyers came among others to the Baptism of John, but when they hear his sharp reprehensions of their Viperous Opinions and Practices, they nauseate his Doctrine, repudiate his Baptism, calumniate his Conversation, Luke 7. 30. Herodias hath an inward grudge and a quarrel against him, because he found fault with her incestuous Marriage, Mar. 6. 19. Yea, that very Age and Generation of the Jews, were like to a company of surly, sullen and froward children, whom no Musick can please, they neither dance after the Pipe, nor make lamentation after the mourner. They inveigh against John's austerity, saying that he was transported with diabolical fury, and was an enemy to humane society: and they do as much distaste and abhor Christ's gentleness and familiarity, traducing him, as being a sensual and voluptuous person, given to intemperance and luxury, and a Patron and Abettor of looseness and profaneness, Mat. 11. 16–19. Thus doth the frowardness and stubbornness of man, resist and oppose the wisdome and goodness of God, who useth various wayes and instruments to compass poor sinners, but they through their folly and perverseness, frustrate, disanul and abrogate the counsel of God against themselves. The evil spirit that troubled Saul, was quieted and allayed by the sweet Melody of David's Harp: but the mad and outragious fury that transports men against the Truth and the Ministry thereof, cannot be quieted and allayed by the voice of the Charmers, charm they never so wisely.

Branch II. When men abate and cool in their affection to the pure Worship of God, which they went into the Wilderness to enjoy, the Lord calls upon them seriously and thoroughly to examine themselves, what it was that drew them into the Wilderness, and to consider that it was not the expectation of ludicrous levity, nor of Courtly pomp and delicacy, but of the free and clear dispensation of the Gospel and Kingdome of God. Our Saviour knowing that the people had lost their first love and singular affection to the revelation of his grace by the Ministry of his Herauld John, He is very intense in examining them, what expectation drew them into the Wilderness: He doth not once nor twice, but thrice propound that Question, What went ye out into the Wilderness to see? Yea, in particular he enquires whether it were to see a man that was like to a Reed shaken with the wind? or whether it were to see a man clothed like a Courtier, or whether it were to see a Prophet, and then determines the Question, concluding that it was to see a great and excellent Prophet, and that had not they seen rare and admirable things in him, they would never have gone out into the Wilderness unto him.

The Reason is, Because the serious consideration of the inestimable grace and mercy of God in the free and clear dispensation of the Gospel and Kingdome of God, is a special means to convince men of their folly and perverseness in undervaluing the same, and a sanctified remedy to recover their affections thereunto. The Lord foreseeing the defection of Israel after Moses his death, commands him to write that Prophetical Song, recorded in Deut. 32. as a Testimony against them: wherein the chief remedy, which he prescribes for the prevention and healing of their Apostacy, is their calling to remembrance Gods great and signal love in manifesting himself to them in the Wilderness, in conducting them safely and mercifully and giving them possession of their promised Inheritance, ver. 7–14. And when Israel was apostatized and fallen, the Lord to convince them of their ingratitude and folly, brings to their remembrance his deliverance of them out of Egypt, his leading them through the Wilderness for the space of forty years, and not onely giving them possession of their Enemies Land, but also raising up, even of their own Sons, Prophets, faithful and eminent Ministers, and of their young men Nazarites, who being separated from worldly delights and encumbrances, were Paterns of Purity and Holiness: all which were great and obliging mercies. Yea, the Lord appeals to their own Consciences, whether these his favours were not real and signal, Amos 2. 10, 11. The Prophet Jeremiah, that he might reduce the people from their back-slidings, cries in the ears of Jerusalem, with earnestness and boldness declaring unto them, that the Lord remembered how well they stood affected towards him, when he first chose them to be his people and espoused them to himself, how they followed him in the Wilderness, and kept close to him in their long and wearisome passage through the uncultured Desert; how they were then consecrated to God, and set apart for his Worship and Service; as the first-fruits are wont to be sequestred and devoted to God: and thereupon expostulates with them for their forsaking the Lord, and following after their Idols, Jer. 2. 2, 3, 5, 6. Surely our Saviour's Dialogism with his Hearers in my

Text, is not a meer Rhetorical Elegancy to adorn his Testimony concerning John, but a clear and strong conviction of their folly in slighting and despising that which they sometime so highly pretended unto, and a wholesome admonition and direction how to recover their primitive affection to his Doctrine and Administration.

USE I. Of solemn and serious Enquiry to us all in this general Assembly, Whether we have not in a great measure forgotten our Errand into the Wilderness. You have solemnly professed before God, Angels and Men, that the Cause of your leaving your Country, Kindred and Fathers houses, and transporting your selves with your Wives, Little Ones and Substance over the vast Ocean into this waste and howling Wilderness, was your Liberty to walk in the Faith of the Gospel with all good Conscience according to the Order of the Gospel, and your enjoyment of the pure Worship of God according to his Institution, without humane Mixtures and Impositions. Now let us sadly consider whether our ancient and primitive affections to the Lord Jesus, his glorious Gospel, his pure and Spiritual Worship and the Order of his House, remain, abide and continue firm, constant, entire and inviolate. Our Saviour's reiteration of this Question, What went ye out into the Wilderness to see? is no idle repetition, but a sad conviction of our dulness and backwardness to this great duty, and a clear demonstration of the weight and necessity thereof. It may be a grief to us to be put upon such an Inquisition; as it is said of Peter, Joh. 21. 17. Peter was grieved, because he said unto him the third time, Lovest thou me? but the Lord knoweth that a strict and rigid examination of our hearts in this point, is no more than necessary. Wherefore let us call to remembrance the former dayes, and consider whether it was not then better with us, then it is now....

But who is there left among you, that saw these Churches in their first glory, and how do you see them now? Are they not in your eyes in comparison thereof, as nothing? How is the gold become dim! how is the most fine gold changed! Is not the Temper, Complexion and Countenance of the Churches strangely altered? Doth not a careless, remiss, flat, dry, cold, dead frame of spirit, grow in upon us secretly, strongly, prodigiously? They that have Ordinances, are as though they had none; and they that hear the Word, as though they heard it not; and they that pray, as though they prayed not; and they that receive Sacraments, as though they received them not; and they that are exercised in the holy things, using them by the by, as matters of custome and ceremony, so as not to hinder their eager prosecution of other things which their hearts are set upon. Yea and in some particular Congregations amongst us, is there not in stead of a sweet smell, a stink? and in stead of a girdle, a rent? and in stead of a stomacher, a girding with sackcloth? and burning instead of beauty? yea the Vineyard is all overgrown with thorns, and nettles cover the face thereof, and the stone-wall thereof is broken down, Prov. 24. 31. yea, and that which is the most sad and certain sign of calamity approaching. Iniquity aboundeth, and the love of many waxeth cold, Mat. 24. 12. Pride, Contention, Worldliness, Covetousness, Luxury, Drunkenness and Uncleanness break in like a flood upon us, and good men grow cold in their love to God and to one another. If a man be cold in his bed, let them lay on the more clothes, that he may get heat: but we are like to David in his old age, they covered him with clothes, but he gat no heat, 1 King 1.

Hebraic Sources

Samuel Danforth thunderingly reminded his audience of the Israelites' tendency to lose their way time and time again – coming out of Egypt, wandering in the Wilderness, settling in the Land, growing fat in exile. He quoted the prophets, through whom God chastised the Hebrew nation for their syncretism, rebellion, and neglect of God and the Temple, and continuing in that tradition, called on his audience to mind their purpose and mend their ways.

Exodus 32

(ז) וַיְדַבֵּר ה' אֶל מֹשֶׁה לֶךְ רֵד כִּי שִׁחֵת עַמְּךָ אֲשֶׁר הֶעֱלֵיתָ מֵאֶרֶץ מִצְרָיִם.

(ח) סָרוּ מַהֵר מִן הַדֶּרֶךְ אֲשֶׁר צִוִּיתִם עָשׂוּ לָהֶם עֵגֶל מַסֵּכָה וַיִּשְׁתַּחֲווּ לוֹ וַיִּזְבְּחוּ לוֹ וַיֹּאמְרוּ אֵלֶּה אֱ-לֹהֶיךָ יִשְׂרָאֵל אֲשֶׁר הֶעֱלוּךָ מֵאֶרֶץ מִצְרָיִם.

[7] And the Lord said unto Moses, Go, get thee down; for thy people, which thou broughtest out of the land of Egypt, have corrupted themselves:
[8] They have turned aside quickly out of the way which I commanded them: they have made them a molten calf, and have worshipped it, and have sacrificed thereunto, and said, These be thy gods, O Israel, which have brought thee up out of the land of Egypt.

Amos 5

(כה) הַזְּבָחִים וּמִנְחָה הִגַּשְׁתֶּם לִי בַמִּדְבָּר אַרְבָּעִים שָׁנָה בֵּית יִשְׂרָאֵל.
(כו) וּנְשָׂאתֶם אֵת סִכּוּת מַלְכְּכֶם וְאֵת כִּיּוּן צַלְמֵיכֶם כּוֹכַב אֱלֹהֵיכֶם אֲשֶׁר עֲשִׂיתֶם לָכֶם.

[25] Have ye offered unto me sacrifices and offerings in the wilderness forty years, O house of Israel?
[26] But ye have borne the tabernacle of your Moloch and Chiun your images, the star of your god, which ye made to yourselves.

Psalm 95

(ח) אַל תַּקְשׁוּ לְבַבְכֶם כִּמְרִיבָה כְּיוֹם מַסָּה בַּמִּדְבָּר.
(ט) אֲשֶׁר נִסּוּנִי אֲבוֹתֵיכֶם בְּחָנוּנִי גַּם רָאוּ פָעֳלִי.
(י) אַרְבָּעִים שָׁנָה אָקוּט בְּדוֹר וָאֹמַר עַם תֹּעֵי לֵבָב הֵם וְהֵם לֹא יָדְעוּ דְרָכָי.

[8] Harden not your heart, as in the provocation, and as in the day of temptation in the wilderness:
[9] When your fathers tempted me, proved me, and saw my work.
[10] Forty years long was I grieved with this generation, and said, It is a people that do err in their heart, and they have not known my ways:

II Samuel 7

(ב) וַיֹּאמֶר הַמֶּלֶךְ אֶל נָתָן הַנָּבִיא רְאֵה נָא אָנֹכִי יוֹשֵׁב בְּבֵית אֲרָזִים וַאֲרוֹן הָאֱ-לֹהִים יֹשֵׁב בְּתוֹךְ הַיְרִיעָה.

[2] That the king said unto Nathan the prophet: See now, I dwell in a house of cedar, but the ark of God dwelleth within curtains.

Haggai 1

(א) בִּשְׁנַת שְׁתַּיִם לְדָרְיָוֶשׁ הַמֶּלֶךְ בַּחֹדֶשׁ הַשִּׁשִּׁי בְּיוֹם אֶחָד לַחֹדֶשׁ הָיָה דְבַר ה' בְּיַד חַגַּי הַנָּבִיא אֶל זְרֻבָּבֶל בֶּן שְׁאַלְתִּיאֵל פַּחַת יְהוּדָה וְאֶל יְהוֹשֻׁעַ בֶּן יְהוֹצָדָק הַכֹּהֵן הַגָּדוֹל לֵאמֹר.
(ב) כֹּה אָמַר ה' צְבָאוֹת לֵאמֹר הָעָם הַזֶּה אָמְרוּ לֹא עֵת בֹּא עֵת בֵּית ה' לְהִבָּנוֹת.
(ג) וַיְהִי דְּבַר ה' בְּיַד חַגַּי הַנָּבִיא לֵאמֹר.
(ד) הַעֵת לָכֶם אַתֶּם לָשֶׁבֶת בְּבָתֵּיכֶם סְפוּנִים וְהַבַּיִת הַזֶּה חָרֵב.
(ה) וְעַתָּה כֹּה אָמַר ה' צְבָאוֹת שִׂימוּ לְבַבְכֶם עַל דַּרְכֵיכֶם.

¹ In the second year of Darius the king, in the sixth month, in the first day of the month, came the word of the Lord by Haggai the prophet unto Zerubbabel the son of Shealtiel, governor of Judah, and to Joshua the son of Jehozadak, the high priest, saying:

² Thus speaketh the Lord of hosts, saying: This people say: The time is not come, the time that the Lord's house should be built.

³ Then came the word of the Lord by Haggai the prophet, saying:

⁴ Is it a time for you yourselves to dwell in your cieled houses, while this house lieth waste?

⁵ Now therefore thus saith the Lord of hosts: Consider your ways.

Deuteronomy 32

(ז) זְכֹר יְמוֹת עוֹלָם בִּינוּ שְׁנוֹת דּוֹר וָדוֹר שְׁאַל אָבִיךָ וְיַגֵּדְךָ זְקֵנֶיךָ וְיֹאמְרוּ לָךְ.

(ח) בְּהַנְחֵל עֶלְיוֹן גּוֹיִם בְּהַפְרִידוֹ בְּנֵי אָדָם יַצֵּב גְּבֻלֹת עַמִּים לְמִסְפַּר בְּנֵי יִשְׂרָאֵל.

(ט) כִּי חֵלֶק ה' עַמּוֹ יַעֲקֹב חֶבֶל נַחֲלָתוֹ.

(י) יִמְצָאֵהוּ בְּאֶרֶץ מִדְבָּר וּבְתֹהוּ יְלֵל יְשִׁמֹן יְסֹבְבֶנְהוּ יְבוֹנְנֵהוּ יִצְּרֶנְהוּ כְּאִישׁוֹן עֵינוֹ.

(יא) כְּנֶשֶׁר יָעִיר קִנּוֹ עַל גּוֹזָלָיו יְרַחֵף יִפְרֹשׂ כְּנָפָיו יִקָּחֵהוּ יִשָּׂאֵהוּ עַל אֶבְרָתוֹ.

(יב) ה' בָּדָד יַנְחֶנּוּ וְאֵין עִמּוֹ אֵל נֵכָר.

(יג) יַרְכִּבֵהוּ עַל במותי [בָּמֳתֵי] אָרֶץ וַיֹּאכַל תְּנוּבֹת שָׂדָי וַיֵּנִקֵהוּ דְבַשׁ מִסֶּלַע וְשֶׁמֶן מֵחַלְמִישׁ צוּר.

(יד) חֶמְאַת בָּקָר וַחֲלֵב צֹאן עִם חֵלֶב כָּרִים וְאֵילִים בְּנֵי בָשָׁן וְעַתּוּדִים עִם חֵלֶב כִּלְיוֹת חִטָּה וְדַם עֵנָב תִּשְׁתֶּה חָמֶר.

(טו) וַיִּשְׁמַן יְשֻׁרוּן וַיִּבְעָט שָׁמַנְתָּ עָבִיתָ כָּשִׂיתָ וַיִּטֹּשׁ אֱ-לוֹהַּ עָשָׂהוּ וַיְנַבֵּל צוּר יְשֻׁעָתוֹ.

⁷ Remember the days of old, consider the years of many generations; ask thy father, and he will declare unto thee, thine elders, and they will tell thee.

⁸ When the Most High gave to the nations their inheritance, when He separated the children of men, He set the borders of the peoples according to the number of the children of Israel.

⁹ For the portion of the Lord is His people, Jacob the lot of His inheritance.

¹⁰ He found him in a desert land, and in the waste, a howling wilderness; He compassed him about, He cared for him, He kept him as the apple of His eye.

¹¹ As an eagle that stirreth up her nest, hovereth over her young, spreadeth abroad her wings, taketh them, beareth them on her pinions –

¹² The Lord alone did lead him, and there was no strange god with Him.

¹³ He made him ride on the high places of the earth, and he did eat the fruitage of the field; and He made him to suck honey out of the crag, and oil out of the flinty rock;

¹⁴ Curd of kine, and milk of sheep, with fat of lambs, and rams of the breed of Bashan, and he-goats, with the kidney-fat of wheat; and of the blood of the grape thou drankest foaming wine.

¹⁵ But Jeshurun waxed fat, and kicked – thou didst wax fat, thou didst grow thick, thou didst become gross – and he forsook God who made him, and contemned the Rock of his salvation.

Amos 2

(ט) וְאָנֹכִי הִשְׁמַדְתִּי אֶת הָאֱמֹרִי מִפְּנֵיהֶם אֲשֶׁר כְּגֹבַהּ אֲרָזִים גָּבְהוֹ וְחָסֹן הוּא כָּאַלּוֹנִים וָאַשְׁמִיד פִּרְיוֹ מִמַּעַל וְשָׁרָשָׁיו מִתָּחַת.
(י) וְאָנֹכִי הֶעֱלֵיתִי אֶתְכֶם מֵאֶרֶץ מִצְרָיִם וָאוֹלֵךְ אֶתְכֶם בַּמִּדְבָּר אַרְבָּעִים שָׁנָה לָרֶשֶׁת אֶת אֶרֶץ הָאֱמֹרִי.
(יא) וָאָקִים מִבְּנֵיכֶם לִנְבִיאִים וּמִבַּחוּרֵיכֶם לִנְזִרִים הַאַף אֵין זֹאת בְּנֵי יִשְׂרָאֵל נְאֻם ה'.

⁹ Yet I destroyed the Amorite before them, whose height was like the height of the cedars, and he was strong as the oaks; yet I destroyed his fruit from above, and his roots from beneath.
¹⁰ Also I brought you up out of the land of Egypt, and led you forty years in the wilderness, to possess the land of the Amorites.
¹¹ And I raised up of your sons for prophets, and of your young men for Nazirites. Is it not even thus, O ye children of Israel? saith the Lord.

Jeremiah 2

(א) וַיְהִי דְבַר ה' אֵלַי לֵאמֹר.
(ב) הָלֹךְ וְקָרָאתָ בְאָזְנֵי יְרוּשָׁלִַם לֵאמֹר כֹּה אָמַר ה' זָכַרְתִּי לָךְ חֶסֶד נְעוּרַיִךְ אַהֲבַת כְּלוּלֹתָיִךְ לֶכְתֵּךְ אַחֲרַי בַּמִּדְבָּר בְּאֶרֶץ לֹא זְרוּעָה.
(ג) קֹדֶשׁ יִשְׂרָאֵל לַה' רֵאשִׁית תְּבוּאָתֹה כָּל אֹכְלָיו יֶאְשָׁמוּ רָעָה תָּבֹא אֲלֵיהֶם נְאֻם ה'.
(ד) שִׁמְעוּ דְבַר ה' בֵּית יַעֲקֹב וְכָל מִשְׁפְּחוֹת בֵּית יִשְׂרָאֵל.
(ה) כֹּה אָמַר ה' מַה מָּצְאוּ אֲבוֹתֵיכֶם בִּי עָוֶל כִּי רָחֲקוּ מֵעָלָי וַיֵּלְכוּ אַחֲרֵי הַהֶבֶל וַיֶּהְבָּלוּ.
(ו) וְלֹא אָמְרוּ אַיֵּה ה' הַמַּעֲלֶה אֹתָנוּ מֵאֶרֶץ מִצְרָיִם הַמּוֹלִיךְ אֹתָנוּ בַּמִּדְבָּר בְּאֶרֶץ עֲרָבָה וְשׁוּחָה בְּאֶרֶץ צִיָּה וְצַלְמָוֶת בְּאֶרֶץ לֹא עָבַר בָּהּ אִישׁ וְלֹא יָשַׁב אָדָם שָׁם.

¹ And the word of the Lord came to me, saying:
² Go, and cry in the ears of Jerusalem, saying: Thus saith the Lord: I remember for thee the affection of thy youth, the love of thine espousals; how thou wentest after Me in the wilderness, in a land that was not sown.
³ Israel is the Lord's hallowed portion, His first-fruits of the increase; all that devour him shall be held guilty, evil shall come upon them, saith the Lord.
⁴ Hear ye the word of the Lord, O house of Jacob, and all the families of the house of Israel;

⁵ Thus saith the Lord: What unrighteousness have your fathers found in Me, that they are gone far from Me, and have walked after things of nought, and are become nought?

⁶ Neither said they: Where is the Lord that brought us up out of the land of Egypt; that led us through the wilderness, through a land of deserts and of pits, through a land of drought and of the shadow of death, through a land that no man passed through, and where no man dwelt?

JONATHAN EDWARDS (1703–1758)

The Puritans were not the only religious group in America. While all the English in the New World were Christian, there were many different denominations. And there was hardly any love lost between them. Indeed, the difference between a Quaker and a Reformed Puritan was seen as so great, and such a threat, that Quaker proselytizing was forbidden, and those who attempted it were whipped. Between 1659 and 1661, four Quakers were hung for sedition. The Baptists had a relatively small presence in the colonies, until the Great Awakening in the 1740s. The first Baptist settlement in the colonies was led by Roger Williams (1603–1683), who was supposedly more tolerant than other members of the Massachusetts colonies. Yet he too felt great antipathy toward the Quakers and lambasted their pacifism. Williams believed in a radical break with the Church of England and that local church affairs should be locally controlled. John Winthrop arranged to have Williams banished when he tried to proliferate his dissenting views, including the idea that those who did not confess may not attend church, and that the Puritans had no right to the Native American lands in the New World. Anne Hutchinson, who asserted that Christians do not need the moral law for salvation and that salvation was by grace and not by works, was also banished. The battles of the Reformation and within the Reformation still raged in America, and these episodes indicate that America was far from a place of easy toleration and pure religious freedom. The advantage of the vast country was that if one did not like a given religion, one could leave and start one's own community. Freedom was thus the product of the great expanse of the New World. Indeed, in 1681, William Penn acquired land from the King to found a haven for religious freedom, Pennsylvania, and it was the most secure place for religious toleration in the world.

The beginning of the Americanization of Protestantism began with the First Great Awakening (c. 1730-1755), the first religious movement in the New World that had a distinctly New World feel to it. The Second Great

Awakening (c. 1790–1840) tinged Protestantism with more individualism and activism; it became more open to the power of religious emotion, lay-led services, and individual Bible readings. With a booming American population – growing from around 240,000 to over one million from the late seventeenth to the mid-eighteenth century – there were a large number of new people to bring into the faith. The period was called the First Great Awakening because of an upsurge in piety: Baptists, Presbyterians, and Dutch Reformed populations all grew. The extent of this upsurge, however, has been questioned. In Connecticut during the First Great Awakening, about the same number of people joined churches as left them. And there is thus some exaggeration in the numbers of those who joined. In fact, some studies suggest that church attendance declined gradually from 1700 to the time of the Revolution.[5]

The First Great Awakening produced two very captivating figures: George Whitefield, a charismatic preacher, and the theologically astute Jonathan Edwards. Whitefield, so squinty-eyed that his nickname was Dr. Squintum, was the more charismatic figure, able to make crowds weep with his honeyed words. Edwards was the deeper thinker, a reader of Locke and Newton, and America's greatest early theologian. His most famous sermon is "Sinners in the Hands of an Angry God," in which he depicts mankind as depraved sinners:

> *Your wickedness makes you as it were heavy as lead, and to tend downwards with great weight and pressure towards hell; and if God should let you go, you would immediately sink and swiftly descend and plunge into the bottomless gulf, and your healthy constitution, and your own care and prudence, and best contrivance, and all your righteousness, would have no more influence to uphold you and keep you out of hell, than a spider's web would have to stop a falling rock. Were it not for the sovereign pleasure of God, the earth would not bear you one moment; for you are a burden to it; the creation groans with you; the creature is made subject to the bondage of your corruption, not willingly; the sun does not willingly shine upon you to give*

---

5. On religion in early America, see especially Mark A. Noll, *America's God: From Jonathan Edwards to Abraham Lincoln* (Oxford: Oxford University Press, 2005) and Nathan O. Hatch, *The Democratization of American Christianity* (New Haven: Yale University Press, 1991).

you light to serve sin and Satan; the earth does not willingly yield her increase to satisfy your lusts; nor is it willingly a stage for your wickedness to be acted upon; the air does not willingly serve you for breath to maintain the flame of life in your vitals, while you spend your life in the service of God's enemies.

Despite his traditionally Calvinist depiction of the depravity of mankind and the unfathomable and absolute grace of God, Edwards also turned, as did others of his generation, to the inner workings of the heart and the importance of subjective religious experience. He died at the age of fifty-four, just as he was assuming the presidency of Princeton College. His grandson was Aaron Burr, vice president under Thomas Jefferson and notorious for killing Alexander Hamilton in a duel.

The following is an excerpt from Edwards's Some Thoughts concerning the Present Revival of Religion in New England (1742). The epitaph of the book is from Isaiah 40:3: "Prepare ye the way of the Lord, make straight in the desert a highway for our God."

The Latter Day Glory Is Probably to Begin in America (1742)

It is not unlikely that this work of God's Spirit, so extraordinary and wonderful, is the dawning, or, at least, a prelude of that glorious work of God, so often foretold in Scripture, which, in the progress and issue of it, shall renew the world of mankind. If we consider how long since the things foretold as what should precede this great event, have been accomplished; and how long this event has been expected by the church of God, and thought to be nigh by the most eminent men of God in the church; and withal consider what the state of things now is, and has for a considerable time been, in the church of God, and the world of mankind; we cannot reasonably think otherwise, than that the beginning of this great work of God must be near. And there are many things that make it probable that this work will begin in America. It is signified that it shall begin in some very remote part of the world, with which other parts have no communication but by navigation, in Isa. lx. 9. "Surely the isles shall wait for me, and the ships of Tarshish first, to bring my sons from far." It is exceeding manifest that this chapter is a prophecy of the prosperity of the church, in its most glorious state on earth, in the latter days; and I cannot think that any thing else can be here intended but America by the isles that are far off, from whence the first-born sons of that glorious day shall be brought. Indeed, by the isles, in prophecies of gospel-times, is very often meant Europe. It is so in prophecies of that great spreading of the gospel that should be soon after Christ's time, because it was far separated from that part of the world where the church of God had till then been, by the sea. But this prophecy cannot have respect to the conversion of Europe, in the time of that great work of God, in the primitive ages of the Christian church; for it was not fulfilled then. The isles and ships of Tarshish, thus understood, did not wait for God first; that glorious work did not begin in Europe, but in Jerusalem, and had for a considerable time been very wonderfully carried on in Asia, before it reached Europe. And as it is not that work of God which is chiefly intended in this chapter, but some more glorious work that should be in the latter ages of the Christian church; therefore, some other part of the world is here intended by the isles, that should be, as Europe then was, far separated from that part of the world where the church had before been, and with which it can have no communication but by the ships of Tarshish. And what is chiefly intended is not the British isles, nor any isles near the other continent; for they are spoken of as at a great distance from that part of the world where the church had till then been. This prophecy therefore seems plainly to point out America, as the first-fruits of that glorious day.

God has made as it were two worlds here below, two great habitable continents, far separated one from the other: The latter is as it were now but newly created; it has been, till of late, wholly the possession of Satan, the church of God having never been in it, as it has been in the other continent, from the beginning of the world. This new world is probably now discovered, that the new and most glorious state of God's church on earth might commence there; that God might in it begin a new world in a spiritual respect, when he creates the new heavens and new earth.

God has already put that honour upon the other continent, that Christ was born there literally and there made the purchase of redemption. So, as Providence observes a kind of equal distribution of things, it is not unlikely that the great spiritual birth of Christ, and the most glorious application of redemption, is to begin in this. The elder sister brought forth Judah, of whom Christ came, and so she was the mother of Christ; but the younger sister, after long barrenness, brought forth Joseph and Benjamin, the beloved children. Joseph who had the most glorious apparel, the coat of many colours; who was separated from his brethren, and was exalted to great glory out of a dark dungeon – who fed and saved the world when ready to perish with famine, and was as fruitful bough by a well, whose branches ran over the wall, and was blessed with all manner of blessings and precious things of heaven and earth, through the good-will of him that dwelt in the bush – was, as by the horns of an unicorn, to push the people together, to the ends of the earth, i.e., conquer the world. See Gen. xlix. 22, &c. and Deut. xxxiii. 13, &c. And Benjamin, whose mess was five times so great as that of any of his brethren, and to whom Joseph, that type of Christ, gave wealth and raiment far beyond all the rest, Gen. xlv. 22.

The other continent hath slain Christ, and has from age to age shed the blood of the saints and martyrs of Jesus, and has often been as it were deluged with the church's blood. God has therefore probably reserved the honour of building the glorious temple to the daughter that has not shed so much blood, when those times of the peace, prosperity, and glory of the church, typified by the reign of Solomon, shall commence.

The Gentiles first received the true religion from the Jews: God's church of ancient times had been among them, and Christ was of them. But, that there may be a kind of equality in the dispensations of providence, God has so ordered it, that when the Jews come to be admitted to the benefits of the evangelical dispensation, and to receive their highest privileges of all, they should receive the gospel from the Gentiles. Though Christ was of them, yet they have been guilty of crucifying him; it is therefore the will of God, that the Jews should not have the honour of communicating the blessing of the kingdom of God in its most glorious state to the Gentiles; but on the contrary, they shall receive the gospel in the beginning of that glorious day from the Gentiles. In some analogy to this, I apprehend, God's dealings will be with the two continents. America has received the true religion of the old continent; the church of ancient times has been there, and Christ is from thence. But that there may be an equality, and inasmuch as that continent has crucified Christ, they shall not have the honour of communicating religion in its most glorious state to us, but we to them.

The old continent has been the source and original of mankind, in several respects. The first parents of mankind dwelt there; and there dwelt Noah and his sons; there the second Adam was born, and crucified and raised again: and 'tis probable that, in some measure to balance these things, the most glorious renovation of the world shall originate from the new continent, and the church of God in that respect be from hence. And so it is probable that will come to pass in spirituals, which has taken place in temporals, with respect to America; that whereas, till of late, the world was supplied with its silver, and gold, and earthly treasures from the old continent, now it is supplied chiefly from the new; so the course of things in spiritual respects will be in like manner turned. – And it is worthy to be noted, that America was discovered about the time of the reformation, or but little before: which reformation was the first thing that God did towards the glorious renovation of the world, after it had sunk into the depths of darkness and ruin, under the great anti-Christian apostacy. So that, as soon as this new world stands forth in view, God presently goes about doing some great thing in order to make way for the introduction of the church's latter-day glory – which is to have its first seat in, and is to take its rise from, that new world.

It is agreeable to God's manner, when he accomplishes any glorious work in the world, in order to introduce a new and more excellent state of his church, to begin where no foundation had been already laid, that the power of God might be the more conspicuous; that the work might appear to be entirely God's, and be more manifestly a creation out of nothing; agreeable to Hos. i. 10 [2:1]. "And it shall come to pass, that in the place where it was said unto them, Ye are not my people, there it shall be said unto them, Ye are the sons of the living God." When God is about to turn the earth into a paradise, he does not begin his work where there is some good growth already, but in the wilderness, where nothing grows, and nothing is to be seen but dry sand and barren rocks; that the light may shine out of darkness, the world be replenished from emptiness, and the earth watered by springs from a droughty desert; agreeable to many prophecies of Scripture, as Isa. xxxii. 15. "Until the Spirit be poured from on high, and the wilderness become a fruitful field." And chap. xli. 18, 19. "I will open rivers in high places, and fountains in the midst of the valleys: I will make the wilderness a pool of water, and the dry land springs of water. I will plant in the wilderness the cedar, the shittah-tree, and the myrtle, and oil-tree: I will set in the desert the fir-tree, and the pine, and the box-tree together." And chap. xliii. 20. "I will give waters in the wilderness, and rivers in the desert, to give drink to my people, my chosen." And many other parallel scriptures might be mentioned. Now as, when God is about to do some great work for his church, his manner is to begin at the lower end; so, when he is about to renew the whole habitable earth, it is probable that he will begin in this utmost, meanest, youngest, and weakest part of it, where the church of God has been planted last of all; and so the first shall be last: and that will be fulfilled in an eminent manner in Isa. xxiv. 19. "From the uttermost part of the earth have we heard songs, even glory to the righteous."

There are several things that seem to me to argue, that the Sun of righteousness, the Sun of the new heavens and new earth, when he rises – and comes forth as the bridegroom of his church, rejoicing as a strong man to run his race, having his going forth from the end of heaven, and his circuit to the end of it, that nothing may be hid from the light and heat of it – shall rise in the west, contrary to the course of things in the old heavens and earth. The movements of Providence shall in the day be so wonderfully altered in many respects, that God will as it were change the course of nature, in answer to the prayers of his church; as he caused the sun to go from the west to the east, when he promised to do such great things for his church; a deliverance out of the hand of the king of Assyria, is often used by the prophet Isaiah, as a type of the glorious deliverance of the church from her enemies in the latter days. The resurrection as it were of Hezekiah, the king and captain of the church (as he is called, 2 Kings xx. 5.) is given as an earnest of the church's resurrection and salvation, Isa. xxxviii. 6. And is a type of the resurrection of Christ. At the same time there is a resurrection of the sun, or coming back and rising again from the west, whither it had gone down, which is also a type of the sun of righteousness. The sun was brought back ten

45

degrees; which probably brought it to the meridian. The Sun of righteousness has long been going down from east to west; and probably when the time comes of the church's deliverance from her enemies, so often typified by the Assyrians, the light will rise in the west, till it shines through the world like the sun in its meridian brightness.

The same seems also to be represented by the course of the waters of the sanctuary, Ezek. xlvii. Which was from west to east; which waters undoubtedly represented the Holy spirit, in the progress of his saving influences, in the latter ages of the world: for it is manifest, that the whole of those last chapters of Ezekiel treat concerning the glorious state of the church at that time. And if we may suppose that this glorious work of God shall begin in any part of America, I think, if we consider the circumstances of the settlement of New England, it must needs appear the most likely, of all American colonies, to be the place whence this work shall principally take its rise. And, if these things be so, it gives us more abundant reason to hope that what is now seen in America, and especially in New England, may prove the dawn of that glorious day; and the very uncommon and wonderful circumstances and events of this work, seem to me strongly to argue that God intends it as the beginning or forerunner of something vastly great.

Edwards's Miscellanies *constitutes the voluminous collection of his personal notebooks, in which he wrote on all manner of topics. They afford us a window onto his innermost theological ruminations.*

Miscellanies (1722)

439. Covenants. Testaments.

The covenant that God made of old with the children of Israel is spoken of in Scripture as different from that which he makes with his people in these gospel times. We will consider what difference there was. And here,

1. God proposed a covenant to them that was essentially and entirely different, which was the covenant of works: he

promulgated the moral law to them, together with many positive precepts of the ceremonial and judicial law, that answered to the prohibition of eating the forbidden fruit; which God proposed to them with the threatening of death, and the curse affixed to the least defect in obedience. If it be inquired, in what sense God gave this covenant to them more than to us, I answer, that although it was as much impossible for them to be saved by it as it is for us, yet it was really proposed to them as a covenant for them, for their trial (Exodus 20:20 [20:16]), that they might this way be brought to despair of obtaining life by this covenant, and might see their necessity of free grace and a Mediator. God chose this way to convince them, by Proposing the covenant of works to them, as though he expected they should seek and obtain life in this way, that everyone, when he came to apply it to himself, might see its impracticableness; as being a way of conviction to that ignorant and infantile state of the church. God did with them as Christ did with the young man, when he came and inquired what he should do to inherit eternal life: Christ bid him keep the commandments. There was this difference also: the law, or covenant of works, was more fully and plainly revealed to them than the gospel, or covenant of grace, was.

2. The covenant which God made with them, and by which they indeed obtained blessings of God, though in some respects it was the same, yet in other respects it was different. Covenants that God makes with men can be different but these two ways, by having different conditions, and different things promised upon those conditions. Now the conditions were the same with respect to the general nature of them, that is, the exercise of the same spirit of true holiness, and gracious respect to God in faith, and a sincere and universal obedience; but yet the particular matter of that faith [and] obedience was in considerable part different. Such explicit acts of faith with respect to the Mediator and the gospel doctrines, was in no wise necessary then. And the obedience was not the same, because the commands were different. There were innumerable laws that they of old must obey in order to their salvation, that now are abolished; all those laws came into the

terms of the covenant, Jeremiah 34:13–14. And [there are] some duties we are now obliged to do in order to our salvation, that they could be saved without; some moral duties that though they were obliged to, yet they could then be saved in great neglect of them, that we cannot now, by reason of our being under so much stronger obligations to perform them now, and by reason of the much clearer revelations of them and the foundation of them. And so there are duties that respect the Messias and his salvation and another world that are necessary now to salvation, that were not then, by reason of the different state of the church and of revelation. Though they could not be saved without the same principle and spirit, of old, yet they might be saved without such exercises and explicit acts thereof. So that the covenant is a new covenant, because the conditions of it are in some respect new.

3. There were also things promised that were different. The covenant, as it was made with the nation as a nation, had the promises of Canaan, and of prosperity, and many public tokens of God's favor in it.

4. And as to particular persons, the promises of eternal life and immortality, which are the great and main things promised in the gospel, they are in a respect new. For, though they of old had general promises of God's grace and favor, that did indeed infer a future state, yet there were no express promises in the law of Moses, of any discoveries or fruits of that grace and favor after this life; the other were very much kept out of sight: all that was expressly promised, either of outward or spiritual blessings, extended not beyond this present state of mankind in this world.

5. That which is more primarily the condition of the covenant of grace (see explication of Jeremiah 31:33), viz. faith, was not so fully revealed. Herein the church now has the advantage of the Old Testament church as to comfort, in the advantages they are under of being assured of their justification. Then, the secondary conditions, the fruits of faith, were more fully revealed and insisted on than the primary.

Hebraic Sources

In the New World as Jonathan Edwards depicted it, the pregnant possibilities of
the period were rendered tangible. Owing to his Protestantism, he mostly cited
the Hebrew Bible, finding old promises, blessings, and covenants that he believed
were being fulfilled in his day. For Edwards, America was the new Israel.

Genesis 49

(כב) בֵּן פֹּרָת יוֹסֵף בֵּן פֹּרָת עֲלֵי עָיִן בָּנוֹת צָעֲדָה עֲלֵי שׁוּר.

(כג) וַיְמָרֲרֻהוּ וָרֹבּוּ וַיִּשְׂטְמֻהוּ בַּעֲלֵי חִצִּים.

(כד) וַתֵּשֶׁב בְּאֵיתָן קַשְׁתּוֹ וַיָּפֹזּוּ זְרֹעֵי יָדָיו מִידֵי אֲבִיר יַעֲקֹב מִשָּׁם רֹעֶה אֶבֶן יִשְׂרָאֵל.

(כה) מֵאֵל אָבִיךָ וְיַעְזְרֶךָּ וְאֵת שַׁדַּי וִיבָרֲכֶךָּ בִּרְכֹת שָׁמַיִם מֵעָל בִּרְכֹת תְּהוֹם רֹבֶצֶת תָּחַת בִּרְכֹת שָׁדַיִם וָרָחַם.

(כו) בִּרְכֹת אָבִיךָ גָּבְרוּ עַל בִּרְכֹת הוֹרַי עַד תַּאֲוַת גִּבְעֹת עוֹלָם תִּהְיֶיןָ לְרֹאשׁ יוֹסֵף וּלְקָדְקֹד נְזִיר אֶחָיו.

22 Joseph is a fruitful vine, a fruitful vine by a fountain; its branches run over the wall.

23 The archers have dealt bitterly with him, and shot at him, and hated him;

24 But his bow abode firm, and the arms of his hands were made supple, by the hands of the Mighty One of Jacob, from thence, from the Shepherd, the Stone of Israel,

25 Even by the God of thy father, who shall help thee, and by the Almighty, who shall bless thee, with blessings of heaven above, blessings of the deep that coucheth beneath, blessings of the breasts, and of the womb.

26 The blessings of thy father are mighty beyond the blessings of my progenitors unto the utmost bound of the everlasting hills; they shall be on the head of Joseph, and on the crown of the head of the prince among his brethren.

Deuteronomy 33

(יג) וּלְיוֹסֵף אָמַר מְבֹרֶכֶת ה' אַרְצוֹ מִמֶּגֶד שָׁמַיִם מִטָּל וּמִתְּהוֹם רֹבֶצֶת תָּחַת.

(יד) וּמִמֶּגֶד תְּבוּאֹת שָׁמֶשׁ וּמִמֶּגֶד גֶּרֶשׁ יְרָחִים.

(טו) וּמֵרֹאשׁ הַרְרֵי קֶדֶם וּמִמֶּגֶד גִּבְעוֹת עוֹלָם.

(טז) וּמִמֶּגֶד אֶרֶץ וּמְלֹאָהּ וּרְצוֹן שֹׁכְנִי סְנֶה תָּבוֹאתָה לְרֹאשׁ יוֹסֵף וּלְקָדְקֹד נְזִיר אֶחָיו.

(יז) בְּכוֹר שׁוֹרוֹ הָדָר לוֹ וְקַרְנֵי רְאֵם קַרְנָיו בָּהֶם עַמִּים יְנַגַּח יַחְדָּו אַפְסֵי אָרֶץ וְהֵם רִבְבוֹת אֶפְרַיִם וְהֵם אַלְפֵי מְנַשֶּׁה.

13 And of Joseph he said: Blessed of the Lord be his land; for the precious things of heaven, for the dew, and for the deep that coucheth beneath,

14 And for the precious things of the fruits of the sun, and for the precious things of the yield of the moons,

¹⁵ And for the tops of the ancient mountains, and for the precious things of the everlasting hills,

¹⁶ And for the precious things of the earth and the fullness thereof, and the good will of Him that dwelt in the bush; let the blessing come upon the head of Joseph, and upon the crown of the head of him that is prince among his brethren.

¹⁷ His firstling bullock, majesty is his; and his horns are the horns of the wild-ox; with them he shall gore the peoples all of them, even the ends of the earth; and they are the ten thousands of Ephraim, and they are the thousands of Manasseh.

Genesis 45

(כב) לְכֻלָּם נָתַן לָאִישׁ חֲלִפוֹת שְׂמָלֹת וּלְבִנְיָמִן נָתַן שְׁלֹשׁ מֵאוֹת כֶּסֶף וְחָמֵשׁ חֲלִפֹת שְׂמָלֹת.

²² To all of them he gave each man changes of raiment; but to Benjamin he gave three hundred pieces of silver, and five changes of raiment.

II Kings 20

(א) בַּיָּמִים הָהֵם חָלָה חִזְקִיָּהוּ לָמוּת וַיָּבֹא אֵלָיו יְשַׁעְיָהוּ בֶן אָמוֹץ הַנָּבִיא וַיֹּאמֶר אֵלָיו כֹּה אָמַר ה' צַו לְבֵיתֶךָ כִּי מֵת אַתָּה וְלֹא תִחְיֶה.

(ב) וַיַּסֵּב אֶת פָּנָיו אֶל הַקִּיר וַיִּתְפַּלֵּל אֶל ה' לֵאמֹר.

(ג) אָנָּה ה' זְכָר נָא אֵת אֲשֶׁר הִתְהַלַּכְתִּי לְפָנֶיךָ בֶּאֱמֶת וּבְלֵבָב שָׁלֵם וְהַטּוֹב בְּעֵינֶיךָ עָשִׂיתִי וַיֵּבְךְּ חִזְקִיָּהוּ בְּכִי גָדוֹל.

(ד) וַיְהִי יְשַׁעְיָהוּ לֹא יָצָא הָעִיר [חָצֵר] הַתִּיכֹנָה וּדְבַר ה' הָיָה אֵלָיו לֵאמֹר.

(ה) שׁוּב וְאָמַרְתָּ אֶל חִזְקִיָּהוּ נְגִיד עַמִּי כֹּה אָמַר ה' אֱ-לֹהֵי דָּוִד אָבִיךָ שָׁמַעְתִּי אֶת תְּפִלָּתֶךָ רָאִיתִי אֶת דִּמְעָתֶךָ הִנְנִי רֹפֶא לָךְ בַּיּוֹם הַשְּׁלִישִׁי תַּעֲלֶה בֵּית ה'.

(ו) וְהֹסַפְתִּי עַל יָמֶיךָ חֲמֵשׁ עֶשְׂרֵה שָׁנָה וּמִכַּף מֶלֶךְ אַשּׁוּר אַצִּילְךָ וְאֵת הָעִיר הַזֹּאת וְגַנּוֹתִי עַל הָעִיר הַזֹּאת לְמַעֲנִי וּלְמַעַן דָּוִד עַבְדִּי.

(ז) וַיֹּאמֶר יְשַׁעְיָהוּ קְחוּ דְּבֶלֶת תְּאֵנִים וַיִּקְחוּ וַיָּשִׂימוּ עַל הַשְּׁחִין וַיֶּחִי.

(ח) וַיֹּאמֶר חִזְקִיָּהוּ אֶל יְשַׁעְיָהוּ מָה אוֹת כִּי יִרְפָּא ה' לִי וְעָלִיתִי בַּיּוֹם הַשְּׁלִישִׁי בֵּית ה'.

(ט) וַיֹּאמֶר יְשַׁעְיָהוּ זֶה לְּךָ הָאוֹת מֵאֵת ה' כִּי יַעֲשֶׂה ה' אֶת הַדָּבָר אֲשֶׁר דִּבֵּר הָלַךְ הַצֵּל עֶשֶׂר מַעֲלוֹת אִם יָשׁוּב עֶשֶׂר מַעֲלוֹת.

(י) וַיֹּאמֶר יְחִזְקִיָּהוּ נָקֵל לַצֵּל לִנְטוֹת עֶשֶׂר מַעֲלוֹת לֹא כִי יָשׁוּב הַצֵּל אֲחֹרַנִּית עֶשֶׂר מַעֲלוֹת.

(יא) וַיִּקְרָא יְשַׁעְיָהוּ הַנָּבִיא אֶל ה' וַיָּשֶׁב אֶת הַצֵּל בַּמַּעֲלוֹת אֲשֶׁר יָרְדָה בְּמַעֲלוֹת אָחָז אֲחֹרַנִּית עֶשֶׂר מַעֲלוֹת.

[1] In those days was Hezekiah sick unto death. And the prophet Isaiah the son of Amoz came to him, and said unto him, Thus saith the Lord, Set thine house in order; for thou shalt die, and not live.

[2] Then he turned his face to the wall, and prayed unto the Lord, saying,

[3] I beseech thee, O Lord, remember now how I have walked before thee in truth and with a perfect heart, and have done that which is good in thy sight. And Hezekiah wept sore.

[4] And it came to pass, afore Isaiah was gone out into the middle court, that the word of the Lord came to him, saying,

[5] Turn again, and tell Hezekiah the captain of my people, Thus saith the Lord, the God of David thy father, I have heard thy prayer, I have seen thy tears: behold, I will heal thee: on the third day thou shalt go up unto the house of the Lord.

[6] And I will add unto thy days fifteen years; and I will deliver thee and this city out of the hand of the king of Assyria; and I will defend this city for mine own sake, and for my servant David's sake.

[7] And Isaiah said, Take a lump of figs. And they took and laid it on the boil, and he recovered.

[8] And Hezekiah said unto Isaiah, What shall be the sign that the Lord will heal me, and that I shall go up into the house of the Lord the third day?

[9] And Isaiah said, This sign shalt thou have of the Lord, that the Lord will do the thing that he hath spoken: shall the shadow go forward ten degrees, or go back ten degrees?

[10] And Hezekiah answered, It is a light thing for the shadow to go down ten degrees: nay, but let the shadow return backward ten degrees.

[11] And Isaiah the prophet cried unto the Lord: and he brought the shadow ten degrees backward, by which it had gone down in the dial of Ahaz.

Isaiah 38

(א) בַּיָּמִים הָהֵם חָלָה חִזְקִיָּהוּ לָמוּת וַיָּבוֹא אֵלָיו יְשַׁעְיָהוּ בֶן אָמוֹץ הַנָּבִיא וַיֹּאמֶר אֵלָיו כֹּה אָמַר ה' צַו לְבֵיתֶךָ כִּי מֵת אַתָּה וְלֹא תִחְיֶה.

(ב) וַיַּסֵּב חִזְקִיָּהוּ פָּנָיו אֶל הַקִּיר וַיִּתְפַּלֵּל אֶל ה'.

(ג) וַיֹּאמַר אָנָּה ה' זְכָר נָא אֵת אֲשֶׁר הִתְהַלַּכְתִּי לְפָנֶיךָ בֶּאֱמֶת וּבְלֵב שָׁלֵם וְהַטּוֹב בְּעֵינֶיךָ עָשִׂיתִי וַיֵּבְךְּ חִזְקִיָּהוּ בְּכִי גָדוֹל.

(ד) וַיְהִי דְּבַר ה' אֶל יְשַׁעְיָהוּ לֵאמֹר.

(ה) הָלוֹךְ וְאָמַרְתָּ אֶל חִזְקִיָּהוּ כֹּה אָמַר ה' אֱ-לֹהֵי דָּוִד אָבִיךָ שָׁמַעְתִּי אֶת תְּפִלָּתֶךָ רָאִיתִי אֶת דִּמְעָתֶךָ הִנְנִי יוֹסִף עַל יָמֶיךָ חֲמֵשׁ עֶשְׂרֵה שָׁנָה.

(ו) וּמִכַּף מֶלֶךְ אַשּׁוּר אַצִּילְךָ וְאֵת הָעִיר הַזֹּאת וְגַנּוֹתִי עַל הָעִיר הַזֹּאת.

(ז) וְזֶה לְּךָ הָאוֹת מֵאֵת ה' אֲשֶׁר יַעֲשֶׂה ה' אֶת הַדָּבָר הַזֶּה אֲשֶׁר דִּבֵּר.

(ח) הִנְנִי מֵשִׁיב אֶת צֵל הַמַּעֲלוֹת אֲשֶׁר יָרְדָה בְמַעֲלוֹת אָחָז בַּשֶּׁמֶשׁ אֲחֹרַנִּית עֶשֶׂר מַעֲלוֹת וַתָּשָׁב הַשֶּׁמֶשׁ עֶשֶׂר מַעֲלוֹת בַּמַּעֲלוֹת אֲשֶׁר יָרָדָה.

¹ In those days was Hezekiah sick unto death. And Isaiah the prophet the son of Amoz came unto him, and said unto him, Thus saith the Lord, Set thine house in order: for thou shalt die, and not live.

² Then Hezekiah turned his face toward the wall, and prayed unto the Lord,

³ And said, Remember now, O Lord, I beseech thee, how I have walked before thee in truth and with a perfect heart, and have done that which is good in thy sight. And Hezekiah wept sore.

⁴ Then came the word of the Lord to Isaiah, saying,

⁵ Go, and say to Hezekiah, Thus saith the Lord, the God of David thy father, I have heard thy prayer, I have seen thy tears: behold, I will add unto thy days fifteen years.

⁶ And I will deliver thee and this city out of the hand of the king of Assyria: and I will defend this city.

⁷ And this shall be a sign unto thee from the Lord, that the Lord will do this thing that he hath spoken;

⁸ Behold, I will bring again the shadow of the degrees, which is gone down in the sun dial of Ahaz, ten degrees backward. So the sun returned ten degrees, by which degrees it was gone down.

Exodus 20

(טז) וַיֹּאמֶר מֹשֶׁה אֶל הָעָם אַל תִּירָאוּ כִּי לְבַעֲבוּר נַסּוֹת אֶתְכֶם בָּא הָאֱ־לֹהִים וּבַעֲבוּר תִּהְיֶה יִרְאָתוֹ עַל פְּנֵיכֶם לְבִלְתִּי תֶחֱטָאוּ.

¹⁶ And Moses said unto the people: Fear not; for God is come to prove you, and that His fear may be before you, that ye sin not.

Jeremiah 34

(יב) וַיְהִי דְבַר ה' אֶל יִרְמְיָהוּ מֵאֵת ה' לֵאמֹר.

(יג) כֹּה אָמַר ה' אֱ־לֹהֵי יִשְׂרָאֵל אָנֹכִי כָּרַתִּי בְרִית אֶת אֲבוֹתֵיכֶם בְּיוֹם הוֹצִאִי אוֹתָם מֵאֶרֶץ מִצְרַיִם מִבֵּית עֲבָדִים לֵאמֹר.

(יד) מִקֵּץ שֶׁבַע שָׁנִים תְּשַׁלְּחוּ אִישׁ אֶת אָחִיו הָעִבְרִי אֲשֶׁר יִמָּכֵר לְךָ וַעֲבָדְךָ שֵׁשׁ שָׁנִים וְשִׁלַּחְתּוֹ חָפְשִׁי מֵעִמָּךְ וְלֹא שָׁמְעוּ אֲבוֹתֵיכֶם אֵלַי וְלֹא הִטּוּ אֶת אָזְנָם.

(טו) וַתָּשֻׁבוּ אַתֶּם הַיּוֹם וַתַּעֲשׂוּ אֶת הַיָּשָׁר בְּעֵינַי לִקְרֹא דְרוֹר אִישׁ לְרֵעֵהוּ וַתִּכְרְתוּ בְרִית לְפָנַי בַּבַּיִת אֲשֶׁר נִקְרָא שְׁמִי עָלָיו.

(טז) וַתָּשֻׁבוּ וַתְּחַלְּלוּ אֶת שְׁמִי וַתָּשִׁבוּ אִישׁ אֶת עַבְדּוֹ וְאִישׁ אֶת שִׁפְחָתוֹ אֲשֶׁר שִׁלַּחְתֶּם חָפְשִׁים לְנַפְשָׁם וַתִּכְבְּשׁוּ אֹתָם לִהְיוֹת לָכֶם לַעֲבָדִים וְלִשְׁפָחוֹת.

(יז) לָכֵן כֹּה אָמַר ה' אַתֶּם לֹא שְׁמַעְתֶּם אֵלַי לִקְרֹא דְרוֹר אִישׁ לְאָחִיו וְאִישׁ לְרֵעֵהוּ הִנְנִי קֹרֵא לָכֶם דְּרוֹר נְאֻם ה' אֶל הַחֶרֶב אֶל הַדֶּבֶר וְאֶל הָרָעָב וְנָתַתִּי אֶתְכֶם לזועה [לְזַעֲוָה] לְכֹל מַמְלְכוֹת הָאָרֶץ.

¹² Therefore the word of the Lord came to Jeremiah from the Lord, saying,

¹³ Thus saith the Lord, the God of Israel; I made a covenant with your fathers in the day that I brought them forth out of the land of Egypt, out of the house of bondmen, saying,

¹⁴ At the end of seven years let ye go every man his brother an Hebrew, which hath been sold unto thee; and when he hath served thee six years, thou shalt let him go free from thee: but your fathers hearkened not unto me, neither inclined their ear.

¹⁵ And ye were now turned, and had done right in my sight, in proclaiming liberty every man to his neighbour; and ye had made a covenant before me in the house which is called by my name:

¹⁶ But ye turned and polluted my name, and caused every man his servant, and every man his handmaid, whom ye had set at liberty at their pleasure, to return, and brought them into subjection, to be unto you for servants and for handmaids.

¹⁷ Therefore thus saith the Lord; Ye have not hearkened unto me, in proclaiming liberty, every one to his brother, and every man to his neighbour: behold, I proclaim a liberty for you, saith the Lord, to the sword, to the pestilence, and to the famine; and I will make you to be removed into all the kingdoms of the earth.

Jeremiah 31

(ל) הִנֵּה יָמִים בָּאִים נְאֻם ה' וְכָרַתִּי אֶת בֵּית יִשְׂרָאֵל וְאֶת בֵּית יְהוּדָה בְּרִית חֲדָשָׁה.
(לא) לֹא כַבְּרִית אֲשֶׁר כָּרַתִּי אֶת אֲבוֹתָם בְּיוֹם הֶחֱזִיקִי בְיָדָם לְהוֹצִיאָם מֵאֶרֶץ מִצְרָיִם אֲשֶׁר הֵמָּה הֵפֵרוּ אֶת בְּרִיתִי וְאָנֹכִי בָּעַלְתִּי בָם נְאֻם ה'.
(לב) כִּי זֹאת הַבְּרִית אֲשֶׁר אֶכְרֹת אֶת בֵּית יִשְׂרָאֵל אַחֲרֵי הַיָּמִים הָהֵם נְאֻם ה' נָתַתִּי אֶת תּוֹרָתִי בְּקִרְבָּם וְעַל לִבָּם אֶכְתֲּבֶנָּה וְהָיִיתִי לָהֶם לֵא-לֹהִים וְהֵמָּה יִהְיוּ לִי לְעָם.

³⁰ Behold, the days come, saith the Lord, that I will make a new covenant with the house of Israel, and with the house of Judah;

³¹ Not according to the covenant that I made with their fathers in the day that I took them by the hand to bring them out of the land of Egypt; forasmuch as they broke My covenant, although I was a lord over them, saith the Lord.

³² But this is the covenant that I will make with the house of Israel after those days, saith the Lord, I will put My law in their inward parts, and in their heart will I write it; and I will be their God, and they shall be My people.

Part Two

Revolutionary America

Introduction

As mentioned earlier, the great French philosopher Alexis de Tocqueville championed the idea that America had two foundings, the Puritan and the Revolutionary. It is easy to oppose them as contrary moments that represent divergent tendencies in American culture. The Puritan founding was religious and Christian, the Revolutionary secular and republican; the Puritans were religiously intolerant, the revolutionaries established religious liberty; the former were insular, the latter were worldly and enlightened. This opposition, however, is largely false. The vast majority of the revolutionaries were devout men, and churchmen were central figures who played important roles in the Revolution. Though far from a religious war, the Revolution was partially conceived and justified in explicitly religious terminology, as a fight for God-given rights and for a divine mission. In addition, the new Republic, they believed, should be grounded in the solid morality of its citizenry, a morality they thought derived from religious faith and observance. Self-government meant democratic political institutions. But it also meant self-control and moral living. In truth, the American Revolution continued the Puritan founding, albeit in modified ways.

For all its glory, the American Revolution was a painful civil war: cities were burned and suspicious neighbors turned against each other; homes were looted and families expelled from their houses; property was confiscated and lost; food shortages, disease, and bad harvests were common; and sick soldiers trudged on with little provisions in the dead of winter. In these agonizing moments of national struggle, it is unsurprising that a people would turn to their religion for succor. And the Americans did. The men and women who fought the Revolution really did think that they were carrying out a divine task, though the final victory was not assured; they thought themselves a people of destiny, embarking upon an experiment in free government that was, somehow, the object of divine providence. Individual events were interpreted in religious terms. For example, in late August 1776, only a month after the triumphant signing of the Declaration of Independence, the British landed an army on Long Island, cornering the Continental army at Brooklyn Heights. George Washington, aided by a miraculously dense morning fog, was able to ferry his army to Manhattan and save the Revolution from failure. The Continental army's escape from Brooklyn was later interpreted as an act of divine providence. In addition, the church was a locus of political gathering, the pulpit the focus of political discourse. Men like Samuel Langdon and Ezra Stiles – presidents of American centers of religious learning, Harvard and Yale – spoke of the Revolution in biblical terms. In the Revolution the spirit of religion and the spirit of politics were intimately intertwined. Certainly not all, but much of the rhetoric of the Revolutionary period was saturated with Hebraic themes.[1]

The American Revolution, like the regime itself, did not have one single major influence or spring from one major source. James Madison and Thomas Jefferson were influenced by John Locke and the European Enlightenment, but also by the Whig opposition and classical antiquity, especially Rome. They read the ancient Greek essayist Plutarch, they read Montesquieu, a great eighteenth-century French political philosopher, and Blackstone, the late eighteenth-century British legal philosopher. But they also read and knew the Bible. Madison stayed on at Princeton to deepen his understanding of the Bible under then-president John Witherspoon. Donald Lutz conducted a study demonstrating that of

---

1. See Eric Nelson, *The Royalist Revolution: Themes in American Political Thought* (Cambridge: Harvard University Press, 2014).

all works, the Bible – and the Hebrew Bible especially – was by far the most-cited document during the Revolutionary period.[2] The task for the student of the Revolution is not to argue for the influence of the Bible, which is incontrovertible, but to determine the relation of, tension among, and synergies between the various influences in what some scholars have called the "American amalgam."[3]

The Hebraic influence on the Revolution was even in the symbolism of the early Republic. An early proposal for the national seal by Franklin was decidedly Hebraic, with imagery of the exodus. Even the final version mixes Hebraic and Masonic themes and exemplifies the dynamism of the American amalgam. After the adoption of the Declaration on July 4, 1776, a committee was formed to design a seal. Jefferson and Benjamin Franklin both chose scenes from the Hebrew Bible. Franklin chose "Moses [in the dress of a high priest] standing on the shore, and extending his hand over the sea, thereby causing the same to overwhelm Pharaoh who is sitting in an open Chariot, a crown on his Head and a sword in his hand. Rays from a Pillar of Fire in the clouds reaching to Moses, to express that he acts by the command of the Deity. Motto: Rebellion to tyrants is obedience to God." Jefferson chose the Israelites in the wilderness being led by a cloud by day and a pillar of fire by night. John Adams, though the most religious of the three, chose a scene from Roman mythology. The seal that was eventually adopted included strong themes from Masonry, including the number thirteen, the eye of wisdom, and an eagle reminiscent of Rome. These themes were conjoined with some from the Hebrew Bible: the exodus from Egypt is denoted by the wasteland and desert behind the pyramid and the shrubbery and fertility beyond it. But these references are not purely Hebraic. Gideon sits next to Cincinnatus, the Roman general. America of the Revolutionary period was eclectic. It remains an open question whether influences of Rome, English opposition, Enlightenment philosophy, and the Hebrew Bible form a coherent whole or whether they exist in productive tension.

---

2. Lutz, 189–97.
3. See Michael Zuckert, *The Natural Rights Republic* (Notre Dame: University of Notre Dame Press, 1996).

While it is relatively straightforward to show that the Hebrew Bible was influential during the Revolution, it is more difficult to determine the work that the Bible actually did: How did it influence the founding generation? What did they believe were the lessons of the Hebrew Bible? Were they even good interpreters of it? How was the influence of the Bible during the days of the Puritans continued, changed, or modified by the time of the Revolution? Historical analysis is an inexact science. But to take just the Puritan example, perhaps one could say this: by the time the Revolution occurred, Americans already had a long tradition stretching back to the Puritan past of using the Hebrew Bible as a means of understanding and cementing their communal identity. The Puritans believed that their destiny was to create a city upon a hill; the founders thought the same. But while the Puritans believed their destiny was to be a shining exemplar of Christian charity, the American revolutionaries, though not of course speaking with a single voice, thought themselves to be embarking on a providential quest to prove that self-government was possible. Each thought it had a God-given destiny, but the color of that destiny changed hue.

Apart from the theological question of whether in fact America is part of a divine plan, like the Puritans, Americans of the Revolutionary period interpreted the events of their own times through the lens of biblical stories and figures. For the Revolutionary generation the Bible was a political text they found meaningful and immediately contemporary. As mentioned earlier, when Revolutionary pastors read of the corruption of Persia in the book of Esther, they thought of Britain and its court; when they thought of British tyranny, they were reminded of the power-hungry Haman. When Thomas Paine wanted to make a case to the colonies that monarchy was a primitive, outdated, and illegitimate form of government, he cited the book of Samuel. George Washington was portrayed as a modern Moses and Gideon.

There were also writers who thought that the Hebrew Republic was an actual model for the new American one. The idea that the Hebrew Republic is a political model is an old one, stretching back to the development of Protestant political philosophy in the sixteenth century. Along the road it has had a few permutations. In Protestant Europe and in the American colonies before the Revolution, the Hebrew Republic was used to justify limited monarchy. During the American Revolution, the model of the Israelite regime was understood to be more republican and less monarchical.[4] The sermon below by Samuel Langdon, pastor and president of Harvard, exemplifies this idea. For further examples of the republican turn in Protestant biblical interpretation, one could also look to sermons by Samuel Cooper, such as "A Sermon Preached before His Excellency John Hancock" (Oct. 25, 1780), and Joseph Huntington's "A Discourse Adapted to the Present Day" (April 1781), in which he claims that God gave the Israelites the "most perfect form of Civil Government."[5] Huntington argues that the Hebraic Constitution was a mixed government that combined elements of democracy, aristocracy, and monarchy (judges, Sanhedrin, and assemblies of the people), with federal and tribal elements, and that had a separation of powers.

These notions resonated with the American colonists who were in the midst of creating a confederated Republic with a separation of powers. But what regime exactly did the Hebrew Republic endorse, if any? Was it the Articles of Confederation? The Constitution? Both? Neither? Was the Bible the inspiration, or was it really the Enlightenment and the Bible was used to justify it? Was the Bible influence or justification? While the colonists used the Hebrew Bible to support their regime, how do we know what regime the Bible supports, if any? Perhaps it is better to claim, with Eran Shalev, that the Bible provided an overarching "moral language of liberty" that crystallized the American cultural and political identity rather than directly supported the text of any particular document.[6]

Therefore, we can say with some confidence that Revolutionary America was a biblical Republic. But this raises yet another difficult question: Which Bible? Influence from the Hebrew Bible was mixed with Christian themes and Christian religious fervor more generally. This was true in the Christianizing of Hebraic themes already present in the Protestant Reformation, which was brought to the New World

---

4. Samuel Phillips, "Political Rulers authorized and influenced by God our savior to Decree and Execute Justice," a sermon preached at Boston, 1750.
5. Shalev, 63.
6. Ibid., 48.

by Puritanism. In addition to specifically Christian themes, there was also a general sense among the founding generation that religion was important to the maintenance of a free regime. In their minds virtue was key to republican government, and that virtue was most easily attained by a religious people because a religious upbringing best instilled those habits of character and cast of mind that inclined one toward morality, self-sacrifice, and orderliness. Currents of American culture during the Revolution were a mix of Hebraic, Christian, and general religiosity.

The difference between biblical influence and religion in the colonies should not be overstated. It is wrong to see a neat division between religion and politics in the colonial era, as the numerous prayers, thanksgiving days, days of repentance, and the importance of religious men as men of public affairs attest. Simultaneously, it is all too easy to overstate their significance. Madison and Jefferson both struggled with, and were at times steadfastly against, the president issuing days of thanksgiving and prayer.[7] It is certainly wrong to see the Revolution in the minds of its undertakers as a purely secular event. It is also wrong to think that they thought it was a religious war. It little resembled Cromwell's Protestant war in England against the Crown in the seventeenth century. It is also wrong to view the America of the Revolution as the same as the America of the Puritan colonies. There is a shift from the encoding of Mosaic laws in the New Haven legal codes to the Constitution of the United States, the First Amendment, and provisions excluding religious tests for office. The First Amendment did much to enshrine the principle of religious freedom, but one should not be mistaken into believing that it created a "wall of separation" between religion and the government (in this case the federal government). The phrase "wall of separation" comes from a private letter by Jefferson. In fact, the common understanding at the time was that there would be no national establishment and that the Constitution left the states free to do as they chose. Indeed, there was

---

7. Jefferson's letter to Rev. S. Miller, Jan. 23, 1808; Madison, in 1820, wrote that "religious proclamations by the executive recommending thanksgiving and fasts are shoots from the same root with the legislative acts reviewed. Altho' recommendations only, they imply a religious agency, making no part of the trust delegated to political rulers." See https://founders.archives.gov/documents/Madison/04-01-02-0549.

state-established religion at the time of the First Amendment that the amendment did not overturn.[8] America had changed since John Winthrop. It was more religiously, intellectually, and culturally diverse. But it was still a very religious place.

BENJAMIN FRANKLIN (1706–1790)

There were few figures in the middle of the eighteenth century who had colony-wide fame, and even fewer who were internationally known. The two most famous men of such stature were George Whitefield and Benjamin Franklin. The former is largely forgotten today, but he was the most celebrated itinerant preacher of what has become known as the First Great Awakening. Crowds would gather in the tens of thousands to hear him speak. At one such meeting, all of Philadelphia assembled to hear his sermons. Ben Franklin was among the crowd, as he relates in his autobiography, holding a few pieces of change in his pocket that he was determined not to give to the charity basket when it was passed around. And yet even Franklin could not resist the mellifluous language of Whitefield and, with some embellishment in the telling, gave over the contents of his pocket. What Franklin saw in Whitefield was not religious conversion but business opportunity. Franklin made himself the exclusive publisher of Whitefield's sermons, and made his pockets much heavier by it.

Franklin is the archetypal man of the American and Enlightenment spirit, perhaps the first "American." He was self-consciously foundational in shaping the American mythology and ethos, especially the ideal of the self-made man, the quintessential "rags to riches" story. He did so, on his own account, by means of frugality, industry, and planning. He was the consummate spokesman for himself and was able to draw a public picture of a man who had some resemblance, but not a full congruence, with the private man. The private Franklin was a man of looser morals and laxer frugality, a consummate bon vivant and the star networker of his day. Franklin was a man of many talents: an entrepreneur, he was the first media mogul in America, controlling a large publishing conglomerate that was a colony-wide business; a famous inventor, he invented devices based on electricity, some of which – like

---

8. Michael McConnell, "The Origins and Understanding of the Free Exercise of Religion," *Harvard Law Review* 103:7 (May 1990): 1409–517.

the lightning rod – confronted the religious sensibility of his day, which believed lightning to be a divine occurrence. He was also a man of true civic talent. Franklin founded the University of Pennsylvania, the first public library in America, public lighting and sanitation projects, and a fire brigade. During the Revolution Franklin was a skillful ambassador to France, charming them with his faux rusticity to secure their aid that was instrumental in victory. Franklin knew the minds of men and how to speak to their concerns, perhaps to the point of manipulation. For instance, he suggested the Constitutional Convention be opened with a prayer. Perhaps he believed in a Providence that oversaw men's affairs; perhaps this was the public Franklin only; perhaps he thought grand public occasions should be solemn and that religion was crucial to that. Like Odysseus, Franklin had many sides.

Franklin wrote much throughout his life. In the following excerpt, taken from his autobiography (written over the course of seventeen years), Franklin recounts his attempt to achieve moral perfection.

The Autobiography of Benjamin Franklin (1791)

I had been religiously educated as a Presbyterian; and tho' some of the dogmas of that persuasion, such as the eternal decrees of God, election, reprobation, etc., appeared to me unintelligible, others doubtful, and I early absented myself from the public assemblies of the sect, Sunday being my studying day, I never was without some religious principles. I never doubted, for instance, the existence of the Deity; that he made the world, and govern'd it by his Providence; that the most acceptable service of God was the doing good to man; that our souls are immortal; and that all crime will be punished, and virtue rewarded, either here or hereafter. These I esteem'd the essentials of every religion; and, being to be found in all the religions we had in our country, I respected them all, tho' with different degrees of respect, as I found them more or less mix'd with other articles, which, without any tendency to inspire, promote, or confirm morality, serv'd principally to divide us, and make us unfriendly to one another. This respect to all, with an opinion that the worst had some good effects, induc'd me to avoid all discourse that might tend to lessen the good opinion another might have of his own religion; and as our province increas'd in people, and new places of worship were continually wanted, and generally erected by voluntary contributions, my mite for such purpose, whatever might be the sect, was never refused.

Tho' I seldom attended any public worship, I had still an opinion of its propriety, and of its utility when rightly conducted, and I regularly paid my annual subscription for the support of the only Presbyterian minister or meeting we had in Philadelphia. He us'd to visit me sometimes as a friend, and admonish me to attend his administrations, and I was now and then prevail'd on to do so, once for five Sundays successively. Had he been in my opinion a good preacher, perhaps I might have continued, notwithstanding the occasion I had for the Sunday's leisure in my course of study; but his discourses were chiefly either polemic arguments, or explications of the peculiar doctrines of our sect, and were all to me very dry, uninteresting, and unedifying, since not a single moral principle was inculcated or enforc'd, their aim seeming to be rather to make us Presbyterians than good citizens.

At length he took for his text that verse of the fourth chapter of Philippians, "Finally, brethren, whatsoever things are true, honest, just, pure, lovely, or of good report, if there be any virtue, or any praise, think on these things." And I imagin'd, in a sermon on such a text, we could not miss of having some morality. But he confin'd himself to five points only, as meant by the apostle, viz.: 1. Keeping holy the Sabbath day. 2. Being diligent in reading the holy Scriptures. 3. Attending duly the publick worship. 4. Partaking of the Sacrament. 5. Paying a due respect to God's ministers.

These might be all good things; but, as they were not the kind of good things that I expected from that text, I despaired of ever meeting with them from any other, was disgusted, and attended his preaching no more. I had some years before compos'd a little Liturgy, or form of prayer, for my own private use (viz., in 1728), entitled, "Articles of Belief and Acts of Religion." I return'd to the use of this, and went no more to the public assemblies. My conduct might be blameable, but I leave it, without attempting further to excuse it; my present purpose being to relate facts, and not to make apologies for them.

It was about this time I conceiv'd the bold and arduous project of arriving at moral perfection. I wish'd to live without committing any fault at any time; I would conquer all that either natural inclination, custom, or company might lead me into. As I knew, or thought I knew, what was right and wrong, I did not see why I might not always do the one and avoid the other. But I soon found I had undertaken a task of more difficulty than I had imagined. While my care was employ'd in guarding against one fault, I was often surprised by another; habit took the advantage of inattention; inclination was sometimes too strong for reason. I concluded, at length, that the mere speculative conviction that it was our interest to be completely virtuous was not sufficient to prevent our slipping, and that the contrary habits must be broken, and good ones acquired and established, before we can have any dependence on a steady, uniform rectitude of conduct. For this purpose I therefore contrived the following method.

In the various enumerations of the moral virtues I had met with in my reading, I found the catalogue more or less numerous, as different writers included more or fewer ideas under the same name. Temperance, for example, was by some confined to eating and drinking, while by others it was extended to mean the moderating every other pleasure, appetite, inclination, or passion, bodily or mental, even to our avarice and ambition. I propos'd to myself, for the sake of clearness, to use rather more names, with fewer ideas annex'd to each, than a few names with more ideas; and I included under thirteen names of virtues all that at that time occurr'd to me as necessary or desirable, and annexed to each a short precept, which fully express'd the extent I gave to its meaning.

These names of virtues, with their precepts, were:

1. TEMPERANCE. Eat not to dullness; drink not to elevation.
2. SILENCE. Speak not but what may benefit others or yourself; avoid trifling conversation.
3. ORDER. Let all your things have their places; let each part of your business have its time.
4. RESOLUTION. Resolve to perform what you ought; perform without fail what you resolve.
5. FRUGALITY. Make no expense but to do good to others or yourself; i.e., waste nothing.
6. INDUSTRY. Lose no time; be always employ'd in something useful; cut off all unnecessary actions.

7. SINCERITY. Use no hurtful deceit; think innocently and justly, and, if you speak, speak accordingly.
8. JUSTICE. Wrong none by doing injuries, or omitting the benefits that are your duty.
9. MODERATION. Avoid extreams; forbear resenting injuries so much as you think they deserve.
10. CLEANLINESS. Tolerate no uncleanliness in body, cloaths, or habitation.
11. TRANQUILLITY. Be not disturbed at trifles, or at accidents common or unavoidable.
12. CHASTITY. Rarely use venery but for health or offspring, never to dulness, weakness, or the injury of your own or another's peace or reputation.
13. HUMILITY. Imitate Jesus and Socrates.

My intention being to acquire the habitude of all these virtues, I judg'd it would be well not to distract my attention by attempting the whole at once, but to fix it on one of them at a time; and, when I should be master of that, then to proceed to another, and so on, till I should have gone thro' the thirteen; and, as the previous acquisition of some might facilitate the acquisition of certain others, I arrang'd them with that view, as they stand above. Temperance first, as it tends to procure that coolness and clearness of head, which is so necessary where constant vigilance was to be kept up, and guard maintained against the unremitting at traction of ancient habits, and the force of perpetual temptations. This being acquir'd and establish'd, Silence would be more easy; and my desire being to gain knowledge at the same time that I improv'd in virtue, and considering that in conversation it was obtain'd rather by the use of the ears than of the tongue, and therefore wishing to break a habit I was getting into of prattling, punning, and joking, which only made me acceptable to trifling company, I gave Silence the second place. This and the next, Order, I expected would allow me more time for attending to my project and my studies. Resolution, once become habitual, would keep me firm in my endeavors to obtain all the subsequent virtues; Frugality and Industry freeing me from my remaining debt and producing affluence and independence, would make more easy the practice of Sincerity and Justice, etc., etc. Conceiving then, that, agreeably to the advice of Pythagoras in his Golden Verses, daily examination would be necessary, I contrived the following method for conducting that examination.

I made a little book, in which I allotted a page for each of the virtues. I rul'd each page with red ink, so as to have seven columns, one for each day of the week, marking each column with a letter for the day. I cross'd these columns with thirteen red lines, marking the beginning of each line with the first letter of one of the virtues, on which line, and in its proper column, I might mark, by a little black spot, every fault I found upon examination to have been committed respecting that virtue upon that day.

I determined to give a week's strict attention to each of the virtues successively. Thus, in the first week, my great guard was to avoid every the least offence against Temperance, leaving the other virtues to their ordinary chance, only marking every evening the faults of the day. Thus, if in the first week I could keep my first line, marked T, clear of spots, I suppos'd the habit of that virtue so much strengthen'd and its opposite weaken'd, that I might venture extending my attention to include the next, and for the following week keep both lines clear of spots. Proceeding thus to the last, I could go thro' a course compleat in thirteen weeks, and four courses in a year. And like him who, having a garden to weed, does not attempt to eradicate all the bad herbs at once, which would exceed his reach and his strength, but works on one of the beds at a time, and, having accomplish'd the first, proceeds to a second, so I should have, I hoped, the encouraging pleasure of seeing on my pages the progress I made in virtue, by clearing successively my lines of their spots, till in the end, by a number of courses, I should be happy in viewing a clean book, after a thirteen weeks' daily examination.

This my little book had for its motto these lines from Addison's Cato:

> "Here will I hold. If there's a power above us (And that there is all nature cries aloud Thro' all her works), He must delight in virtue; And that which he delights in must be happy."

Another from Cicero:

"O vitae Philosophia dux! O virtutum indagatrix expultrixque vitiorum! Unus dies, bene et ex praeceptis tuis actus, peccanti immortalitati est anteponendus." ["Oh philosophy, guide of life! Diligent inquirer after virtue, and banisher of vice! A single day well spent, and as thy precepts direct, is to be preferred to an eternity of sin."]

Another from the Proverbs of Solomon, speaking of wisdom or virtue:

"Length of days is in her right hand, and in her left hand riches and honour. Her ways are ways of pleasantness, and all her paths are peace." iii. 16, 17.

And conceiving God to be the fountain of wisdom, I thought it right and necessary to solicit his assistance for obtaining it; to this end I formed the following little prayer, which was prefix'd to my tables of examination, for daily use. "O powerful Goodness! bountiful Father! merciful Guide! increase in me that wisdom which discovers my truest interest. Strengthen my resolutions to perform what that wisdom dictates. Accept my kind offices to thy other children as the only return in my power for thy continual favors to me"...

I enter'd upon the execution of this plan for self-examination, and continu'd it with occasional intermissions for some time. I was surpris'd to find myself so much fuller of faults than I had imagined; but I had the satisfaction of seeing them diminish. To avoid the trouble of renewing now and then my little book, which, by scraping out the marks on the paper of old faults to make room for new ones in a new course, became full of holes, I transferr'd my tables and precepts to the ivory leaves of a memorandum book, on which the lines were drawn with red ink, that made a durable stain, and on those lines I mark'd my faults with a black-lead pencil, which marks I could easily wipe out with a wet sponge. After a while I went thro' one course only in a year, and afterward only one in several years, till at length I omitted them entirely, being employ'd in voyages and business abroad with a multiplicity of affairs that interfered; but I always carried my little book with me.

...This article [Order], therefore, cost me so much painful attention, and my faults in it vexed me so much, and I made so little progress in amendment, and had such frequent relapses, that I was almost ready to give up the attempt, and content myself with a faulty character in that respect, the man who, in buying an ax of a smith, my neighbour, desired to have the whole of its surface as bright as the edge. The smith consented to grind it bright for him if he would turn the wheel; he turn'd, while the smith press'd the broad face of the ax hard and heavily on the stone, which made the turning of it very fatiguing. The man came every now and then from the wheel to see how the work went on, and at length would take his ax as it was, without farther grinding. "No," said the smith, "turn on, turn on; we shall have it bright by-and-by; as yet, it is only speckled." "Yes," said the man, "but I think I like a speckled ax best." And I believe this may have been the case with many, who, having, for want of some such means as I employ'd, found the difficulty of obtaining good and breaking bad habits in other points of vice and virtue, have given up the struggle, and concluded that "a speckled ax was best"; for something, that pretended to be reason, was every now and then suggesting to me that such extream nicety as I exacted of myself might be a kind of foppery in morals, which, if it were known, would make me ridiculous; that a perfect character might be attended with the inconvenience of being envied and hated; and that a benevolent man should allow a few faults in himself, to keep his friends in countenance.

Opening Prayer at the Constitutional Convention (July 28, 1787)

Franklin was a master of public relations and public perceptions. In the following speech, given at the Constitutional Convention in 1787, three years before his death, Franklin appealed to Providence. What might the juxtaposition with his self-portrait in the Autobiography *tell you about Franklin's personal and public beliefs? (His motion, proposed below, did not pass.)*

Mr. President:

The small progress we have made after 4 or five weeks close attendance & continual reasonings with each other – our different sentiments on almost every question, several of the last producing as many noes as ays, is methinks a melancholy proof of the imperfection of the Human Understanding. We indeed seem to feel our own wont of political wisdom, since we have been running about in search of it. We have gone back to ancient history for models of government, and examined the different forms of those Republics which having been formed with the seeds of their own dissolution now no longer exist. And we have viewed Modern States all round Europe, but find none of their Constitutions suitable to our circumstances.

In this situation of this Assembly groping as it were in the dark to find political truth, and scarce able to distinguish it when to us, how has it happened, Sir, that we have not hitherto once thought of humbly applying to the Father of lights to illuminate our understandings? In the beginning of the contest with G. Britain, when we were sensible of danger we had daily prayer in this room for the Divine Protection. – Our prayers, Sir, were heard, and they were graciously answered. All of us who were engaged in the struggle must have observed frequent instances of a Superintending providence in our favor. To that kind providence we owe this happy opportunity of consulting in peace on the means of establishing our future national felicity. And have we now forgotten that powerful friend? or do we imagine that we no longer need His assistance.

I have lived, Sir, a long time and the longer I live, the more convincing proofs I see of this truth – that *God governs in the affairs of men.* And if a sparrow cannot fall to the ground without His notice, is it probable that an empire can rise without His aid? We have been assured, Sir, in the sacred writings that "except the Lord build they labor in vain that build it" [Ps. 127:1]. I firmly believe this; and I also believe that without His concurring aid we shall succeed in this political building no better than the Builders of Babel: We shall be divided by our little partial local interests; our projects will be confounded, and we ourselves shall be become a reproach and a bye word down to future age. And what is worse, mankind may hereafter this unfortunate instance, despair of establishing Governments by Human Wisdom, and leave it to chance, war, and conquest.

> I therefore beg leave to move – that henceforth prayers imploring the assistance of Heaven, and its blessings on our deliberations, be held in this Assembly every morning before we proceed to business, and that one or more of the Clergy of this City be requested to officiate in that service.

Hebraic Sources

Benjamin Franklin fittingly drew a comparison to the tower of Babel as a warning against disorder and confusion. Franklin appealed to the faith in divine providence shared by most of his fellow delegates, at least publicly, to establish a ritual that would inspire unity.

Psalm 127

(א) שִׁיר הַמַּעֲלוֹת לִשְׁלֹמֹה אִם ה' לֹא יִבְנֶה בַיִת שָׁוְא עָמְלוּ בוֹנָיו בּוֹ אִם ה' לֹא יִשְׁמָר עִיר שָׁוְא שָׁקַד שׁוֹמֵר.
(ב) שָׁוְא לָכֶם מַשְׁכִּימֵי קוּם מְאַחֲרֵי שֶׁבֶת אֹכְלֵי לֶחֶם הָעֲצָבִים כֵּן יִתֵּן לִידִידוֹ שֵׁנָא.

[1] A Song of Ascents; of Solomon. Except the Lord build the house, they labour in vain that build it; except the Lord keep the city, the watchman waketh but in vain.
[2] It is vain for you that ye rise early, and sit up late, ye that eat the bread of toil; so He giveth unto His beloved in sleep.

Genesis 11

(א) וַיְהִי כָל הָאָרֶץ שָׂפָה אֶחָת וּדְבָרִים אֲחָדִים.
(ב) וַיְהִי בְּנָסְעָם מִקֶּדֶם וַיִּמְצְאוּ בִקְעָה בְּאֶרֶץ שִׁנְעָר וַיֵּשְׁבוּ שָׁם.
(ג) וַיֹּאמְרוּ אִישׁ אֶל רֵעֵהוּ הָבָה נִלְבְּנָה לְבֵנִים וְנִשְׂרְפָה לִשְׂרֵפָה וַתְּהִי לָהֶם הַלְּבֵנָה לְאָבֶן וְהַחֵמָר הָיָה לָהֶם לַחֹמֶר.
(ד) וַיֹּאמְרוּ הָבָה נִבְנֶה לָּנוּ עִיר וּמִגְדָּל וְרֹאשׁוֹ בַשָּׁמַיִם וְנַעֲשֶׂה לָּנוּ שֵׁם פֶּן נָפוּץ עַל פְּנֵי כָל הָאָרֶץ.
(ה) וַיֵּרֶד ה' לִרְאֹת אֶת הָעִיר וְאֶת הַמִּגְדָּל אֲשֶׁר בָּנוּ בְּנֵי הָאָדָם.
(ו) וַיֹּאמֶר ה' הֵן עַם אֶחָד וְשָׂפָה אַחַת לְכֻלָּם וְזֶה הַחִלָּם לַעֲשׂוֹת וְעַתָּה לֹא יִבָּצֵר מֵהֶם כֹּל אֲשֶׁר יָזְמוּ לַעֲשׂוֹת.
(ז) הָבָה נֵרְדָה וְנָבְלָה שָׁם שְׂפָתָם אֲשֶׁר לֹא יִשְׁמְעוּ אִישׁ שְׂפַת רֵעֵהוּ.
(ח) וַיָּפֶץ ה' אֹתָם מִשָּׁם עַל פְּנֵי כָל הָאָרֶץ וַיַּחְדְּלוּ לִבְנֹת הָעִיר.

(ט) עַל כֵּן קָרָא שְׁמָהּ בָּבֶל כִּי שָׁם בָּלַל ה' שְׂפַת כָּל הָאָרֶץ וּמִשָּׁם הֱפִיצָם ה' עַל פְּנֵי כָּל הָאָרֶץ.

[1] And the whole earth was of one language, and of one speech.

[2] And it came to pass, as they journeyed from the east, that they found a plain in the land of Shinar; and they dwelt there.

[3] And they said one to another, Go to, let us make brick, and burn them throughly. And they had brick for stone, and slime had they for morter.

[4] And they said, Go to, let us build us a city and a tower, whose top may reach unto heaven; and let us make us a name, lest we be scattered abroad upon the face of the whole earth.

[5] And the Lord came down to see the city and the tower, which the children of men builded.

[6] And the Lord said, Behold, the people is one, and they have all one language; and this they begin to do: and now nothing will be restrained from them, which they have imagined to do.

[7] Go to, let us go down, and there confound their language, that they may not understand one another's speech.

[8] So the Lord scattered them abroad from thence upon the face of all the earth: and they left off to build the city.

[9] Therefore is the name of it called Babel; because the Lord did there confound the language of all the earth: and from thence did the Lord scatter them abroad upon the face of all the earth.

The Revolution and
Its Aftermath

JOHN ADAMS (1735–1826)

In the following letter we see the power of covenantal thinking to unite disparate groups. John Adams describes how, when the Continental Congress first met in 1774, it was proposed that they unite in prayer, but John Jay argued that the theological differences between them were too great. Sam Adams then said that he is no bigot and would hear a prayer from anyone who was a man of piety and virtue. They brought in an Episcopal clergyman to read Psalm 35, about the care and protection God shows David and Israel against their enemies.

The Prayer that Began the Continental Congress:
John Adams's Letter to Abigail Adams (September 16, 1774)

Having a Leisure Moment, while the Congress is assembling, I gladly embrace it to write you a Line.

When the Congress first met, Mr. Cushing made a Motion, that it should be opened with Prayer. It was opposed by Mr. Jay of N. York and Mr. Rutledge of South Carolina, because we were so divided in religious Sentiments, some Episcopalians, some Quakers, some Anabaptists, some Presbyterians and some Congregationalists, so that We could not join in the same Act of Worship. – Mr. S. Adams arose and said he was no Bigot, and could hear a Prayer from a Gentleman of Piety and Virtue, who was at the same Time a Friend to his Country. He was a Stranger in Phyladelphia, but had heard that Mr. Duche (Dushay they pronounce it) deserved that Character, and therefore he moved that Mr. Duche, an episcopal Clergyman, might be desired, to read Prayers to the Congress, tomorrow Morning. The Motion was seconded and passed in the Affirmative. Mr. Randolph our President, waited on Mr. Duche, and received for Answer that if his Health would permit, he certainly would. Accordingly next Morning he appeared with his Clerk and in his Pontificallibus, and read several Prayers, in the established Form; and then read the Collect for the seventh day of September, which was the Thirty fifth Psalm. – You must remember this was the next Morning after we heard the horrible Rumour, of the Cannonade of Boston. – I never saw a greater Effect upon an Audience. It seemed as if Heaven had ordained that Psalm to be read on that Morning.

After this Mr. Duche, unexpected to every Body struck out into an extemporary Prayer, which filled the Bosom of every Man present. I must confess I never heard a better Prayer or one, so well pronounced. Episcopalian as he is, Dr. Cooper himself never prayed with such fervour, such Ardor, such Earnestness and Pathos, and in Language so elegant and sublime – for America, for the Congress, for The Province of Massachusetts Bay, and especially the Town of Boston. It has had an excellent Effect upon every Body here.

I must beg you to read that Psalm. If there was any Faith in the sortes Virgilianae, or sortes Homericae, or especially the Sortes biblicae, it would be thought providential.

It will amuse your Friends to read this Letter and the 35th. Psalm to them. Read it to your Father and Mr. Wibirt. – I wonder what our Braintree Churchmen would think of this? – Mr. Duche is one of the most ingenious Men, and best Characters, and greatest orators in the Episcopal order, upon this Continent – Yet a Zealous Friend of Liberty and his Country.

I long to see my dear Family – God bless, preserve and prosper it.
Adieu.   John Adams

Hebraic Source
Psalm 35

(א) לְדָוִד רִיבָה ה׳ אֶת יְרִיבַי לְחַם אֶת לֹחֲמָי.

(ב) הַחֲזֵק מָגֵן וְצִנָּה וְקוּמָה בְּעֶזְרָתִי.

(ג) וְהָרֵק חֲנִית וּסְגֹר לִקְרַאת רֹדְפָי אֱמֹר לְנַפְשִׁי יְשֻׁעָתֵךְ אָנִי.

(ד) יֵבֹשׁוּ וְיִכָּלְמוּ מְבַקְשֵׁי נַפְשִׁי יִסֹּגוּ אָחוֹר וְיַחְפְּרוּ חֹשְׁבֵי רָעָתִי.

(ה) יִהְיוּ כְּמֹץ לִפְנֵי רוּחַ וּמַלְאַךְ ה׳ דֹּחֶה.

(ו) יְהִי דַרְכָּם חֹשֶׁךְ וַחֲלַקְלַקֹּת וּמַלְאַךְ ה׳ רֹדְפָם.

(ז) כִּי חִנָּם טָמְנוּ לִי שַׁחַת רִשְׁתָּם חִנָּם חָפְרוּ לְנַפְשִׁי.

(ח) תְּבוֹאֵהוּ שׁוֹאָה לֹא יֵדָע וְרִשְׁתּוֹ אֲשֶׁר טָמַן תִּלְכְּדוֹ בְּשׁוֹאָה יִפָּל בָּהּ.

(ט) וְנַפְשִׁי תָּגִיל בַּה׳ תָּשִׂישׂ בִּישׁוּעָתוֹ.

(י) כָּל עַצְמֹתַי תֹּאמַרְנָה ה׳ מִי כָמוֹךָ מַצִּיל עָנִי מֵחָזָק מִמֶּנּוּ וְעָנִי וְאֶבְיוֹן מִגֹּזְלוֹ.

(יא) יְקוּמוּן עֵדֵי חָמָס אֲשֶׁר לֹא יָדַעְתִּי יִשְׁאָלוּנִי.

(יב) יְשַׁלְּמוּנִי רָעָה תַּחַת טוֹבָה שְׁכוֹל לְנַפְשִׁי.

(יג) וַאֲנִי בַּחֲלוֹתָם לְבוּשִׁי שָׂק עִנֵּיתִי בַצּוֹם נַפְשִׁי וּתְפִלָּתִי עַל חֵיקִי תָשׁוּב.

(יד) כְּרֵעַ כְּאָח לִי הִתְהַלָּכְתִּי כַּאֲבֶל אֵם קֹדֵר שַׁחוֹתִי.

(טו) וּבְצַלְעִי שָׂמְחוּ וְנֶאֱסָפוּ נֶאֶסְפוּ עָלַי נֵכִים וְלֹא יָדַעְתִּי קָרְעוּ וְלֹא דָמּוּ.

(טז) בְּחַנְפֵי לַעֲגֵי מָעוֹג חָרֹק עָלַי שִׁנֵּימוֹ.

(יז) אֲדֹנָי כַּמָּה תִרְאֶה הָשִׁיבָה נַפְשִׁי מִשֹּׁאֵיהֶם מִכְּפִירִים יְחִידָתִי.

(יח) אוֹדְךָ בְּקָהָל רָב בְּעַם עָצוּם אֲהַלְלֶךָּ.

(יט) אַל יִשְׂמְחוּ לִי אֹיְבַי שֶׁקֶר שֹׂנְאַי חִנָּם יִקְרְצוּ עָיִן.

(כ) כִּי לֹא שָׁלוֹם יְדַבֵּרוּ וְעַל רִגְעֵי אֶרֶץ דִּבְרֵי מִרְמוֹת יַחֲשֹׁבוּן.

(כא) וַיַּרְחִיבוּ עָלַי פִּיהֶם אָמְרוּ הֶאָח הֶאָח רָאֲתָה עֵינֵינוּ.

(כב) רָאִיתָה ה׳ אַל תֶּחֱרַשׁ אֲדֹנָי אַל תִּרְחַק מִמֶּנִּי.

(כג) הָעִירָה וְהָקִיצָה לְמִשְׁפָּטִי אֱ־לֹהַי וַאדֹנָי לְרִיבִי.

(כד) שָׁפְטֵנִי כְצִדְקְךָ ה׳ אֱ־לֹהָי וְאַל יִשְׂמְחוּ לִי.

(כה) אַל יֹאמְרוּ בְלִבָּם הֶאָח נַפְשֵׁנוּ אַל יֹאמְרוּ בִּלַּעֲנוּהוּ.

(כו) יֵבֹשׁוּ וְיַחְפְּרוּ יַחְדָּו שְׂמֵחֵי רָעָתִי יִלְבְּשׁוּ בֹשֶׁת וּכְלִמָּה הַמַּגְדִּילִים עָלָי.

(כז) יָרֹנּוּ וְיִשְׂמְחוּ חֲפֵצֵי צִדְקִי וְיֹאמְרוּ תָמִיד יִגְדַּל ה׳ הֶחָפֵץ שְׁלוֹם עַבְדּוֹ.

(כח) וּלְשׁוֹנִי תֶּהְגֶּה צִדְקֶךָ כָּל הַיּוֹם תְּהִלָּתֶךָ.

---

[1] Plead my cause, O Lord, with them that strive with me: fight against them that fight against me.

[2] Take hold of shield and buckler, and stand up for mine help.

[3] Draw out also the spear, and stop the way against them that persecute me: say unto my soul, I am thy salvation.

[4] Let them be confounded and put to shame that seek after my soul: let them be turned back and brought to confusion that devise my hurt.

[5] Let them be as chaff before the wind: and let the angel of the Lord chase them.

[6] Let their way be dark and slippery: and let the angel of the Lord persecute them.

[7] For without cause have they hid for me their net in a pit, which without cause they have digged for my soul.

[8] Let destruction come upon him at unawares; and let his net that he hath hid catch himself: into that very destruction let him fall.

[9] And my soul shall be joyful in the Lord: it shall rejoice in his salvation.

[10] All my bones shall say, Lord, who is like unto thee, which deliverest the poor from him that is too strong for him, yea, the poor and the needy from him that spoileth him?

[11] False witnesses did rise up; they laid to my charge things that I knew not.

[12] They rewarded me evil for good to the spoiling of my soul.

[13] But as for me, when they were sick, my clothing was sackcloth: I humbled my soul with fasting; and my prayer returned into mine own bosom.

[14] I behaved myself as though he had been my friend or brother: I bowed down heavily, as one that mourneth for his mother.

[15] But in mine adversity they rejoiced, and gathered themselves together: yea, the abjects gathered themselves together against me, and I knew it not; they did tear me, and ceased not:

[16] With hypocritical mockers in feasts, they gnashed upon me with their teeth.

[17] Lord, how long wilt Thou look on? rescue my soul from their destructions, my darling from the lions.

[18] I will give Thee thanks in the great congregation: I will praise thee among much people.

[19] Let not them that are mine enemies wrongfully rejoice over me: neither let them wink with the eye that hate me without a cause.

[20] For they speak not peace: but they devise deceitful matters against them that are quiet in the land.

[21] Yea, they opened their mouth wide against me, and said, Aha, aha, our eye hath seen it.

[22] This thou hast seen, O Lord: keep not silence: O Lord, be not far from me.

[23] Stir up thyself, and awake to my judgment, even unto my cause, my God and my Lord.

[24] Judge me, O Lord my God, according to thy righteousness; and let them not rejoice over me.

[25] Let them not say in their hearts, Ah, so would we have it: let them not say, We have swallowed him up.

[26] Let them be ashamed and brought to confusion together that rejoice at mine hurt: let them be clothed with shame and dishonour that magnify themselves against me.

[27] Let them shout for joy, and be glad, that favour my righteous cause: yea, let them say continually, Let the Lord be magnified, which hath pleasure in the prosperity of his servant.

[28] And my tongue shall speak of thy righteousness and of thy praise all the day long.

THOMAS PAINE (1737–1809)

Thomas Paine lived a rough-and-tumble life. He was an Englishman who immigrated to America in 1774. Unsuccessful at all other ventures, he became extremely successful as the author of the pro-Revolutionary pamphlets Common Sense *(1776) and* The American Crisis *(1776–1783, seven issues).* Common Sense *sold 500,000 copies – 120,000 in the first three months – an astounding feat given that the entire colonial population was only 2.5 million.*[1] Common Sense *(excerpted below) is a distillation, and simplification, of Enlightenment arguments for natural rights, legitimate government elected by the people, and the illegitimacy of monarchy. It is amazing that such a philosophical tract was a bestseller in colonial America. In* Common Sense *Paine argued that monarchy was born in the ancient world and was now antiquated and anachronistic. But he also used biblical arguments to buttress his case. He cites the book of Samuel as demonstrating that the Hebrew Bible is anti-monarchical. Scholar Nathan Perl-Rosenthal notes that "Paine drew heavily on the Hebraic republican tradition. Indeed he devoted more space in his pamphlet to Hebraic republican arguments than to almost any of his other lines of attack against monarchy. These arguments helped persuade at least some patriots to reject monarchy. Hebraic republican arguments also became a significant part of the broader public debate over the merits of monarchy and a kingless form of government."*[2] *Paine knew his audience extremely well. He knew what types of arguments would sit well with the American public, and what type of authority they respected.*

After the American Revolution, Paine worked for the Continental Congress as a secretary but was expelled for revealing the contents of negotiations with France. After moving to England, he published The Rights of Man *as a response to Edmund Burke's* Reflections on the Revolution in France. *He was tried, in abstentia, for seditious libel in England and sentenced to death. By then he was already in France, participating in the French Revolution as a member of the National Convention. He aided the writing of early constitutions for the French Republic but was opposed to the execution of Louis XVI. Paine*

1. http://www2.census.gov/prod2/decennial/documents/00165897ch01.pdf.
2. Nathan Perl-Rosenthal, "The 'Divine Right of Republics': Hebraic Republicanism and the Debate over Kingless Government in Revolutionary America," *The William and Mary Quarterly*, 3rd series, vol. 66, no. 3 (July 2009): 535–64.

fell out of favor with the leaders of the French Revolution and was imprisoned. In prison he completed his Age of Reason, *which was to be his final testament and statement of his beliefs. He wrote it expecting that he would be executed at any moment. In fact, Paine was scheduled to be guillotined, but the jailer, in a fit of absentmindedness, chalked the sign indicating he was to be executed the next day on the inside instead of the outside of Paine's door. The following day, since the mark was not visible, Paine was passed over, while those to his left and right were killed. The day after Robespierre fell and the Terror was over, Paine was saved.[3] The American minister in Paris, James Monroe, secured his release. He then rejoined the tumult of French politics, arguing for universal suffrage, and when Napoleon seized power Paine wrote books to aid him in planning the invasion of England. He returned to the United States in 1802 when invited back by his closest intellectual ally of the founding generation, Thomas Jefferson. He died in 1809 in Greenwich Village, New York. Only eight people attended his funeral.*

Paine's use of the Bible raises the question of his sincerity. John Adams reports the following conversation with Paine: "I told him further that his Reasoning from the Old Testament [in Common Sense*] was ridiculous, and I could hardly think him sincere. At this he laughed, and said he had taken his ideas in part from Milton: and then expressed a contempt for the Old Testament and indeed of the Bible at large, which surprised me."[4]*

Common Sense (1776)

Part I: On the Origin and Design of Government in General

SOME writers have so confounded society with government, as to leave little or no distinction between them; whereas they are not only different, but have different origins. Society is produced by our wants, and government by wickedness; the former promotes our happiness *positively* by uniting our affections, the latter *negatively* by restraining our vices. The one encourages intercourse, the other creates distinctions. The first is a patron, the last a punisher.

---

3. Daniel E. Wheeler, ed., *The Life and Writings of Thomas Paine* (New York: Vincent Park, 1908).

4. Nelson, *Hebrew Republic*, 165 n.104; and see John Adams, *Diary and Autobiography of John Adams*, 3 vols., ed. L. H. Butterfield (Cambridge, MA: Harvard University Press, 1961), 3:333.

1

Society in every state is a blessing, but government even in its best state is but a necessary evil; in its worst state an intolerable one; for when we suffer, or are exposed to the same miseries *by a government*, which we might expect in a country *without government*, our calamity is heightened by reflecting that we furnish the means by which we suffer. Government, like dress, is the badge of lost innocence; the palaces of kings are built on the ruins of the bowers of paradise. For were the impulses of conscience clear, uniform, and irresistibly obeyed, man would need no other lawgiver; but that not being the case, he finds it necessary to surrender up a part of his property to furnish means for the protection of the rest; and this he is induced to do by the same prudence which in every other case advises him out of two evils to choose the least. *Wherefore*, security being the true design and end of government, it unanswerably follows that whatever *form* thereof appears most likely to ensure it to us, with the least expence and greatest benefit, is preferable to all others.

2

In order to gain a clear and just idea of the design and end of government, let us suppose a small number of persons settled in some sequestered part of the earth, unconnected with the rest, they will then represent the first peopling of any country, or of the world. In this state of natural liberty, society will be their first thought. A thousand motives will excite them thereto, the strength of one man is so unequal to his wants, and his mind so unfitted for perpetual solitude, that he is soon obliged to seek assistance and relief of another, who in his turn requires the same. Four or five united would be able to raise a tolerable dwelling in the midst of a wilderness, but *one* man might labour out the common period of life without accomplishing any thing; when he had felled his timber he could not remove it, nor erect it after it was removed; hunger in the mean time would urge him from his work, and every different want call him a different way. Disease, nay even misfortune would be death, for though neither might be mortal, yet either would disable him from living, and reduce him to a state in which he might rather be said to perish than to die....

Part II: Of Monarchy and Hereditary Succession

MANKIND being originally equals in the order of creation, the equality could only be destroyed by some subsequent circumstance; the distinctions of rich, and poor, may in a great measure be accounted for, and that without having recourse to the harsh ill sounding names of oppression and avarice. Oppression is often the *consequence*, but seldom or never the *means* of riches; and though avarice will preserve a man from being necessitously poor, it generally makes him too timorous to be wealthy.

1

But there is another and greater distinction for which no truly natural or religious reason can be assigned, and that is, the distinction of men into KINGS and SUBJECTS. Male and female are the distinctions of nature, good and bad the distinctions of heaven; but how a race of men came into the world so exalted above the rest, and distinguished like some new species, is worth enquiring into, and whether they are the means of happiness or of misery to mankind.

2

In the early ages of the world, according to the scripture chronology, there were no kings; the consequence of which was there were no wars; it is the pride of kings which throw mankind into confusion. Holland without a king hath enjoyed more peace for this last century than any of the monarchical governments in Europe. Antiquity favors the same remark; for the quiet and rural lives of the first patriarchs hath a happy something in them, which vanishes away when we come to the history of Jewish royalty.

3

Government by kings was first introduced into the world by the Heathens, from whom the children of Israel copied the custom. It was the most prosperous invention the Devil ever set on foot for the promotion of idolatry. The Heathens paid divine honors to their deceased kings, and the christian world hath improved on the plan by doing the same to their living ones. How impious is the title of sacred majesty applied to a worm, who in the midst of his splendor is crumbling into dust!

4

As the exalting one man so greatly above the rest cannot be justified on the equal rights of nature, so neither can it be defended on the authority of scripture; for the will of the Almighty, as declared by Gideon and the prophet Samuel, expressly disapproves of government by kings. All anti-monarchical parts of scripture have been very smoothly glossed over in monarchical governments, but they undoubtedly merit the attention of countries which have their governments yet to form. *"Render unto Caesar the things which are Caesar's"* is the scripture doctrine of courts, yet it is no support of monarchical government, for the Jews at that time were without a king, and in a state of vassalage to the Romans.

5

Near three thousand years passed away from the Mosaic account of the creation, till the Jews under a national delusion requested a king. Till then their form of government (except in extraordinary cases, where the Almighty interposed) was a kind of republic administered by a judge and the elders of the tribes. Kings they had none, and it was held sinful to acknowledge any being under that title but the Lord of Hosts. And when a man seriously reflects on the idolatrous homage which is paid to the persons of Kings, he need not wonder, that the Almighty ever jealous of his honor, should disapprove of a form of government which so impiously invades the prerogative of heaven.

6

Monarchy is ranked in scripture as one of the sins of the Jews, for which a curse in reserve is denounced against them. The history of that transaction is worth attending to.

7

The children of Israel being oppressed by the Midianites, Gideon marched against them with a small army, and victory, thro' the divine interposition, decided in his favour. The Jews elate with success, and attributing it to the generalship of Gideon, proposed making him a king, saying, *Rule thou over us, thou and thy son and thy son's son* [Judg. 8:22]. Here was temptation in its fullest extent; not a kingdom only, but an hereditary one, but Gideon in the piety of his soul replied, *I will not rule over you, neither shall my son rule over you.* THE Lord SHALL RULE OVER YOU [Judg. 8:23]. Words need not be more explicit; Gideon doth not *decline* the honor, but denieth their right to give it; neither doth he compliment them with invented declarations of his thanks, but in the positive stile of a prophet charges them with disaffection to their proper Sovereign, the King of heaven.

8

About one hundred and thirty years after this, they fell again into the same error. The hankering which the Jews had for the idolatrous customs of the Heathens, is something exceedingly unaccountable; but so it was, that laying hold of the misconduct of Samuel's two sons, who were entrusted with some secular concerns, they came in an abrupt and clamorous manner to Samuel, saying, *Behold thou art old, and thy sons walk not in thy ways, now make us a king to judge us like all the other nations* [I Sam. 8:5]. And here we cannot but observe that their motives were bad, viz. that they might be *like* unto other nations, i.e. the Heathens, whereas their true glory laid in being as much *unlike* them as possible. *But the thing displeased Samuel when they said, Give us a king to judge us; and Samuel prayed unto the Lord, and the Lord said unto Samuel, Hearken unto the voice of the people in all that they say unto thee, for they have not rejected thee, but they have rejected me,* THAT I SHOULD NOT REIGN OVER THEM. *According to all the works which they have done since the day that I brought them up out of Egypt, even unto this day; wherewith they have forsaken me and served other Gods; so do they also unto thee. Now therefore hearken unto their voice, howbeit, protest solemnly unto them and shew them the manner of the king that shall reign over them* [I Sam. 8:6-9], i.e. not of any particular king, but the general manner of the kings of the earth, whom Israel was so eagerly copying after. And notwithstanding the great distance of time and difference of manners, the character is still in fashion. *And Samuel told all the words of the Lord unto the people, that asked of him a king. And he said, This shall be the manner of the king that shall reign over you; he will take your sons and appoint them for himself, for his chariots, and to be his horsemen, and some shall run before his chariots* (this description agrees with the present mode of impressing men) *and he will appoint him captains over thousands and captains over fifties, and will set them to ear his ground and to reap his harvest, and to make his instruments of war, and instruments of his chariots; and he will take your daughters to be confectionaries, and to be cooks and to be bakers* (this describes the expence and luxury as well as the oppression of kings) *and he will take your fields and your olive yards, even the best of them, and give them to his servants; and he will take the tenth of your feed, and of your vineyards, and give them to his officers and to his servants* (by which we see that bribery, corruption, and favoritism are the standing vices of kings) *and he will take the tenth of your men servants, and your maid servants, and your goodliest young men and your asses, and put them to his work; and he will take the tenth of your sheep, and ye shall be his servants, and ye shall cry out in that day because of your king which ye shall have chosen,* AND THE Lord WILL NOT HEAR YOU IN THAT DAY [I Sam. 8:10-18]. This accounts for the continuation of monarchy; neither do the characters of the few good kings which have lived since, either sanctify the title, or blot out the sinfulness of the origin; the high encomium given of David takes no notice of him *officially as a king,* but only as a *man* after God's own heart. *Nevertheless the People refused to obey the voice of Samuel, and they said, Nay, but we will have a king over us, that we may be like all the nations, and that our king may judge us, and go out before us, and fight our battles* [I Sam. 8:19-20]. Samuel continued to reason with them, but to no purpose; he set before them their ingratitude, but all would not avail; and seeing them fully bent on their folly, he cried out, *I will call unto the Lord, and he shall send thunder and rain* (which then was a punishment, being in the time of wheat harvest) *that ye may perceive and see that your wickedness is great which ye have done in the sight of the Lord,* IN ASKING YOU A KING. *So Samuel called unto the Lord, and the Lord sent thunder and rain that day, and all the people greatly feared the Lord and Samuel. And all the people said unto*

> Samuel, Pray for thy servants unto the Lord thy God that we die not, for
> WE HAVE ADDED UNTO OUR SINS THIS EVIL, TO ASK A KING
> [I Sam. 12:17-19]. These portions of scripture are direct and positive.
> They admit of no equivocal construction. That the Almighty hath here
> entered his protest against monarchical government is true, or the
> scripture is false. And a man hath good reason to believe that there
> is as much of kingcraft, as priestcraft, in withholding the scripture
> from the public in Popish countries. For monarchy in every instance
> is the Popery of government.

Hebraic Sources

Paine recruited the most explicitly anti-monarchical parts of the Hebrew Bible
to make his argument. However, he conveniently ended his citation before God
ultimately acceded to the Israelites' request, failed to mention the emphasis
on continued obedience of God, and wholly omitted Deuteronomy 17:14–20,
which seemingly contains a commandment to appoint a king hedged in by
prohibitions against excess. The Rabbis of late antiquity struggled with the
manifest contradiction between biblical sources on this issue, and, like Paine,
mostly took a dim view of monarchy.

I Samuel 8

(ד) וַיִּתְקַבְּצוּ כֹּל זִקְנֵי יִשְׂרָאֵל וַיָּבֹאוּ אֶל שְׁמוּאֵל הָרָמָתָה.

(ה) וַיֹּאמְרוּ אֵלָיו הִנֵּה אַתָּה זָקַנְתָּ וּבָנֶיךָ לֹא הָלְכוּ בִּדְרָכֶיךָ עַתָּה שִׂימָה לָּנוּ מֶלֶךְ לְשָׁפְטֵנוּ כְּכָל הַגּוֹיִם.

(ו) וַיֵּרַע הַדָּבָר בְּעֵינֵי שְׁמוּאֵל כַּאֲשֶׁר אָמְרוּ תְּנָה לָּנוּ מֶלֶךְ לְשָׁפְטֵנוּ וַיִּתְפַּלֵּל שְׁמוּאֵל אֶל ה'.

(ז) וַיֹּאמֶר ה' אֶל שְׁמוּאֵל שְׁמַע בְּקוֹל הָעָם לְכֹל אֲשֶׁר יֹאמְרוּ אֵלֶיךָ כִּי לֹא אֹתְךָ מָאָסוּ כִּי אֹתִי מָאֲסוּ מִמְּלֹךְ עֲלֵיהֶם.

(ח) כְּכָל הַמַּעֲשִׂים אֲשֶׁר עָשׂוּ מִיּוֹם הַעֲלֹתִי אֹתָם מִמִּצְרַיִם וְעַד הַיּוֹם הַזֶּה וַיַּעַזְבֻנִי וַיַּעַבְדוּ אֱלֹהִים אֲחֵרִים כֵּן הֵמָּה עֹשִׂים גַּם לָךְ.

(ט) וְעַתָּה שְׁמַע בְּקוֹלָם אַךְ כִּי הָעֵד תָּעִיד בָּהֶם וְהִגַּדְתָּ לָהֶם מִשְׁפַּט הַמֶּלֶךְ אֲשֶׁר יִמְלֹךְ עֲלֵיהֶם.

(י) וַיֹּאמֶר שְׁמוּאֵל אֵת כָּל דִּבְרֵי ה' אֶל הָעָם הַשֹּׁאֲלִים מֵאִתּוֹ מֶלֶךְ.

(יא) וַיֹּאמֶר זֶה יִהְיֶה מִשְׁפַּט הַמֶּלֶךְ אֲשֶׁר יִמְלֹךְ עֲלֵיכֶם אֶת בְּנֵיכֶם יִקָּח וְשָׂם לוֹ בְּמֶרְכַּבְתּוֹ וּבְפָרָשָׁיו וְרָצוּ לִפְנֵי מֶרְכַּבְתּוֹ.

(יב) וְלָשׂוּם לוֹ שָׂרֵי אֲלָפִים וְשָׂרֵי חֲמִשִּׁים וְלַחֲרֹשׁ חֲרִישׁוֹ וְלִקְצֹר קְצִירוֹ וְלַעֲשׂוֹת כְּלֵי מִלְחַמְתּוֹ וּכְלֵי רִכְבּוֹ.

(יג) וְאֶת בְּנוֹתֵיכֶם יִקָּח לְרַקָּחוֹת וּלְטַבָּחוֹת וּלְאֹפוֹת.

(יד) וְאֶת שְׂדוֹתֵיכֶם וְאֶת כַּרְמֵיכֶם וְזֵיתֵיכֶם הַטּוֹבִים יִקָּח וְנָתַן לַעֲבָדָיו.

(טו) וְזַרְעֵיכֶם וְכַרְמֵיכֶם יַעְשֹׂר וְנָתַן לְסָרִיסָיו וְלַעֲבָדָיו.

(טז) וְאֶת עַבְדֵיכֶם וְאֶת שִׁפְחוֹתֵיכֶם וְאֶת בַּחוּרֵיכֶם הַטּוֹבִים וְאֶת חֲמוֹרֵיכֶם יִקָּח וְעָשָׂה לִמְלַאכְתּוֹ.

(יז) צֹאנְכֶם יַעְשֹׂר וְאַתֶּם תִּהְיוּ לוֹ לַעֲבָדִים.

(יח) וּזְעַקְתֶּם בַּיּוֹם הַהוּא מִלִּפְנֵי מַלְכְּכֶם אֲשֶׁר בְּחַרְתֶּם לָכֶם וְלֹא יַעֲנֶה ה' אֶתְכֶם בַּיּוֹם הַהוּא.

(יט) וַיְמָאֲנוּ הָעָם לִשְׁמֹעַ בְּקוֹל שְׁמוּאֵל וַיֹּאמְרוּ לֹא כִּי אִם מֶלֶךְ יִהְיֶה עָלֵינוּ.

(כ) וְהָיִינוּ גַם אֲנַחְנוּ כְּכָל הַגּוֹיִם וּשְׁפָטָנוּ מַלְכֵּנוּ וְיָצָא לְפָנֵינוּ וְנִלְחַם אֶת מִלְחֲמֹתֵנוּ.

(כא) וַיִּשְׁמַע שְׁמוּאֵל אֵת כָּל דִּבְרֵי הָעָם וַיְדַבְּרֵם בְּאָזְנֵי ה'.

(כב) וַיֹּאמֶר ה' אֶל שְׁמוּאֵל שְׁמַע בְּקוֹלָם וְהִמְלַכְתָּ לָהֶם מֶלֶךְ וַיֹּאמֶר שְׁמוּאֵל אֶל אַנְשֵׁי יִשְׂרָאֵל לְכוּ אִישׁ לְעִירוֹ.

[4] Then all the elders of Israel gathered themselves together, and came to Samuel unto Ramah,

[5] And said unto him: Behold, thou art old, and thy sons walk not in thy ways; now make us a king to judge us like all the nations.

[6] But the thing displeased Samuel, when they said: Give us a king to judge us. And Samuel prayed unto the Lord.

[7] And the Lord said unto Samuel: Hearken unto the voice of the people in all that they say unto thee; for they have not rejected thee, but they have rejected Me, that I should not reign over them.

[8] According to all the works which they have done since the day that I brought them up out of Egypt even unto this day, wherewith they have forsaken Me, and served other gods, so do they also unto thee.

[9] Now therefore hearken unto their voice: howbeit yet protest solemnly unto them, and show them the manner of the king that shall reign over them.

[10] And Samuel told all the words of the Lord unto the people that asked of him a king.

[11] And he said: This will be the manner of the king that shall reign over you: He will take your sons, and appoint them for himself, for his chariots, and to be his horsemen; and some shall run before his chariots.

[12] And he will appoint him captains over thousands, and captains over fifties; and will set them to plow his ground, and to reap his harvest, and to make his instruments of war, and instruments of his chariots.

[13] And he will take your daughters to be confectionaries, and to be cooks, and to be bakers.

[14] And he will take your fields, and your vineyards, and your oliveyards, even the best of them, and give them to his servants.

¹⁵ And he will take the tenth of your seed, and of your vineyards, and give to his officers, and to his servants.

¹⁶ And he will take your menservants, and your maidservants, and your goodliest young men, and your asses, and put them to his work.

¹⁷ He will take the tenth of your sheep; and ye shall be his servants.

¹⁸ And ye shall cry out in that day because of your king which ye shall have chosen you; and the Lord will not hear you in that day.

¹⁹ Nevertheless the people refused to obey the voice of Samuel; and they said: Nay, but we will have a king over us;

²⁰ That we also may be like all the nations; and that our king may judge us, and go out before us, and fight our battles.

²¹ And Samuel heard all the words of the people, and he rehearsed them in the ears of the Lord.

²² And the Lord said to Samuel: Hearken unto their voice, and make them a king. And Samuel said unto the men of Israel: Go ye every man unto his city.

I Samuel 12

(ו) וַיֹּאמֶר שְׁמוּאֵל אֶל הָעָם ה' אֲשֶׁר עָשָׂה אֶת מֹשֶׁה וְאֶת אַהֲרֹן וַאֲשֶׁר הֶעֱלָה אֶת אֲבֹתֵיכֶם מֵאֶרֶץ מִצְרָיִם.

(ז) וְעַתָּה הִתְיַצְּבוּ וְאִשָּׁפְטָה אִתְּכֶם לִפְנֵי ה' אֵת כָּל צִדְקוֹת ה' אֲשֶׁר עָשָׂה אִתְּכֶם וְאֶת אֲבוֹתֵיכֶם.

(ח) כַּאֲשֶׁר בָּא יַעֲקֹב מִצְרָיִם וַיִּזְעֲקוּ אֲבוֹתֵיכֶם אֶל ה' וַיִּשְׁלַח ה' אֶת מֹשֶׁה וְאֶת אַהֲרֹן וַיּוֹצִיאוּ אֶת אֲבֹתֵיכֶם מִמִּצְרַיִם וַיֹּשִׁבוּם בַּמָּקוֹם הַזֶּה.

(ט) וַיִּשְׁכְּחוּ אֶת ה' אֱ-לֹהֵיהֶם וַיִּמְכֹּר אֹתָם בְּיַד סִיסְרָא שַׂר צְבָא חָצוֹר וּבְיַד פְּלִשְׁתִּים וּבְיַד מֶלֶךְ מוֹאָב וַיִּלָּחֲמוּ בָּם.

(י) וַיִּזְעֲקוּ אֶל ה' [וַיֹּאמְרוּ] ויאמר חָטָאנוּ כִּי עָזַבְנוּ אֶת ה' וַנַּעֲבֹד אֶת הַבְּעָלִים וְאֶת הָעַשְׁתָּרוֹת וְעַתָּה הַצִּילֵנוּ מִיַּד אֹיְבֵינוּ וְנַעַבְדֶךָּ.

(יא) וַיִּשְׁלַח ה' אֶת יְרֻבַּעַל וְאֶת בְּדָן וְאֶת יִפְתָּח וְאֶת שְׁמוּאֵל וַיַּצֵּל אֶתְכֶם מִיַּד אֹיְבֵיכֶם מִסָּבִיב וַתֵּשְׁבוּ בֶּטַח.

(יב) וַתִּרְאוּ כִּי נָחָשׁ מֶלֶךְ בְּנֵי עַמּוֹן בָּא עֲלֵיכֶם וַתֹּאמְרוּ לִי לֹא כִּי מֶלֶךְ יִמְלֹךְ עָלֵינוּ וַה' אֱ-לֹהֵיכֶם מַלְכְּכֶם.

(יג) וְעַתָּה הִנֵּה הַמֶּלֶךְ אֲשֶׁר בְּחַרְתֶּם אֲשֶׁר שְׁאֶלְתֶּם וְהִנֵּה נָתַן ה' עֲלֵיכֶם מֶלֶךְ.

(יד) אִם תִּירְאוּ אֶת ה' וַעֲבַדְתֶּם אֹתוֹ וּשְׁמַעְתֶּם בְּקֹלוֹ וְלֹא תַמְרוּ אֶת פִּי ה' וִהְיִתֶם גַּם אַתֶּם וְגַם הַמֶּלֶךְ אֲשֶׁר מָלַךְ עֲלֵיכֶם אַחַר ה' אֱ-לֹהֵיכֶם.

(טו) וְאִם לֹא תִשְׁמְעוּ בְּקוֹל ה' וּמְרִיתֶם אֶת פִּי ה' וְהָיְתָה יַד ה' בָּכֶם וּבַאֲבֹתֵיכֶם.

(טז) גַּם עַתָּה הִתְיַצְּבוּ וּרְאוּ אֶת הַדָּבָר הַגָּדוֹל הַזֶּה אֲשֶׁר ה' עֹשֶׂה לְעֵינֵיכֶם.

(יז) הֲלוֹא קְצִיר חִטִּים הַיּוֹם אֶקְרָא אֶל ה' וְיִתֵּן קֹלוֹת וּמָטָר וּדְעוּ וּרְאוּ כִּי רָעַתְכֶם רַבָּה אֲשֶׁר עֲשִׂיתֶם בְּעֵינֵי ה' לִשְׁאוֹל לָכֶם מֶלֶךְ.

(יח) וַיִּקְרָא שְׁמוּאֵל אֶל ה' וַיִּתֵּן ה' קֹלֹת וּמָטָר בַּיּוֹם הַהוּא וַיִּירָא כָל הָעָם מְאֹד אֶת ה' וְאֶת שְׁמוּאֵל.

(יט) וַיֹּאמְרוּ כָל הָעָם אֶל שְׁמוּאֵל הִתְפַּלֵּל בְּעַד עֲבָדֶיךָ אֶל ה' אֱ-לֹהֶיךָ וְאַל נָמוּת כִּי יָסַפְנוּ עַל כָּל חַטֹּאתֵינוּ רָעָה לִשְׁאֹל לָנוּ מֶלֶךְ.

(כ) וַיֹּאמֶר שְׁמוּאֵל אֶל הָעָם אַל תִּירָאוּ אַתֶּם עֲשִׂיתֶם אֵת כָּל הָרָעָה הַזֹּאת אַךְ אַל תָּסוּרוּ מֵאַחֲרֵי ה' וַעֲבַדְתֶּם אֶת ה' בְּכָל לְבַבְכֶם.

(כא) וְלֹא תָּסוּרוּ כִּי אַחֲרֵי הַתֹּהוּ אֲשֶׁר לֹא יוֹעִילוּ וְלֹא יַצִּילוּ כִּי תֹהוּ הֵמָּה.

(כב) כִּי לֹא יִטֹּשׁ ה' אֶת עַמּוֹ בַּעֲבוּר שְׁמוֹ הַגָּדוֹל כִּי הוֹאִיל ה' לַעֲשׂוֹת אֶתְכֶם לוֹ לְעָם.

(כג) גַּם אָנֹכִי חָלִילָה לִּי מֵחֲטֹא לַה' מֵחֲדֹל לְהִתְפַּלֵּל בַּעַדְכֶם וְהוֹרֵיתִי אֶתְכֶם בְּדֶרֶךְ הַטּוֹבָה וְהַיְשָׁרָה.

(כד) אַךְ יְראוּ אֶת ה' וַעֲבַדְתֶּם אֹתוֹ בֶּאֱמֶת בְּכָל לְבַבְכֶם כִּי רְאוּ אֵת אֲשֶׁר הִגְדִּל עִמָּכֶם.

(כה) וְאִם הָרֵעַ תָּרֵעוּ גַּם אַתֶּם גַּם מַלְכְּכֶם תִּסָּפוּ.

[6] And Samuel said unto the people: It is the Lord that advanced Moses and Aaron, and that brought your fathers up out of the land of Egypt.

[7] Now therefore stand still, that I may reason with you before the Lord of all the righteous acts of the Lord, which He did to you and to your fathers.

[8] When Jacob was come into Egypt, and your fathers cried unto the Lord, then the Lord sent Moses and Aaron, which brought forth your fathers out of Egypt, and made them dwell in this place.

[9] And when they forgot the Lord their God, he sold them into the hand of Sisera, captain of the host of Hazor, and into the hand of the Philistines, and into the hand of the king of Moab, and they fought against them.

[10] And they cried unto the Lord, and said: We have sinned, because we have forsaken the Lord, and have served Baalim and Ashtaroth; but now deliver us out of the hand of our enemies, and we will serve thee.

[11] And the Lord sent Jerubbaal, and Bedan, and Jephthah, and Samuel, and delivered you out of the hand of your enemies on every side, and ye dwelled safe.

[12] And when ye saw that Nahash the king of the children of Ammon came against you, ye said unto me: Nay, but a king shall reign over us; when the Lord your God was your king.

[13] Now therefore behold the king whom ye have chosen, and whom ye have desired! and, behold, the Lord hath set a king over you.

[14] If ye will fear the Lord, and serve Him, and obey His voice, and not rebel against the commandment of the Lord, then shall both ye and also the king that reigneth over you continue following the Lord your God:

[15] But if ye will not obey the voice of the Lord, but rebel against the commandment of the Lord, then shall the hand of the Lord be against you, as it was against your fathers.

[16] Now therefore stand and see this great thing, which the Lord will do before your eyes.

¹⁷ Is it not wheat harvest to day? I will call unto the Lord, and He shall send thunder and rain; that ye may perceive and see that your wickedness is great, which ye have done in the sight of the Lord, in asking you a king.

¹⁸ So Samuel called unto the Lord; and the Lord sent thunder and rain that day; and all the people greatly feared the Lord and Samuel.

¹⁹ And all the people said unto Samuel: Pray for thy servants unto the Lord thy God, that we die not; for we have added unto all our sins this evil, to ask us a king.

²⁰ And Samuel said unto the people: Fear not; ye have done all this wickedness; yet turn not aside from following the Lord, but serve the Lord with all your heart;

²¹ And turn ye not aside; for then should ye go after vain things, which cannot profit nor deliver, for they are vain.

²² For the Lord will not forsake His people for His great name's sake; because it hath pleased the Lord to make you his people.

²³ Moreover as for me, God forbid that I should sin against the Lord in ceasing to pray for you; but I will teach you the good and the right way:

²⁴ Only fear the Lord, and serve Him in truth with all your heart; for consider how great things He hath done for you.

²⁵ But if ye shall still do wickedly, ye shall be consumed, both ye and your king.

Deuteronomy Rabba 5

[ח.] "ואמרת אשימה עלי מלך"... אמ' הקב"ה לישראל, בני, כך חשבתי שתהיו חירות מן המלכיות, שנאמ' "פרא למוד מדבר" (ירמיהו ב:כד), כשם שהערוד הזה גדל במדבר ואין אימת מלכות עליו, כך חשבתי שלא תהא אימת מלכות עליכם, אבל אתם לא חשבתם כן, אלא "באות נפשה שאפה רוח" (שם), ואין רוח אלא מלכיות, מנין, שנא' "וארו ארבע רוחי שמיא מגיחן לימא רבה" (דניאל ז:ב), אמ' הקב"ה, ואם תאמרו שאיני יודע שסופכם לעזבני, כבר הזהרתי על ידי משה ואמרתי לו, הואיל וסופן לבקש להם מלך בש"ו, מהם ימליכו עליהם ולא מלך נכרי, מנין, ממה שקרינו בענין, "ואמרת אשימה עלי מלך וגו'".

[ט.] ד"א "ואמרת אשימה עלי מלך וגו'"... "ממלוך אדם חנף" (איוב לד:ל), רבנין אמרי כיון שעמדו מלכים על ישראל התחילו משעבדי' בהם, אמ' הקב"ה, לא אתם עזבתם אותי ובקשתם לכם מלך, הוי "אשימה עלי מלך". ד"א "אשימה עלי מלך", הה"ד "אל תבטחו בנדיבים וגו'" (תהלים קמו:ג)... כל מי שנשען בבש"ו עובר, אף פרוסטטמיא שלו עוברת, שנא' "בבן אדם שאין לו תשועה" (שם), מה כתי' אחריו, "תצא רוחו ישוב לאדמתו" (תהלים קמו:ד). אמ' הקב"ה ויודעין שאין בש"ו כלום, ומניחין כבודי ואומרי', שימה לנו מלך, מה אתם מבקשים מלך, חייכם, סופכם להרגיש מה עתיד להגיע לכם מתחת מלכיכם, שנא' "כל מלכיהם נפלו ואין קורא בהם אלי" (הושע ז:ז)....

[יא.] ד"א "אשימה עלי מלך", רבנן אמרי, אמ' הקב"ה, בעה"ז בקשתם מלכים, ועמדו המלכים והפילו אתכם בחרב, שאול הפילן בהר הגלבוע, שנא' "וינוסו

אנשי ישראל מפני פלשתים ויפילו חללים בהר הגלבוע" (שמואל א' לא:א),
דוד נתן בהם מגפה, שנא' "ויתן ה' דבר בישראל" (שמואל ב' כד:טו). אחאב
עצר עליהם את הגשמים, שנא' "אם יהיה השנים האלה טל וגו'" (מלכים א'
יז:א), צדקיהו החריב בית המקדש, כיון שראו מה הגיען מתחת ידי מלכיהם,
התחילו צווחין, אין אנו מבקשים מלך, למלכנו הראשון אנו מבקשים, שנא'
"כי ה' שופטנו ה' מחוקקנו ה' מלכנו הוא יושיענו" (ישעיהו לג:כב), אמ' להם
הקב"ה כך אני עושה, מנין, שנא' "והיה ה' למלך על כל הארץ" (זכריה יד:ט).

[8] "If you say, I will set a king over me": ...The Holy One said to Israel: My children, I endeavored that you be free of the monarchy [*malkhut*]. Where [is this derived] from? As
written, "A wild ass used to the desert" (Jer. 2:24): just as the wild ass grows up in the wilderness, without fear of humanity, so I intended you to be without fear of monarchy. You,
however, endeavored otherwise: "snuffing the wind in her eagerness" (Jer. 2:24) – "wind"
signifying kingdoms [*malkhuyot*]. Where [is this derived] from? As written, "I saw the
four winds of heaven," etc. (Dan. 7:2ff.). The Holy One said: Do you think I did not know
that in the end you will forsake Me? [In anticipation] I already instructed Moses, saying:
"Seeing that in the end they will seek a king of flesh and blood, they should appoint one
of their own, not a foreigner." Where [is this derived] from? From what we read in this
section, "If you say...be sure to set as king over yourself one of your own people."

[9] Another view, "If you say, I will set a king over me": ... "Impious man reigns from the
people's folly" (Job 34:30). When kings arose over Israel and began to enslave them, the
Holy One said: Was it not you who forsook Me to seek a king for yourselves? As written,
"I will set a king over me." Another view, "If you say, I will set a king over me": As Scripture
says, "Put not your trust in the great," etc. (Ps. 146:3) ... Whenever one relies upon flesh
and blood, as he fails so does his word fail, as written, "In mortal man who cannot save"
(Ps. 146:3). What is written next? "His breath departs; he returns to the dust; on that day
his plans come to nothing" (Ps. 146:4). The Holy One said: Though they know that flesh
and blood is nought, they abandon My glory and say: "Set a king over us." Why do you
seek a king? By your life, in the end you will experience what befalls you under your kings,
as written, "All their kings have fallen – none of them calls to me" (Hos. 7:7)....

[11] Another view, "If you say, I will set a king over me": The rabbis say: The Holy One said,
In this world you sought kings, and the kings arose and caused you to fall by the sword.
Saul caused them to fall on Mount Gilboa, as written, "The men of Israel fled before the
Philistines and fell on Mount Gilboa" (I Sam. 31:1); David brought upon them a plague,
as written, "The Lord sent a pestilence upon Israel" (II Sam. 24:15); Ahab caused them to
suffer a drought, as written, "There will be no dew or rain" (I Kings 17:1); Zedekiah caused
the destruction of the Temple. When Israel saw what befell them because of their kings,
they started screaming, "We do not seek a king, it is our first king that we seek!" as written,
"For the Lord shall be our ruler, the Lord shall be our prince, the Lord shall be our king;
he shall deliver us!" (Is. 33:22). The Holy One replied: So shall I do. As written, "And the
Lord shall be king over all the earth" (Zech. 14: 9).

PROPOSALS FOR THE SEAL OF THE UNITED STATES (1776)

After the Declaration of Independence was adopted on July 4, 1776, a committee was formed to design a national seal. Thomas Jefferson and Benjamin Franklin both proposed basing the seal on scenes from the Hebrew Bible while John Adams proposed a scene from Roman mythology, each described in Adams's letter below. Jefferson's and Franklin's suggestions reflect two different aspects of covenantal history: Franklin emphasized the miraculous and the providential while Jefferson stressed the covenantal loyalty of people to God and their mission.

Letter from John Adams to Abigail Adams (August 14, 1776)

I am put upon a committee, to prepare a device for a golden medal, to commemorate the surrender of Boston to the American arms, and upon another, to prepare devices for a great seal, for the confederated States.... Doctor F. [Benjamin Franklin] proposes a device for a seal. Moses lifting up his wand, and dividing the red sea, and Pharaoh in his chariot overwhelmed with the waters. This motto, "Rebellion to tyrants is obedience to God." Mr. Jefferson proposed, The children of Israel in the wilderness, led by a cloud by day, and a pillar of fire by night, and on the other side Hengist and Horsa, the Saxon Chiefs, from whom We claim the Honour of being descended and whose Political Principles and Form of Government We have assumed.

I proposed the Choice of Hercules, as engraved by Gribeline in some Editions of Lord Shaftsburys Works. The Hero resting on his Clubb. Virtue pointing to her rugged Mountain, on one Hand, and perswading him to ascend. Sloth, glancing at her flowery Paths of Pleasure, wantonly reclining on the Ground, displaying the Charms both of her Eloquence and Person, to seduce him into Vice. But this is too complicated a Group for a Seal or Medal, and it is not original.

Hebraic Sources
Exodus 14

(כא) וַיֵּט מֹשֶׁה אֶת יָדוֹ עַל הַיָּם וַיּוֹלֶךְ ה' אֶת הַיָּם בְּרוּחַ קָדִים עַזָּה כָּל הַלַּיְלָה וַיָּשֶׂם אֶת הַיָּם לֶחָרָבָה וַיִּבָּקְעוּ הַמָּיִם.
(כב) וַיָּבֹאוּ בְנֵי יִשְׂרָאֵל בְּתוֹךְ הַיָּם בַּיַּבָּשָׁה וְהַמַּיִם לָהֶם חוֹמָה מִימִינָם וּמִשְּׂמֹאלָם.

(כג) וַיִּרְדְּפוּ מִצְרַיִם וַיָּבֹאוּ אַחֲרֵיהֶם כֹּל סוּס פַּרְעֹה רִכְבּוֹ וּפָרָשָׁיו אֶל תּוֹךְ הַיָּם.
(כד) וַיְהִי בְּאַשְׁמֹרֶת הַבֹּקֶר וַיַּשְׁקֵף ה' אֶל מַחֲנֵה מִצְרַיִם בְּעַמּוּד אֵשׁ וְעָנָן וַיָּהָם אֵת מַחֲנֵה מִצְרָיִם.
(כה) וַיָּסַר אֵת אֹפַן מַרְכְּבֹתָיו וַיְנַהֲגֵהוּ בִּכְבֵדֻת וַיֹּאמֶר מִצְרַיִם אָנוּסָה מִפְּנֵי יִשְׂרָאֵל כִּי ה' נִלְחָם לָהֶם בְּמִצְרָיִם.
(כו) וַיֹּאמֶר ה' אֶל מֹשֶׁה נְטֵה אֶת יָדְךָ עַל הַיָּם וְיָשֻׁבוּ הַמַּיִם עַל מִצְרַיִם עַל רִכְבּוֹ וְעַל פָּרָשָׁיו.
(כז) וַיֵּט מֹשֶׁה אֶת יָדוֹ עַל הַיָּם וַיָּשָׁב הַיָּם לִפְנוֹת בֹּקֶר לְאֵיתָנוֹ וּמִצְרַיִם נָסִים לִקְרָאתוֹ וַיְנַעֵר ה' אֶת מִצְרַיִם בְּתוֹךְ הַיָּם.
(כח) וַיָּשֻׁבוּ הַמַּיִם וַיְכַסּוּ אֶת הָרֶכֶב וְאֶת הַפָּרָשִׁים לְכֹל חֵיל פַּרְעֹה הַבָּאִים אַחֲרֵיהֶם בַּיָּם לֹא נִשְׁאַר בָּהֶם עַד אֶחָד.
(כט) וּבְנֵי יִשְׂרָאֵל הָלְכוּ בַיַּבָּשָׁה בְּתוֹךְ הַיָּם וְהַמַּיִם לָהֶם חֹמָה מִימִינָם וּמִשְּׂמֹאלָם.

[21] And Moses stretched out his hand over the sea; and the Lord caused the sea to go back by a strong east wind all that night, and made the sea dry land, and the waters were divided. [22] And the children of Israel went into the midst of the sea upon the dry ground: and the waters were a wall unto them on their right hand, and on their left. [23] And the Egyptians pursued, and went in after them to the midst of the sea, even all Pharaoh's horses, his chariots, and his horsemen. [24] And it came to pass, that in the morning watch the Lord looked unto the host of the Egyptians through the pillar of fire and of the cloud, and troubled the host of the Egyptians, [25] And took off their chariot wheels, that they drave them heavily: so that the Egyptians said, Let us flee from the face of Israel; for the Lord fighteth for them against the Egyptians. [26] And the Lord said unto Moses, Stretch out thine hand over the sea, that the waters may come again upon the Egyptians, upon their chariots, and upon their horsemen. [27] And Moses stretched forth his hand over the sea, and the sea returned to his strength when the morning appeared; and the Egyptians fled against it; and the Lord overthrew the Egyptians in the midst of the sea. [28] And the waters returned, and covered the chariots, and the horsemen, and all the host of Pharaoh that came into the sea after them; there remained not so much as one of them. [29] But the children of Israel walked upon dry land in the midst of the sea; and the waters were a wall unto them on their right hand, and on their left.

Exodus 13

(יח) וַיַּסֵּב אֱ־לֹהִים אֶת הָעָם דֶּרֶךְ הַמִּדְבָּר יַם סוּף וַחֲמֻשִׁים עָלוּ בְנֵי יִשְׂרָאֵל מֵאֶרֶץ מִצְרָיִם.
(יט) וַיִּקַּח מֹשֶׁה אֶת עַצְמוֹת יוֹסֵף עִמּוֹ כִּי הַשְׁבֵּעַ הִשְׁבִּיעַ אֶת בְּנֵי יִשְׂרָאֵל לֵאמֹר פָּקֹד יִפְקֹד אֱ־לֹהִים אֶתְכֶם וְהַעֲלִיתֶם אֶת עַצְמֹתַי מִזֶּה אִתְּכֶם.

(כ) וַיִּסְעוּ מִסֻּכֹּת וַיַּחֲנוּ בְאֵתָם בִּקְצֵה הַמִּדְבָּר.

(כא) וַה' הֹלֵךְ לִפְנֵיהֶם יוֹמָם בְּעַמּוּד עָנָן לַנְחֹתָם הַדֶּרֶךְ וְלַיְלָה בְּעַמּוּד אֵשׁ לְהָאִיר לָהֶם לָלֶכֶת יוֹמָם וָלָיְלָה.

(כב) לֹא יָמִישׁ עַמּוּד הֶעָנָן יוֹמָם וְעַמּוּד הָאֵשׁ לָיְלָה לִפְנֵי הָעָם.

[18] But God led the people about, through the way of the wilderness of the Red Sea: and the children of Israel went up harnessed out of the land of Egypt.

[19] And Moses took the bones of Joseph with him: for he had straitly sworn the children of Israel, saying, God will surely visit you; and ye shall carry up my bones away hence with you.

[20] And they took their journey from Succoth, and encamped in Etham, in the edge of the wilderness.

[21] And the Lord went before them by day in a pillar of a cloud, to lead them the way; and by night in a pillar of fire, to give them light; to go by day and night:

[22] He took not away the pillar of the cloud by day, nor the pillar of fire by night, from before the people.

DAYS OF FASTING, THANKSGIVING, AND REPENTANCE

Thanksgiving is a harvest festival, but in the early Republic, days of thanksgiving were conjoined with days of fasting and repentance. This covenantal element of American life was carried through from the Puritans in the way that the early Continental Congress and George Washington thought it important for the nation to have national days of fasting and repentance together as a community. Below are some examples of proclamations from the Revolutionary era.

Continental Congress Fast Day Proclamation (December 11, 1776)

Whereas, the war in which the United States are engaged with Great Britain, has not only been prolonged, but is likely to be carried to the greatest extremity; and whereas, it becomes all public bodies, as well as private persons, to reverence the Providence of God, and look up to him as the supreme disposer of all events, and the arbiter of the fate of nations; therefore,

Resolved, That it be recommended to all the United States, as soon as possible, to appoint a day of solemn fasting and humiliation; to implore of Almighty God the forgiveness of the many sins prevailing among all ranks, and to beg the countenance and assistance of his Providence in the prosecution of the present just and necessary war.

The Congress do also, in the most earnest manner, recommend to all the members of the United States, and particularly the officers civil and military under them, the exercise of repentance and reformation; and further, require of them the strict observation of the articles of war, and particularly, that part of the said articles, which forbids profane swearing, and all immorality, of which all such officers are desired to take notice.

It is left to each state to issue out proclamations fixing the days that appear most proper within their several bounds...

General Washington, General Orders (July 9, 1776)

...The Hon. Continental Congress having been pleased to allow a Chaplain to each Regiment, with the pay of Thirty-three Dollars and one third pr month – The Colonels or commanding officers of each regiment are directed to procure Chaplains accordingly; persons of good Characters and exemplary lives – To see that all inferior officers and soldiers pay them a suitable respect and attend carefully upon religious exercises. The blessing and protection of Heaven are at all times necessary but especially so in times of public distress and danger – The General hopes and trusts, that every officer and man, will endeavour so to live, and act, as becomes a Christian Soldier defending the dearest Rights and Liberties of his country.

The Hon. Continental Congress, impelled by the dictates of duty, policy and necessity, having been pleased to dissolve the Connection which subsisted between this Country, and Great Britain, and to declare the United Colonies of North America, free and independent States: The several brigades are to be drawn up this evening on their respective Parades, at Six OClock, when the declaration of Congress, shewing the grounds and reasons of this measure, is to be read with an audible voice....

Continental Congress Thanksgiving Proclamation (October 26, 1781)

By the United States, in Congress Assembled.

PROCLAMATION.

Whereas it hath pleased Almighty God, the Father of Mercies, remarkably to assist and support the United States of America in their important struggle for liberty against the long-continued efforts of a powerful nation, it is the duty of all ranks to observe and thankfully acknowledge the interpositions of his Providence in their behalf; – Through the whole of the contest from its first rise to this time the influence of Divine Providence may be clearly perceived in many signal instances, of which we mention but a few:

In revealing the counsels of our enemies, when the discoveries were seasonable and important, and the means seemingly inadequate or fortuitous.

In preserving and even improving the union of the several states on the breach of which our enemies placed their greatest dependence,

In increasing the number and adding to the zeal and attachment of friends of liberty,

In granting remarkable deliverances and blessings with the most signal success, when affairs seemed to have the most discouraging appearance,

In raising up for us a most powerful and generous ally in one of the first of European Powers,

In confounding the counsels of our enemies and suffering them to pursue such measures as have most directly contributed to frustrate their own desires and expectations: above all

In making their extreme cruelty to the inhabitants of those states when in their power and their savage devastation of property the very means of cementing our Union and adding vigor to every effort in opposition to them; and as we cannot help leading the good people of these states to a retrospect on the events which have taken place since the beginning of the war so we may recommend in a particular manner to their observation the goodness of God in the year now drawing to a conclusion in which the Confederation of the United States has been completed,

In which there have been so many instances of prowess and success in our armies, particularly in the southern states, where, notwithstanding the difficulties with which they had to struggle, they have recovered the whole country which the enemy had overrun, leaving them only a post or two on or near the sea,

In which we have been so powerfully and effectually assisted by our allies, while in all the unjust operations, the most perfect harmony has subsisted in the allied army: In which there has been so plentiful a harvest, and so great abundance of the fruits of the earth of every kin, as not only enable us easily to supply the wants of our army, but gives comfort and happiness to the whole people,

And in which, after the success of our allies by sea, a general of the first rank with his whole army has been captured by the allied forces under the direction of our commander-in-chief.

It is therefore recommended to the several states to set apart the THIRTEENTH day of DECEMBER next, to be religiously observed as a day of THANKSGIVING and PRAYER; that all the people may assemble on that day with grateful hearts to celebrate the praises of our glorious Benefactor, to confess our manifold sins, to offer up our most fervent supplications to the God of all grace that it may please Him to pardon our offense, and incline our hearts for the future, to keep all His laws, to comfort and relieve all our brethren who are in distress or captivity, to prosper our husbandmen, and give strength to all engaged in lawful commerce; to impart wisdom and integrity to our counselors, judgment and fortitude to our officers and soldiers; to protect and prosper our illustrious ally and favor our united exertions for the speedy establishment of a safe, honorable, and lasting peace, to bless our seminaries of learning, and cause the knowledge of God to cover the earth as the waters cover the seas.

Done in Congress the 26th day of October, in the year of our Lord, one thousand seven hundred and eighty-one, and in the sixth year of the Independence of America.

Thomas McKean, *President*
Attest, Charles Thomson, *Secretary*

George Washington, Thanksgiving Day Proclamation (October 3, 1789)

By the President of the United States of America, a Proclamation.

Whereas it is the duty of all Nations to acknowledge the providence of Almighty God, to obey his will, to be grateful for his benefits, and humbly to implore his protection and favor – and whereas both Houses of Congress have by their joint Committee requested me to recommend to the People of the United States a day of public thanksgiving and prayer to be observed by acknowledging with grateful hearts the many signal favors of Almighty God especially by affording them an opportunity peaceably to establish a form of government for their safety and happiness.

Now therefore I do recommend and assign Thursday the 26th day of November next to be devoted by the People of these States to the service of that great and glorious Being, who is the beneficent Author of all the good that was, that is, or that will be; that we may then all unite in rendering unto him our sincere and humble thanks for his kind care and protection of the People of this Country previous to their becoming a Nation; for the signal and manifold mercies, and the favorable interpositions of his Providence which we experienced in the course and conclusion of the late war; for the great degree of tranquility, union, and plenty, which we have since enjoyed; for the peaceable and rational manner, in which we have been enabled to establish constitutions of government for our safety and happiness, and particularly the national One now lately instituted; for the civil and religious liberty with which we are blessed, and the means we have of acquiring and diffusing useful knowledge; and in general for all the great and various favors which he hath been pleased to confer upon us.

And also that we may then unite in most humbly offering our prayers and supplications to the great Lord and Ruler of Nations and beseech him to pardon our national and other transgressions; to enable us all, whether in public or private stations, to perform our several and relative duties properly and punctually; to render our national government a blessing to all the people, by constantly being a Government of wise, just, and constitutional laws, discreetly and faithfully executed and obeyed; to protect and guide all Sovereigns and Nations (especially such as have shewn kindness unto us) and to bless them with good government, peace, and concord; to promote the knowledge and practice of true religion and virtue, and the encrease of science among them and us; and, generally, to grant unto all Mankind such a degree of temporal prosperity as he alone knows to be best.

Given under my hand at the City of New York the third day of October in the year of our Lord 1789.

Go. Washington

Hebraic Sources

In conducting the war, the Continental Congress ordered the observance of traditional religious rituals intended to enlist, maintain, and recognize divine assistance, all of which have deep roots in the Hebrew Bible: fasting and repenting, policing the army's morality, and expressing thanksgiving. A few years after the war's conclusion and the successful formation of the government, President George Washington declared the first national Thanksgiving be celebrated on Thursday, November 26, 1789.

Ezra 8

(כא) וָאֶקְרָא שָׁם צוֹם עַל הַנָּהָר אַהֲוָא לְהִתְעַנּוֹת לִפְנֵי אֱ־לֹהֵינוּ לְבַקֵּשׁ מִמֶּנּוּ דֶּרֶךְ יְשָׁרָה לָנוּ וּלְטַפֵּנוּ וּלְכָל רְכוּשֵׁנוּ.
(כב) כִּי בֹשְׁתִּי לִשְׁאוֹל מִן הַמֶּלֶךְ חַיִל וּפָרָשִׁים לְעָזְרֵנוּ מֵאוֹיֵב בַּדָּרֶךְ כִּי אָמַרְנוּ לַמֶּלֶךְ לֵאמֹר יַד אֱ־לֹהֵינוּ עַל כָּל מְבַקְשָׁיו לְטוֹבָה וְעֻזּוֹ וְאַפּוֹ עַל כָּל עֹזְבָיו.

99

(כג) וַנָּצוּמָה וַנְּבַקְשָׁה מֵאֱ-לֹהֵינוּ עַל זֹאת וַיֵּעָתֵר לָנוּ.
(לא) וַנִּסְעָה מִנְּהַר אַהֲוָא בִּשְׁנֵים עָשָׂר לַחֹדֶשׁ הָרִאשׁוֹן לָלֶכֶת יְרוּשָׁלָם וְיַד אֱ-לֹהֵינוּ הָיְתָה עָלֵינוּ וַיַּצִּילֵנוּ מִכַּף אוֹיֵב וְאוֹרֵב עַל הַדָּרֶךְ.

²¹ Then I proclaimed a fast there, at the river of Ahava, that we might afflict ourselves before our God, to seek of him a right way for us, and for our little ones, and for all our substance. ²² For I was ashamed to require of the king a band of soldiers and horsemen to help us against the enemy in the way: because we had spoken unto the king, saying, The hand of our God is upon all them for good that seek him; but his power and his wrath is against all them that forsake him.

²³ So we fasted and besought our God for this: and he was intreated of us.

³¹ Then we departed from the river of Ahava on the twelfth day of the first month, to go unto Jerusalem: and the hand of our God was upon us, and he delivered us from the hand of the enemy, and of such as lay in wait by the way.

Deuteronomy 23

(י) כִּי תֵצֵא מַחֲנֶה עַל אֹיְבֶיךָ וְנִשְׁמַרְתָּ מִכֹּל דָּבָר רָע.
(יא) כִּי יִהְיֶה בְךָ אִישׁ אֲשֶׁר לֹא יִהְיֶה טָהוֹר מִקְּרֵה לָיְלָה וְיָצָא אֶל מִחוּץ לַמַּחֲנֶה לֹא יָבֹא אֶל תּוֹךְ הַמַּחֲנֶה.
(יב) וְהָיָה לִפְנוֹת עֶרֶב יִרְחַץ בַּמָּיִם וּכְבֹא הַשֶּׁמֶשׁ יָבֹא אֶל תּוֹךְ הַמַּחֲנֶה.
(יג) וְיָד תִּהְיֶה לְךָ מִחוּץ לַמַּחֲנֶה וְיָצָאתָ שָׁמָּה חוּץ.
(יד) וְיָתֵד תִּהְיֶה לְךָ עַל אֲזֵנֶךָ וְהָיָה בְּשִׁבְתְּךָ חוּץ וְחָפַרְתָּה בָהּ וְשַׁבְתָּ וְכִסִּיתָ אֶת צֵאָתֶךָ.
(טו) כִּי ה' אֱ-לֹהֶיךָ מִתְהַלֵּךְ בְּקֶרֶב מַחֲנֶךָ לְהַצִּילְךָ וְלָתֵת אֹיְבֶיךָ לְפָנֶיךָ וְהָיָה מַחֲנֶיךָ קָדוֹשׁ וְלֹא יִרְאֶה בְךָ עֶרְוַת דָּבָר וְשָׁב מֵאַחֲרֶיךָ.

⁹ ⁽¹⁰⁾ When the host goeth forth against thine enemies, then keep thee from every wicked thing.

¹⁰ ⁽¹¹⁾ If there be among you any man, that is not clean by reason of uncleanness that chanceth him by night, then shall he go abroad out of the camp, he shall not come within the camp:

¹¹ ⁽¹²⁾ But it shall be, when evening cometh on, he shall wash himself with water: and when the sun is down, he shall come into the camp again.

¹² ⁽¹³⁾ Thou shalt have a place also without the camp, whither thou shalt go forth abroad:

¹³ ⁽¹⁴⁾ And thou shalt have a paddle upon thy weapon; and it shall be, when thou wilt ease thyself abroad, thou shalt dig therewith, and shalt turn back and cover that which cometh from thee:

¹⁴ ⁽¹⁵⁾ For the Lord thy God walketh in the midst of thy camp, to deliver thee, and to give up thine enemies before thee; therefore shall thy camp be holy: that he see no unclean thing in thee, and turn away from thee.

Deuteronomy 26

(א) וְהָיָה כִּי־תָבוֹא אֶל־הָאָרֶץ אֲשֶׁר ה' אֱ־לֹהֶיךָ נֹתֵן לְךָ נַחֲלָה וִירִשְׁתָּהּ וְיָשַׁבְתָּ בָּהּ.

(ב) וְלָקַחְתָּ מֵרֵאשִׁית כָּל־פְּרִי הָאֲדָמָה אֲשֶׁר תָּבִיא מֵאַרְצְךָ אֲשֶׁר ה' אֱ־לֹהֶיךָ נֹתֵן לָךְ וְשַׂמְתָּ בַטֶּנֶא וְהָלַכְתָּ אֶל־הַמָּקוֹם אֲשֶׁר יִבְחַר ה' אֱ־לֹהֶיךָ לְשַׁכֵּן שְׁמוֹ שָׁם.

(ג) וּבָאתָ אֶל־הַכֹּהֵן אֲשֶׁר יִהְיֶה בַּיָּמִים הָהֵם וְאָמַרְתָּ אֵלָיו הִגַּדְתִּי הַיּוֹם לַה' אֱ־לֹהֶיךָ כִּי־בָאתִי אֶל־הָאָרֶץ אֲשֶׁר נִשְׁבַּע ה' לַאֲבֹתֵינוּ לָתֶת לָנוּ.

(ד) וְלָקַח הַכֹּהֵן הַטֶּנֶא מִיָּדֶךָ וְהִנִּיחוֹ לִפְנֵי מִזְבַּח ה' אֱ־לֹהֶיךָ.

(ה) וְעָנִיתָ וְאָמַרְתָּ לִפְנֵי ה' אֱ־לֹהֶיךָ אֲרַמִּי אֹבֵד אָבִי וַיֵּרֶד מִצְרַיְמָה וַיָּגָר שָׁם בִּמְתֵי מְעָט וַיְהִי שָׁם לְגוֹי גָּדוֹל עָצוּם וָרָב.

(ו) וַיָּרֵעוּ אֹתָנוּ הַמִּצְרִים וַיְעַנּוּנוּ וַיִּתְּנוּ עָלֵינוּ עֲבֹדָה קָשָׁה.

(ז) וַנִּצְעַק אֶל־ה' אֱ־לֹהֵי אֲבֹתֵינוּ וַיִּשְׁמַע ה' אֶת־קֹלֵנוּ וַיַּרְא אֶת־עָנְיֵנוּ וְאֶת־עֲמָלֵנוּ וְאֶת־לַחֲצֵנוּ.

(ח) וַיּוֹצִאֵנוּ ה' מִמִּצְרַיִם בְּיָד חֲזָקָה וּבִזְרֹעַ נְטוּיָה וּבְמֹרָא גָּדֹל וּבְאֹתוֹת וּבְמֹפְתִים.

(ט) וַיְבִאֵנוּ אֶל־הַמָּקוֹם הַזֶּה וַיִּתֶּן־לָנוּ אֶת־הָאָרֶץ הַזֹּאת אֶרֶץ זָבַת חָלָב וּדְבָשׁ.

(י) וְעַתָּה הִנֵּה הֵבֵאתִי אֶת־רֵאשִׁית פְּרִי הָאֲדָמָה אֲשֶׁר נָתַתָּה לִּי ה' וְהִנַּחְתּוֹ לִפְנֵי ה' אֱ־לֹהֶיךָ וְהִשְׁתַּחֲוִיתָ לִפְנֵי ה' אֱ־לֹהֶיךָ.

(יא) וְשָׂמַחְתָּ בְכָל־הַטּוֹב אֲשֶׁר נָתַן לְךָ ה' אֱ־לֹהֶיךָ וּלְבֵיתֶךָ אַתָּה וְהַלֵּוִי וְהַגֵּר אֲשֶׁר בְּקִרְבֶּךָ.

---

[1] And it shall be, when thou art come in unto the land which the Lord thy God giveth thee for an inheritance, and possessest it, and dwellest therein;

[2] That thou shalt take of the first of all the fruit of the earth, which thou shalt bring of thy land that the Lord thy God giveth thee, and shalt put it in a basket, and shalt go unto the place which the Lord thy God shall choose to place His name there.

[3] And thou shalt go unto the priest that shall be in those days, and say unto him, I profess this day unto the Lord thy God, that I am come unto the country which the Lord sware unto our fathers for to give us.

[4] And the priest shall take the basket out of thine hand, and set it down before the altar of the Lord thy God.

[5] And thou shalt speak and say before the Lord thy God: A Syrian ready to perish was my father, and he went down into Egypt, and sojourned there with a few, and became there a nation, great, mighty, and populous;

[6] And the Egyptians evil entreated us, and afflicted us, and laid upon us hard bondage;

[7] And when we cried unto the Lord God of our fathers, the Lord heard our voice, and looked on our affliction, and our labour, and our oppression;

[8] And the Lord brought us forth out of Egypt with a mighty hand, and with an outstretched arm, and with great terribleness, and with signs, and with wonders;

[9] And He hath brought us into this place, and hath given us this land, even a land that floweth with milk and honey.

¹⁰ And now, behold, I have brought the firstfruits of the land, which thou, O Lord, hast given me. And thou shalt set it before the Lord thy God, and worship before the Lord thy God.
¹¹ And thou shalt rejoice in every good thing which the Lord thy God hath given unto thee, and unto thine house, thou, and the Levite, and the stranger that is among you.

A LETTER FROM JONAS PHILLIPS TO THE PRESIDENT AND MEMBERS OF THE CONSTITUTIONAL CONVENTION (SEPTEMBER 7, 1787)

Originally from what is now western Germany, Jonas Phillips (1736-1783) fought in the Revolutionary War and was a prominent member of Mikveh Israel, an early Spanish-Portuguese Synagogue in Philadelphia. Excited by the ideals and business opportunities that arose during the Revolutionary War, Phillips wrote to a friend and business partner in the Netherlands in Yiddish, asking for a list of things to import to the United States. He included a copy of the Declaration of Independence, in Yiddish. The British intercepted the letter and thought it was in code. He had over twenty children with his wife, Rebecca. A grandson, Franklin J. Moses, Jr., became the governor of South Carolina during Reconstruction. In the following letter to the Constitutional Convention, Phillips, concerned about religious oaths for office, asked the Constitutional Convention to protect religious freedom with more expansive rights.

With leave and submission I address myself To those in whome there is wisdom understanding and knowledge. They are the honourable personages appointed and Made overseers of a part of the terrestrial globe of the Earth, Namely the 13 united states of america in Convention Assembled, the Lord preserve them amen.

I the subscriber being one of the people called Jews of the City of Philadelphia, a people scattered and dispersed among all nations do behold with Concern that among the laws in the Constitution of Pennsylvania their is a Clause Sect. 10 to viz – I do believe in one God the Creator and governour of the universe the Rewarder of the good and the punisher of the wicked – and I do acknowledge the scriptures of the old and New testament to be given by a divine inspiration – to swear and believe that the new testament was given by divine inspiration is absolutely against the religious principle of a Jew, and is against his Conscience to take any such oath – By the above law a Jew is deprived of holding any publick office or place of Goverment which is a Contradictory to the bill of Right Sect 2. viz:

That all men have a natural and unalienable Right To worship almighty God according to the dictates of their own Conscience and understanding, and that no man aught or of Right can be Compelled to attend any Religious Worship or Erect or support any place of worship or Maintain any minister contrary to or against his own free will and Consent nor Can any man who acknowledges the being of a God be Justly deprived or abridged of any Civil Right as a Citizen on account of his Religious sentiments or peculiar mode of Religious Worship, and that no authority Can or aught to be vested in or assumed by any power what ever that shall in any Case interfere or in any manner Control the Right of Conscience in the free Exercise of Religious Worship –

It is well known among all the Citizens of the 13 united States that the Jews have been true and faithful whigs, and during the late Contest with England they have been foremost in aiding and assisting the States with their lifes and fortunes, they have supported the Cause, have bravely faught and bleed for liberty which they Can not Enjoy –

Therefore if the honourable Convention shall in ther Wisdom think fit and alter the said oath and leave out the words to viz – and I do acknoweledge the scripture of the new testament to be given by devine inspiration then the Israeletes will think them self happy to live under a goverment where all Religious societys are on an Equal footing – I solicit this favour for my self my Childreen and posterity and for the benefit of all the Israelites through the 13 united States of america

My prayers is unto the Lord. May the people of this States Rise up as a great and young lion, May they prevail against their Enemies, May the degrees of honour of his Excellencey the president of the Convention George Washington, be Extollet and Raise up. May Every one speak of his glorious Exploits. May God prolong his days among us in this land of Liberty – May he lead the armies against his Enemys as he has done hereuntofore – May God Extend peace unto the united States – May they get up to the highest Prosperetys – May God Extend peace to them and their seed after them so long as the Sun and moon Endureth – and may the almighty God of our father Abraham Isaac and Jacob endow this Noble Assembly with wisdom Judgement and unamity in their Councels, and may they have the Satisfaction to see that their present toil and labour for the welfare of the united States may be approved of, Through all the world and particular by the united States of america is the ardent prayer of Sires

Your Most devoted obed. Servant

Jonas Phillips[5]

Philadelphia 24th Ellul 5547 or Sepr 7th 1787

A LETTER FROM GEORGE WASHINGTON
TO THE HEBREW CONGREGATION AT NEWPORT
(AUGUST 18, 1790)

Gentlemen:

While I received with much satisfaction your address replete with expressions of esteem, I rejoice in the opportunity of assuring you that I shall always retain grateful remembrance of the cordial welcome I experienced on my visit to Newport from all classes of citizens.

The reflection on the days of difficulty and danger which are past is rendered the more sweet from a consciousness that they are succeeded by days of uncommon prosperity and security.

If we have wisdom to make the best use of the advantages with which we are now favored, we cannot fail, under the just administration of a good government, to become a great and happy people.

The citizens of the United States of America have a right to applaud themselves for having given to mankind examples of an enlarged and liberal policy – a policy worthy of imitation. All possess alike liberty of conscience and immunities of citizenship.

It is now no more that toleration is spoken of as if it were the indulgence of one class of people that another enjoyed the exercise of their inherent natural rights, for, happily, the Government of the United States, which gives to bigotry no sanction, to persecution no

---

5. From *The Documentary History of the Constitution of the United States of America, 1786 – 1870*, vol. 1 (Washington, DC: Department of State, 1901), 281–82.

assistance, requires only that they who live under its protection should demean themselves as good citizens in giving it on all occasions their effectual support.

It would be inconsistent with the frankness of my character not to avow that I am pleased with your favorable opinion of my administration and fervent wishes for my felicity.

May the children of the stock of Abraham who dwell in this land continue to merit and enjoy the good will of the other inhabitants – while every one shall sit in safety under his own vine and fig tree and there shall be none to make him afraid.

May the father of all mercies scatter light, and not darkness, upon our paths, and make us all in our several vocations useful here, and in His own due time and way everlastingly happy.

G. Washington

PRESIDENT WASHINGTON, FAREWELL ADDRESS (1796)

I have already intimated to you the danger of parties in the State, with particular reference to the founding of them on geographical discriminations. Let me now take a more comprehensive view, and warn you in the most solemn manner against the baneful effects of the spirit of party generally.

This spirit, unfortunately, is inseparable from our nature, having its root in the strongest passions of the human mind. It exists under different shapes in all governments, more or less stifled, controlled, or repressed; but, in those of the popular form, it is seen in its greatest rankness, and is truly their worst enemy.

The alternate domination of one faction over another, sharpened by the spirit of revenge, natural to party dissension, which in different ages and countries has perpetrated the most horrid enormities, is itself a frightful despotism. But this leads at length to a more formal and permanent despotism. The disorders and miseries which result gradually incline the minds of men to seek security and repose in the absolute power of an individual; and sooner or later the chief of some prevailing faction, more able or more fortunate than his competitors, turns this disposition to the purposes of his own elevation, on the ruins of public liberty.

Without looking forward to an extremity of this kind (which nevertheless ought not to be entirely out of sight), the common and continual mischiefs of the spirit of party are sufficient to make it the interest and duty of a wise people to discourage and restrain it.

It serves always to distract the public councils and enfeeble the public administration. It agitates the community with ill-founded jealousies and false alarms, kindles the animosity of one part against another, foments occasionally riot and insurrection. It opens the door to foreign influence and corruption, which finds a facilitated access to the government itself through the channels of party passions. Thus the policy and the will of one country are subjected to the policy and will of another.

There is an opinion that parties in free countries are useful checks upon the administration of the government and serve to keep alive the spirit of liberty. This within certain limits is probably true; and in governments of a monarchical cast, patriotism may look with indulgence, if not with favor, upon the spirit of party. But in those of the popular character, in governments purely elective, it is a spirit not to be encouraged. From their natural tendency, it is certain there will always be enough of that spirit for every salutary purpose. And there being constant danger of excess, the effort ought to be by force of public opinion, to mitigate and assuage it. A fire not to be quenched, it demands a uniform vigilance to prevent its bursting into a flame, lest, instead of warming, it should consume.

It is important, likewise, that the habits of thinking in a free country should inspire caution in those entrusted with its administration, to confine themselves within their respective constitutional spheres, avoiding in the exercise of the powers of one department to encroach upon another. The spirit of encroachment tends to consolidate the powers of all the departments in one, and thus to create, whatever the form of government, a real despotism. A just estimate of that love of power, and proneness to abuse it, which predominates in the human heart, is sufficient to satisfy us of the truth of this position. The necessity of reciprocal checks in the exercise of political power, by dividing and distributing it into different depositaries, and constituting each the guardian of the public weal against invasions by the others, has been evinced by experiments ancient and modern; some of them in our country and under our own eyes. To preserve them must be as necessary as to institute them. If, in the opinion of the people, the distribution or modification of the constitutional powers be in any particular wrong, let it be corrected by an amendment in the way which the Constitution designates. But let there be no change by usurpation; for though this, in one instance, may be the instrument of good, it is the customary weapon by which free governments are destroyed. The precedent must always greatly overbalance in permanent evil any partial or transient benefit, which the use can at any time yield.

Of all the dispositions and habits which lead to political prosperity, religion and morality are indispensable supports. In vain would that man claim the tribute of patriotism, who should labor to subvert these great pillars of human happiness, these firmest props of the duties of men and citizens. The mere politician, equally with the pious man, ought to respect and to cherish them. A volume could not trace all their connections with private and public felicity. Let it simply be asked: Where is the security for property, for reputation, for life, if the sense of religious obligation desert the oaths which are the instruments of investigation in courts of justice? And let us with caution indulge the supposition that morality can be maintained without religion. Whatever may be conceded to the influence of refined education on minds of peculiar structure, reason and experience both forbid us to expect that national morality can prevail in exclusion of religious principle.

It is substantially true that virtue or morality is a necessary spring of popular government. The rule, indeed, extends with more or less force to every species of free government. Who that is a sincere friend to it can look with indifference upon attempts to shake the foundation of the fabric?

Promote then, as an object of primary importance, institutions for the general diffusion of knowledge. In proportion as the structure of a government gives force to public opinion, it is essential that public opinion should be enlightened.

As a very important source of strength and security, cherish public credit. One method of preserving it is to use it as sparingly as possible, avoiding occasions of expense by cultivating peace, but remembering also that timely disbursements to prepare for danger frequently prevent much greater disbursements to repel it, avoiding likewise the accumulation of debt, not only by shunning occasions of expense, but by vigorous exertion in time of peace to discharge the debts which unavoidable wars may have occasioned, not ungenerously throwing upon posterity the burden which we ourselves ought to bear. The execution of these maxims belongs to your representatives, but it is necessary that public opinion should co-operate. To facilitate to them the performance of their duty, it is essential that you should practically bear in mind that towards the payment of debts there must be revenue; that to have revenue there must be taxes; that no taxes can be devised which are not more or less inconvenient and unpleasant; that the intrinsic embarrassment, inseparable from the selection of the proper objects (which is always a choice of difficulties), ought to be a decisive motive for a candid construction of the conduct of the government in making it, and for a spirit of acquiescence in the measures for obtaining revenue, which the public exigencies may at any time dictate....

THE LETTERS OF JOHN ADAMS AND THOMAS JEFFERSON

The letters of John Adams and Thomas Jefferson, both to one another and to others, are among some of the most interesting and touching missives in American public life. They put on display the wide-ranging learning and curiosity of two powerful minds. On January 21, 1812, Jefferson wrote to Adams that "I have given up newspapers in exchange for Tacitus and Thucydides, for Newton and Euclid; and I find myself much the happier. Sometimes indeed I look back to former occurrences, in remembrance of our old friends and fellow laborers, who have fallen before us. Of the signers of the Declaration of Independence I see now living not more than half a dozen on your side of the Potomak, and, on this side, myself alone." Ranging from history and philosophy to education and politics, the letters between once bitter enemies are a testament to the founding generation's respect for learning and great eloquence. Below are some excerpts from their letters that discuss the nature and impact of the Hebrew Bible on Western civilization.

John Adams to F. A. Vanderkemp (February 16, 1809)

...The two most powerful, active, and enterprising nations that ever existed are now contending with us. The two nations, to whom mankind are under more obligations for the progress of science and civilization than to any others, except the Hebrews. This consideration affects me more than the danger from either or both. I excepted the Hebrews, for in spite of Bolingbroke and Voltaire, I will insist that the Hebrews have done more to civilize men than any other nation. If I were an atheist, and believed in blind eternal fate, I should still believe that fate had ordained the Jews to be the most essential instrument for civilizing the nations. If I were an atheist of the other sect, who believe or pretend to believe that all is ordered by chance, I should believe that chance had ordered the Jews to preserve and propagate to all mankind the doctrine of a supreme, intelligent, wise, almighty sovereign of the universe, which I believe to be the great essential principle of all morality, and consequently of all civilization. I cannot say that I love the Jews very much neither, nor the French, nor the English, nor the Romans, nor the Greeks. We must love all nations as well as we can, but it is very hard to love most of them....

Thomas Jefferson to John Adams (October 12, 1813)

DEAR SIR,

Since mine of Aug. 22. I have recieved your favors of Aug. 16. Sep. 2. 14. 15. and – and Mrs. Adams's of Sep. 20. I now send you, according to your request a copy of the Syllabus. To fill up this skeleton with arteries, with veins, with nerves, muscles and flesh, is really beyond my time and information. Whoever could undertake it would find great aid in Enfield's judicious abridgment of Brucker's history of Philosophy, in which he has reduced 5. or 6. quarto vols. of 1000. pages each of Latin closely printed, to two moderate 8 vos. of English, open, type.

To compare the morals of the old, with those of the new testament, would require an attentive study of the former, a search thro' all its books for its precepts, and through all its history for its practices, and the principles they prove. As commentaries too on these, the philosophy of the Hebrews must be enquired into, their Mishna, their Gemara, Cabbala, Jezirah, Sohar, Cosri, and their Talmud must be examined and understood, in order to do them full justice. Brucker, it should seem, has gone deeply into these Repositories of their ethics, and Enfield, his epitomiser, concludes in these words. "Ethics were so little studied among the Jews, that, in their whole compilation called the Talmud, there is only one treatise on moral subjects. Their books of Morals chiefly consisted in a minute enumeration of duties. From the law of Moses were deduced 613. precepts, which were divided into two classes, affirmative and negative, 248 in the former, and 365 in the latter. It may serve to give the reader some idea of the low state of moral philosophy among the Jews in the Middle age, to add, that of the 248. affirmative precepts, only 3. were considered as obligatory upon women; and that, in order to obtain salvation, it was judged sufficient to fulfill any one single law in the hour of death; the observance of the rest being deemed necessary, only to increase the felicity of the future life. What a wretched depravity of sentiment and manners must have prevailed before such corrupt maxims could have obtained credit! It is impossible to collect from these writings a consistent series of moral Doctrine." Enfield, B. 4. chap. 3. It was the reformation of this "wretched depravity" of morals which Jesus undertook. In extracting the pure principles which he taught, we should have to strip off the artificial vestments in which they have been muffled by priests, who have travestied them into various forms, as instruments of riches and power to them. We must dismiss the Platonists and Plotinists, the Stagyrites and Gamalielites, the Eclectics the Gnostics and Scholastics, their essences and emanations, their Logos and Demi-urgos, Aeons and Daemons male and female, with a long train of Etc. Etc. Etc. or, shall I say at once, of Nonsense. We must reduce our volume to the simple evangelists, select, even from them, the very words only of Jesus, paring off the Amphibologisms into which they have been led by forgetting often, or not understanding, what had fallen from him, by giving their own misconceptions as his dicta, and expressing unintelligibly for others what they had not understood themselves. There will be found remaining the most sublime and benevolent code of morals which has ever been offered to man. I have performed this operation for my own use, by cutting verse by verse out of the printed book, and arranging, the matter which is evidently his, and which is as easily distinguishable as diamonds in a dunghill. The result is an 8 vo. of 46. pages of pure and unsophisticated doctrines, such as were professed and acted on by the *unlettered* apostles, the Apostolic fathers, and the Christians of the 1st. century. Their Platonising successors indeed, in after times, in order to legitimate the corruptions which they had incorporated into the doctrines of Jesus, found it necessary to disavow the primitive Christians, who had taken their principles from the mouth of Jesus himself, of his Apostles, and the Fathers cotemporary with them. They excommunicated their followers as heretics, branding them with the opprobrious name of Ebionites or Beggars.

For a comparison of the Graecian philosophy with that of Jesus, materials might be largely drawn from the same source. Enfield gives a history, and detailed account of the opinions and principles of the different sects. These relate to

> the gods, their natures, grades, places and powers;
> the demi-gods and daemons, and their agency with man;
> the Universe, its structure, extent, production and duration;
> the origin of things from the elements of fire, water, air and earth;
> the human soul, its essence and derivation;
> the summum bonum and finis bonorum; with a thousand idle dreams and fancies on these and other subjects the knowlege of which is withheld from man, leaving but a short chapter for his moral duties, and the principal section of that given to what he owes himself, to precepts for rendering him impassible, and unassailable by the evils of life, and for preserving his mind in a state of constant serenity.

Such a canvas is too broad for the age of seventy, and especially of one whose chief occupations have been in the practical business of life. We must leave therefore to others, younger and more learned than we are, to prepare this euthanasia for Platonic Christianity, and its restoration to the primitive simplicity of its founder. I think you give a just outline of the theism of the three religions when you say that the principle of the Hebrew was the fear, of the Gentile the honor, and of the Christian the love of God.

An expression in your letter of Sep. 14. that "the human under-standing is a revelation from its maker" gives the best solution, that I believe can be given, of the question, What did Socrates mean by his Daemon? He was too wise to believe, and too honest to pretend that he had real and familiar converse with a superior and invisible being. He probably considered the suggestions of his conscience, or reason, as revelations, or inspirations from the Supreme mind, bestowed, on important occasions, by a special superintending providence.

I acknolege all the merit of the hymn of Cleanthes to Jupiter, which you ascribe to it. It is as highly sublime as a chaste and cor-rect imagination can permit itself to go. Yet in the contemplation of a being so superlative, the hyperbolic flights of the Psalmist may often be followed with approbation, even with rapture; and I have no hesitation in giving him the palm over all the Hymnists of every language, and of every time. Turn to the 148th. psalm, in Brady and Tate's version. Have such conceptions been ever before expressed? Their version of the 15th. psalm is more to be esteemed for it's pithi-ness, than it's poetry. Even Sternhold, the leaden Sternhold, kindles, in a single instance, with the sublimity of his original, and expresses the majesty of God descending on the earth, in terms not unworthy of the subject.

> The Lord descended from above
> And underneath his feet he cast
> On Cherubim and Seraphim
> And on the wings of mighty winds
> And bowed the heav'ns most high;
> The darkness of the sky.
> Full royally he rode;
> Came flying all abroad.
>
> Psalm xviii. 9. 10.

The Latin versions of this passage by Buchanan and by Johnston, are but mediocres. But the Greek of Duport is worthy of quotation.

Ορανον αγκλνας κατεβη νπο ποςςι δ' εοιςιν Αχλυς αμφι μελαινα χυθη, και νυξ ερεβεννη. Ριμφα ποτατο Χερουβψ οχευμενος, ωςπερ εφ' ιππψ Ιπτατο δε πτερυγεςςι πολυπλαγκτου ανεμοιο.

The best collection of these psalms is that of the Octagonian dissenters of Liverpool, in their printed Form of prayer; but they are not always the best versions. Indeed bad is the best of the English versions; not a ray of poetical genius having ever been employed on them. And how much depends on this may be seen by comparing Brady and Tate's XVth. psalm with Blacklock's Justum et tenacem propositi virum ["a man just and steadfast of purpose"] of Horace, quoted in Hume's history, Car. 2. ch. 65. A translation of David in this style, or in that of Pompei's Cleanthes, might give us some idea of the merit of the original. The character too of the poetry of these hymns is singular to us. Written in monostichs, each divided into strophe and antistrophe, the sentiment of the 1st. member responded with amplification or antithesis in the second.

On the subject of the Postscript of yours of Aug. 16. and of Mrs. Adams's letter, I am silent. I know the depth of the affliction it has caused, and can sympathise with it the more sensibly, inasmuch as there is no degree of affliction, produced by the loss of those dear to us, which experience has not taught me to estimate. I have ever found time and silence the only medecine, and these but assuage, they never can suppress, the deep-drawn sigh which recollection for ever brings up, until recollection and life are extinguished together.

Every affectionately yours,

Th. Jefferson

P.S. Your's of Sep – just received

John Adams to Thomas Jefferson (November 14, 1813)

Dear Sir

Accept my thanks for the comprehensive Syllabus, in your favour of Oct. 12.

The Psalms of David, in Sublimity beauty, pathos and originality, or in one Word, in poetry, are Superiour to all the Odes Hymns and Songs in any language. But I had rather read them in our prose translation, than in any version I have Seen. His Morality however, often Shocks me, like *Tristram Shandy*'s execrations.

Blacklocks translation of Horace's "Justum" is admirable; Superiour to Addisons. Could David be translated as well; his Superiority would be universally acknowledged. We cannot compare the Sybbiline Poetry. By Virgils Pollio we may conjecture, there was Prophecy as well as Sublimity. Why have those Verses been annihilated? I Suspect platonick Christianity, pharisaical Judaism, or machiavilian Politicks, in this case; as in all other cases of the destruction of records and litterary monuments. The Auri Sacra fames, et dominandi Sæva cupido.

Among all your researches in Hebrew History and Controversy have you ever met a book, the design of which is to prove, that the ten Commandments, as We have them in our Catechisms and hung up in our Churches, were not the Ten Commandments written by the Finger of God upon tables, delivered to Moses on mount Sinai and broken by him in a passion with Aaron for his golden calf, nor those afterwards engraved by him on Tables of Stone; but a very different Sett of Commandments?

There is such a book by J. W. Goethens Schristen. Berlin 1775–1779. I wish to See this Book.

You will See the Subject and perceive the question in Exodus 20. 1–17. 22–28. chapter 24. 3 &c ch. 24. 12. ch. 25. 31 ch. 31. 18. ch. 31. 19. [32:19] ch. 34. 1. ch. 34. 10 &c.

I will make a Covenant with all this People. Observe that which I command this day.

1

Thou Shall not adore any other God. Therefore take heed, not to enter into covenant, with the Inhabitants of this country; neither take for your Sons, their daughters in marriage. They would allure thee to the Worship of false Gods. Much less Shall you in any place, erect Images.

2

The Feast of unleavened bread, Shall thou keep. Seven days, Shall thou eat unleavened bread, at the time of the month Abib; to remember that about that time, I delivered thee from Egypt.

3

Every first born of the mother is mine; the male of thine herd, be it Stock or flock. But you Shall replace the first born of an Ass with a Sheep. The first born of your Sons Shall you redeem. No Man Shall appear before me with empty hands.

4

Six days Shall thou labour: the Seventh day, thou shall rest from ploughing and gathering.

5

The Feast of Weeks shalt thou keep, with the firstlings of the wheat Harvest: and the Feast of Harvesting, at the end of the year.

6

Thrice, in every year, all male persons shall appear before the Lord. Nobody shall invade your Country, as long as you obey this Command.

7

Thou shall not Sacrifice the blood of a Sacrifice of mine, upon leavened bread.

8

The Sacrifice of the Passover Shall not remain, till the next day.

9

The Firstlings of the produce of your land, thou Shalt bring to the House of the Lord.

10

Thou shalt not boil the kid, while it is yet Sucking.

  And the Lord Spake to Moses: Write these Words; as, after these Words I made with you, and with Israel a Covenant.

  I know not whether Goethens translated or abridged from the Hebrew, or whether he used any translation Greek, Latin, or German. But he differs in form and Words, Somewhat from our Version. Exod.

34. 10. to 28. The Sense Seems to be the Same. The Tables were the evidence of the covenant, by which the Almighty attached the People of Israel to himself. By these laws they were Seperated from all other nations, and were reminded of the principal Epochas of their History.

When and where originated our Ten commandments? The Tables and The Ark were lost. Authentic copies, in few, if any hands; the ten Precepts could not be observed, and were little remembered.

If the Book of Deuteronomy was compiled, during or after the Babilonian Captivity, from Traditions, the Error or amendment might come in there.

But you must be weary, as I am at present, of Problems, conjectures, and paradoxes, concerning Hebrew, Grecian and Christian and all other Antiquities; but while We believe that the finis bonorum will be happy, We may leave learned men to this disquisition and Criticism.

I admire your Employment, in Selecting the Philosophy and Divinity of Jesus and Seperating it from all intermixtures. If I had Eyes and Nerves, I would go through both Testaments and mark all that I understand. To examine the Mishna Gemara Cabbala Jezirah, Sohar Cosri and Talmud of the Hebrews would require the life of Methuselah, and after all, his 969 years would be wasted to very little purpose. The Dæmon of Hierarchical despotism has been at Work, both with the Mishna and Gemara. In 1238 a French Jew, made a discovery to the Pope (Gregory 9th) of the heresies of the Talmud. The Pope Sent 35 Articles of Error, to the Archbishops of France, requiring them to Seize the books of the Jews, and burn all that contained any Errors. He wrote in the same terms to the Kings of France, England Arragon, Castile Leon, Navarre and Portugal. In consequence of this Order 20 Cartloads of Hebrew Books were burnt in France: and how many times 20 cartloads were destroyed in the other Kingdoms? The Talmud of Babylon and that of Jerusalem were composed from 120 to 500 years after the destruction of Jerusalem. If Lightfoot derived Light from what escaped from Gregory's fury in explaining many passages in the New Testament, by comparing the Expressions of the Mishna, with those of the Apostles and Evangelists, how many proofs of the Corruptions of Christianity might We find in the Passages burnt?

John Adams

/n

Hebraic Sources

The correspondence between Adams and Jefferson demonstrates the extent to which the history, morality, and aesthetics of the Hebrew Bible were the subject of intense interest to the Founding Fathers.

Exodus 20

(א) וַיְדַבֵּר אֱ־לֹהִים אֵת כָּל הַדְּבָרִים הָאֵלֶּה לֵאמֹר.

(ב) אָנֹכִי ה' אֱ־לֹהֶיךָ אֲשֶׁר הוֹצֵאתִיךָ מֵאֶרֶץ מִצְרַיִם מִבֵּית עֲבָדִים לֹא יִהְיֶה לְךָ אֱלֹהִים אֲחֵרִים עַל פָּנָי.

(ג) לֹא תַעֲשֶׂה לְךָ פֶסֶל וְכָל תְּמוּנָה אֲשֶׁר בַּשָּׁמַיִם מִמַּעַל וַאֲשֶׁר בָּאָרֶץ מִתַּחַת וַאֲשֶׁר בַּמַּיִם מִתַּחַת לָאָרֶץ.

(ד) לֹא תִשְׁתַּחֲוֶה לָהֶם וְלֹא תָעָבְדֵם כִּי אָנֹכִי ה' אֱ־לֹהֶיךָ אֵ־ל קַנָּא פֹּקֵד עֲוֹן אָבֹת עַל בָּנִים עַל שִׁלֵּשִׁים וְעַל רִבֵּעִים לְשֹׂנְאָי.

(ה) וְעֹשֶׂה חֶסֶד לַאֲלָפִים לְאֹהֲבַי וּלְשֹׁמְרֵי מִצְוֹתָי.

(ו) לֹא תִשָּׂא אֶת שֵׁם ה' אֱ־לֹהֶיךָ לַשָּׁוְא כִּי לֹא יְנַקֶּה ה' אֵת אֲשֶׁר יִשָּׂא אֶת שְׁמוֹ לַשָּׁוְא.

(ז) זָכוֹר אֶת יוֹם הַשַּׁבָּת לְקַדְּשׁוֹ.

(ח) שֵׁשֶׁת יָמִים תַּעֲבֹד וְעָשִׂיתָ כָּל מְלַאכְתֶּךָ.

(ט) וְיוֹם הַשְּׁבִיעִי שַׁבָּת לַה' אֱ־לֹהֶיךָ לֹא תַעֲשֶׂה כָל מְלָאכָה אַתָּה וּבִנְךָ וּבִתֶּךָ עַבְדְּךָ וַאֲמָתְךָ וּבְהֶמְתֶּךָ וְגֵרְךָ אֲשֶׁר בִּשְׁעָרֶיךָ.

(י) כִּי שֵׁשֶׁת יָמִים עָשָׂה ה' אֶת הַשָּׁמַיִם וְאֶת הָאָרֶץ אֶת הַיָּם וְאֶת כָּל אֲשֶׁר בָּם וַיָּנַח בַּיּוֹם הַשְּׁבִיעִי עַל כֵּן בֵּרַךְ ה' אֶת יוֹם הַשַּׁבָּת וַיְקַדְּשֵׁהוּ.

(יא) כַּבֵּד אֶת אָבִיךָ וְאֶת אִמֶּךָ לְמַעַן יַאֲרִכוּן יָמֶיךָ עַל הָאֲדָמָה אֲשֶׁר ה' אֱ־לֹהֶיךָ נֹתֵן לָךְ.

(יב) לֹא תִרְצָח לֹא תִנְאָף לֹא תִגְנֹב לֹא תַעֲנֶה בְרֵעֲךָ עֵד שָׁקֶר.

(יג) לֹא תַחְמֹד בֵּית רֵעֶךָ לֹא תַחְמֹד אֵשֶׁת רֵעֶךָ וְעַבְדּוֹ וַאֲמָתוֹ וְשׁוֹרוֹ וַחֲמֹרוֹ וְכֹל אֲשֶׁר לְרֵעֶךָ.

---

[1] And God spake all these words, saying,

[2] [2] I am the Lord thy God, which have brought thee out of the land of Egypt, out of the house of bondage.

[3] Thou shalt have no other gods before me.

[4] [3] Thou shalt not make unto thee any graven image, or any likeness of any thing that is in heaven above, or that is in the earth beneath, or that is in the water under the earth:

[5] [4] Thou shalt not bow down thyself to them, nor serve them: for I the Lord thy God am a jealous God, visiting the iniquity of the fathers upon the children unto the third and fourth generation of them that hate me;

117

⁶ [5] And shewing mercy unto thousands of them that love me, and keep my commandments.

⁷ [6] Thou shalt not take the name of the Lord thy God in vain; for the Lord will not hold him guiltless that taketh his name in vain.

⁸ [7] Remember the sabbath day, to keep it holy.

⁹ [8] Six days shalt thou labour, and do all thy work:

¹⁰ [9] But the seventh day is the sabbath of the Lord thy God: in it thou shalt not do any work, thou, nor thy son, nor thy daughter, thy manservant, nor thy maidservant, nor thy cattle, nor thy stranger that is within thy gates:

¹¹ [10] For in six days the Lord made heaven and earth, the sea, and all that in them is, and rested the seventh day: wherefore the Lord blessed the sabbath day, and hallowed it.

¹² [11] Honour thy father and thy mother: that thy days may be long upon the land which the Lord thy God giveth thee.

¹³ [12] Thou shalt not kill.

¹⁴ Thou shalt not commit adultery.

¹⁵ Thou shalt not steal.

¹⁶ Thou shalt not bear false witness against thy neighbour.

¹⁷ [13] Thou shalt not covet thy neighbour's house, thou shalt not covet thy neighbour's wife, nor his manservant, nor his maidservant, nor his ox, nor his ass, nor any thing that is thy neighbour's.

Exodus 22

(כח) מְלֵאָתְךָ וְדִמְעֲךָ לֹא תְאַחֵר בְּכוֹר בָּנֶיךָ תִּתֶּן לִי.

(כט) כֵּן תַּעֲשֶׂה לְשֹׁרְךָ לְצֹאנֶךָ שִׁבְעַת יָמִים יִהְיֶה עִם אִמּוֹ בַּיוֹם הַשְּׁמִינִי תִּתְּנוֹ לִי.

²⁹ [28] Thou shalt not delay to offer the first of thy ripe fruits, and of thy liquors: the firstborn of thy sons shalt thou give unto me.

³⁰ [29] Likewise shalt thou do with thine oxen, and with thy sheep: seven days it shall be with his dam; on the eighth day thou shalt give it me.

Exodus 24

(ג) וַיָּבֹא מֹשֶׁה וַיְסַפֵּר לָעָם אֵת כָּל דִּבְרֵי ה' וְאֵת כָּל הַמִּשְׁפָּטִים וַיַּעַן כָּל הָעָם קוֹל אֶחָד וַיֹּאמְרוּ כָּל הַדְּבָרִים אֲשֶׁר דִּבֶּר ה' נַעֲשֶׂה.

(ד) וַיִּכְתֹּב מֹשֶׁה אֵת כָּל דִּבְרֵי ה' וַיַּשְׁכֵּם בַּבֹּקֶר וַיִּבֶן מִזְבֵּחַ תַּחַת הָהָר וּשְׁתֵּים עֶשְׂרֵה מַצֵּבָה לִשְׁנֵים עָשָׂר שִׁבְטֵי יִשְׂרָאֵל.

(ה) וַיִּשְׁלַח אֶת נַעֲרֵי בְּנֵי יִשְׂרָאֵל וַיַּעֲלוּ עֹלֹת וַיִּזְבְּחוּ זְבָחִים שְׁלָמִים לַה' פָּרִים.

(ו) וַיִּקַּח מֹשֶׁה חֲצִי הַדָּם וַיָּשֶׂם בָּאַגָּנֹת וַחֲצִי הַדָּם זָרַק עַל הַמִּזְבֵּחַ.

(ז) וַיִּקַּח סֵפֶר הַבְּרִית וַיִּקְרָא בְּאָזְנֵי הָעָם וַיֹּאמְרוּ כֹּל אֲשֶׁר דִּבֶּר ה' נַעֲשֶׂה וְנִשְׁמָע.

(ח) וַיִּקַּח מֹשֶׁה אֶת הַדָּם וַיִּזְרֹק עַל הָעָם וַיֹּאמֶר הִנֵּה דַם הַבְּרִית אֲשֶׁר כָּרַת ה׳
עִמָּכֶם עַל כָּל הַדְּבָרִים הָאֵלֶּה.

(ט) וַיַּעַל מֹשֶׁה וְאַהֲרֹן נָדָב וַאֲבִיהוּא וְשִׁבְעִים מִזִּקְנֵי יִשְׂרָאֵל.

(י) וַיִּרְאוּ אֵת אֱ־לֹהֵי יִשְׂרָאֵל וְתַחַת רַגְלָיו כְּמַעֲשֵׂה לִבְנַת הַסַּפִּיר וּכְעֶצֶם הַשָּׁמַיִם
לָטֹהַר.

(יא) וְאֶל אֲצִילֵי בְּנֵי יִשְׂרָאֵל לֹא שָׁלַח יָדוֹ וַיֶּחֱזוּ אֶת הָאֱ־לֹהִים וַיֹּאכְלוּ וַיִּשְׁתּוּ.

(יב) וַיֹּאמֶר ה׳ אֶל מֹשֶׁה עֲלֵה אֵלַי הָהָרָה וֶהְיֵה שָׁם וְאֶתְּנָה לְךָ אֶת לֻחֹת הָאֶבֶן
וְהַתּוֹרָה וְהַמִּצְוָה אֲשֶׁר כָּתַבְתִּי לְהוֹרֹתָם.

(יג) וַיָּקָם מֹשֶׁה וִיהוֹשֻׁעַ מְשָׁרְתוֹ וַיַּעַל מֹשֶׁה אֶל הַר הָאֱ־לֹהִים.

(יד) וְאֶל הַזְּקֵנִים אָמַר שְׁבוּ לָנוּ בָזֶה עַד אֲשֶׁר נָשׁוּב אֲלֵיכֶם וְהִנֵּה אַהֲרֹן וְחוּר
עִמָּכֶם מִי בַעַל דְּבָרִים יִגַּשׁ אֲלֵהֶם.

(טו) וַיַּעַל מֹשֶׁה אֶל הָהָר וַיְכַס הֶעָנָן אֶת הָהָר.

(טז) וַיִּשְׁכֹּן כְּבוֹד ה׳ עַל הַר סִינַי וַיְכַסֵּהוּ הֶעָנָן שֵׁשֶׁת יָמִים וַיִּקְרָא אֶל מֹשֶׁה
בַּיּוֹם הַשְּׁבִיעִי מִתּוֹךְ הֶעָנָן.

(יז) וּמַרְאֵה כְּבוֹד ה׳ כְּאֵשׁ אֹכֶלֶת בְּרֹאשׁ הָהָר לְעֵינֵי בְּנֵי יִשְׂרָאֵל.

(יח) וַיָּבֹא מֹשֶׁה בְּתוֹךְ הֶעָנָן וַיַּעַל אֶל הָהָר וַיְהִי מֹשֶׁה בָּהָר אַרְבָּעִים יוֹם וְאַרְבָּעִים
לָיְלָה.

[3] And Moses came and told the people all the words of the Lord, and all the judgments: and all the people answered with one voice, and said, All the words which the Lord hath said will we do.

[4] And Moses wrote all the words of the Lord, and rose up early in the morning, and builded an altar under the hill, and twelve pillars, according to the twelve tribes of Israel.

[5] And he sent young men of the children of Israel, which offered burnt offerings, and sacrificed peace offerings of oxen unto the Lord.

[6] And Moses took half of the blood, and put it in basons; and half of the blood he sprinkled on the altar.

[7] And he took the book of the covenant, and read in the audience of the people: and they said, All that the Lord hath said will we do, and be obedient.

[8] And Moses took the blood, and sprinkled it on the people, and said, Behold the blood of the covenant, which the Lord hath made with you concerning all these words.

[9] Then went up Moses, and Aaron, Nadab, and Abihu, and seventy of the elders of Israel:

[10] And they saw the God of Israel: and there was under his feet as it were a paved work of a sapphire stone, and as it were the body of heaven in his clearness.

[11] And upon the nobles of the children of Israel he laid not his hand: also they saw God, and did eat and drink.

[12] And the Lord said unto Moses, Come up to me into the mount, and be there: and I will give thee tables of stone, and a law, and commandments which I have written; that thou mayest teach them.

¹³ And Moses rose up, and his minister Joshua: and Moses went up into the mount of God.

¹⁴ And he said unto the elders, Tarry ye here for us, until we come again unto you: and, behold, Aaron and Hur are with you: if any man have any matters to do, let him come unto them.

¹⁵ And Moses went up into the mount, and a cloud covered the mount.

¹⁶ And the glory of the Lord abode upon mount Sinai, and the cloud covered it six days: and the seventh day he called unto Moses out of the midst of the cloud.

¹⁷ And the sight of the glory of the Lord was like devouring fire on the top of the mount in the eyes of the children of Israel.

¹⁸ And Moses went into the midst of the cloud, and gat him up into the mount: and Moses was in the mount forty days and forty nights.

Exodus 31

(יח) וַיִּתֵּן אֶל מֹשֶׁה כְּכַלֹּתוֹ לְדַבֵּר אִתּוֹ בְּהַר סִינַי שְׁנֵי לֻחֹת הָעֵדֻת לֻחֹת אֶבֶן כְּתֻבִים בְּאֶצְבַּע אֱ-לֹהִים.

¹⁸ And he gave unto Moses, when he had made an end of communing with him upon mount Sinai, two tables of testimony, tables of stone, written with the finger of God.

Exodus 32

(יט) וַיְהִי כַּאֲשֶׁר קָרַב אֶל הַמַּחֲנֶה וַיַּרְא אֶת הָעֵגֶל וּמְחֹלֹת וַיִּחַר אַף מֹשֶׁה וַיַּשְׁלֵךְ מִיָּדָו אֶת הַלֻּחֹת וַיְשַׁבֵּר אֹתָם תַּחַת הָהָר.

¹⁹ And it came to pass, as soon as he came nigh unto the camp, that he saw the calf, and the dancing: and Moses' anger waxed hot, and he cast the tables out of his hands, and brake them beneath the mount.

Exodus 34

(א) וַיֹּאמֶר ה' אֶל מֹשֶׁה פְּסָל לְךָ שְׁנֵי לֻחֹת אֲבָנִים כָּרִאשֹׁנִים וְכָתַבְתִּי עַל הַלֻּחֹת אֶת הַדְּבָרִים אֲשֶׁר הָיוּ עַל הַלֻּחֹת הָרִאשֹׁנִים אֲשֶׁר שִׁבַּרְתָּ.

(י) וַיֹּאמֶר הִנֵּה אָנֹכִי כֹּרֵת בְּרִית נֶגֶד כָּל עַמְּךָ אֶעֱשֶׂה נִפְלָאֹת אֲשֶׁר לֹא נִבְרְאוּ בְכָל הָאָרֶץ וּבְכָל הַגּוֹיִם וְרָאָה כָל הָעָם אֲשֶׁר אַתָּה בְקִרְבּוֹ אֶת מַעֲשֵׂה ה' כִּי נוֹרָא הוּא אֲשֶׁר אֲנִי עֹשֶׂה עִמָּךְ.

(יא) שְׁמָר לְךָ אֵת אֲשֶׁר אָנֹכִי מְצַוְּךָ הַיּוֹם הִנְנִי גֹרֵשׁ מִפָּנֶיךָ אֶת הָאֱמֹרִי וְהַכְּנַעֲנִי וְהַחִתִּי וְהַפְּרִזִּי וְהַחִוִּי וְהַיְבוּסִי.

(יב) הִשָּׁמֶר לְךָ פֶּן תִּכְרֹת בְּרִית לְיוֹשֵׁב הָאָרֶץ אֲשֶׁר אַתָּה בָּא עָלֶיהָ פֶּן יִהְיֶה לְמוֹקֵשׁ בְּקִרְבֶּךָ.

(יג) כִּי אֶת מִזְבְּחֹתָם תִּתֹּצוּן וְאֶת מַצֵּבֹתָם תְּשַׁבֵּרוּן וְאֶת אֲשֵׁרָיו תִּכְרֹתוּן.

(יד) כִּי לֹא תִשְׁתַּחֲוֶה לְאֵל אַחֵר כִּי ה' קַנָּא שְׁמוֹ אֵ-ל קַנָּא הוּא.

(טו) פֶּן תִּכְרֹת בְּרִית לְיוֹשֵׁב הָאָרֶץ וְזָנוּ אַחֲרֵי אֱלֹהֵיהֶם וְזָבְחוּ לֵאלֹהֵיהֶם וְקָרָא לְךָ וְאָכַלְתָּ מִזִּבְחוֹ.

(טז) וְלָקַחְתָּ מִבְּנֹתָיו לְבָנֶיךָ וְזָנוּ בְנֹתָיו אַחֲרֵי אֱלֹהֵיהֶן וְהִזְנוּ אֶת בָּנֶיךָ אַחֲרֵי אֱלֹהֵיהֶן.

(יז) אֱלֹהֵי מַסֵּכָה לֹא תַעֲשֶׂה לָךְ.

(יח) אֶת חַג הַמַּצּוֹת תִּשְׁמֹר שִׁבְעַת יָמִים תֹּאכַל מַצּוֹת אֲשֶׁר צִוִּיתִךָ לְמוֹעֵד חֹדֶשׁ הָאָבִיב כִּי בְּחֹדֶשׁ הָאָבִיב יָצָאתָ מִמִּצְרָיִם.

(יט) כָּל פֶּטֶר רֶחֶם לִי וְכָל מִקְנְךָ תִּזָּכָר פֶּטֶר שׁוֹר וָשֶׂה.

(כ) וּפֶטֶר חֲמוֹר תִּפְדֶּה בְשֶׂה וְאִם לֹא תִפְדֶּה וַעֲרַפְתּוֹ כֹּל בְּכוֹר בָּנֶיךָ תִּפְדֶּה וְלֹא יֵרָאוּ פָנַי רֵיקָם.

(כא) שֵׁשֶׁת יָמִים תַּעֲבֹד וּבַיּוֹם הַשְּׁבִיעִי תִּשְׁבֹּת בֶּחָרִישׁ וּבַקָּצִיר תִּשְׁבֹּת.

(כב) וְחַג שָׁבֻעֹת תַּעֲשֶׂה לְךָ בִּכּוּרֵי קְצִיר חִטִּים וְחַג הָאָסִיף תְּקוּפַת הַשָּׁנָה.

(כג) שָׁלֹשׁ פְּעָמִים בַּשָּׁנָה יֵרָאֶה כָּל זְכוּרְךָ אֶת פְּנֵי הָאָדֹן ה' אֱ-לֹהֵי יִשְׂרָאֵל.

(כד) כִּי אוֹרִישׁ גּוֹיִם מִפָּנֶיךָ וְהִרְחַבְתִּי אֶת גְּבֻלֶךָ וְלֹא יַחְמֹד אִישׁ אֶת אַרְצְךָ בַּעֲלֹתְךָ לֵרָאוֹת אֶת פְּנֵי ה' אֱ-לֹהֶיךָ שָׁלֹשׁ פְּעָמִים בַּשָּׁנָה.

(כה) לֹא תִשְׁחַט עַל חָמֵץ דַּם זִבְחִי וְלֹא יָלִין לַבֹּקֶר זֶבַח חַג הַפָּסַח.

(כו) רֵאשִׁית בִּכּוּרֵי אַדְמָתְךָ תָּבִיא בֵּית ה' אֱ-לֹהֶיךָ לֹא תְבַשֵּׁל גְּדִי בַּחֲלֵב אִמּוֹ.

(כז) וַיֹּאמֶר ה' אֶל מֹשֶׁה כְּתָב לְךָ אֶת הַדְּבָרִים הָאֵלֶּה כִּי עַל פִּי הַדְּבָרִים הָאֵלֶּה כָּרַתִּי אִתְּךָ בְּרִית וְאֶת יִשְׂרָאֵל.

(כח) וַיְהִי שָׁם עִם ה' אַרְבָּעִים יוֹם וְאַרְבָּעִים לַיְלָה לֶחֶם לֹא אָכַל וּמַיִם לֹא שָׁתָה וַיִּכְתֹּב עַל הַלֻּחֹת אֵת דִּבְרֵי הַבְּרִית עֲשֶׂרֶת הַדְּבָרִים.

[1] And the Lord said unto Moses, Hew thee two tables of stone like unto the first: and I will write upon these tables the words that were in the first tables, which thou brakest.

[10] And he said, Behold, I make a covenant: before all thy people I will do marvels, such as have not been done in all the earth, nor in any nation: and all the people among which thou art shall see the work of the Lord: for it is a terrible thing that I will do with thee.

[11] Observe thou that which I command thee this day: behold, I drive out before thee the Amorite, and the Canaanite, and the Hittite, and the Perizzite, and the Hivite, and the Jebusite.

[12] Take heed to thyself, lest thou make a covenant with the inhabitants of the land whither thou goest, lest it be for a snare in the midst of thee:

[13] But ye shall destroy their altars, break their images, and cut down their groves:

[14] For thou shalt worship no other god: for the Lord, whose name is Jealous, is a jealous God:

[15] Lest thou make a covenant with the inhabitants of the land, and they go a whoring after their gods, and do sacrifice unto their gods, and one call thee, and thou eat of his sacrifice;

[16] And thou take of their daughters unto thy sons, and their daughters go a whoring after their gods, and make thy sons go a whoring after their gods.

[17] Thou shalt make thee no molten gods.

[18] The feast of unleavened bread shalt thou keep. Seven days thou shalt eat unleavened bread, as I commanded thee, in the time of the month Abib: for in the month Abib thou camest out from Egypt.

[19] All that openeth the matrix is mine; and every firstling among thy cattle, whether ox or sheep, that is male.

[20] But the firstling of an ass thou shalt redeem with a lamb: and if thou redeem him not, then shalt thou break his neck. All the firstborn of thy sons thou shalt redeem. And none shall appear before me empty.

[21] Six days thou shalt work, but on the seventh day thou shalt rest: in earing time and in harvest thou shalt rest.

[22] And thou shalt observe the feast of weeks, of the firstfruits of wheat harvest, and the feast of ingathering at the year's end.

[23] Thrice in the year shall all your men children appear before the Lord God, the God of Israel.

[24] For I will cast out the nations before thee, and enlarge thy borders: neither shall any man desire thy land, when thou shalt go up to appear before the Lord thy God thrice in the year.

[25] Thou shalt not offer the blood of my sacrifice with leaven; neither shall the sacrifice of the feast of the passover be left unto the morning.

[26] The first of the firstfruits of thy land thou shalt bring unto the house of the Lord thy God. Thou shalt not seethe a kid in his mother's milk.

[27] And the Lord said unto Moses, Write thou these words: for after the tenor of these words I have made a covenant with thee and with Israel.

[28] And he was there with the Lord forty days and forty nights; he did neither eat bread, nor drink water. And he wrote upon the tables the words of the covenant, the ten commandments.

BENJAMIN RUSH (1746–1813)

A signer of the Declaration of Independence, Benjamin Rush was a prominent figure during the early American Republic. Rush was a well-known and respected doctor from Philadelphia. He was the chief surgeon of the Continental Army, taught medicine at the University of Pennsylvania, and advanced the causes of women's education and abolitionism.

Observations on the Fourth of July Procession in Philadelphia (July 15, 1788)

My dear Friend, Herewith you will receive an account of our late procession in honor of the establishment of the Fœderal Government. It was drawn up by Judge Hopkinson, a gentleman to whose patriotism, ingenuity, and taste, our city is much indebted for the entertainment.

To this account I cannot help adding a few facts and remarks that occurred during the day, and which were of too minute or speculative a nature to be introduced in the general account published by order of the committee of arrangement.... The Clergy formed a very agreeable part of the Procession – They manifested, by their attendance, their sense of the connection between religion and good government. They amounted to seventeen in number. Four and five of them marched arm in arm with each other, to exemplify the Union. Pains were taken to connect Ministers of the most dissimilar religious principles together, thereby to shew the influence of a free government in promoting christian charity. The Rabbi of the Jews, locked in the arms of two ministers of the gospel, was a most delightful sight. There could not have been a more happy emblem contrived, of that section of the new constitution, which opens all its power and offices alike, not only to every sect of christians, but to worthy men of every religion....

Thoughts upon the Mode of Education Proper in a Republic (1786)

I proceed, in the next place, to inquire what mode of education we shall adopt so as to secure to the state all the advantages that are to be derived from the proper instruction of youth; and here I beg leave to remark that the only foundation for a useful education in a republic is to be laid in RELIGION. Without this, there can be no virtue, and without virtue there can be no liberty, and liberty is the object and life of all republican governments.

Such is my veneration for every religion that reveals the attributes of the Deity, or a future state of rewards and punishments, that I had rather see the opinions of Confucius or Mohammed inculcated upon our youth than see them grow up wholly devoid of a system of religious principles. But the religion I mean to recommend in this place is the religion of JESUS CHRIST.

It is foreign to my purpose to hint at the arguments which establish the truth of the Christian revelation. My only business is to declare that all its doctrines and precepts are calculated to promote the happiness of society and the safety and well-being of civil government. A Christian cannot fail of being a republican. The history of the creation of man and of the relation of our species to each other by birth, which is recorded in the Old Testament, is the best refutation that can be given to the divine right of kings and the strongest argument that can be used in favor of the original and natural equality of all mankind.

Hebraic Sources
Genesis 1

(כו) וַיֹּאמֶר אֱ־לֹהִים נַעֲשֶׂה אָדָם בְּצַלְמֵנוּ כִּדְמוּתֵנוּ וְיִרְדּוּ בִדְגַת הַיָּם וּבְעוֹף הַשָּׁמַיִם וּבַבְּהֵמָה וּבְכָל הָאָרֶץ וּבְכָל הָרֶמֶשׂ הָרֹמֵשׂ עַל הָאָרֶץ.
(כז) וַיִּבְרָא אֱ־לֹהִים אֶת הָאָדָם בְּצַלְמוֹ בְּצֶלֶם אֱ־לֹהִים בָּרָא אֹתוֹ זָכָר וּנְקֵבָה בָּרָא אֹתָם.

[26] And God said, Let us make man in our image, after our likeness: and let them have dominion over the fish of the sea, and over the fowl of the air, and over the cattle, and over all the earth, and over every creeping thing that creepeth upon the earth.
[27] So God created man in his own image, in the image of God created he him; male and female created he them.

Proverbs 22

(ב) עָשִׁיר וָרָשׁ נִפְגָּשׁוּ עֹשֵׂה כֻלָּם ה'.

[2] The rich and poor meet together: the Lord is the maker of them all.

Letter to His Wife Julia about the Marriage of Rachel Phillips (June 27, 1787)

Philadelphia, June 27, 1787
My Dear Julia,
Being called a few days ago to attend in the family of Jonas Phillips, I was honored this morning with an invitation to the attend the marriage of his daughter to a young man of the name of Levy from Virginia. I accepted the invitation with great pleasure, for you know I love to be in the way of adding to my stock of ideas upon all subjects. At 1 o'clock the company, consisting of 30 or 40 men, assembled in

Mr. Philips' common parlor, which was accommodated with benches for the purpose. The ceremony began with prayers in the Hebrew language, which were chanted by an old rabbi and in which he was followed by the whole company. As I did not understand a word except now and then an Amen or Hallelujah, my attention was directed to the haste with which they covered their heads with their hats as soon as the prayers began, and to the freedom with which some of them conversed with each other during the whole time of this part of their worship.

As soon as these prayers were ended, which took up about 20 minutes, a small piece of parchment was produced, written in Hebrew, which contained a deed of settlement and which the groom subscribed in the presence of four witnesses. In this deed he conveyed a part of his fortune to his bride, by which she was provided for after his death in case she survived him.

This ceremony was followed by the erection of a beautiful canopy composed of white and red silk in the middle of the floor. It was supported by four young men (by means of four poles), who put on white gloves for the purpose. As soon as this canopy was fixed, the bride, accompanied with her mother, sister, and a long train of female relations, came downstairs. Her face was covered with a veil which reached halfways down her body. She was handsome at all times, but the occasion and her dress rendered her in a peculiar manner a most lovely and affecting object. I gazed with delight upon her. Innocence, modesty, fear, respect, and devotion appeared all at once in her countenance.

Upon my taking leave of the company, Mrs. Phillips put a large piece of cake into my pocket for you, which she begged I would present to you with her best compliments.[6]

---

6. *Letters of Benjamin Rush*, ed. L. H. Butterfield, vol. 1: 1761–1792 (Princeton: Princeton University Press, 1951), 429–32.

Sermons of the Founding Era

Early America was a religious place. The church was a politicized pulpit where preachers would discourse on the Bible's relation to the present state of political affairs. Many of the pamphlets of the era were reproduced sermons.[1] And many of the more famous sermons that touch on political issues were given in front of elected representatives to start a government session. It is therefore no exaggeration to say that religious men played central roles in the early American political drama and in American culture generally. For instance, John Witherspoon, the most influential academic in American history, was also a famous pastor. At Princeton he taught one president (James Madison), "one vice-president, twelve members of the continental congress, five delegates to the Constitutional Convention, forty-nine US representatives, twenty-eight US Senators; three supreme court justices, eight district judges, three attorney generals and one secretary of state, two foreign ministers and scores of officers in the continental army."[2]

---

1. Ellis Sandoz, *Political Sermons of the Founding Era*, vol. 1 (Indianapolis: Liberty Fund, 1998), xi.
2. Novak, 15.

Below are excerpts of a selection of sermons. It should of course be kept in mind that what follows are representations of political sermons and that there was great variety among them.

EZRA STILES, "THE UNITED STATES ELEVATED TO GLORY AND HONOR" (1783)

Except for the University of Pennsylvania, founded by Benjamin Franklin on nonsectarian grounds, the vast majority of America's institutions of higher learning were founded for the religious instruction of ministers: Harvard, Yale, Princeton, and Brown were all founded by Puritans for this purpose. Many of the most prominent learned men of early America were ministers and presidents of Harvard (Samuel Langdon), Princeton (John Witherspoon), and Yale (Ezra Stiles, 1727–1795, who also helped found Brown University).

There was a small Jewish congregation in Newport, Rhode Island, famous for receiving the letter from George Washington in 1790, reprinted above. Stiles befriended the rabbi of the congregation and they corresponded in Hebrew. He became president of Yale in 1778. While president, he delivered the following sermon to the Connecticut General Assembly, comparing the United States to biblical Israel. The sermon is over one hundred pages long, and it must have tried human patience to listen to it. For Stiles, American democracy was the wave of the future, the destiny of both America and the world.

DEUT. XXVI. 19.

> And to make thee high above all nations, which he hath made in praise, and in name, and in honor; and that thou mayest be an holy people unto the Lord thy God.

TAUGHT by the omniscient Deity, Moses foresaw and predicted the capital events relative to Israel, through the successive changes of depression and glory, until their final elevation to the first dignity and eminence among the empires of the world. These events have been so ordered as to become a display of retribution and sovereignty; for while the good and evil, hitherto felt by this people, have been dispensed in the way of exact national retribution, their ultimate glory and honor will be of the divine sovereignty, with a not for your sakes, do I this, saith the Lord, be it known unto you – but for mine holy name's sake [cf. Ezek. 36:22,32].

However it may be doubted, whether political Communities are rewarded and punished in this world only; and whether the prosperity and decline of other Empires have corresponded with their moral state, as to virtue and vice: yet the history of the hebrew theocracy shews, that the secular welfare of God's ancient people depended upon their virtue, their religion, their observance of that holy covenant, which Israel entered into with God, on the plains at the foot of Nebo on the other side Jordan. Here Moses the man of God assembled three million of people, the number of the united states, recapitulated and gave them a second publication of the sacred jural institute, delivered thirty-eight years before, with the most awful solemnity at mount Sinai. A Law dictated with sovereign authority by the Most High to a people, a world, a universe, becomes of invincible force and obligation without any reference to the consent of the governed: it is obligatory for three reasons, viz. its *original justice* and unerring equity, the *omnipotent Authority* by which it is enforced, and the sanctions of *rewards and punishments*. But in the case of Israel, he condescended to a mutual covenant; and by the hand of Moses lead his people to avouch the Lord Jehovah to be their God, and in the most public and explicit manner voluntarily to engage and covenant with God to keep and obey his Law. Thereupon this great prophet, whom God had raised up for so solemn a transaction, declared in the name of the Lord, that the Most High avouched, acknowledged and took them for a peculiar people to himself; promising to be their God and Protector, and upon their obedience, to make them prosperous and happy. Deut. xxix. 10 & 14. C. xxx. 9 & 19. He foresaw indeed their rejection of God, and predicted the judicial chastisement of apostacy; a chastisement involving the righteous with the wicked. But as well to comfort and support the righteous in every age and under every calamity, as to make his power known among all nations, God determined that a remnant should be saved. Whence Moses and the Prophets, by divine direction interspersed their writings with promises, that, when the ends of God's moral government should be answered in a series of national punishments, inflicted for a succession of ages, he would by his irresistible power and sovereign grace, subdue the hearts of his people to a free, willing, joyful obedience; *turn* their *captivity; –* recover and *gather* them *from all the nations wither the Lord had scattered them in his fierce anger – bring them into the land which their fathers possessed – and multiply* them *above* their *fathers – and rejoice over* them *for good, as he rejoiced over* their fathers. Deut. xxx. 3. Then the words of Moses, hitherto accomplished but in part, will be literally fulfilled; when this branch of the posterity of Abraham shall be nationally collected, and become a very distinguished and glorious people, under the great Messiah the Prince of Peace. He will then *make* them *high above all nations which he hath made in praise, and in name, and in honor* [Deut. 26:19], and they shall become *a key people unto the Lord* their *God.*

I shall enlarge no further upon the primary sense and Eternal accomplishment of this and numerous other prophecies respecting both Jews and Gentiles, in the latter day glory of the church. For I have assumed the text, only as introductory to a discourse upon the political welfare of God's American Israel; and as allusively prophetic of the future prosperity and splendor of the United States. We may then consider

I. What reason we have to expect that, by the blessing of God, these States may prosper and flourish into a great American Republic; and ascend into high and distinguished honor among the nations of the earth. *To make thee high above all nations, which he hath made in praise, and in name, and in honor.*

II. That our system of dominion and CIVIL POLITY would be imperfect, without the true RELIGION; or, that from the diffusion of virtue among the people of any community, would arise their greatest secular happiness: which will terminate in this conclusion, that Holiness ought to be the end of all civil government. *That thou mayest be an holy people unto the Lord thy God...* [Deut. 26:19].

Dominion is founded in property; and resides where that is, whether in the hands of the few or many. The Dominion founded in the feudal tenure of estate, is suited to hold a conquered country in subjection, but is not adapted to the circumstances of free citizens.

Large territorial property vested in individuals is pernicious to society. Civilians, in contemplating the principles of government, have judged superior and inferior partition of property necessary in order to pre- serve the subordination of society, and establish a permanent system of dominion. This makes the public defence the interest of a few landholders only.

A free tenure of lands, an equable distribution of property, enters into the foundation of a happy State: so far I mean, as that the body of the people may have it in their power, by industry, to become possessed of real freehold fee-simple estate. For connected with this will be a general spirit and principle of self-defence – defence of our *property, liberty, country*. This has been singularly verified in New-England; where we have realized the capital ideas of Harrington's Oceana.

But numerous *population*, as well as *industry*, is necessary towards giving value to land; to judiciously partitioned territory. The public weal requires the encouragement of both. A very inconsiderable value arose from the sparse thin settlement of the American aboriginals; of whom there are not fifty thousand souls on this side the Mississippi. The protestant Europeans have generally bought the native right of soil, as far as they have settled, and paid the value ten fold; and are daily increasing the value of the remaining Indian territory a thousand fold; and in this manner we are a constant increasing revenue to the Sachems and original Lords of the Soil. How much must the value of lands, reserved to the natives of North and South-America, be increased to remaining Indians, by the inhabitation of two or three hundred millions of Europeans? ...

Great and extensive will be the happy effects of this warfare, in which we have been called in providence to fight out, not the liberties of america only, but the liberties of the world itself. The spirited and successful stand which we have made against tyranny, will prove the salvation of *england* and *ireland*: and by teaching all sovereigns the danger of irritating and trifling with the affections and loyalty of their subjects, introduce clemency, moderation and justice into public government at large through europe. Already have we learned ireland and all other nations the road to liberty; the way to a redress of grievances, by open *systematical measures, committees of correspondence*, and *military discipline* of an armed people. ...

Hebraic Sources

Stiles puts before his audience the Israelite nation detailed in the Bible and the danger of breaking the covenant with God. Holiness should be one of the goals of the American community.

Deuteronomy 29–30

(ט) אַתֶּם נִצָּבִים הַיּוֹם כֻּלְּכֶם לִפְנֵי ה' אֱ־לֹהֵיכֶם רָאשֵׁיכֶם שִׁבְטֵיכֶם זִקְנֵיכֶם וְשֹׁטְרֵיכֶם כֹּל אִישׁ יִשְׂרָאֵל.

(י) טַפְּכֶם נְשֵׁיכֶם וְגֵרְךָ אֲשֶׁר בְּקֶרֶב מַחֲנֶיךָ מֵחֹטֵב עֵצֶיךָ עַד שֹׁאֵב מֵימֶיךָ.

(יא) לְעָבְרְךָ בִּבְרִית ה' אֱ־לֹהֶיךָ וּבְאָלָתוֹ אֲשֶׁר ה' אֱ־לֹהֶיךָ כֹּרֵת עִמְּךָ הַיּוֹם.

(יב) לְמַעַן הָקִים אֹתְךָ הַיּוֹם לוֹ לְעָם וְהוּא יִהְיֶה לְךָ לֵא־לֹהִים כַּאֲשֶׁר דִּבֶּר לָךְ וְכַאֲשֶׁר נִשְׁבַּע לַאֲבֹתֶיךָ לְאַבְרָהָם לְיִצְחָק וּלְיַעֲקֹב.

(יג) וְלֹא אִתְּכֶם לְבַדְּכֶם אָנֹכִי כֹּרֵת אֶת הַבְּרִית הַזֹּאת וְאֶת הָאָלָה הַזֹּאת.

(יד) כִּי אֶת אֲשֶׁר יֶשְׁנוֹ פֹּה עִמָּנוּ עֹמֵד הַיּוֹם לִפְנֵי ה' אֱ־לֹהֵינוּ וְאֵת אֲשֶׁר אֵינֶנּוּ פֹּה עִמָּנוּ הַיּוֹם.

(טו) כִּי אַתֶּם יְדַעְתֶּם אֵת אֲשֶׁר יָשַׁבְנוּ בְּאֶרֶץ מִצְרָיִם וְאֵת אֲשֶׁר עָבַרְנוּ בְּקֶרֶב הַגּוֹיִם אֲשֶׁר עֲבַרְתֶּם.

(טז) וַתִּרְאוּ אֶת שִׁקּוּצֵיהֶם וְאֵת גִּלֻּלֵיהֶם עֵץ וָאֶבֶן כֶּסֶף וְזָהָב אֲשֶׁר עִמָּהֶם.

(יז) פֶּן יֵשׁ בָּכֶם אִישׁ אוֹ אִשָּׁה אוֹ מִשְׁפָּחָה אוֹ שֵׁבֶט אֲשֶׁר לְבָבוֹ פֹנֶה הַיּוֹם מֵעִם ה' אֱ־לֹהֵינוּ לָלֶכֶת לַעֲבֹד אֶת אֱלֹהֵי הַגּוֹיִם הָהֵם פֶּן יֵשׁ בָּכֶם שֹׁרֶשׁ פֹּרֶה רֹאשׁ וְלַעֲנָה.

(יח) וְהָיָה בְּשָׁמְעוֹ אֶת דִּבְרֵי הָאָלָה הַזֹּאת וְהִתְבָּרֵךְ בִּלְבָבוֹ לֵאמֹר שָׁלוֹם יִהְיֶה לִּי כִּי בִּשְׁרִרוּת לִבִּי אֵלֵךְ לְמַעַן סְפוֹת הָרָוָה אֶת הַצְּמֵאָה.

(יט) לֹא יֹאבֶה ה' סְלֹחַ לוֹ כִּי אָז יֶעְשַׁן אַף ה' וְקִנְאָתוֹ בָּאִישׁ הַהוּא וְרָבְצָה בּוֹ כָּל הָאָלָה הַכְּתוּבָה בַּסֵּפֶר הַזֶּה וּמָחָה ה' אֶת שְׁמוֹ מִתַּחַת הַשָּׁמָיִם.

(כ) וְהִבְדִּילוֹ ה' לְרָעָה מִכֹּל שִׁבְטֵי יִשְׂרָאֵל כְּכֹל אָלוֹת הַבְּרִית הַכְּתוּבָה בְּסֵפֶר הַתּוֹרָה הַזֶּה.

(כא) וְאָמַר הַדּוֹר הָאַחֲרוֹן בְּנֵיכֶם אֲשֶׁר יָקוּמוּ מֵאַחֲרֵיכֶם וְהַנָּכְרִי אֲשֶׁר יָבֹא מֵאֶרֶץ רְחוֹקָה וְרָאוּ אֶת מַכּוֹת הָאָרֶץ הַהִוא וְאֶת תַּחֲלֻאֶיהָ אֲשֶׁר חִלָּה ה' בָּהּ.

(כב) גָּפְרִית וָמֶלַח שְׂרֵפָה כָל אַרְצָהּ לֹא תִזָּרַע וְלֹא תַצְמִחַ וְלֹא יַעֲלֶה בָהּ כָּל עֵשֶׂב כְּמַהְפֵּכַת סְדֹם וַעֲמֹרָה אַדְמָה וּצְבֹיִים [וּצְבוֹיִם] אֲשֶׁר הָפַךְ ה' בְּאַפּוֹ וּבַחֲמָתוֹ.

(כג) וְאָמְרוּ כָּל הַגּוֹיִם עַל מֶה עָשָׂה ה' כָּכָה לָאָרֶץ הַזֹּאת מֶה חֳרִי הָאַף הַגָּדוֹל הַזֶּה.

(כד) וְאָמְרוּ עַל אֲשֶׁר עָזְבוּ אֶת בְּרִית ה' אֱ־לֹהֵי אֲבֹתָם אֲשֶׁר כָּרַת עִמָּם בְּהוֹצִיאוֹ אֹתָם מֵאֶרֶץ מִצְרָיִם.

(כה) וַיֵּלְכוּ וַיַּעַבְדוּ אֱלֹהִים אֲחֵרִים וַיִּשְׁתַּחֲווּ לָהֶם אֱלֹהִים אֲשֶׁר לֹא יְדָעוּם וְלֹא חָלַק לָהֶם.

(כו) וַיִּחַר אַף ה' בָּאָרֶץ הַהִוא לְהָבִיא עָלֶיהָ אֶת כָּל הַקְּלָלָה הַכְּתוּבָה בַּסֵּפֶר הַזֶּה.

(כז) וַיִּתְּשֵׁם ה׳ מֵעַל אַדְמָתָם בְּאַף וּבְחֵמָה וּבְקֶצֶף גָּדוֹל וַיַּשְׁלִכֵם אֶל אֶרֶץ אַחֶרֶת כַּיּוֹם הַזֶּה.

(כח) הַנִּסְתָּרֹת לַה׳ אֱ-לֹהֵינוּ וְהַנִּגְלֹת לָנוּ וּלְבָנֵינוּ עַד עוֹלָם לַעֲשׂוֹת אֶת כָּל דִּבְרֵי הַתּוֹרָה הַזֹּאת.

(א) וְהָיָה כִי יָבֹאוּ עָלֶיךָ כָּל הַדְּבָרִים הָאֵלֶּה הַבְּרָכָה וְהַקְּלָלָה אֲשֶׁר נָתַתִּי לְפָנֶיךָ וַהֲשֵׁבֹתָ אֶל לְבָבֶךָ בְּכָל הַגּוֹיִם אֲשֶׁר הִדִּיחֲךָ ה׳ אֱ-לֹהֶיךָ שָׁמָּה.

(ב) וְשַׁבְתָּ עַד ה׳ אֱ-לֹהֶיךָ וְשָׁמַעְתָּ בְקֹלוֹ כְּכֹל אֲשֶׁר אָנֹכִי מְצַוְּךָ הַיּוֹם אַתָּה וּבָנֶיךָ בְּכָל לְבָבְךָ וּבְכָל נַפְשֶׁךָ.

(ג) וְשָׁב ה׳ אֱ-לֹהֶיךָ אֶת שְׁבוּתְךָ וְרִחֲמֶךָ וְשָׁב וְקִבֶּצְךָ מִכָּל הָעַמִּים אֲשֶׁר הֱפִיצְךָ ה׳ אֱ-לֹהֶיךָ שָׁמָּה.

(ד) אִם יִהְיֶה נִדַּחֲךָ בִּקְצֵה הַשָּׁמָיִם מִשָּׁם יְקַבֶּצְךָ ה׳ אֱ-לֹהֶיךָ וּמִשָּׁם יִקָּחֶךָ.

(ה) וֶהֱבִיאֲךָ ה׳ אֱ-לֹהֶיךָ אֶל הָאָרֶץ אֲשֶׁר יָרְשׁוּ אֲבֹתֶיךָ וִירִשְׁתָּהּ וְהֵיטִבְךָ וְהִרְבְּךָ מֵאֲבֹתֶיךָ.

(ו) וּמָל ה׳ אֱ-לֹהֶיךָ אֶת לְבָבְךָ וְאֶת לְבַב זַרְעֶךָ לְאַהֲבָה אֶת ה׳ אֱ-לֹהֶיךָ בְּכָל לְבָבְךָ וּבְכָל נַפְשְׁךָ לְמַעַן חַיֶּיךָ.

(ז) וְנָתַן ה׳ אֱ-לֹהֶיךָ אֵת כָּל הָאָלוֹת הָאֵלֶּה עַל אֹיְבֶיךָ וְעַל שֹׂנְאֶיךָ אֲשֶׁר רְדָפוּךָ.

(ח) וְאַתָּה תָשׁוּב וְשָׁמַעְתָּ בְּקוֹל ה׳ וְעָשִׂיתָ אֶת כָּל מִצְוֹתָיו אֲשֶׁר אָנֹכִי מְצַוְּךָ הַיּוֹם.

(ט) וְהוֹתִירְךָ ה׳ אֱ-לֹהֶיךָ בְּכֹל מַעֲשֵׂה יָדֶךָ בִּפְרִי בִטְנְךָ וּבִפְרִי בְהֶמְתְּךָ וּבִפְרִי אַדְמָתְךָ לְטֹבָה כִּי יָשׁוּב ה׳ לָשׂוּשׂ עָלֶיךָ לְטוֹב כַּאֲשֶׁר שָׂשׂ עַל אֲבֹתֶיךָ.

(י) כִּי תִשְׁמַע בְּקוֹל ה׳ אֱ-לֹהֶיךָ לִשְׁמֹר מִצְוֹתָיו וְחֻקֹּתָיו הַכְּתוּבָה בְּסֵפֶר הַתּוֹרָה הַזֶּה כִּי תָשׁוּב אֶל ה׳ אֱ-לֹהֶיךָ בְּכָל לְבָבְךָ וּבְכָל נַפְשֶׁךָ.

[10] [9] Ye stand this day all of you before the Lord your God; your captains of your tribes, your elders, and your officers, with all the men of Israel,

[11] [10] Your little ones, your wives, and thy stranger that is in thy camp, from the hewer of thy wood unto the drawer of thy water;

[12] [11] That thou shouldest enter into covenant with the Lord thy God, and into His oath, which the Lord thy God maketh with thee this day;

[13] [12] That he may establish thee today for a people unto Himself, and that He may be unto thee a God, as He hath said unto thee, and as He hath sworn unto thy fathers, to Abraham, to Isaac, and to Jacob.

[14] [13] Neither with you only do I make this covenant and this oath;

[15] [14] But with him that standeth here with us this day before the Lord our God, and also with him that is not here with us this day:

[16] [15] For ye know how we have dwelt in the land of Egypt; and how we came through the nations which ye passed by,

[17] [16] And ye have seen their abominations, and their idols, wood and stone, silver and gold, which were among them;

18 [17] Lest there should be among you man, or woman, or family, or tribe, whose heart turneth away this day from the Lord our God, to go and serve the gods of these nations; lest there should be among you a root that beareth gall and wormwood;

19 [18] And it come to pass, when he heareth the words of this curse, that he bless himself in his heart, saying, I shall have peace, though I walk in the imagination of mine heart, to add drunkenness to thirst:

20 [19] The Lord will not spare him, but then the anger of the Lord and His jealousy shall smoke against that man, and all the curses that are written in this book shall lie upon him, and the Lord shall blot out his name from under heaven.

21 [20] And the Lord shall separate him unto evil out of all the tribes of Israel, according to all the curses of the covenant that are written in this book of the law:

22 [21] So that the generation to come of your children that shall rise up after you, and the stranger that shall come from a far land, shall say, when they see the plagues of that land, and the sicknesses which the Lord hath laid upon it;

23 [22] And that the whole land thereof is brimstone, and salt, and burning, that it is not sown, nor beareth, nor any grass groweth therein, like the overthrow of Sodom, and Gomorrah, Admah, and Zeboim, which the Lord overthrew in His anger, and in His wrath;

24 [23] Even all nations shall say: Wherefore hath the Lord done thus unto this land? What meaneth the heat of this great anger?

25 [24] Then men shall say: Because they have forsaken the covenant of the Lord God of their fathers, which He made with them when He brought them forth out of the land of Egypt:

26 [25] For they went and served other gods, and worshipped them, gods whom they knew not, and whom He had not given unto them;

27 [26] And the anger of the Lord was kindled against this land, to bring upon it all the curses that are written in this book;

28 [27] And the Lord rooted them out of their land in anger, and in wrath, and in great indignation, and cast them into another land, as it is this day.

29 [28] The secret things belong unto the Lord our God: but those things which are revealed belong unto us and to our children for ever, that we may do all the words of this law.

1 And it shall come to pass, when all these things are come upon thee, the blessing and the curse, which I have set before thee, and thou shalt call them to mind among all the nations, whither the Lord thy God hath driven thee,

2 And shalt return unto the Lord thy God, and shalt obey His voice according to all that I command thee this day, thou and thy children, with all thine heart, and with all thy soul;

3 That then the Lord thy God will turn thy captivity, and have compassion upon thee, and will return and gather thee from all the nations, whither the Lord thy God hath scattered thee.

4 If any of thine be driven out unto the outmost parts of heaven, from thence will the Lord thy God gather thee, and from thence will He fetch thee.

5 And the Lord thy God will bring thee into the land which thy fathers possessed, and thou shalt possess it; and He will do thee good, and multiply thee above thy fathers.

6 And the Lord thy God will circumcise thine heart, and the heart of thy seed, to love the Lord thy God with all thine heart, and with all thy soul, that thou mayest live.

⁷ And the Lord thy God will put all these curses upon thine enemies, and on them that hate thee, which persecuted thee.

⁸ And thou shalt return and obey the voice of the Lord, and do all His commandments which I command thee this day.

⁹ And the Lord thy God will make thee plenteous in every work of thine hand, in the fruit of thy body, and in the fruit of thy cattle, and in the fruit of thy land, for good: for the Lord will again rejoice over thee for good, as He rejoiced over thy fathers:

¹⁰ If thou shalt hearken unto the voice of the Lord thy God, to keep His commandments and His statutes which are written in this book of the law, and if thou turn unto the Lord thy God with all thine heart, and with all thy soul.

Deuteronomy 26

(טז) הַיּוֹם הַזֶּה ה' אֱ-לֹהֶיךָ מְצַוְּךָ לַעֲשׂוֹת אֶת הַחֻקִּים הָאֵלֶּה וְאֶת הַמִּשְׁפָּטִים וְשָׁמַרְתָּ וְעָשִׂיתָ אוֹתָם בְּכָל לְבָבְךָ וּבְכָל נַפְשֶׁךָ.

(יז) אֶת ה' הֶאֱמַרְתָּ הַיּוֹם לִהְיוֹת לְךָ לֵא-לֹהִים וְלָלֶכֶת בִּדְרָכָיו וְלִשְׁמֹר חֻקָּיו וּמִצְוֹתָיו וּמִשְׁפָּטָיו וְלִשְׁמֹעַ בְּקֹלוֹ.

(יח) וַה' הֶאֱמִירְךָ הַיּוֹם לִהְיוֹת לוֹ לְעַם סְגֻלָּה כַּאֲשֶׁר דִּבֶּר לָךְ וְלִשְׁמֹר כָּל מִצְוֹתָיו.

(יט) וּלְתִתְּךָ עֶלְיוֹן עַל כָּל הַגּוֹיִם אֲשֶׁר עָשָׂה לִתְהִלָּה וּלְשֵׁם וּלְתִפְאָרֶת וְלִהְיֹתְךָ עַם קָדֹשׁ לַה' אֱ-לֹהֶיךָ כַּאֲשֶׁר דִּבֵּר.

¹⁶ This day the Lord thy God hath commanded thee to do these statutes and judgments: thou shalt therefore keep and do them with all thy heart, and with all thy soul.

¹⁷ Thou hast avouched the Lord this day to be thy God, and to walk in His ways, and to keep His statutes, and His commandments, and His judgments, and to hearken unto His voice.

¹⁸ And the Lord hath avouched thee this day to be His treasure, as He hath promised thee, and that thou shouldest keep all His commandments;

¹⁹ And to make thee high above all nations which He hath made, in praise, and in name, and in honor; and that thou mayest be a holy people unto the Lord thy God, as He hath spoken.

Ezekiel 36

(כב) לָכֵן אֱמֹר לְבֵית יִשְׂרָאֵל כֹּה אָמַר אֲדֹנָי ה' לֹא לְמַעַנְכֶם אֲנִי עֹשֶׂה בֵּית יִשְׂרָאֵל כִּי אִם לְשֵׁם קָדְשִׁי אֲשֶׁר חִלַּלְתֶּם בַּגּוֹיִם אֲשֶׁר בָּאתֶם שָׁם.

(כג) וְקִדַּשְׁתִּי אֶת שְׁמִי הַגָּדוֹל הַמְחֻלָּל בַּגּוֹיִם אֲשֶׁר חִלַּלְתֶּם בְּתוֹכָם וְיָדְעוּ הַגּוֹיִם כִּי אֲנִי ה' נְאֻם אֲדֹנָי ה' בְּהִקָּדְשִׁי בָכֶם לְעֵינֵיהֶם.

(כד) וְלָקַחְתִּי אֶתְכֶם מִן הַגּוֹיִם וְקִבַּצְתִּי אֶתְכֶם מִכָּל הָאֲרָצוֹת וְהֵבֵאתִי אֶתְכֶם אֶל אַדְמַתְכֶם.

(כה) וְזָרַקְתִּי עֲלֵיכֶם מַיִם טְהוֹרִים וּטְהַרְתֶּם מִכֹּל טֻמְאוֹתֵיכֶם וּמִכָּל גִּלּוּלֵיכֶם אֲטַהֵר אֶתְכֶם.

(כו) וְנָתַתִּי לָכֶם לֵב חָדָשׁ וְרוּחַ חֲדָשָׁה אֶתֵּן בְּקִרְבְּכֶם וַהֲסִרֹתִי אֶת לֵב הָאֶבֶן
מִבְּשַׂרְכֶם וְנָתַתִּי לָכֶם לֵב בָּשָׂר.
(כז) וְאֶת רוּחִי אֶתֵּן בְּקִרְבְּכֶם וְעָשִׂיתִי אֶת אֲשֶׁר בְּחֻקַּי תֵּלֵכוּ וּמִשְׁפָּטַי תִּשְׁמְרוּ
וַעֲשִׂיתֶם.
(כח) וִישַׁבְתֶּם בָּאָרֶץ אֲשֶׁר נָתַתִּי לַאֲבֹתֵיכֶם וִהְיִיתֶם לִי לְעָם וְאָנֹכִי אֶהְיֶה לָכֶם
לֵא-לֹהִים.

[22] Therefore say unto the house of Israel: Thus saith the Lord God; I do not this for your sakes, O house of Israel, but for My holy name's sake, which ye have profaned among the heathen, whither ye went.

[23] And I will sanctify My great name, which was profaned among the heathen, which ye have profaned in the midst of them; and the heathen shall know that I am the Lord, saith the Lord God, when I shall be sanctified in you before their eyes.

[24] For I will take you from among the heathen, and gather you out of all countries, and will bring you into your own land.

[25] Then will I sprinkle clean water upon you, and ye shall be clean: from all your filthiness, and from all your idols, will I cleanse you.

[26] A new heart also will I give you, and a new spirit will I put within you: and I will take away the stony heart out of your flesh, and I will give you a heart of flesh.

[27] And I will put My spirit within you, and cause you to walk in My statutes, and ye shall keep My judgments, and do them.

[28] And ye shall dwell in the land that I gave to your fathers; and ye shall be My people, and I will be your God.

SAMUEL SHERWOOD, "THE CHURCH'S FLIGHT FROM THE WILDERNESS" (1776)

Only two of the sermons of Samuel Sherwood (1730–1783) survive. That is surprising given that this sermon was considered one of the most popular and often reproduced during the Revolutionary period. The text that launches the sermon is Revelation 12:14–17, a discussion of the cause of the apocalypse. Sherwood depicted America as God's chosen people, whom He will defend against the British Antichrist, depicted as a dragon. The sermon was preached in January 1776. The war was underway, Boston besieged, but independence had yet to be declared. It was widely reprinted in April of 1776.[3]

---

3. This introduction is indebted to Sandoz's introduction to *Political Sermons of the Founding Era*, 2 vols. (Indianapolis: Liberty Fund, 1998).

There seems an evident allusion here, to what God said to the children of Israel, Exod. xix. 4. after their deliverance from cruel oppressive slavery in Egypt, when encamp'd before Sinai, and on their way to the good land of Canaan, "Ye have seen what I did unto the Egyptians, and how I bore you on eagles wings, and brought you unto myself." He was not conducting them from a land of liberty, peace, and tranquility, into a state of bondage, persecution and distress; but on the contrary, had wrought out a very glorious deliverance for them, and set them free from the cruel hand of tyranny and oppression, by executing his judgments in a most terrible and awful manner, on the Egyptians, their enemies; and was now, by his kind providence, leading them to the good land of Canaan, which he gave them by promise, for an everlasting inheritance. Hence, as the trials and sufferings of the Christian church were parallel in some measure, with those of the Jewish, and there is a great similarity and likeness in the manner of God's dealings with the one to the other.... The passage, in its most natural, genuine construction, contains as full and absolute a promise of this land, to the Christian church, as ever was made to the Jewish, of the land of Canaan....

Thus the church, in this difficult, distressed season, whenever it happened, was supported and carried, as it were, on eagles wings, to a distant remote wilderness, for safety and protection. And what period or event is there in all the history of her trials and persecutions, which these expressions more exactly describe, and to which they can be applied with more truth and propriety, than to the flight of our forefathers into this then howling wilderness, which was a land not sown nor occupied by any ruling power on earth, except by savages and wild beasts? It is an indisputable fact, that the cruel hand of oppression, tyranny and persecution drove them out from their pleasant seats and habitations, in the land of their nativity; and that the purest principles of religion and liberty, led them to make the bold adventure across the wide Atlantic ocean; for which they surely needed the two wings of the great eagle, to speed their flight, and to shelter and cover them from danger, while seeking a safe retreat from the relentless fury and shocking cruelty of the persecuting dragon, and a secure abode for unadulterated christianity, liberty and peace....

As the church has such a gift and grant of this good land, from that God to whom the earth belongs, and the fulness thereof; the present war set on foot by the British ministry and parliament, against her true and worthy members, the American sons of liberty, to dispossess them hereof, is not only felonious and murderous, as stiled by the noble lord mayor of London, in his excellent speech on this subject; but seems likewise a very bold and daring attack upon the sovereign prerogative of that Being, who is the Great Lord Proprietor of all, to whom vengeance belongeth; who has already interposed in a very signal manner, to display his awful vengeance against this wicked nefarious undertaking, by plunging four thousand of these our malignant foes in the ocean, with an hundred and fifty thousand pounds sterling of their property; by setting fire to two of their ships with lightening from heaven; and by a late very sweeping storm on the coasts of Great-Britain, to an immense destruction of both men and shipping; by which, and other remarkable providences in our favour, we have incontestible evidence, that God Almighty, with all the powers of heaven, are on our side. Great numbers of angels, no doubt, are encamping round our coast, for our defence and protection. Michael stands ready; with all the artillery of heaven, to encounter the dragon, and to vanquish this black host.

Hebraic Source
Exodus 19

(ג) וּמֹשֶׁה עָלָה אֶל הָאֱלֹהִים וַיִּקְרָא אֵלָיו ה' מִן הָהָר לֵאמֹר כֹּה תֹאמַר לְבֵית יַעֲקֹב וְתַגֵּיד לִבְנֵי יִשְׂרָאֵל.

(ד) אַתֶּם רְאִיתֶם אֲשֶׁר עָשִׂיתִי לְמִצְרָיִם וָאֶשָּׂא אֶתְכֶם עַל כַּנְפֵי נְשָׁרִים וָאָבִא אֶתְכֶם אֵלָי.

(ה) וְעַתָּה אִם שָׁמוֹעַ תִּשְׁמְעוּ בְּקֹלִי וּשְׁמַרְתֶּם אֶת בְּרִיתִי וִהְיִיתֶם לִי סְגֻלָּה מִכָּל הָעַמִּים כִּי לִי כָּל הָאָרֶץ.

(ו) וְאַתֶּם תִּהְיוּ לִי מַמְלֶכֶת כֹּהֲנִים וְגוֹי קָדוֹשׁ אֵלֶּה הַדְּבָרִים אֲשֶׁר תְּדַבֵּר אֶל בְּנֵי יִשְׂרָאֵל.

[3] And Moses went up unto God, and the Lord called unto him out of the mountain, saying: Thus shalt thou say to the house of Jacob, and tell the children of Israel;

4 Ye have seen what I did unto the Egyptians, and how I bare you on eagles' wings, and brought you unto Myself.

5 Now therefore, if ye will obey My voice indeed, and keep My covenant, then ye shall be a treasure unto Me above all people; for all the earth is Mine:

6 And ye shall be unto Me a kingdom of priests, and an holy nation. These are the words which thou shalt speak unto the children of Israel.

JOHN WITHERSPOON, "THE DOMINION OF PROVIDENCE OVER THE PASSIONS OF MEN" (1776)

Originally from Scotland, John Witherspoon (1723–1794) was elected to the Continental Congress, where he held a seat until 1782. He then served in the New Jersey legislature and in the Constitutional Convention. Because of the number of Witherspoon's former Princeton students who became congressmen, presidents, and Supreme Court justices, Witherspoon can probably be considered one of the most influential men of the founding era. In the following sermon, Witherspoon draws a tight connection between the cause of American liberty and true religion.

> Surely the Wrath of Man shall praise thee;
> the remainder of Wrath shalt thou restrain.
> Psalm LXXVI. 10 [11].

There is not a greater evidence either of the reality or the power of religion, than a firm belief of God's universal presence, and a constant attention to the influence and operation of his providence. It is by this means that the Christian may be said, in the emphatical scripture language, "to walk with God, and to endure as seeing him who is invisible."

The doctrine of divine providence is very full and complete in the sacred oracles. It extends not only to things which we may think of great moment, and therefore worthy of notice, but to things the most indifferent and inconsiderable; "Are not two sparrows sold for a farthing," says our Lord, "and one of them falleth not to the ground without your heavenly Father"; nay, "the very hairs of your head are all numbered.["] It extends not only to things beneficial and salutary, or to the direction and assistance of those who are the servants of the living God; but to things seemingly most hurtful and destructive, and to persons the most refractory and disobedient. He overrules all his creatures, and all their actions. Thus we are told, that "fire, hail, snow, vapour, and stormy wind, fulfil his word" [Ps. 148:8], in the course of nature; and even so the most impetuous and disorderly passions of men, that are under no restraint from themselves, are yet perfectly subject to the dominion of Jehovah. They carry his commission, they obey his orders, they are limited and restrained by his authority, and they conspire with every thing else in promoting his glory. There is the greater need to take notice of this, that men are not generally sufficiently aware of the distinction between the law of God and his purpose; they are apt to suppose, that as the temper of the sinner is contrary to the one, so the outrages of the sinner are able to defeat the other; than which nothing can be more false. The truth is plainly asserted, and nobly expressed by the psalmist in the text, "Surely the wrath of man shall praise thee; the remainder of wrath shalt thou restrain."

This psalm was evidently composed as a song of praise for some signal victory obtained, which was at the same time a remarkable deliverance from threatening danger. The author was one or other of the later prophets, and the occasion probably the unsuccessful assault of Jerusalem, by the army of Sennacherib king of Assyria, in the days of Hezekiah. Great was the insolence and boasting of his generals and servants against the city of the living God, as may be seen in the thirty-sixth chapter of Isaiah. Yet it pleased God to destroy their enemies, and, by his own immediate interposition, to grant them deliverance. Therefore the Psalmist says in the fifth and sixth verses [6-7] of this psalm, "The stout-hearted are spoiled, they have slept their sleep. None of the men of might have found their hands. At thy rebuke, O God of Jacob! both the chariot and the horse are cast into a deep sleep." After a few more remarks to the same purpose, he draws the inference, or makes the reflection in the text, "Surely the wrath of man shall praise thee; the remainder of wrath shalt thou restrain["]: which may be paraphrased thus, The fury and injustice of oppressors shall bring in a tribute of praise to thee; the influence of thy righteous providence shall be clearly discerned; the countenance and support thou wilt give to thine own people shall be gloriously illustrated; thou shalt set the bounds which the boldest cannot pass.

I am sensible, my brethren, that the time and occasion of this psalm, may seem to be in one respect ill suited to the interesting circumstances of this country at present. It was composed after the victory was obtained; whereas we are now but putting on the harness and entering upon an important contest, the length of which it is impossible to foresee, and the issue of which it will perhaps be thought presumption to foretell. But as the truth, with respect to God's moral government, is the same and unchangeable; as the issue, in the case of Sennacherib's invasion, did but lead the prophet to acknowledge it; our duty and interest conspire in calling upon us to improve it. And I have chosen to insist upon it on this day of solemn humiliation, as it will probably help us to a clear and explicit view of what should be the chief subject of our prayers and endeavors, as well as the great object of our hope and trust, in our present situation.

The truth, then, asserted in this text, which I propose to illustrate and improve, is, That all the disorderly passions of men, whether exposing the innocent to private injury, or whether they are the arrows of divine judgment in public calamity, shall, in the end, be to the praise of God: Or, to apply it more particularly to the present state of the American colonies, and the plague of war, The ambition of mistaken princes, the cunning and cruelty of oppressive and corrupt ministers, and even the inhumanity of brutal soldiers, however dreadful, shall finally promote the glory of God, and in the mean time, while the storm continues, his mercy and kindness shall appear in prescribing bounds to their rage and fury.

In discoursing on this subject, it is my intention, through the assistance of divine grace,

I. To point out to you in some particulars, how the wrath of man praises God.

II. To apply these principles to our present situation, by inferences of truth for your instruction and comfort, and by suitable exhortations to duty in the important crisis.

In the first place, I am to point out to you in some particulars, how the wrath of man praises God. I say in some instances, because it is far from being in my power, either to mention or explain the whole. There is an unsearchable depth in the divine counsels, which it is impossible for us to penetrate. It is the duty of every good man to place the most unlimited confidence in divine wisdom, and to believe that those measures of providence that are most unintelligible to him, are yet planned with the same skill, and directed to the same great purposes as others, the reason and tendency of which he can explain in the clearest manner. But where revelation and experience enables us to discover the wisdom, equity, or mercy of divine providence, nothing can be more delightful or profitable to a serious mind, and therefore I beg your attention to the following remarks.

In the first place, the wrath of man praises God, as it is an example and illustration of divine truth, and clearly points out the corruption of our nature, which is the foundation stone of the doctrine of redemption. Nothing can be more absolutely necessary to true religion, than a clear and full conviction of the sinfulness of our nature and state. Without this there can be neither repentance in the sinner, nor humility in the believer. Without this all that is said in scripture of the wisdom and mercy of God in providing a Saviour, is without force and without meaning. Justly does our Saviour say, "The whole have no need of a physician, but those that are sick. I came not to call the righteous, but sinners to repentance." Those who are not sensible that they are sinners, will treat every exhortation to repentance, and every offer of mercy, with disdain or defiance.

But where can we have a more affecting view of the corruption of our nature, than in the wrath of man, when exerting itself in oppression, cruelty and blood? It must be owned, indeed, that this truth is abundantly manifest in times of the greatest tranquility. Others may, if they please, treat the corruption of our nature as a chimera: for my part, I see it every where, and I feel it every day. All the disorders in human society, and the greatest part even of the unhappiness we are exposed to, arises from the envy, malice, covetousness, and other lusts of man. If we and all about us were just what we ought to be in all respects, we should not need to go any further for heaven, for it would be upon earth. But war and violence present a spectacle still more awful. How affecting is it to think, that the lust of domination should be so violent and universal? That men should so rarely be satisfied with their own possessions and acquisitions, or even with the benefit that would arise from mutual service, but should look upon the happiness and tranquility of others, as an obstruction to their own? That, as if the great law of nature, were not enough, "Dust thou art, and to dust thou shalt return" [Gen. 3:19], they should be so furiously set for the destruction of each other? It is shocking to think, since the first murder of Abel by his brother Cain, what havock has been made of man by man in every age. What is it that fills the pages of history, but the wars and contentions of princes and empires? What vast numbers has lawless ambition brought into the field, and delivered as a prey to the destructive sword?

If we dwell a little upon the circumstances, they become deeply affecting. The mother bears a child with pain, rears him by the laborious attendance of many years; yet in the prime of life, in the vigor of health, and bloom of beauty, in a moment he is cut down by the dreadful instruments of death. "Every battle of the warrior is with confused noise, and garments rolled in blood" [Is. 9:4]; but the horror of the scene is not confined to the field of slaughter. Few go there unrelated, or fall unlamented; in every hostile encounter, what must be the impression upon the relations of the deceased? The bodies of the dead can only be seen, or the cries of the dying heard for a single day, but many days shall not put an end to the mourning of a parent for a beloved son, the joy and support of his age, or of the widow and helpless offspring, for a father taken away in the fullness of health and vigor.

But if this may be justly said of all wars between man and man, what shall we be able to say that is suitable to the abhorred scene of civil war between citizen and citizen? How deeply affecting is it, that those who are the same in complexion, the same in blood, in language, and in religion, should, notwithstanding, butcher one another with unrelenting rage, and glory in the deed? That men should lay waste the fields of their fellow subjects, with whose provision they themselves had been often fed, and consume with devouring fire those houses in which they had often found a hospitable shelter.

These things are apt to overcome a weak mind with fear, or overwhelm it with sorrow, and in the greatest number are apt to excite the highest indignation, and kindle up a spirit of revenge. If this last has no other tendency than to direct and invigorate the measures of self-defence, I do not take upon me to blame it, on the contrary, I call it necessary and laudable.

But what I mean at this time to prove by the preceding reflections, and wish to impress on your minds, is the depravity of our nature. James iv. i. "From whence come wars and fighting among you? come they not hence even from your lusts that war in your members?" Men of lax and corrupt principles, take great delight in speaking to the praise of human nature, and extolling its dignity, without distinguishing what it was, at its first creation, from what it is in its present fallen state. These fine speculations are very grateful to a worldly mind. They are also much more pernicious to uncautious and unthinking youth, than even the temptations to a dissolute and sensual life, against which they are fortified by the dictates of natural conscience, and a sense of public shame. But I appeal from these visionary reasonings to the history of all ages, and the inflexible testimony of daily experience. These will tell us what men have been in their practice, and from thence you may judge what they are by nature, while unrenewed. If I am not mistaken, a cool and candid attention, either to the past history, or present state of the world, but above all, to the ravages of lawless power, ought to humble us in the dust. It should at once lead us to acknowlege the just view given us in scripture of our lost state; to desire the happy influence of renewing grace each for ourselves; and to long for the dominion of righteousness and peace, when "men shall beat their swords into plow-shares, and their spears into pruning hooks; when nation shall not lift up sword against nation, neither shall they learn war any more." Mic iv. 3.

2. The wrath of man praiseth God, as it is the instrument in his hand for bringing sinners to repentance, and for the correction and improvement of his own children. Whatever be the nature of the affliction with which he visits either persons, families, or nations; whatever be the disposition or intention of those whose malice he employs as a scourge; the design on his part is, to rebuke men for iniquity, to bring them to repentance, and to promote their holiness and peace. The salutary nature and sanctifying influence of affliction in general, is often taken notice of in scripture, both as making a part of the purpose

of God, and the experience of his saints. Heb. xii. 11. "Now, no affliction for the present seemeth to be joyous, but grievous: Nevertheless, afterwards it yieldeth the peaceable fruit of righteousness unto
them which are exercised thereby." But what we are particularly led
to observe by the subject of this discourse is, that the wrath of man,
or the violence of the oppressor that praiseth God in this respect, it
has a peculiar tendency to alarm the secure conscience, to convince
and humble the obstinate sinner. This is plain from the nature of the
thing, and from the testimony of experience. Public calamities, particularly the destroying sword, is so awful that it cannot but have a
powerful influence in leading men to consider the presence and the
power of God. It threatens them not only in themselves, but touches
them in all that is dear to them, whether relations or possessions. The
prophet Isaiah says, Is. xxvi. 8, 9. "Yea, in the way of thy judgments,
O Lord, have we waited for thee, for when thy judgments are in
the earth, the inhabitants of the world will learn righteousness." He
considers it as the most powerful mean of alarming the secure and
subduing the obstinate. Is. xxvi. 11. "Lord when thy hand is lifted up,
they will not see, but they shall see and be ashamed for their envy at
the people, yea the fire of thine enemies shall devour them." It is also
sometimes represented as a symptom of a hopeless and irrecoverable
state, when public judgments have no effect. Thus says the prophet
Jeremiah, Jer. v. 3. "O Lord, are not thine eyes upon the truth? thou
hast stricken them, but they have not grieved; thou hast consumed
them, but they have refused to receive correction: they have made
their faces harder than a rock, they have refused to return." We can
easily see in the history of the children of Israel, how severe strokes
brought them to submission and penitence, Ps. lxxviii. 34, 35. "When
he slew them, then they sought him, and they returned and inquired
early after God, and they remembered that God was their rock, and
the high God their redeemer."

Both nations in general, and private persons, are apt to grow
remiss and lax in a time of prosperity and seeming security; but when
their earthly comforts are endangered or withdrawn, it lays them under
a kind of necessity to seek for something better in their place. Men
must have comfort from one quarter or another. When earthly things

are in a pleasing and promising condition, too many are apt to find their rest, and be satisfied with them as their only portion. But when the vanity and passing nature of all created comfort is discovered, they are compelled to look for something more durable as well as valuable. What therefore, can be more to the praise of God, than that when a whole people have forgotten their resting place, when they have abused their privileges, and despised their mercies, they should by distress and suffering be made to hearken to the rod, and return to their duty?

There is an inexpressible depth and variety in the judgments of God, as in all his other works; but we may lay down this as a certain principle, that if there were no sin, there could be no suffering. Therefore they are certainly for the correction of sin, or for the trial, illustration, and perfecting of the grace and virtue of his own people. We are not to suppose, that those who suffer most, or who suffer soonest, are therefore more criminal than others. Our Saviour himself thought it necessary to give a caution against this rash conclusion, as we are informed by the evangelist Luke, Luke xiii. 1. "There were present at that season some that told him of the Galileans, whose blood Pilate had mingled with their sacrifices. And Jesus answering said unto them, Suppose ye that these Galileans were sinners above all the Galileans, because they suffered such things? I tell you nay, but except ye repent, ye shall all likewise perish." I suppose we may say with sufficient warrant, that it often happens, that those for whom God hath designs of the greatest mercy, are first brought to the trial, that they may enjoy in due time the salutary effect of the unpalatable medicine.

I must also take leave to observe, and I hope no pious humble sufferer will be unwilling to make the application, that there is often a discernible mixture of sovereignty and righteousness in providential dispensations. It is the prerogative of God to do what he will with his own, but he often displays his justice itself, by throwing into the furnace those, who though they may not be visibly worse than others, may yet have more to answer for, as having been favored with more distinguished privileges, both civil and sacred. It is impossible for us to make a just and full comparison of the character either of persons or nations, and it would be extremely foolish for any to attempt it, either for increasing their own security, or impeaching the justice of the Supreme Ruler. Let us therefore neither forget the truth, nor go beyond it. "His mercy fills the earth" [Ps. 119:64]. He is also "known by the judgment which he executeth" [Ps. 9:17]. The wrath of man in its most tempestuous rage, fulfills his will, and finally promotes the good of his chosen.

3. The wrath of man praiseth God, as he sets bounds to it, or restrains it by his providence, and sometimes makes it evidently a mean of promoting and illustrating his glory.

There is no part of divine providence in which a greater beauty and majesty appears, than when the Almighty Ruler turns the counsels of wicked men into confusion, and makes them militate against themselves. If the psalmist may be thought to have had a view in this text to the truths illustrated in the two former observations, there is no doubt at all that he had a particular view to this, as he says in the latter part of the verse, "the remainder of wrath shalt thou restrain." The scripture abounds with instances, in which the designs of oppressors were either wholly disappointed, or in execution fell far short of the malice of their intention, and in some they turned out to the honor and happiness of the persons or the people, whom they were intended to destroy. We have an instance of the first of these in the history to which my text relates. We have also an instance in Esther, in which the most mischievous designs of Haman, the son of Hammedatha the Agagite against Mordecai the Jew, and the nation from which he sprung, turned out at last to his own destruction, the honor of Mordecai, and the salvation and peace of his people.

From the New Testament I will make choice of that memorable event on which the salvation of believers in every age rests as its foundation, the death and sufferings of the Son of God. This the great adversary and all his agents and instruments prosecuted with unrelenting rage. When they had blackened him with slander, when they scourged him with shame, when they had condemned him in judgment, and nailed him to the cross, how could they help esteeming their victory complete? But oh the unsearchable wisdom of God! they were but perfecting the great design laid for the salvation of sinners. Our blessed Redeemer by his death finished his work, overcame principalities and powers, and made a shew of them openly, triumphing over them in his cross. With how much justice do the apostles and their company offer this doxology to God, "They lift up their voice with one accord, and said, Lord thou art God which hast made heaven and earth, and the sea, and all that in them is; Who by the mouth of thy servant David hast said, Why did the Heathen rage, and the people imagine vain things? The kings of the earth stood up, and the rulers were gathered together against the Lord, and against his Christ. For of a truth, against thy holy child Jesus, whom thou hast anointed, both Herod and Pontius Pilate, with the Gentiles, and the people of Israel were gathered together, for to do whatsoever thy hand and thy counsel determined before to be done." Acts iv. 24. 28.

In all after ages, in conformity to this, the deepest laid contrivances of the prince of darkness, have turned out to the confusion of their author; and I know not, but considering his malice and pride, this perpetual disappointment, and the superiority of divine wisdom, may be one great source of his suffering and torment. The cross hath still been the banner of truth, under which it hath been carried through the world. Persecution has been but as the furnace to the gold, to purge it of its dross, to manifest its purity, and increase its lustre. It was taken notice of very early, that the blood of the martyrs was the seed of christianity; the more abundantly it was shed, the more plentifully did the harvest grow.

So certain has this appeared, that the most violent infidels, both of early and later ages, have endeavored to account for it, and have observed that there is a spirit of obstinacy in man which inclines him to resist violence, and that severity doth but increase opposition, be the cause what it will. They suppose that persecution is equally proper to propagate truth and error. This though in part true, will by no means generally hold. Such an apprehension, however, gave occasion to a glorious triumph of divine providence of an opposite kind, which I must shortly relate to you. One of the Roman emperors, Julian, surnamed the apostate, perceiving how impossible it was to suppress the gospel by violence, endeavored to extinguish it by neglect and scorn. He left the Christians unmolested for sometime, but gave all manner of encouragement to those of opposite principles, and particularly to the

Jews, out of hatred to the Christians; and that he might bring public disgrace upon the Galileans, as he affected to stile them, he encouraged the Jews to rebuild the temple of Jerusalem, and visibly refute the prophecy of Christ, that it should lie under perpetual desolation. But this profane attempt was so signally frustrated, that it served, as much as any one circumstance, to spread the glory of our Redeemer, and establish the faith of his saints. It is affirmed by some ancient authors, particularly by Ammianus Marcellinus, a heathen historian, that fire came out of the earth and consumed the workmen when laying the foundation. But in whatever way it was prevented, it is beyond all controversy, from the concurring testimony of heathens and Christians, that little or no progress was ever made in it, and that in a short time, it was entirely defeated.

It is proper here to observe, that at the time of the reformation, when religion began to revive, nothing contributed more to facilitate its reception and increase its progress than the violence of its persecutors. Their cruelty and the patience of the sufferers, naturally disposed men to examine and weigh the cause to which they adhered with so much constancy and resolution. At the same time also, when they were persecuted in one city, they fled to another, and carried the discoveries of popish fraud to every part of the world. It was by some of those who were persecuted in Germany, that the light of the reformation was brought so early into Britain.

The power of divine providence appears with the most distinguished lustre, when small and inconsiderable circumstances, and sometimes, the weather and seasons, have defeated the most formidable armaments, and frustrated the best concerted expeditions. Near two hundred years ago, the monarchy of Spain was in the height of its power and glory, and determined to crush the interest of the reformation. They sent out a powerful armament against Britain, giving it ostentatiously, and in my opinion profanely, the name of the Invincible Armada. But it pleased God so entirely to discomfit it by tempests, that a small part of it returned home, though no British force had been opposed to it at all.

We have a remarkable instance of the influence of small circumstances in providence in the English history. The two most remarkable persons in the civil wars, had earnestly desired to withdraw themselves from the contentions of the times, Mr. Hampden and Oliver Cromwell. They had actually taken their passage in a ship for New England, when by an arbitrary order of council they were compelled to remain at home. The consequence of this was, that one of them was the soul of the republican opposition to monarchical usurpation during the civil wars, and the other in the course of that contest, was the great instrument in bringing the tyrant to the block.

The only other historical remark I am to make, is, that the violent persecution which many eminent Christians met with in England from their brethren, who called themselves Protestants, drove them in great numbers to a distant part of the world, where the light of the gospel and true religion were unknown. Some of the American settlements, particularly those in New-England, were chiefly made by them; and as they carried the knowledge of Christ to the dark places of the earth, so they continue themselves in as great a degree of purity, of faith, and strictness of practice, or rather a greater, than is to be found in any protestant church now in the world. Does not the wrath of man in this instance praise God? Was not the accuser of the brethren, who stirs up their enemies, thus taken in his own craftiness, and his kingdom shaken by the very means which he employed to establish it.

II. Proceed now to the second general head, which was to apply the principles illustrated above to our present situation, by inferences of truth for your instruction and comfort, and by suitable exhortations to duty in this important crisis. And,

In the first place, I would take the opportunity on this occasion, and from this subject, to press every hearer to a sincere concern for his own soul's salvation. There are times when the mind may be expected to be more awake to divine truth, and the conscience more open to the arrows of conviction, than at others. A season of public judgment is of this kind, as appears from what has been already said. That curiosity and attention at least are raised in some degree, is plain from the unusual throng of this assembly. Can you have a clearer view of the sinfulness of your nature, than when the rod of the oppressor is lifted up, and when you see men putting on the habit of the warrior, and collecting on every hand the weapons of hostility and instruments of death? I do not blame your ardor in preparing for the resolute defence of your temporal rights. But consider I beseech you, the truly infinite importance of the salvation of your souls. Is it of much moment whether you and your children shall be rich or poor, at liberty or in bonds? Is it of much moment whether this beautiful country shall increase in fruitfulness from year to year, being cultivated by active industry, and possessed by independent freemen, or the scanty produce of the neglected fields shall be eaten up by hungry publicans, while the timid owner trembles at the tax gatherers approach? And is it of less moment my brethren, whether you shall be the heirs of glory or the heirs of hell? Is your state on earth for a few fleeting years of so much moment? And is it of less moment, what shall be your state through endless ages? Have you assembled together willingly to hear what shall be said on public affairs, and to join in imploring the blessing of God on the counsels and arms of the united colonies, and can you be unconcerned, what shall become of you for ever, when all the monuments of human greatness shall be laid in ashes, for "the earth *itself* and all the works that are therein shall be burnt up."

Wherefore my beloved hearers, as the ministry of reconciliation is committed to me, I beseech you in the most earnest manner, to attend to "the things that belong to your peace, before they are hid from your eyes." How soon and in what manner a seal shall be set upon the character and state of every person here present, it is impossible to know; for he who only can know does not think proper to reveal it. But you may rest assured that there is no time more suitable, and there is none so safe, as that which is present, since it is wholly uncertain whether any other shall be your's. Those who shall first fall in battle, have not many more warnings to receive. There are some few daring and hardened sinners who despise eternity itself, and set their Maker at defiance, but the far greater number by staving off their convictions to a more convenient season, have been taken unprepared, and thus eternally lost. I would therefore earnestly press the apostles exhortation, 2 Cor. vi. i, 2. "We then, as workers together with him, beseech you also, that ye receive not the grace of God in vain: For he saith, I have heard thee in a time accepted, and in the day of salvation have I succoured thee: Behold, now is the accepted time; behold, now is the day of salvation."

Suffer me to beseech you, or rather to give you warning, not to rest satisfied with a form of godliness, denying the power thereof. There can be no true religion, till there be a discovery of your lost state by nature and practice, and an unfeigned acceptance of Christ Jesus, as he is offered in the gospel. Unhappy they who either despise his mercy, or are ashamed of his cross! Believe it, "there is no salvation in any other. There is no other name under heaven given amongst men by which we must be saved." Unless you are united to him by a lively faith, not the resentment of a haughty monarch, but the sword of divine justice hangs over you, and the fulness of divine vengeance shall speedily overtake you. I do not speak this only to the heaven, daring profligate, or grovelling sensualist, but to every insensible secure sinner; to all those, however decent and orderly in their civil deportment, who live to themselves and have their part and portion in this life; in fine to all who are yet in a state of nature, for "except a man be born again, he cannot see the kingdom of God." The fear of man may make you hide your profanity: prudence and experience may make you abhor intemperance and riot; as you advance in life, one vice may supplant another and hold its place; but nothing less than the sovereign grace of God can produce a saving change of heart and temper, or fit you for his immediate presence.

2. From what has been said upon this subject, you may see what ground there is to give praise to God for his favors already bestowed on us, respecting the public cause. It would be a criminal inattention not to observe the singular interposition of Providence hitherto, in behalf of the American colonies. It is however impossible for me, in a single discourse, as well as improper at this time, to go through every step of our past transactions, I must therefore content myself with a few remarks. How many discoveries have been made of the designs of enemies in Britain and among ourselves, in a manner as unexpected to us as to them, and in such season as to prevent their effect? What surprising success has attended our encounters in almost every instance? Has not the boasted discipline of regular and veteran soldiers been turned into confusion and dismay, before the new and maiden courage of freemen, in defence of their property and right? In what great mercy has blood

been spared on the side of this injured country? Some important victories in the south have been gained with so little loss, that enemies will probably think it has been dissembled; as many, even of ourselves thought, till time rendered it undeniable. But these were comparatively of small moment. The signal advantage we have gained by the evacuation of Boston, and the shameful flight of the army and navy of Britain, was brought about without the loss of a man. To all this we may add, that the counsels of our enemies have been visibly confounded, so that I believe that I may say with truth, that there is hardly any step which they have taken, but it has operated strongly against themselves, and been more in our favor, than if they had followed a contrary course.

While we give praise to God the supreme disposer of all events, for his interposition in our behalf, let us guard against the dangerous error of trusting in, or boasting of an arm of flesh. I could earnestly wish, that while our arms are crowned with success, we might content ourselves with a modest ascription of it to the power of the Highest. It has given me great uneasiness to read some ostentatious, vaunting expressions in our news-papers, though happily I think, much restrained of late. Let us not return to them again. If I am not mistaken, not only the holy scriptures in general, and the truths of the glorious gospel in particular, but the whole course of providence, seem intended to abase the pride of man, and lay the vain-glorious in the dust. How many instances does history furnish us with, of those who after exulting over, and despising their enemies, were signally and shamefully defeated. The truth is, I believe, the remark may be applied universally, and we may say, that through the whole frame of nature, and the whole system of human life, that which promises most, performs the least. The flowers of finest colour seldom have the sweetest fragrance. The trees of quickest groweth or fairest form, are seldom of the greatest value or duration. Deep waters move with least noise. Men who think most are seldom talkative. And I think it holds as much in war as in any thing, that every boaster is a coward.

Pardon me, my brethren, for insisting so much upon this, which may seem but an immaterial circumstance. It is in my opinion of very great moment. I look upon ostentation and confidence to be a sort of outrage upon Providence, and when it becomes general, and infuses itself into the spirit of a people, it is a forerunner of destruction. How does Goliath the champion armed in a most formidable manner, express his disdain of David the stripling with his sling and his stone, 1 Sam. xvii. 42, 43, 44, 45. "And when the Philistine looked about and saw David, he disdained him: for he was but a youth, and ruddy, and of a fair countenance. And the Philistine said unto David, Am I a dog, that thou comest to me with staves? And the Philistine cursed David by his gods, and the Philistine said to David, come to me, and I will give thy flesh unto the fowls of the air, and to the beasts of the field." But how just and modest the reply? ["]Then said David to the Philistine, thou comest to me with a sword and with a spear, and with a shield, but I come unto thee in the name of the Lord of hosts, the God of the armies of Israel, whom thou hast defied." I was well pleased with a remark of this kind thirty years ago in a pamphlet, in which it was observed, that there was a great deal of profane ostentation in the names given to ships of war, as the Victory, the Valient, the Thunderer, the Dreadnought, the Terrible, the Firebrand, the Furnace, the Lightning, the Infernal, and many more of the same kind. This the author considered as a symptom of the national character and manners very unfavorable, and not likely to obtain the blessing of the God of heaven.

3. From what has been said you may learn what encouragement you have to put your trust in God, and hope for his assistance in the present important conflict. He is the Lord of hosts, great in might, and strong in battle. Whoever hath his countenance and approbation, shall have the best at last. I do not mean to speak prophetically, but agreeably to the analogy of faith, and the principles of God's moral government. Some have observed that true religion, and in her train, dominion, riches, literature, and arts, have taken their course in a slow and gradual manner, from east to west, since the earth was settled after the flood, and from thence forebode the future glory of America. I leave this as a matter rather of conjecture than certainty, but observe, that if your cause is just, if your principles are pure, and if your conduct is prudent, you need not fear the multitude of opposing hosts.

If your cause is just – you may look with confidence to the Lord and intreat him to plead it as his own. You are all my witnesses, that this is the first time of my introducing any political subject into the pulpit. At this season however, it is not only lawful but necessary, and I willingly embrace the opportunity of declaring my opinion without any hesitation, that the cause in which America is now in arms, is the cause of justice, of liberty, and of human nature. So far as we have hitherto proceeded, I am satisfied that the confederacy of the colonies, has not been the effect of pride, resentment, or sedition, but of a deep and general conviction, that our civil and religious liberties, and consequently in a great measure the temporal and eternal happiness of us and our posterity, depended on the issue. The knowledge of God and his truths have from the beginning of the world been chiefly, if not entirely, confined to those parts of the earth, where some degree of liberty and political justice were to be seen, and great were the difficulties with which they had to struggle from the imperfection of human society, and the unjust decisions of usurped authority. There is not a single instance in history in which civil liberty was lost, and religious liberty preserved entire. If therefore we yield up our temporal property, we at the same time deliver the conscience into bondage.

You shall not, my brethren, hear from me in the pulpit, what you have never heard from me in conversation, I mean railing at the king personally, or even his ministers and the parliament, and people of Britain, as so many barbarous savages. Many of their actions have probably been worse than their intentions. That they should desire unlimited dominion, if they can obtain or preserve it, is neither new nor wonderful. I do not refuse submission to their unjust claims, because they are corrupt or profligate, although probably many of them are so, but because they are men, and therefore liable to all the selfish bias inseparable from human nature. I call this claim unjust, of making laws to bind us in all cases whatsoever, because they are separated from us, independent of us, and have an interest in opposing us. Would any man who could prevent it, give up his estate, person, and family, to the disposal of his neighbour, although he had liberty to chuse the wisest and the best master? Surely not. This is the true and proper hinge of the controversy between Great-Britain and America. It is however to be added, that such is their distance from us, that a wise and prudent administration of our affairs is as impossible as the claim of authority is unjust. Such is and must be their ignorance of the state of things here, so much time must elapse before an error can be seen and remedied, and so much injustice and partiality must be expected from the arts and misrepresentation of interested persons, that for these colonies to depend wholly upon the legislature of Great-Britain, would be like many other oppressive connexions, injury to the master, and ruin to the slave.

The management of the war itself on their part, would furnish new proof of this, if any were needful. Is it not manifest with what absurdity and impropriety they have conducted their own designs? We had nothing so much to fear as dissension, and they have by wanton and unnecessary cruelty forced us into union. At the same time to let us see what we have to expect, and what would be the fatal consequence of unlimited submission, they have uniformly called those acts *lenity*, which filled this whole continent with resentment and horror. The ineffable disdain expressed by our fellow subject, in saying, "That he would not harken to America, till she was at his feet," has armed more men, and inspired more deadly rage, than could have been done by laying waste a whole province with fire and sword. Again we wanted not numbers, but time, and they sent over handful after handful till we were ready to oppose a multitude greater than they have to send. In fine, if there was one place stronger than the rest, and more able and willing to resist, there they made the attack, and left the others till they were duly informed, completely incensed, and fully furnished with every instrument of war.

I mention these things, my brethren, not only as grounds of confidence in God, who can easily overthrow the wisdom of the wise, but as decisive proofs of the impossibility of these great and growing states, being safe and happy when every part of their internal polity is dependant on Great Britain. If, on account of their distance, and ignorance of our situation, they could not conduct their own quarrel with propriety for one year, how can they give direction and vigor to every department of our civil constitutions from age to age? There are fixed bounds to every human thing. When the branches of a tree grow very large and weighty, they fall off from the trunk. The sharpest sword will not pierce when it cannot reach. And there is a certain distance from the seat of government, where an attempt to rule will either produce tyranny and helpless subjection, or provoke resistance and effect a separation.

I have said, if your principles are pure – the meaning of this is, if your present opposition to the claims of the British ministry does not arise from a seditious and turbulent spirit, or a wanton contempt of legal authority; from a blind and factious attachment to particular persons or parties; or from a selfish rapacious disposition, and a desire to turn public confusion to private profit – but from a concern for the interest of your country, and the safety of yourselves and your posterity. On this subject I cannot help observing, that though it would be a miracle if there were not many selfish persons among us, and discoveries now and then made of mean and interested transactions, yet they have been comparatively inconsiderable both in number and effect. In general, there has been so great a degree of public spirit, that we have much more reason to be thankful for its vigor and prevalence, than to wonder at the few appearances of dishonesty or disaffection. It would be very uncandid to ascribe the universal ardor that has prevailed among all ranks of men, and the spirited exertions in the most distant colonies, to any thing else than public spirit. Nor was there ever perhaps in history so general a commotion from which religious differences have been so entirely excluded. Nothing of this kind has as yet been heard, except of late in the absurd, but malicious and detestable attempts of our few remaining enemies to introduce them. At the same time I must also, for the honor of this country observe, that though government in the ancient forms has been so long unhinged, and in some colonies not sufficient care taken to substitute another in its place; yet has there been, by common consent, a much greater degree of order and public peace, than men of reflection and experience foretold or expected. From all these circumstances I conclude favorably of the principles of the friends of liberty, and do earnestly exhort you to adopt and act upon those which have been described, and resist the influence of every other.

Once more, if to the justice of your cause, and the purity of your principles, you add prudence in your conduct, there will be the greatest reason to hope, by the blessing of God, for prosperity and success. By prudence in conducting this important struggle, I have chiefly in view union, firmness, and patience. Every body must perceive the absolute necessity of union. It is indeed in every body's mouth, and therefore instead of attempting to convince you of its importance, I will only caution you against the usual causes of division. If persons of every rank, instead of implicitly complying with the orders of those whom they themselves have chosen to direct, will needs judge every measure over again, when it comes to be put in execution; if different classes of men intermix their little private views, or clashing interest with public affairs, and marshal into parties, the merchant against the landholder, and the landholder against the merchant; if local provincial pride and jealousy arise, and you allow yourselves to speak with contempt of the courage, character, manners, or even language of particular places, you are doing a greater injury to the common cause, than you are aware of. If such practices are admitted among us, I shall look upon it as one of the most dangerous symptoms, and if they become general, a presage of approaching ruin.

By firmness and patience, I mean a resolute adherence to your duty, and laying your account with many difficulties, as well as occasional disappointments. In a former part of this discourse, I have cautioned you against ostentation and vain glory. Be pleased farther to observe that extremes often beget one another, the same persons who exult extravagantly on success, are generally most liable to despondent timidity on every little inconsiderable defeat. Men of this character are the bane and corruption of every society or party to which they belong, but they are especially the ruin of an army, if suffered to continue in it. Remember the vicissitude of human things, and the usual course of providence. How often has a just cause been reduced to the lowest ebb, and yet when firmly adhered to, has become finally triumphant. I speak this now while the affairs of the colonies are in so prosperous a state, lest this propriety itself should render you less able to bear unexpected misfortunes – the sum of the whole is, that the blessing of God is only to be looked for by those who are not wanting in the discharge of their own duty. I would neither have you to trust in an arm of flesh, nor sit with folded hands and expect that miracles should be wrought in your defence – this is a sin which is in scripture stiled tempting God. In opposition to it, I would exhort you as Joab did the host of Israel, who, though he does not appear to have had a spotless character throughout, certainly in this instance spoke like a prudent general and a pious man. 2 Sam. x. 12. "Be of good courage, and let us behave ourselves valiantly for our people and for the cities of our God, and let the Lord do that which is good in his sight."

I shall now conclude this discourse by some exhortations to duty, founded upon the truths which have been illustrated above, and suited to the interesting state of this country at the present time; and,

1. Suffer me to recommend to you an attention to the public interest of religion, or in other words, zeal for the glory of God and the good of others. I have already endeavored to exhort sinners to repentance; what I have here in view is to point out to you the concern which every good man ought to take in the national character and manners, and the means which he ought to use for promoting public virtue, and bearing down impiety and vice. This is a matter of the utmost moment, and which ought to be well understood, both in its nature and principles. Nothing is more certain than that a general profligacy and corruption of manners make a people ripe for destruction. A good form of government may hold the rotten materials together for some time, but beyond a certain pitch, even the best constitution will be ineffectual, and slavery must ensue. On the other hand, when the manners of a nation are pure, when true religion and internal principles maintain their vigour, the attempts of the most powerful enemies to oppress them are commonly baffled and disappointed. This will be found equally certain, whether we consider the great principles of God's moral government, or the operation and influence of natural causes.

What follows from this? That he is the best friend to American liberty, who is most sincere and active in promoting true and undefiled religion, and who sets himself with the greatest firmness to bear down profanity and immorality of every kind. Whoever is an avowed enemy to God, I scruple not to call him an enemy to his country. Do not suppose, my brethren, that I mean to recommend a furious and angry zeal for the circumstantials of religion, or the contentions of one sect with another about their peculiar distinctions. I do not wish you to oppose any body's religion, but every body's wickedness. Perhaps there are few surer marks of the reality of religion, than when a man feels himself more joined in spirit to a true holy person of a different denomination, than to an irregular liver of his own. It is therefore your duty in this important and critical season to exert yourselves, every one in his proper sphere, to stem the tide of prevailing vice, to promote the knowledge of God, the reverence of his name and worship, and obedience to his laws.

Perhaps you will ask, what it is that you are called to do for this purpose farther than your own personal duty? I answer this itself when taken in its proper extent is not a little. The nature and obligation of visible religion is, I am afraid, little understood and less attended to.

Many from a real or pretended fear of the imputation of hypocrisy, banish from their conversation and carriage every appearance of respect and submission to the living God. What a weakness and meanness of spirit does it discover, for a man to be ashamed in the presence of his fellow sinners, to profess that reverence to almighty God which he inwardly feels: The truth is, he makes himself truly liable to the accusation which he means to avoid. It is as genuine and perhaps a more culpable hypocrisy to appear to have less religion than you really have, than to appear to have more. This false shame is a more extensive evil than is commonly apprehended. We contribute constantly, though insensibly, to form each others character and manners; and therefore, the usefulness of a strictly holy and conscientious deportment is not confined to the possessor, but spreads its happy influence to all that are within its reach. I need scarcely add, that in proportion as men are distinguished by understanding, literature, age, rank, office, wealth, or any other circumstance, their example will be useful on the one hand, or pernicious on the other.

But I cannot content myself with barely recommending a silent example. There is a dignity in virtue which is entitled to authority, and ought to claim it. In many cases it is the duty of a good man, by open reproof and opposition, to wage war with profaneness. There is a scripture precept delivered in very singular terms, to which I beg your attention; "Thou shalt not hate thy brother in thy heart, but shalt in any wise rebuke him, and not suffer sin upon him" [Lev. 19:17]. How prone are many to represent reproof as flowing from ill nature and surliness of temper? The spirit of God, on the contrary, considers it as the effect of inward hatred, or want of genuine love, to forbear reproof, when it is necessary or may be useful. I am sensible there may in some cases be a restraint from prudence, agreeably to that caution of our Saviour, "Cast not your pearls before swine, lest they trample them under their feet, and turn again and rent you." Of this every man must judge as well as he can for himself; but certainly, either by open reproof, or expressive silence, or speedy departure from such society, we ought to guard against being partakers of other men's sins.

To this let me add, that if all men are bound in some degree, certain classes of men are under peculiar obligations, to the discharge of this duty. Magistrates, ministers, parents, heads of families, and those whom age has rendered venerable, are called to use their authority and influence for the glory of God and the good of others. Bad men themselves discover an inward conviction of this, for they are often liberal in their reproaches of persons of grave characters or religious profession, if they bear with patience the profanity of others. Instead of enlarging on the duty of men in authority in general, I must particularly recommend this matter to those who have the command of soldiers inlisted for the defence of their country. The cause is sacred, and the champions for it ought to be holy. Nothing is more grieving to the heart of a good man, than to hear from those who are going to the field, the horrid sound of cursing and blasphemy; it cools the ardor of his prayers, as well as abates his confidence and hope in God. Many more circumstances affect me in such a case, than I can enlarge upon, or indeed easily enumerate at present; the glory of God, the interest of the deluded sinner, going like a devoted victim, and imprecating vengeance on his own head, as well as the cause itself committed to his care. We have sometimes taken the liberty to forebode the downfall of the British empire, from the corruption and degeneracy of the people. Unhappily the British soldiers have been distinguished among all the nations in Europe, for the most shocking profanity. Shall we then pretend to emulate them in this internal distinction, or rob them of the horrid privilege? God forbid. Let the officers of the army in every degree remember, that as military subjection, while it lasts, is the most complete of any, it is in their power greatly to restrain, if not wholly to banish, this flagrant enormity.

2. I exhort all who are not called to go into the field, to apply themselves with the utmost diligence to works of industry. It is in your power by this mean not only to supply the necessities, but to add to the strength of your country. Habits of industry prevailing in a society, not only increase its wealth, as their immediate effect, but they prevent the

introduction of many vices, and are intimately connected with sobriety and good morals. Idleness is the mother or nurse of almost every vice; and want, which is its inseparable companion, urges men on to the most abandoned and destructive courses. Industry, therefore is a moral duty of the greatest moment, absolutely necessary to national prosperity, and the sure way of obtaining the blessing of God. I would also observe, that in this, as in every other part of God's government, obedience to his will is as much a natural mean, as a meritorious cause, of the advantage we wish to reap from it. Industry brings up a firm and hardy race. He who is inured to the labor of the field, is prepared for the fatigues of a campaign. The active farmer who rises with the dawn and follows his team or plow, must in the end be an overmatch for those effeminate and delicate soldiers, who are nursed in the lap of self-indulgence, and whose greatest exertion is in the important preparation for, and tedious attendance on, a masquerade, or midnight ball.

3. In the last place, suffer me to recommend to you frugality in your families, and every other article of expence. This the state of things among us renders absolutely necessary, and it stands in the most immediate connexion both with virtuous industry, and active public spirit. Temperance in meals, moderation and decency in dress, furniture and equipage, have, I think, generally been characteristics of a distinguished patriot. And when the same spirit pervades a people in general, they are fit for every duty, and able to encounter the most formidable enemy. The general subject of the preceding discourse has been the wrath of man praising God. If the unjust oppression of your enemies, which withholds from you many of the usual articles of luxury and magnificence, shall contribute to make you clothe yourselves and your children with the works of your own hands, and cover your tables with the salutary productions of your own soil, it will be a new illustration of the same truth, and a real happiness to yourselves and your country.

I could wish to have every good thing done from the purest principles and the noblest views. Consider, therefore, that the Christian character, particularly the self-denial of the gospel, should extend to your whole deportment. In the early times of Christianity, when adult converts were admitted to baptism, they were asked among other questions, Do you renounce the world, its shews, its pomp, and its vanities? I do. The form of this is still preserved in the administration of baptism, where we renounce the devil, the world, and the flesh. This certainly implies not only abstaining from acts of gross intemperance and excess, but a humility of carriage, a restraint and moderation in all your desires. The same thing, as it is suitable to your Christian profession, is also necessary to make you truly independent in yourselves, and to feed the source of liberality and charity to others, or to the public. The riotous and wasteful liver, whose craving appetites make him constantly needy, is and must be subject to many masters, according to the saying of Solomon, "The borrower is servant to the lender" [Prov. 22:7]. But the frugal and moderate person, who guides his affairs with discretion, is able to assist in public counsels by a free and unbiassed judgment, to supply the wants of his poor brethren, and sometimes, by his estate and substance to give important aid to a sinking country.

Upon the whole, I beseech you to make a wise improvement of the present threatening aspect of public affairs, and to remember that your duty to God, to your country, to your families, and to yourselves, is the same. True religion is nothing else but an inward temper and outward conduct suited to your state and circumstances in providence at any time. And as peace with God and conformity to him, adds to the sweetness of created comforts while we possess them, so in times of difficulty and trial, it is in the man of piety and inward principle, that we may expect to find the uncorrupted patriot, the useful citizen, and the invincible soldier. God grant that in America true religion and civil liberty may be inseparable, and that the unjust attempts to destroy the one, may in the issue tend to the support and establishment of both.

Hebraic Source

John Witherspoon's sermon was crafted as a meditation on Psalm 76, which he took to be a song of thanksgiving offered after Sennacherib's vastly superior army was miraculously defeated while besieging Jerusalem. He dwelled on the connections between war and divine providence, especially as evoked by verse 10 [11], but concluded that though divine providence can be seen working on the American side, everyone must perform their duty and should not expect miracles.

Psalm 76

(א) לַמְנַצֵּחַ בִּנְגִינֹת מִזְמוֹר לְאָסָף שִׁיר.

(ב) נוֹדָע בִּיהוּדָה אֱ־לֹהִים בְּיִשְׂרָאֵל גָּדוֹל שְׁמוֹ.

(ג) וַיְהִי בְשָׁלֵם סוּכּוֹ וּמְעוֹנָתוֹ בְצִיּוֹן.

(ד) שָׁמָּה שִׁבַּר רִשְׁפֵי קָשֶׁת מָגֵן וְחֶרֶב וּמִלְחָמָה סֶלָה.

(ה) נָאוֹר אַתָּה אַדִּיר מֵהַרְרֵי טָרֶף.

(ו) אֶשְׁתּוֹלְלוּ אַבִּירֵי לֵב נָמוּ שְׁנָתָם וְלֹא מָצְאוּ כָל אַנְשֵׁי חַיִל יְדֵיהֶם.

(ז) מִגַּעֲרָתְךָ אֱ־לֹהֵי יַעֲקֹב נִרְדָּם וְרֶכֶב וָסוּס.

(ח) אַתָּה נוֹרָא אַתָּה וּמִי יַעֲמֹד לְפָנֶיךָ מֵאָז אַפֶּךָ.

(ט) מִשָּׁמַיִם הִשְׁמַעְתָּ דִּין אֶרֶץ יָרְאָה וְשָׁקָטָה.

(י) בְּקוּם לַמִּשְׁפָּט אֱ־לֹהִים לְהוֹשִׁיעַ כָּל עַנְוֵי אֶרֶץ סֶלָה.

(יא) כִּי חֲמַת אָדָם תּוֹדֶךָּ שְׁאֵרִית חֵמֹת תַּחְגֹּר.

(יב) נִדְרוּ וְשַׁלְּמוּ לַה' אֱ־לֹהֵיכֶם כָּל סְבִיבָיו יֹבִילוּ שַׁי לַמּוֹרָא.

(יג) יִבְצֹר רוּחַ נְגִידִים נוֹרָא לְמַלְכֵי אָרֶץ.

[1] [1-2] (To the chief Musician on Neginoth, A Psalm or Song of Asaph.) In Judah is God known: his name is great in Israel.

[2] [3] In Salem also is his tabernacle, and his dwelling place in Zion.

[3] [4] There brake he the arrows of the bow, the shield, and the sword, and the battle. Selah.

[4] [5] Thou art more glorious and excellent than the mountains of prey.

[5] [6] The stouthearted are spoiled, they have slept their sleep: and none of the men of might have found their hands.

[6] [7] At thy rebuke, O God of Jacob, both the chariot and horse are cast into a dead sleep.

[7] [8] Thou, even thou, art to be feared: and who may stand in thy sight when once thou art angry?

[8] [9] Thou didst cause judgment to be heard from heaven; the earth feared, and was still,

[9] [10] When God arose to judgment, to save all the meek of the earth. Selah.

[10] [11] Surely the wrath of man shall praise thee: the remainder of wrath shalt thou restrain.

[11] [12] Vow, and pay unto the Lord your God: let all that be round about him bring presents unto him that ought to be feared.

[12] [13] He shall cut off the spirit of princes: he is terrible to the kings of the earth.

SAMUEL LANGDON, "THE REPUBLIC OF THE ISRAELITES, AN EXAMPLE TO THE AMERICAN STATES" (1788)

Samuel Langdon (1723–1797) was in the Harvard class of the other famous Samuel of his generation, Samuel Adams. He served as president of Harvard from 1774 to 1780, during the hard days of the Revolution. He was rather unhappy with the

job and glad to leave in order to return to the pulpit in New Hampshire, where he preached for the remaining seventeen years of his life. The following speech was given as an election sermon in 1788. Throughout the Revolution, Americans continued to see themselves in a biblical mold. The following sermon by Samuel Langdon is only the most explicit example of this, but it is one among many.[4]

I think myself happy that, after reiterated invitations from this honourable court, I am at length permitted by divine providence, though under peculiar difficulties, and in the decline of life, to appear in this place, and speak on this public occasion, when the principal officers of government are to be appointed to their several departments, according to the suffrages of the people. I will endeavor to give due honor to the rulers of the people, while I declare, with simplicity of heart and honest freedom, the admonitions which the great Lord of the universe gives; and offer my best thoughts as to the general administration of public affairs, and the way to secure the prosperity and happiness of a nation.

There is a remarkable paragraph in the sacred writings, which may be very well accommodated to my present purpose, and merits particular attention. You have it in Deuteronomy, IV, 5–8.

Behold, I have taught you statutes and judgments, even as the Lord my God commanded me, that ye should do so in the land whither ye go to possess it. Keep therefore and do them; for this is your wisdom and your understanding in the sight of the nations, who shall hear all these statutes, and say, surely this great nation is a wise and understanding people: for what nation is there so great, which hath God so nigh unto them as the Lord our God is in all things that we call upon him for? and what nation is there so great, which hath statutes and judgments so righteous as all this law which I set before you this day.

Here Moses recommends to Israel the strict observance of all the laws which he had delivered to them by God's command, relating

4. See also Abiel Abbot's sermon, *Traits of Resemblance in the People of the United States of America to Ancient Israel.*

both to their civil polity and religion, as the sure way to raise their reputation high among all nations as a wise and understanding people; because no other nation was blessed with such excellent national laws, or the advantage of applying to the oracle of the living God, and praying to him in all difficulties, with assurance that all their requests would be answered.

As to every thing excellent in their constitution of government, except what was peculiar to them as a nation separated to God from the rest of mankind, the Israelites may be considered as a pattern to the world in all ages; and from them we may learn what will exalt our character, and what will depress and bring us to ruin.

Let us therefore look over their constitution and laws, enquire into their practice, and observe how their prosperity and fame depended on their strict observance of the divine commands both as to their government and religion.

They had both a civil and military establishment under divine direction, and a complete body of judicial laws drawn up and delivered to them by Moses in God's name. They had also a form of religious worship, by the same authority, minutely prescribed, designed to preserve among them the knowledge of the great Creator of the Universe, and teach them to love and serve him; while idolatry prevailed through the rest of the world: and this religion contained not only a public ritual, but a perfect, though very concise, system of morals, comprehended in ten commands, which require the perfection of godliness, benevolence, and rectitude of conduct.

When first the Israelites came out from the bondage of Egypt, they were a multitude without any other order than what had been kept up, very feebly, under the ancient patriarchal authority. They were suddenly collected into a body under the conduct of Moses, without any proper national or military regulation. Yet in the short space of about three months after they had passed the red sea, they were reduced into such civil and military order, blended together by the advice of Jethro, as was well adapted to their circumstances in the wilderness while destitute of property. Able men were chosen out of all their tribes, and made captains and rulers of thousands, hundreds, fifties and tens: and these commanded them as military officers, and acted as judges in matters of common controversy.

But the great thing wanting was a permanent constitution, which might keep the people peaceable and obedient while in the desert, and after they had gained possession of the promised land. Therefore, upon the complaint of Moses that the burden of government was too heavy for him, God commanded him to bring seventy men, chosen from among the elders and officers, and present them at the tabernacle; and there he endued them with the same spirit which was in Moses, that they might bear the burden with him. Thus a senate was evidently constituted, as necessary for the future government of the nation, under a chief commander. And as to the choice of this senate, doubtless the people were consulted, who appear to have had a voice in all public affairs from time to time, the whole congregation being called together on all important occasions: the government therefore was a proper republic.

And beside this general establishment, every tribe had elders and a prince according to the patriarchal order, with which Moses did not interfere; and these had an acknowledged right to meet and consult together, and with the consent of the congregation do whatever was necessary to preserve good order, and promote the common interest of the tribe. So that the government of each tribe was very similar to the general government. There was a president and senate at the head of each, and the people assembled and gave their voice in all great matters: for in those ages the people in all republics were entirely unacquainted with the way of appointing delegates to act for them, which is a very excellent modern improvement in the management of republics.

Moreover, to complete the establishment of civil government, courts were to be appointed in every walled city, after their settlement in Canaan, and elders most distinguished for wisdom and integrity were to be made judges, ready always to sit and decide the common controversies within their respective jurisdictions. The people had a right likewise to appoint such other officers as they might think necessary for the more effectual execution of justice, according to that order given in Deut. 16. 18, 19.

Judges and officers shalt thou make thee in all thy gates which the Lord thy God giveth thee throughout thy tribes; and they shall judge the people with just judgment: thou shalt not wrest judgment; thou shalt not respect persons, neither take a gift; for a gift doth blind the eyes of the wise, and pervert the words of the righteous.

But from these courts an appeal was allowed in weighty causes to higher courts appointed over the whole tribe, and in very great and difficult cases to the supreme authority of the general senate and chief magistrate.

A government, thus settled on republican principles, required laws; without which it must have degenerated immediately into aristocracy, or absolute monarchy. But God did not leave a people, wholly unskilled in legislation, to make laws for themselves: he took this important matter wholly into his own hands, and beside the moral laws of the two tables, which directed their conduct as individuals, gave them by Moses a complete code of judicial laws. They were not numerous indeed, but concise and plain, and easily applicable to almost every controversy which might arise between man and man, and every criminal case which might require the judgment of the court. Of these some were peculiarly adapted to their national form, as divided into tribes and families always to be kept distinct; others were especially suited to the peculiar nature of the government as a theocracy, God himself being eminently their king, and manifesting himself among them in a visible manner, by the cloud of glory in the tabernacle and temple. This was the reason why blasphemy, and all obstinate disobedience to his laws, were considered as high treason, and punished with death; especially idolatry, as being a crime against the fundamental principles of the constitution. But far the greater part of the judicial laws were founded on the plain immutable principles of reason, justice, and social virtue; such as are always necessary for civil society. Life and property were well guarded, and punishments were equitably adapted to the nature of every crime: in particular, murder stands foremost among capital crimes, and is defined with such precision, and so clearly distinguished from all cases of accidental and undesigned killing, that the innocent were in no danger of punishment, and the guilty could not escape. And if we still pay regard to this divine law, which is evidently founded on reason and justice, the modern distinction of manslaughter must be rejected as a popish invention, contrived and added in times when superstition reigned and claimed a power above all laws. These laws were sufficient for a nation which had but little commerce abroad; especially as the oracle of Jehovah might be consulted in all cases of a very extraordinary nature.

Let us now consider the national worship which God established among his people; on which their obedience to the moral law very much depended: for unless they paid constant reverence and homage to their God, agreeable to his nature and will, they would soon break loose from all other obligations to morality.

Now as to their ritual; however contemptible, and even ridiculous, it may seem to men whose ideas are all modern, and who proudly contemn divine revelation; and notwithstanding it is now abrogated by a far more glorious revelation of grace and truth by Jesus Christ; no religious institution could be more perfectly accommodated to those early ages of the world, and the situation of the Israelites in the midst of idolaters, or better prepare the way for the truth and mercy of the gospel. In those ages the minds of men were not sufficiently cultivated to receive that religion which is spiritual and simple, detached from sensible objects, and destitute of worldly grandeur. Other nations worshipped their gods with an endless variety of superstitious rites, a multitude of costly sacrifices, and all kinds of external pomp, which they fancied would be acceptable to deities to whom they attributed the imperfections and even the worst vices of men. Their worship gratified all the senses, was accommodated to every passion and lust, and indulgent to gross immoralities; it not only captivated vulgar minds, but bound the greatest heroes, politicians, and philosophers, fast in the chains of superstition. Therefore it was necessary that the worship of the true God should not be destitute of that splendour which, in those ages, struck the minds of men with awe and reverence. Without some magnificence the best religion would have appeared contemptible in the view of the world; and the Israelites themselves, dazzled with the pageantry of idols, would almost inevitably have been captivated; as, notwithstanding every guard which could be placed about them, we find the fashion of the rest of the world had surprising power over them. But the ceremonies of worship which God commanded his people to observe, were not, like those of the heathen, inhuman, frantic, obscene, varied a thousand ways according to the different characters of their gods; no, but by infinite wisdom they were calculated to promote the knowledge of the divine perfections, and obedience to the laws of righteousness, and give the most encouraging hope in the goodness and mercy of God. The ritual of the Israelites was rational, sober, uniform, plainly intended to exhibit the majesty, purity, and mercy of the eternal king; to humble men before him under a continual sense of guilt; and to assure true penitents of free pardon by virtue of the appointed sacrifices, which were types of that one sacrifice which Christ has offered for the sins of the world. And to render their worship more striking in their own view; and in the eyes of the world, their tabernacle and temple, their priesthood with its ornaments, their solemn assemblies and great festivals, were decent and magnificent beyond every thing seen among the nations around.

How unexampled was this quick progress of the Israelites, from abject slavery, ignorance, and almost total want of order, to a national establishment perfected in all its parts far beyond all other kingdoms and states! from a mere mob, to a well regulated nation, under a government and laws far superior to what any other nation could boast!

It was a long time after the law of Moses was given before the rest of the world knew any thing of government by law. Where kings reigned their will was a law. Where popular governments were formed, the capricious humour of the multitude ordered every thing just according to present circumstances; or their senators and judges were left to act according to their best discretion. It was six hundred years after Moses before the Spartans, the most famous of the Grecian republics, received a very imperfect, and in some particulars very absurd code of laws from Lycurgus. After this feeble attempt of legislation, three hundred years more elapsed before Solon appeared and gave laws to Athens, though a city long famous for arms, arts, eloquence, and philosophy. And it was about five hundred years from the first founding of the celebrated Roman empire, and nearly three hundred years after Solon, before the first laws of that empire were imported from Greece in twelve tables, by ten embassadors sent there for that purpose. But even when that empire had attained the summit of glory, and legislation was carried to great perfection, however well adapted to a government so extensive and complicate their laws might be, they were far from being worthy to be compared with the laws of Israel, as to the security of life, liberty, property, and public morals: and as to their religion, which was from the beginning interwoven with the state, instead of receiving any greater perfection from the increase of knowledge, wealth and power, it only became a more abundant congeries of ridiculous and detestable superstitions. Moreover; when the Roman empire was overwhelmed and destroyed by an inundation of barbarous nations, and many kingdoms were erected in Europe out of its ruins by the conquerors, laws were extinct under the feudal system; the will of the barons was a law for their vassals; and but a few centuries have past since kings began to introduce law into their courts of justice. And now, though legislation has been carried to such perfection in Great Britain, that land of knowledge and liberty, yet in a political and judicial view the laws of that kingdom may be charged with many great faults, which ought not to be copied: particularly, the tediousness, voluminous bulk, intricacy, barbarous language, and uncertain operation of many of them as to equity, ought to be avoided by legislators who wish for an easy and speedy course of justice among a free people. And perhaps our own courts might be so reformed as to prevent cases of inconsiderable value, and easy decision, from rising through all the stages of the law. Against these imperfections good provision was made in the law of Moses, and it might be much for our advantage to pay greater attention to that example.

Upon a review of what has been said, must it not appear quite unaccountable, that the Israelites should so speedily attain to such an height of good policy and legislation, beyond all other nations? Are we not constrained to acknowlege an immediate interposition and direction of heaven? Had the unexperienced multitude been left to themselves to draw up a system of civil and military government for themselves, it would have been entirely beyond their abilities to comprehend so complicated a subject; they must have committed innumerable mistakes, in attempting to introduce and establish it; they would have been in danger of jarring opinions, tumults, and insurrections; and probably before the design could be effected, discouragement and confusion would have forced them to surrender into the hands of despotism. But their God provided every thing necessary for their happiness, and nothing more was left to their own wisdom than to submit to his authority, and adhere strictly to his commands: by this, their reputation among the nations would have been equal to the excellency of their laws.

But now you may say, Why then were they not universally celebrated? Why did not princes and politicians from all parts of the world visit them, to learn maxims of polity from so well regulated a nation? Why did not philosophers come, and enquire into that system of religion and morality which carried virtue to such an height of perfection? Surely a nation, of which all the parts were so firmly cemented, must be strong and formidable: a people, who enjoyed the most rational liberty, and yet were under the most voluntary and absolute subjection to authority, free from all the convulsions and revolutions which frequently arise from the raging folly of the populace, must become famous: a wise and impartial administration of justice, according to the most excellent laws, by which all were kept in perfect security and peace, could not but be admired: and the commerce of a people, whose morals were governed by the best precepts, whose word might be trusted, who practised no kind of fraud, and whose behaviour was always benevolent, sober, prudent, and sincere, must be highly valued by the world. Whereas on the contrary, the Israelites were often weak, distressed, and generally despised and hated by all their neighbours. The plain answer to this objection is – They never adhered in practice either to the principles of their civil polity or religion: but on their practice depended the prosperity and honor of the nation. They received their law from God, but they did not keep it. They neglected their government, corrupted their religion, and grew dissolute in their morals, and in such a situation no nation under heaven can prosper.

Let us view their state, in the first place, under the judges. Tho' the national senate was instituted for the assistance of Moses as captain-general and judge of the nation, and this was a plain intimation that in all succeeding times such a senate was necessary for the assistance of the supreme magistrate: yet after Joshua and the elders of his time were dead, it does not appear that they took the least care to fill their places. They left all the affairs of the nation to chance, or extraordinary providence, and had no chief commander, except when God in compassion to them in their troubles raised up judges for their deliverance. And as they suffered the general government to drop, we may well think them as careless of the government of the particular tribes. In each tribe, as we have observed, a government ought to have been kept up similar to the national authority, by the elders and prince of the tribe. But we find this remark repeatedly made in the book of Judges – "In those days there was no king in Israel, but every man did that which was right in his own eyes" [Judg. 17:6, 21:25] – that is in plain terms, there was no authority any where, but every man was left to act as he pleased. No wonder therefore if they were weak in council and war, and exposed on every side to the insults of their neighbours, being unable to unite in their own defence. This neglect of government was wholly inexcusable: for however they might plead, that Moses, and Joshua, and the seventy elders, were of God's immediate appointment, and that they had no warrant to fill up their places; they could not but know they had an undoubted right to provide for their own welfare, especially when there was so plain an intimation that the same government was to be continued. If they were at a loss what to do, they had the greatest oracle in the world among them, and they ought to have enquired of God, their king, how to proceed and what persons to choose. Nay, they were some times sensible enough of their right to appoint a chief commander, and even to make the command hereditary, as appears by the address to Gideon – "Rule thou over us; both thou, and thy son, and thy son's son also" [Judg. 8:22] – by the choice which the Shechemites made of Abimelech to be their king; and by Jephtha's bargain with the Gileadites to be their head and captain, if he fought for them against the Ammonites. By all this we may plainly see that the general neglect of government is to be charged as the fault of the people.

And now we cannot wonder if courts of justice ceased, when the higher powers of government were wanting. These courts, which should have been continued in every walled city, dwindled way and came to nothing; crimes were unpunished, and the most abominable vices spread their infection through all ranks. No law was executed to deter men from murders, robberies, rapes, or any other kind of wickedness. This is evident by the case of the Levite whose concubine was abused to death by the mob of Benjamites at Gibeah: the city in general discovered no disposition to do justice upon the offenders; there were no judges near, to whom complaint might be made; nay, it seems the whole tribe were ready to abett the crime rather than punish it; nor was there any authority in the nation to take cognizance of the matter; and therefore the Levite was obliged to take a method, shocking to humanity, in order to excite the indignation of the other tribes, and bring their forces against the Benjamites to their destruction.

We have also good reason to think the military affairs of the nation were not in a much better state than the civil. They could not wholly omit the care of their militia, because they were continually exposed to wars in their own defence. It was necessary to provide officers, and keep up some degree of discipline; but they were very deficient in this respect, especially as to superior command. In almost every battle, against the most contemptible of their neighbours, they were unsuccessful; and were ravaged, plundered, and brought under tribute by all in their turns, and delivered only when God mercifully interposed by raising up a general in an extraordinary way. On an alarm, instead of forming a regular army, they seem to have ran together suddenly from all quarters, without order, as if to stop a conflagration. Such disunited undirected force was never able to sustain a heavy attack, but gave every invader an easy victory.

But that which was the main force of all their disorder and misery, was their neglecting and corrupting that religion which God commanded. As long as those elders lived, who were with Joshua, and had seen all the great works of the Lord which he did for Israel, the people adhered to the worship of the true God as prescribed in the law: but when they were dead, the impressions which had been made by miracles wore off, as is natural; and they grew regardless of the worship of the sanctuary, gave scope to their own imaginations, and soon made a mixture of all the superstitions and idolatries of the heathen with the worship of Jehovah. They kept up no method of religious instruction; and as they grew more and more ignorant, they thought it too inconvenient to travel so often from all parts of the country, to offer sacrifices at the tabernacle, though it was very centrally placed at Shiloh, not much more than eighty miles distant from the remotest towns; but every man chose to worship nearer home: and so they made groves, and built altars for themselves, and soon set up images of Baal, Ashteroth, and other genteel deities which their neighbours worshipped. By these idols, however, they pretended to worship the true God, and brought sacrifices after their own hearts; for they imagined that all kinds of religion came much to the same thing, and whether precisely agreeable to the command or not, would be acceptable, if they were sincere. Thus Micah made images, and procured a priest in his own house, which the children of Dan afterwards took away, and fixed in their new conquered city, in the northern bounds of Canaan, where this idolatry continued until the ten tribes were carried into captivity; and Joash, the father of Gideon, had a grove, and an altar of Baal, for his own family; like-wise Gideon himself, though highly honoured of God in being the deliverer of Israel from the Midianites, made an ephod, which was soon the occasion of superstitious worship, and drew him and the people from attending at the tabernacle.

Now by the foregoing view of the general state of the nation during the time of the judges, we may plainly see the reason why, instead of rising to fame by the perfection of their polity, religion, and morals, their character sunk into contempt. But let us see whether they conducted better afterwards, under their kings.

It was their crime to demand such a king as was like the kings of other nations, i.e. a king with the same absolute power, to command all according to his own pleasure. In this view God only was their king, and the head of the nation was only to be his viceregent. Therefore as they had implicitly rejected the divine government, God gave them a king in his anger; the consequence of which was, the total loss of their republican form of government, and sad experience of the effects of despotic power. Indeed their religious establishment, which had been very much impaired in the days of the judges, was restored, and brought to its greatest glory, by David the most pious, and Solomon the wisest of kings; and during their reigns, the nation gained the height of grandeur; but no national senate was appointed, and the power of the kings continued to be despotic, and so the days of their prosperity were soon over. As soon as Rehoboam ascended the throne he openly avowed the most despotic principles, so that ten tribes revolted, and made Jeroboam their king. Jeroboam, out of policy, to prevent a reunion with Judah by means of the temple worship, placed two calves at the extremities of his kingdom, and persuaded the people to worship God by them instead of going to Jerusalem: and this false worship, together with a multitude of other idolatries introduced by this means, was the religion of the ten tribes, until they were captivated by the king of Assyria, and dispersed and lost among the nations. Nor did Rehoboam pay greater regard to the law of Moses; for he built high-places, and made images and groves on every high hill and under every green tree, and did according to all the abominations of the heathen; and in consequence of this, every kind of vice, and even sodomy, prevailed in the land. From this time the propensity of the people to idolatry increased, so that they readily followed the examples of succeeding bad kings, and it became a very difficult task for the best to make an effectual reformation. Nor is it to be wondered at that false religion so easily gained ground; for the people grew very ignorant: no care was taken to instruct them, in their several cities, in the law of God; but, being without teachers, they were very little acquainted with their own religious institutions. For this reason when good king Jehoshaphat resolved upon a reformation in church and state, after having taken a circuit thro' his kingdom to *"bring the people back to the Lord God of their fathers, he sent out some of his principal officers, with priests and levites, to teach the people in the cities of Judah; and these carried the book of the law with them, and went about throughout all the cities of Judah, and taught them that religion which God commanded by Moses"* [cf. II Chr. 17:7-9].

It likewise appears by what immediately follows this account of his proceedings, that there had been a long omission of the administration of justice in the cities; that no courts had been kept up by preceeding kings, or such as were corrupt, in which the judges paid little regard to law and equity: for the king set judges in the land, throughout all the fenced cities of Judah, city by city, and said unto the judges, take heed what ye do, for ye judge not for man but for the Lord, who is with you in the judgment: – *"wherefore now let the fear of Lord be upon you, take heed and do it, for there is no iniquity with the Lord our God, nor respect of persons, nor taking of gifts"* [II Chr. 19:5–7].

Repeated attempts were made by the few pious kings, to put a stop to the corruption of religion and morals; but all in vain; the people relapsed again and again into ignorance, idolatry, and wickedness: their vices had increased to the utmost degree of enormity in Jeremiah's time; and their complicated crimes at length brought upon them desolation and a long captivity.

And now let us just take a glance at their general state after the captivity in Babylon. When they returned to their own land they endeavored to conform their religion and government to the mosaic standard; idolatry was entirely purged out; they discovered great zeal for the law of their God and the instituted worship; they appointed a general senate of seventy elders, called by them the Sanhedrin, with a supreme magistrate at the head, for the government of the nation; and while their pious zeal continued they grew and prospered. But, according to the common course of things in the world, religion soon degenerated into mere formality, without proper regard to its principal intention, and became only a shadow of that delivered to their fathers; the affairs of state were badly administered, and the highest honors were gained by favor, bribery, or violence; hypocrisy was substituted in the room of the true fear of God, and the practice of righteousness; all the vices natural to mankind daily increased; and finally they filled up the measure of their sins by crucifying the Lord of Glory, and rejecting his gospel, for which they have been made monuments of the divine displeasure unto this day.

Therefore upon the whole view we see, that the Israelites never attained to that fame and dignity among the nations which their constitution encouraged them to expect, because they took little care to practice agreeably to the good statutes and judgments given them by Moses. Their constitution both of government and religion was excellent in writing, but was never exemplified in fact.

Application

And now, my fellow citizens, and much honored fathers of the State, you may be ready to ask "To what purpose is this long detail of antiquated history on this public occasion?" I answer – Examples are better than precepts; and history is the best instructor both in polity and morals. I have presented you with the portrait of a nation, highly favoured by heaven with civil and religious institutions, who yet, by not improving their advantages, forfeited their blessings, and brought contempt and destruction on themselves. If I am not mistaken, instead of the twelve tribes of Israel, we may substitute the thirteen states of the American union, and see this application plainly offering itself, viz. – That as God in the course of his kind providence hath given you an excellent constitution of government, founded on the most rational, equitable, and liberal principles, by which all that liberty is secured which a people can reasonably claim, and you are impowered to make righteous laws for promoting public order and good morals; and as he has moreover given you by his son Jesus Christ, who is far superior to Moses, a complete revelation of his will, and a perfect system of true religion, plainly delivered in the sacred writings; it will be your wisdom in the eyes of the nations, and your true interest and happiness, to conform your practice in the strictest manner to the excellent principles of your government, adhere faithfully to the doctrines and commands of the gospel, and practice every public and private virtue. By this you will increase in numbers, wealth, and power, and obtain reputation and dignity among the nations: whereas, the contrary conduct will make you poor, distressed, and contemptible.

The God of heaven hath not indeed visibly displayed the glory of his majesty and power before our eyes, as he came down in the sight of Israel on the burning mount; nor has he written with his own finger the laws of our civil polity: but the signal interpositions of divine providence, in saving us from the vengeance of a powerful irritated nation, from which we were unavoidably separated by their inadmissible claim of absolute parliamentary power over us; in giving us a Washington to be captain-general of our armies, in carrying us through the various distressing scenes of war and desolation, and making us twice triumphant over numerous armies, surrounded and captivated in the midst of their career; and finally giving us peace, with a large territory, and acknowledged independence; all these laid together fall little short of real miracles, and an heavenly charter of liberty for these United-States. And when we reflect, how wonderfully the order of these states was preserved when government was dissolved, or supported only by feeble props; with how much sobriety, wisdom, and unanimity they formed and received the diversified yet similar constitutions in the different states; with what prudence, fidelity, patience, and success, the Congress have managed the general government, under the great disadvantages of a very imperfect and impotent confederation; we cannot but acknowledge that God hath graciously patronized our cause, and taken us under his special care, as he did his ancient covenant people.

Or we may consider the hand of God in another view. Wisdom is the gift of God, and social happiness depends on his providential government; therefore, if these states have framed their constitutions with superior wisdom, and secured their natural rights, and all the advantages of society, with greater precaution than other nations, we may with good reason affirm that God hath given us our government; that he hath taught us good statutes and judgments, tending to make us great and respectable in the view of the world. Only one thing more remains to complete his favor toward us; which is, the establishment of a general government, as happily formed as our particular constitutions, for the perfect union of these states. Without this, all that we glory in is lost; but if this should be effected, we may say with the greatest joy, "*God hath done great things for us*" [Ps. 126:3]. The general form of such a constitution hath already been drawn up, and presented to the people, by a convention of the wisest and most celebrated patriots in the land: eight of the states have approved and accepted it, with full testimonies of joy: and if it passes the scrutiny of the whole, and recommends itself to be universally adopted, we shall have abundant reason to offer elevated thanksgivings to the supreme Ruler of the universe for a government completed under his direction.

Now our part is to make a wise improvement of what God grants us, and not neglect or despise our distinguishing privileges: for the best constitution, badly managed, will soon fall, and be changed into anarchy or tyranny. Without constant care of your families, you will have bad servants, and your estates will be wasted. So we must pay constant attention to the great family, if we desire to be a free and happy people.

The power in all our republics is acknowleged to originate in the people: it is delegated by them to every magistrate and officer; and to the people all in authority are accountable, if they deviate from their duty, and abuse their power. Even the man, who may be advanced to the chief command of these United States, according to the proposed constitution; whose office resembles that of a king in other nations, which has always been thought so sacred that they have had no conception of bringing a king before the bar of justice; even he depends on the choice of the people for his temporary and limited power, and will be liable to impeachment, trial, and disgrace for any gross misconduct. On the people, therefore, of these United States it depends whether wise men, or fools, good or bad men, shall govern them; whether they shall have righteous laws, a faithful administration of government, and permanent good order, peace, and liberty; or, on the contrary, feel insupportable burdens, and see all their affairs run to confusion and ruin.

Therefore, I will now lift up my voice, and cry aloud to the people; to the people of this state in particular, whom I will consider as present by their representatives and rulers, and the congregation here collected from various towns. RISE! RISE to fame among all nations, as a wise and understanding people! political life and death are set before you; be a free, numerous, well ordered, and happy people! The way has been plainly set before you; if you pursue it, your prosperity is sure; but if not, distress and ruin will overtake you.

Preserve your government with the utmost attention and solicitude, for it is the remarkable gift of heaven. From year to year be careful in the choice of your representatives, and all the higher powers of government. Fix your eyes upon men of good understanding, and known honesty; men of knowledge, improved by experience; men who fear God, and hate covetousness; who love truth and righteousness, and sincerely wish the public welfare. Beware of such as are cunning rather than wise; who prefer their own interest to every thing; whose judgment is partial, or fickle; and whom you would not willingly trust with your own private interests. When meetings are called for the choice of your rulers, do not carelessly neglect them, or give your votes with indifference, just as any party may persuade, or a sordid treat tempt you; but act with serious deliberation and judgment, as in a most important matter, and let the faithful of the land serve you. Let not men openly irreligious and immoral become your legislators; for how can you expect good laws to be made by men who have no fear of God before their eyes, and who boldly trample on the authority of his commands? And will not the example of their impiety and immorality defeat the efficacy of the best laws which can be made in favour of religion and virtue? If the legislative body are corrupt, you will soon have bad men for counsellors, corrupt judges, unqualified justices, and officers in every department who will dishonor their stations; the consequence of which will be murmurs and complaints from every quarter. Let a superior character point out the man who is to be your head; for much depends on his inspection and care of public affairs and the influence of his judgment, advice and conduct, although his power is circumscribed: in this choice therefore be always on your guard against parties, and the methods taken to make interest for unworthy men, and let distinguished merit always determine your vote. And when all places in government are filled with the best men you can find, behave yourselves as good subjects; obey the laws; cheerfully submit to such taxation as the necessities of the public call for; give tribute to whom tribute is due, custom to whom custom, fear to whom fear, and honor to whom honor, as the gospel commands you. Never give countenance to turbulent men, who wish to distinguish themselves, and rise to power, by forming combinations and exciting insurrections against government: for this can never be the right way to redress real grievances, since you may not only prefer complaints and petitions to the court, but have the very authority, which you think has been misused, in your own power, and may very shortly place it in other hands. How happy was it for this state, that the insurrection, attempted here two years ago, was so seasonably and with so little difficulty suppressed, when the neighbouring state was brought into such a difficult and critical situation by the distracted populace, and has now scarcely recovered from that violent political paroxysm.

I call upon you also to support schools in all your towns, that the rising generation may not grow up in ignorance. Grudge not any expence proportionate to your abilities. It is a debt you owe to your children, and that God to whom they belong; a necessary evidence of your regard for their present and future happiness, and of your concern to transmit the blessings you yourselves enjoy to future generations. The human mind without early and continual cultivation grows wild and savage: knowledge must be instilled as its capacities gradually enlarge, or it cannot expand and extend its sphere of activity. Without instruction men can have no knowledge but what comes from their own observation and experience, and it will be a long time before they can be acquainted even with things most necessary for the support and comfort of the present life. Leave your children untaught to read, write, cypher, &c. teach them no trade, or husbandry; let them grow up wholly without care; and they will be more fit for a savage than civil life, and whatever inheritance you may think to leave them will be of no advantage. But, on the contrary, train them up in the fear of God, in an acquaintance with his word, and all such useful knowledge as your abilities will allow, and they will soon know how to provide for themselves, perhaps may take care of their aged parents, and fill the various stations in life with honor and advantage. Look round and see the growing youth: they are to succeed in your stead; government and religion must be continued by them; from among these will shortly rise up our legislators, judges, ministers of the gospel, and officers of every rank. Can you think of this, and not promote schools, academies, and colleges? Can you leave the youth uninstructed in any thing which may prepare them to act their part well in the world? Will you suffer ignorance to spread its horrid gloom over the land? An ignorant people will easily receive idolatry for their religion, and must bow their necks to the tyrant's yoke, because they are incapable of using rational liberty. Will you then consign over your posterity to foolish and abominable superstitions instead of religion, and to be the slaves of despotism, when a small proportion of the produce of your labours will make them wise, free, and happy?

Will you hear me patiently a little farther, while I say one thing more of very great importance, which I dare not suppress. I call upon you to preserve the knowledge of God in the land, and attend to the revelation written to us from heaven. If you neglect or renounce that religion taught and commanded in the holy scriptures, think no more

of freedom, peace, and happiness; the judgments of heaven will per-
sue you. Religion is not a vain thing for you because it is your life:
it has been the glory and defence of New-England from the infancy
of the settlements; let it be also our glory and protection. I mean no
other religion than what is divinely prescribed, which God himself has
delivered to us with equal evidence of his authority, and even superior
to that given to Israel, and which he has as strictly commanded us to
receive and observe. The holy scriptures are given as the only rule of
our faith, worship and obedience, and if we are guided by this perfect
rule, we shall keep the way of truth and righteousness, and obtain the
heavenly glory. We are now no more at liberty to draw up schemes of
religion for ourselves, according to our own deceitful reasonings and
vain imaginations, or to comply with the traditions and commands of
men, or fall in with the refinements of human wisdom and the fashion-
able sentiments of the world, than Israel was to substitute modes of
serving God different from what he had expressly required. We must
believe what the Son of God, who made the worlds, and was sent by
the Father with a proclamation of mercy to mankind, has declared to
us. He died to redeem men from the servitude of sin, and reconcile
them to God that they may be raised to life eternal; and he is appointed
to be like a second Moses, the captain of our salvation to conduct us
to heaven: to him therefore we must hearken in all things. The principal doctrines of his gospel are quite simple, plain and important. He
teaches us that the commands of God reach to the inward thoughts,
principles, and affections of the heart, as well as the outward conduct,
and are as pure and perfect as the divine nature; that according to the
laws of his moral government all men universally are sinners, and must
repent in order to obtain mercy; that remission of sins is obtained only
by believing on his name, and through his blood shed for us on the
cross; that his disciples must receive his word, and obey whatsoever
he hath commanded, endeavoring to be holy in all manner of conversation and avoid all the vices and corruptions of the world; that there
will be a resurrection from the dead both of the just and unjust; and
a day of solemn judgment, when all mankind must give an account of
their conduct in this world, and receive their sentence from him whom
the Father hath constituted to be the judge; and that in consequence

of their sentence mankind will depart into very opposite states; the wicked into everlasting punishment, and the righteous into life eternal, the present visible system of nature being then dissolved in flames. In the belief of these plain truths, and that worship and obedience connected with them, the religion of Christians consists. As to worship, no multiplied forms, and punctilious ceremonies are prescribed, which only serve to throw a veil over the mind; no certain modes are made necessary; but we must worship God, who is a spirit, in spirit and in truth, by prayer and praise, with love and fear, hope and joy. For such worship christians are united into societies called churches; and are required to assemble every Lord's day, that they may glorify God with one heart and voice, and be instructed and edified by his word, and the two only ordinances of baptism and the Lord's supper; which are very simple, but well adapted to the nature and design of our religion.

The christian religion, therefore, is confined to no particular nation, sect, or denomination; but is designed to call all men to repentance and newness of life; to encourage their hope in the mercy of God, thro' the only mediator Jesus Christ; persuade them to the most cheerful, persevering obedience; and comfort them, under all the labours and sorrows of the world, and the natural dread of death, with the assurance of a glorious immortality. This religion may be believed and practised, so as to answer the main purposes of it, under the various forms in which christian churches now appear: just as the principal ends of civil government may be obtained under the various constitutions which have taken place in different nations, however one may be much more eligible than another.

Therefore, regard not men who are continually crying up their own sect, and employing their utmost zeal and art to proselyte men to their party: they aim to strengthen themselves by your numbers and purses, more than to save your souls. If any say, lo here is Christ! or lo there! go not after them: for wherever his word abides, there is Christ; in and by his word he is already with us, and dwells in the hearts of believers. Listen to no enthusiasts, who instead of enlightening confound your understandings; and substitute folly, nonsense, and hypocritical grimace, in the room of a clear manifestation of truth and conformity of heart and life to the gospel. Take heed of imbibing the licentious principles of men who affect to render all religion doubtful, by persuading you that every kind of religion is equally acceptable to God if a man is but sincere in it; for this renders revelation useless. Beware of receiving new opinions, which militate with the plain and obvious meaning of the word of Christ, however they may pretend to be clearer discoveries of truth, and more comfortable and beneficial to mankind: but adhere to the written word, taken in the most natural sense, without forced allegories, whimsical constructions, or torturing criticisms; especially hold fast those doctrines which meet your eye in almost every page of the new testament. Read and meditate in the word of God day and night, and diligently attend on the public ministrations which Christ hath appointed in his church; and consider that as a true church where the truth as it is in Jesus is preached, and his plain institutions observed, whatever the particular form or denomination may be, avoiding all contentions and uncharitable separations. Be earnest to procure ministers, who preach the uncorrupted doctrines of the gospel, in all your towns: let none of your parishes continue vacant thro' indifference, negligence, or covetousness; and never withhold from faithful ministers a comfortable support. When we look round and see so many churches destitute of teachers, contenting themselves in the total neglect of all divine institutions, have we not reason to fear that God is departing from us? And if our religion is given up, all the liberty we boast of will soon be gone; a profane and wicked people cannot hope for divine blessings, but it may be easily foretold that *"evil will befall them in the latter days"* [cf. Deut. 31:29].

While I thus earnestly exhort you to religion, it must be understood as equally an exhortation to every branch of morality; for without this all religion is vain. That excellent sentence of the wise king ought forever to be in our minds *"Righteousness exalteth a nation, but sin is the reproach of any people"* [Prov. 14:34]. Sobriety, good order, honesty, fidelity, industry, frugality, and the like virtues must prevail; public crimes against person or property must be restrained and punished; or a people cannot be happy. Therefore let all maintain rectitude of conduct, and practise every thing virtuous and praise-worthy among their neighbours, and be just and true in all their intercourse and commerce. Unite in assisting the government in the execution of all good laws: and let all the members of the body politic consider that their own happiness depends on the welfare of the whole.

My subject hath lead me into this long and earnest address to the people. But it suggests some things which may properly be addressed to this honorable court. Will you hear me patiently, while with the utmost respect, I say a few words to excite the wise reflections of your own minds.

You will consider that you assemble from time to time as fathers of the large family, which depends on you to take care of its general welfare, and that no local views ought to govern you, nor partial instructions of your constituents bind you to act contrary to the clear conviction or your own minds. You will be cautious of forming parties for any selfish purposes, and of being too hasty in determining important matters, or too slow in your proceedings when business is urgent. In order to form a wise judgment of every thing that comes before you, you are sensible of the propriety of examining things to the bottom, attending patiently to every argument on both sides, and asking conscience, rather than any friend, what ought to be done. Like frugal householders you will save all unnecessary expences, and take good care of the treasury; but not suffer the faithful servants of the state to be so stinted in their reward as to discourage them from their duty. Lay no grievous burdens on the people beyond their abilities; but take the earliest, easiest, and most righteous methods to reduce and pay off the public debt, unhappily involved in all the perplexities occasioned by boundless emissions of depreciating paper notes. Be liberal, yet frugal in grants of money, according to the exigencies of the public. Let no laws be wanting which good order, and the proper administration of government and justice require; but make no law which establisheth iniquity. And may I propose it, as worthy of your consideration, whether some reformation may not be necessary as to processes in our courts of justice: whether appeals from court to court are not allowed beyond reason and equity, in the plainest cases, and of too trivial value: by which some of our courts are made mere vehicles, justice is delayed, and the law made unnecessarily expensive, tedious and vexatious; and whether some method may not be thought of to determine the judgment of causes in lower or higher courts in proportion to their value and importance. I beg leave to say one word as to religion. With respect to articles of faith or modes of worship, civil authority have no right to establish religion. The people ought to choose their own ministers, and their own denomination, as our laws now permit them; but as far as religion is connected with the morals of the people, and their improvement in knowledge, it becomes of great importance to the state; and legislators may well consider it as part of their concern for the public welfare, to make provision that all the towns may be furnished with good teachers, that they may be impowered to make valid contracts, and that the fulfilment of such contracts should be secured against the fickle humours of men, who are always ready to shift from sect to sect, or make divisions in parishes that they may get free from all legal obligations to their ministers. Perhaps a little addition to the law already in force in this state might sufficiently secure the continuance of religious instruction, enlarge rather than diminish liberty of conscience, and prevent envyings, contentions, and crumbling into parties. Will you permit me now to pray in behalf of the people, that all the departments of government may be constantly filled with the wisest and best men; that his excellency the president may have the assistance of an able and faithful council; that the administration of justice may be in the hands of judges and justices well qualified for their offices, who will not take bribes, or in any manner pervert judgment; in a word, that the constitution established may in every respect be well supported by your care, and that the people may know the blessings of good government by the union of your counsels, and the wisdom of your proceedings. May the Almighty King of kings always be in the midst of you, direct and assist you, impress your hearts with his fear, and grant present and future blessings in reward of your fidelity.

And now if I have delivered words of truth, agreeably to my text; and pointed out the sure way to be a prosperous and happy people; may these things sink deep into your hearts, and be accompanied with the divine blessing! May the general government of these United States, when established, appear to be the best which the nations have yet known, and be exalted by uncorrupted religion and morals! And may the everlasting gospel diffuse its heavenly light, and spread righteousness, liberty, and peace, thro' the whole world.

Amen.

Part Three

The Early Republic and Jacksonian America

Introduction

After the Revolution, the United States underwent a period of rapid growth and dramatic change. The market revolution transformed the economy from subsistence farming to farming for profit, where large farms would deliver their goods to national urban marketplaces that served a growing domestic economy and export industry. Goods traveled on new national engineering feats like the Erie Canal and later the railroads. The nation also experienced large geographic and demographic shifts. Jefferson doubled the country's size with the Louisiana Purchase in 1803, expanding its borders to present-day Colorado and Wyoming; the annexation of Texas in 1845 expanded the nation southward; and the Mexican-American War finally brought the flag to the Pacific coast. As the nation expanded westward so did the population, from the Eastern Seaboard into Pennsylvania and Ohio, and then into Indiana, Illinois, Missouri, and beyond. A wave of new immigrants contributed to a booming population. In 1800 there were slightly more than five million people in the United States; in 1850 there was more than 23 million. Many of the new immigrants were Catholic, which, with the rise of new Protestant denominations like Methodism, added to the religious diversity of the country. The slave population, which many of the founders thought was on the way to ultimate extinction, also experienced rapid growth, despite the fact that the slave trade was abolished in 1807. Finally, in politics, the rise of larger political parties, who fought for the votes of the average citizen on beer-soaked campaign trails, democratized politics beyond the confines of a moneyed elite.

Antebellum America was an age of towering national figures such as Daniel Webster, Henry Clay, and John Calhoun. New parties arose from the ashes of the old. The early Republic was split between the Federalists, led by Washington and Adams, and the Republicans, led by Jefferson and Madison. The defeat of John Adams was the death knell of the Federalists, and the Republicans dominated national politics until the rise of the Whigs. The new political allegiances were ironic commentaries on the first, witnesses to the strange reversals that characterize political life. Members of the Whig Party, called the "ghost of puritanism," were for "internal improvements" both of the individual through temperance and moral perfection, and of the nation through economic growth aided by the national government. They believed self-control was essential to individual morality, economic prosperity, and national greatness. The Democrats were the party of individualism and equality, suspicious of national projects that benefited the wealthy merchant class. The Democrats spoke of Manifest Destiny and the Whigs of divine providence.[1]

Antebellum America was also a time of great optimism and national hope. It was the beginning of a continental intellectual life. The period knew many great novelists and thinkers. These included Nathaniel Hawthorne, Herman Melville, Walt Whitman, Ralph Waldo Emerson, and Henry David Thoreau. During this period the United States generated its first endemic philosophic movement, Transcendentalism.

It was also a time of great reformist energy. Inspired by the successful Revolution, the peaceful change to a new constitution, and the religious revival spirit, Revolutionary moral reform swept the country. Temperance societies, abolitionism, and penal reform were all the rage. Idealistic communities, small idyllic experiments, were formed in places like Oneida, New York; Brook Farm, Massachusetts; and New Harmony, Indiana. Many of these movements had religious underpinnings, inspired by the religious revival called the Second Great Awakening, the name given to a period of intense Protestant evangelization. From upstate New

---

1. McKenna, 105–8.

York to the West, the nation was awash with religious sentiment. New sects arose, such as Methodism and Mormonism, the most successful indigenous American religion. Itinerant preachers stumped at mass tent festivals, where thousands gathered out of the wilderness for intense multiple-day spiritual revivals. Eyewitnesses recount widespread and deep religious feelings that found expression in jerks, where ladies in bonnets and well-dressed gentlemen taken with the spirit would jerk their head to and fro throwing their limbs and clothing wildly; and the barks, where they would get on all fours and "growl, snap the teeth, and bark."[2] Theologically, American Protestantism shifted from predestinarianism, a doctrine ill-suited to mass moral reform, to a more can-do methodism in which human effort prepared the way for grace. Moreover, if the Puritans were keenly aware of their beginnings, the Second Great Awakening was saturated with a sense of endings, the sense that the rapture was nigh and any year might bring the Second Coming. Preachers spoke incessantly of the preparation for the end of days. Whole communities were taken in by those who thought they could predict the exact date of the Second Coming. One was March 21, 1844. Thousands dressed in white and waited on hilltops. Then the sun rose on a very ordinary March 22. It was subsequently called the Great Disappointment of 1844.

Despite the rise in religiosity and the Second Great Awakening, the influence of the Hebrew Bible in Antebellum America was less pronounced than it was during the Puritan and the Revolutionary period. The Second Great Awakening, as well as the transition away from nation building, created a sea change in the focus of American Christianity. The Christianity of the founding generation was less centered upon the figure of Christ than the evangelical movements of the antebellum era, and less focused on the end of days, which takes great inspiration from the book of Revelation.[3] The best-selling books of the nineteenth century were Harriet Beecher Stowe's *Uncle Tom's Cabin,* and Lew Wallace's *Ben Hur: A Tale of the Christ,* both of which were Jesus-centric.[4] The Hebrew Bible became less of a source of national narratives and identity, as the

---

2. Ibid., 84–5.
3. Shalev, 153.
4. Ibid., 163.

intellectual temperament turned toward individual experience, salvation, and the last days. One reason for the decline in the influence of the Hebrew Bible is that it is about a chosen *people*, while the Christian testament is about a chosen *person*. For this reason Christian scripture took pride of place in the backwoods tent revivals where seekers went for individual spiritual rejuvenation, while the Hebrew Bible resonated when a new social group was being formed, such as the Mormons. They appropriated the narrative of the New Israel in their own self-creation, the Exodus in their journey west from Ohio to Utah, where they called their settlement the "New Zion," the new city on the hill.

The narratives of the Hebrew Bible were better suited for territorial expansion. Thus the promised land was extended from rocky New England west across the continent. But here, too, there was a change in cultural appropriation. In the Puritan scheme, God indicates His ways, but they are ultimately unfathomable if not inscrutable. Compare that view to one in which destiny is manifestly clear and need only be fulfilled. In the sparsely populated regions of the vast West, the settler movement was taking and making a nation. But even in the West there was ambiguity about God's role. There was a vacillation between viewing the West as Edenic, a romantic wilderness that testifies to God's goodness and bounty, and viewing it as raw fodder for human innovation, as untapped resources to be tamed and taken by labor. Therefore, while the sense that America was a chosen nation persisted, and motifs of chosenness or election, Eden, and the city on the hill endured, they were transformed and infused with new meaning, reinterpreted in light of new circumstances, social needs, and the emergence of new social groups. During the antebellum age, the Hebrew Bible waned in importance and the nature of its influence changed. Narratives continued but were modified.

The Early Republic

THOMAS JEFFERSON (1743–1826)

After the ratification of the Constitution in 1789, George Washington was elected president. He assembled a cabinet of the great men of the day, with John Adams as vice president, Alexander Hamilton as secretary of the treasury, and Thomas Jefferson as secretary of state. Yet beneath the surface of national unity, faction was emerging. Jefferson thought that America should remain an agrarian Republic with a small central government, no standing army, no central bank, and that the United States should support the French Revolution. Jefferson's vision became the core of the Republican Party, which was led by him and James Madison in Virginia. Hamilton and Washington, and to a lesser extent Adams, thought that the new national government needed strength, which included the ability to levy troops, train a professional army, and maintain a national bank to assume the war debt and prop up American credit, and they maintained that the government should remain neutral in the Napoleonic Wars. These beliefs formed the basis of what became known as the Federalist Party. After the death of Washington, the two parties openly clashed in the election of 1796, with Adams becoming president and Jefferson, who became vice president, undermining Adams from within. Jefferson won the following election against Aaron Burr, the grandson of Jonathan Edwards who eventually killed Alexander Hamilton in a duel. Though Jefferson claimed to support a small federal government, as president he oversaw the Louisiana Purchase in 1803, which expanded the power of the federal government and doubled the size of the country. He also lowered taxes and tried somewhat fecklessly to reduce the size of the national government.

By any account Jefferson was one of the geniuses of his generation. His pen effortlessly poured out lyric phrases and he created architectural designs of understated splendor. Jefferson was a renaissance man, an epicurean who loved the finer things in life (he brought over a chef from France and was said to have had the finest food and collection of wine in America). But his legacy, for all its brilliance, is tainted by his longtime holding of slaves – which, unlike Washington, he did not manumit upon death – and the charge of hypocrisy while in office. He is the primary author of some of the most important documents in American history: the Declaration of Independence, the Virginia Statute of Religious Freedom, and the influential and controversial letter to the Danbury Baptists which advocates for a "wall of separation" between Church and State.

Jefferson's views on religion, as on most things, are not easy to untangle. He did not write a straightforward philosophical treatise. The closest thing to a full-length book he wrote is Notes on the State of Virginia, *a response to a French naturalist. Many of his statements about the meaning of the Declaration, his views on God, and his views on politics are recorded in private letters, where he often writes to the taste and opinions of his audience. Moreover, those views changed over time and, according to cynics, in accordance with Jefferson's own needs. Like Thomas Paine, there was the private Jefferson and the public Jefferson; Jefferson the religious skeptic, and Jefferson the deist. He rewrote the Bible to give good moral lessons and to remove the miracles; and yet he referenced the Bible in his inaugural addresses. Jefferson thus represents much of the richness, and ambiguity, of the American appropriation of biblical tropes.*

Virginia Statute of Religious Freedom (1777)

This act was drafted by Thomas Jefferson in 1777, introduced to the Virginia General Assembly in 1779, and adopted by the Virginia General Assembly on January 16, 1786. Jefferson wanted inscribed on his tombstone that he was the author of the Declaration of Independence, founder of the University of Virginia, and author of the Virginia Statute of Religious Freedom.

An Act for establishing religious Freedom.

Whereas, Almighty God hath created the mind free;

That all attempts to influence it by temporal punishments or bur-
thens, or by civil incapacitations tend only to beget habits of hypocrisy and meanness, and therefore are a departure from the plan of
the holy author of our religion, who being Lord, both of body and
mind yet chose not to propagate it by coercions on either, as was in
his Almighty power to do,

That the impious presumption of legislators and rulers, civil as well as
ecclesiastical, who, being themselves but fallible and uninspired men
have assumed dominion over the faith of others, setting up their own
opinions and modes of thinking as the only true and infallible, and
as such endeavouring to impose them on others, hath established
and maintained false religions over the greatest part of the world and
through all time;

That to compel a man to furnish contributions of money for the
propagation of opinions which he disbelieves is sinful and tyrannical;

That even the forcing him to support this or that teacher of his own religious persuasion is depriving him of the comfortable liberty of giving
his contributions to the particular pastor, whose morals he would make
his pattern, and whose powers he feels most persuasive to righteousness, and is withdrawing from the Ministry those temporary rewards,
which, proceeding from an approbation of their personal conduct are
an additional incitement to earnest and unremitting labours for the
instruction of mankind;

That our civil rights have no dependence on our religious opinions
any more than our opinions in physics or geometry,

That therefore the proscribing any citizen as unworthy the public
confidence, by laying upon him an incapacity of being called to
offices of trust and emolument, unless he profess or renounce this
or that religious opinion, is depriving him injuriously of those privileges and advantages, to which, in common with his fellow citizens,
he has a natural right,

That it tends only to corrupt the principles of that very Religion it is meant to encourage, by bribing with a monopoly of worldly honours and emoluments those who will externally profess and conform to it;

That though indeed, these are criminal who do not withstand such temptation, yet neither are those innocent who lay the bait in their way;

That to suffer the civil magistrate to intrude his powers into the field of opinion, and to restrain the profession or propagation of principles on supposition of their ill tendency, is a dangerous fallacy, which at once destroys all religious liberty; because he being of course judge of that tendency will make his opinions the rule of judgment and approve or condemn the sentiments of others only as they shall square with or differ from his own;

That it is time enough for the rightful purposes of civil government, for its officers to interfere when principles break out into overt acts against peace and good order;

And finally, that Truth is great, and will prevail if left to herself, that she is the proper and sufficient antagonist to error, and has nothing to fear from the conflict, unless by human interposition disarmed of her natural weapons free argument and debate, errors ceasing to be dangerous when it is permitted freely to contradict them:

Be it enacted by General Assembly that no man shall be compelled to frequent or support any religious worship, place, or ministry whatsoever, nor shall be enforced, restrained, molested, or burthened in his body or goods, nor shall otherwise suffer on account of his religious opinions or belief, but that all men shall be free to profess, and by argument to maintain, their opinions in matters of Religion, and that the same shall in no wise diminish, enlarge or affect their civil capacities.

And though we well know that this Assembly elected by the people for the ordinary purposes of Legislation only, have no power to restrain the acts of succeeding Assemblies constituted with powers equal to our own, and that therefore to declare this act irrevocable would be of no effect in law; yet we are free to declare, and do declare, that the rights hereby asserted, are of the natural rights of mankind, and that if any act shall be hereafter passed to repeal the present or to narrow its operation, such act will be an infringement of natural right.

Hebraic Sources

Jefferson strongly and famously professed the equality of all men, which extended as well to their fallibility. The human mind must be at liberty to make its own decisions and not be swayed or imposed upon by others in positions of power. Government is necessary for the maintenance of civil order but should not enforce opinions upon the citizenry.

Exodus 23

(ב) לֹא תִהְיֶה אַחֲרֵי רַבִּים לְרָעֹת וְלֹא תַעֲנֶה עַל רִב לִנְטֹת אַחֲרֵי רַבִּים לְהַטֹּת.

[2] Thou shalt not follow a multitude to do evil; neither shalt thou speak in a cause to decline after many to wrest judgment:

Proverbs 20

(ח) מֶלֶךְ יוֹשֵׁב עַל כִּסֵּא דִין מְזָרֶה בְעֵינָיו כָּל רָע.
(כו) מְזָרֶה רְשָׁעִים מֶלֶךְ חָכָם וַיָּשֶׁב עֲלֵיהֶם אוֹפָן.

[8] A king that sitteth in the throne of judgment scattereth away all evil with his eyes.
[26] A wise king scattereth the wicked, and bringeth the wheel over them.

Proverbs 29

(ד) מֶלֶךְ בְּמִשְׁפָּט יַעֲמִיד אָרֶץ וְאִישׁ תְּרוּמוֹת יֶהֶרְסֶנָּה.

[4] By justice a king gives a country stability, but those who are greedy for bribes tear it down.

First Inaugural Address (March 4, 1801)

CALLED upon to undertake the duties of the first executive office of our country, I avail myself of the presence of that portion of my fellow-citizens which is here assembled to express my grateful thanks for the favor with which they have been pleased to look toward me, to declare a sincere consciousness that the task is above my talents, and that I approach it with those anxious and awful presentiments which the greatness of the charge and the weakness of my powers so justly inspire. A rising nation, spread over a wide and fruitful land, traversing all the seas with the rich productions of their industry, engaged in commerce with nations who feel power and forget right, advancing rapidly to destinies beyond the reach of mortal eye – when I contemplate these transcendent objects, and see the honor, the happiness, and the hopes of this beloved country committed to the issue, and the auspices of this day, I shrink from the contemplation, and humble myself before the magnitude of the undertaking. Utterly, indeed, should I despair did not the presence of many whom I here see remind me that in the other high authorities provided by our Constitution I shall find resources of wisdom, of virtue, and of zeal on which to rely under all difficulties. To you, then, gentlemen, who are charged with the sovereign functions of legislation, and to those associated with you, I look with encouragement for that guidance and support which may enable us to steer with safety the vessel in which we are all embarked amidst the conflicting elements of a troubled world.

Hebraic Source

In his first inaugural address, Jefferson displayed Moses-like humility at the prospect of taking the highest office of this country. As an outgrowth of this humility, he addressed his colleagues of the legislative branch, noting that he could not succeed in this great undertaking without their support.

Exodus 3–4

(י) וְעַתָּה לְכָה וְאֶשְׁלָחֲךָ אֶל פַּרְעֹה וְהוֹצֵא אֶת עַמִּי בְנֵי יִשְׂרָאֵל מִמִּצְרָיִם.
(יא) וַיֹּאמֶר מֹשֶׁה אֶל הָאֱ-לֹהִים מִי אָנֹכִי כִּי אֵלֵךְ אֶל פַּרְעֹה וְכִי אוֹצִיא אֶת בְּנֵי יִשְׂרָאֵל מִמִּצְרָיִם.
(יב) וַיֹּאמֶר כִּי אֶהְיֶה עִמָּךְ וְזֶה לְּךָ הָאוֹת כִּי אָנֹכִי שְׁלַחְתִּיךָ בְּהוֹצִיאֲךָ אֶת הָעָם מִמִּצְרַיִם תַּעַבְדוּן אֶת הָאֱ-לֹהִים עַל הָהָר הַזֶּה.

(א) וַיַּעַן מֹשֶׁה וַיֹּאמֶר וְהֵן לֹא יַאֲמִינוּ לִי וְלֹא יִשְׁמְעוּ בְּקֹלִי כִּי יֹאמְרוּ לֹא נִרְאָה אֵלֶיךָ ה׳.

(ב) וַיֹּאמֶר אֵלָיו ה׳ מזה [מַה זֶּה] בְּיָדֶךָ וַיֹּאמֶר מַטֶּה.

(ג) וַיֹּאמֶר הַשְׁלִיכֵהוּ אַרְצָה וַיַּשְׁלִיכֵהוּ אַרְצָה וַיְהִי לְנָחָשׁ וַיָּנָס מֹשֶׁה מִפָּנָיו.

(ד) וַיֹּאמֶר ה׳ אֶל מֹשֶׁה שְׁלַח יָדְךָ וֶאֱחֹז בִּזְנָבוֹ וַיִּשְׁלַח יָדוֹ וַיַּחֲזֶק בּוֹ וַיְהִי לְמַטֶּה בְּכַפּוֹ.

(ה) לְמַעַן יַאֲמִינוּ כִּי נִרְאָה אֵלֶיךָ ה׳ אֱ‑לֹהֵי אֲבֹתָם אֱ‑לֹהֵי אַבְרָהָם אֱ‑לֹהֵי יִצְחָק וֵא‑לֹהֵי יַעֲקֹב.

(ו) וַיֹּאמֶר ה׳ לוֹ עוֹד הָבֵא נָא יָדְךָ בְּחֵיקֶךָ וַיָּבֵא יָדוֹ בְּחֵיקוֹ וַיּוֹצִאָהּ וְהִנֵּה יָדוֹ מְצֹרַעַת כַּשָּׁלֶג.

(ז) וַיֹּאמֶר הָשֵׁב יָדְךָ אֶל חֵיקֶךָ וַיָּשֶׁב יָדוֹ אֶל חֵיקוֹ וַיּוֹצִאָהּ מֵחֵיקוֹ וְהִנֵּה שָׁבָה כִּבְשָׂרוֹ.

(ח) וְהָיָה אִם לֹא יַאֲמִינוּ לָךְ וְלֹא יִשְׁמְעוּ לְקֹל הָאֹת הָרִאשׁוֹן וְהֶאֱמִינוּ לְקֹל הָאֹת הָאַחֲרוֹן.

(ט) וְהָיָה אִם לֹא יַאֲמִינוּ גַּם לִשְׁנֵי הָאֹתוֹת הָאֵלֶּה וְלֹא יִשְׁמְעוּן לְקֹלֶךָ וְלָקַחְתָּ מִמֵּימֵי הַיְאֹר וְשָׁפַכְתָּ הַיַּבָּשָׁה וְהָיוּ הַמַּיִם אֲשֶׁר תִּקַּח מִן הַיְאֹר וְהָיוּ לְדָם בַּיַּבָּשֶׁת.

(י) וַיֹּאמֶר מֹשֶׁה אֶל ה׳ בִּי אֲדֹנָי לֹא אִישׁ דְּבָרִים אָנֹכִי גַּם מִתְּמוֹל גַּם מִשִּׁלְשֹׁם גַּם מֵאָז דַּבֶּרְךָ אֶל עַבְדֶּךָ כִּי כְבַד פֶּה וּכְבַד לָשׁוֹן אָנֹכִי.

(יא) וַיֹּאמֶר ה׳ אֵלָיו מִי שָׂם פֶּה לָאָדָם אוֹ מִי יָשׂוּם אִלֵּם אוֹ חֵרֵשׁ אוֹ פִקֵּחַ אוֹ עִוֵּר הֲלֹא אָנֹכִי ה׳.

(יב) וְעַתָּה לֵךְ וְאָנֹכִי אֶהְיֶה עִם פִּיךָ וְהוֹרֵיתִיךָ אֲשֶׁר תְּדַבֵּר.

(יג) וַיֹּאמֶר בִּי אֲדֹנָי שְׁלַח נָא בְּיַד תִּשְׁלָח.

(יד) וַיִּחַר אַף ה׳ בְּמֹשֶׁה וַיֹּאמֶר הֲלֹא אַהֲרֹן אָחִיךָ הַלֵּוִי יָדַעְתִּי כִּי דַבֵּר יְדַבֵּר הוּא וְגַם הִנֵּה הוּא יֹצֵא לִקְרָאתֶךָ וְרָאֲךָ וְשָׂמַח בְּלִבּוֹ.

(טו) וְדִבַּרְתָּ אֵלָיו וְשַׂמְתָּ אֶת הַדְּבָרִים בְּפִיו וְאָנֹכִי אֶהְיֶה עִם פִּיךָ וְעִם פִּיהוּ וְהוֹרֵיתִי אֶתְכֶם אֵת אֲשֶׁר תַּעֲשׂוּן.

(טז) וְדִבֶּר הוּא לְךָ אֶל הָעָם וְהָיָה הוּא יִהְיֶה לְּךָ לְפֶה וְאַתָּה תִּהְיֶה לּוֹ לֵאלֹהִים.

(יז) וְאֶת הַמַּטֶּה הַזֶּה תִּקַּח בְּיָדֶךָ אֲשֶׁר תַּעֲשֶׂה בּוֹ אֶת הָאֹתֹת.

---

[10] Come now therefore, and I will send thee unto Pharaoh, that thou mayest bring forth My people the children of Israel out of Egypt.

[11] And Moses said unto God: Who am I, that I should go unto Pharaoh, and that I should bring forth the children of Israel out of Egypt?

[12] And He said: Certainly I will be with thee; and this shall be the token unto thee, that I have sent thee: when thou hast brought forth the people out of Egypt, ye shall serve God upon this mountain.

¹ And Moses answered and said: But, behold, they will not believe me, nor hearken unto my voice; for they will say: The Lord hath not appeared unto thee.

² And the Lord said unto him: What is that in thy hand? And he said: A rod.

³ And He said: Cast it on the ground. And he cast it on the ground, and it became a serpent; and Moses fled from before it.

⁴ And the Lord said unto Moses: Put forth thy hand, and take it by the tail – and he put forth his hand, and laid hold of it, and it became a rod in his hand –

⁵ that they may believe that the Lord, the God of their fathers, the God of Abraham, the God of Isaac, and the God of Jacob, hath appeared unto thee.

⁶ And the Lord said furthermore unto him: Put now thy hand into thy bosom. And he put his hand into his bosom; and when he took it out, behold, his hand was leprous, as white as snow.

⁷ And He said: Put thy hand back into thy bosom. – And he put his hand back into his bosom; and when he took it out of his bosom, behold, it was turned again as his other flesh.

⁸ And it shall come to pass, if they will not believe thee, neither hearken to the voice of the first sign, that they will believe the voice of the latter sign.

⁹ And it shall come to pass, if they will not believe even these two signs, neither hearken unto thy voice, that thou shalt take of the water of the river, and pour it upon the dry land; and the water which thou takest out of the river shall become blood upon the dry land.

¹⁰ And Moses said unto the Lord: Oh Lord, I am not a man of words, neither heretofore, nor since Thou hast spoken unto Thy servant; for I am slow of speech, and of a slow tongue.

¹¹ And the Lord said unto him: Who hath made man's mouth? or who maketh a man dumb, or deaf, or seeing, or blind? is it not I the Lord?

¹² Now therefore go, and I will be with thy mouth, and teach thee what thou shalt speak.

¹³ And he said: Oh Lord, send, I pray Thee, by the hand of him whom Thou wilt send.

¹⁴ And the anger of the Lord was kindled against Moses, and He said: Is there not Aaron thy brother the Levite? I know that he can speak well. And also, behold, he cometh forth to meet thee; and when he seeth thee, he will be glad in his heart.

¹⁵ And thou shalt speak unto him, and put the words in his mouth; and I will be with thy mouth, and with his mouth, and will teach you what ye shall do.

¹⁶ And he shall be thy spokesman unto the people; and it shall come to pass, that he shall be to thee a mouth, and thou shalt be to him in God's stead.

¹⁷ And thou shalt take in thy hand this rod, wherewith thou shalt do the signs.

Second Inaugural Address (March 4, 1805)

In his second inaugural address, Jefferson discussed the quest for neutrality in foreign affairs and the need to diminish the size of the government, and he justified taxing only consumption. He also spoke about US policy toward the Native Americans, affirming the Native Americans' natural rights. After all of this, Jefferson concluded:

I shall now enter on the duties to which my fellow-citizens have again called me, and shall proceed in the spirit of those principles which they have approved. I fear not that any motives of interest may lead me astray; I am sensible of no passion which could seduce me knowingly from the path of justice, but the weaknesses of human nature and the limits of my own understanding will produce errors of judgment sometimes injurious to your interests. I shall need, therefore, all the indulgence which I have heretofore experienced from my constituents; the want of it will certainly not lessen with increasing years. I shall need, too, the favor of that Being in whose hands we are, who led our fathers, as Israel of old, from their native land and planted them in a country flowing with all the necessaries and comforts of life; who has covered our infancy with His providence and our riper years with His wisdom and power, and to whose goodness I ask you to join in supplications with me that He will so enlighten the minds of your servants, guide their councils, and prosper their measures that whatsoever they do shall result in your good, and shall secure to you the peace, friendship, and approbation of all nations.

Hebraic Sources

In his second inaugural address, Jefferson specifically invoked the noncommittal "Being" who guides nations and leaders. This deity embraced ancient Israel in its infancy and brought it to a prosperous land, as summarized at the end of the book of Joshua. Jefferson ended his address in terms reminiscent of the closing of King Solomon's address at the inauguration of the First Temple.

Joshua 24

(ה) וָאֶשְׁלַח אֶת מֹשֶׁה וְאֶת אַהֲרֹן וָאֶגֹּף אֶת מִצְרַיִם כַּאֲשֶׁר עָשִׂיתִי בְּקִרְבּוֹ וְאַחַר הוֹצֵאתִי אֶתְכֶם.

(ו) וָאוֹצִיא אֶת אֲבוֹתֵיכֶם מִמִּצְרַיִם וַתָּבֹאוּ הַיָּמָּה וַיִּרְדְּפוּ מִצְרַיִם אַחֲרֵי אֲבוֹתֵיכֶם בְּרֶכֶב וּבְפָרָשִׁים יַם סוּף.

(ז) וַיִּצְעֲקוּ אֶל ה' וַיָּשֶׂם מַאֲפֵל בֵּינֵיכֶם וּבֵין הַמִּצְרִים וַיָּבֵא עָלָיו אֶת הַיָּם וַיְכַסֵּהוּ וַתִּרְאֶינָה עֵינֵיכֶם אֵת אֲשֶׁר עָשִׂיתִי בְּמִצְרָיִם וַתֵּשְׁבוּ בַמִּדְבָּר יָמִים רַבִּים.

(ח) ואבאה [וָאָבִיא] אֶתְכֶם אֶל אֶרֶץ הָאֱמֹרִי הַיּוֹשֵׁב בְּעֵבֶר הַיַּרְדֵּן וַיִּלָּחֲמוּ אִתְכֶם וָאֶתֵּן אוֹתָם בְּיֶדְכֶם וַתִּירְשׁוּ אֶת אַרְצָם וָאַשְׁמִידֵם מִפְּנֵיכֶם.

(ט) וַיָּקָם בָּלָק בֶּן צִפּוֹר מֶלֶךְ מוֹאָב וַיִּלָּחֶם בְּיִשְׂרָאֵל וַיִּשְׁלַח וַיִּקְרָא לְבִלְעָם בֶּן בְּעוֹר לְקַלֵּל אֶתְכֶם.

(י) וְלֹא אָבִיתִי לִשְׁמֹעַ לְבִלְעָם וַיְבָרֶךְ בָּרוֹךְ אֶתְכֶם וָאַצִּל אֶתְכֶם מִיָּדוֹ.

(יא) וַתַּעַבְרוּ אֶת הַיַּרְדֵּן וַתָּבֹאוּ אֶל יְרִיחוֹ וַיִּלָּחֲמוּ בָכֶם בַּעֲלֵי יְרִיחוֹ הָאֱמֹרִי וְהַפְּרִזִּי וְהַכְּנַעֲנִי וְהַחִתִּי וְהַגִּרְגָּשִׁי הַחִוִּי וְהַיְבוּסִי וָאֶתֵּן אוֹתָם בְּיֶדְכֶם.

(יב) וָאֶשְׁלַח לִפְנֵיכֶם אֶת הַצִּרְעָה וַתְּגָרֶשׁ אוֹתָם מִפְּנֵיכֶם שְׁנֵי מַלְכֵי הָאֱמֹרִי לֹא בְחַרְבְּךָ וְלֹא בְקַשְׁתֶּךָ.

(יג) וָאֶתֵּן לָכֶם אֶרֶץ אֲשֶׁר לֹא יָגַעְתָּ בָּהּ וְעָרִים אֲשֶׁר לֹא בְנִיתֶם וַתֵּשְׁבוּ בָהֶם כְּרָמִים וְזֵיתִים אֲשֶׁר לֹא נְטַעְתֶּם אַתֶּם אֹכְלִים.

[5] Then I sent Moses and Aaron, and I afflicted the Egyptians by what I did there, and I brought you out.

[6] When I brought your people out of Egypt, you came to the sea, and the Egyptians pursued them with chariots and horsemen as far as the Red Sea.

[7] But they cried to the Lord for help, and he put darkness between you and the Egyptians; he brought the sea over them and covered them. You saw with your own eyes what I did to the Egyptians. Then you lived in the wilderness for a long time.

[8] I brought you to the land of the Amorites who lived east of the Jordan. They fought against you, but I gave them into your hands. I destroyed them from before you, and you took possession of their land.

[9] When Balak son of Zippor, the king of Moab, prepared to fight against Israel, he sent for Balaam son of Beor to put a curse on you.

[10] But I would not listen to Balaam, so he blessed you again and again, and I delivered you out of his hand.

[11] Then you crossed the Jordan and came to Jericho. The citizens of Jericho fought against you, as did also the Amorites, Perizzites, Canaanites, Hittites, Girgashites, Hivites and Jebusites, but I gave them into your hands.

[12] I sent the hornet ahead of you, which drove them out before you – also the two Amorite kings. You did not do it with your own sword and bow.

[13] So I gave you a land on which you did not toil and cities you did not build; and you live in them and eat from vineyards and olive groves that you did not plant.

I Kings 8

(נד) וַיְהִי כְּכַלּוֹת שְׁלֹמֹה לְהִתְפַּלֵּל אֶל ה' אֵת כָּל הַתְּפִלָּה וְהַתְּחִנָּה הַזֹּאת קָם מִלִּפְנֵי מִזְבַּח ה' מִכְּרֹעַ עַל בִּרְכָּיו וְכַפָּיו פְּרֻשׂוֹת הַשָּׁמָיִם.

(נה) וַיַּעֲמֹד וַיְבָרֶךְ אֵת כָּל קְהַל יִשְׂרָאֵל קוֹל גָּדוֹל לֵאמֹר.

(נו) בָּרוּךְ ה' אֲשֶׁר נָתַן מְנוּחָה לְעַמּוֹ יִשְׂרָאֵל כְּכֹל אֲשֶׁר דִּבֵּר לֹא נָפַל דָּבָר אֶחָד מִכֹּל דְּבָרוֹ הַטּוֹב אֲשֶׁר דִּבֶּר בְּיַד מֹשֶׁה עַבְדּוֹ.

(נז) יְהִי ה' אֱ-לֹהֵינוּ עִמָּנוּ כַּאֲשֶׁר הָיָה עִם אֲבֹתֵינוּ אַל יַעַזְבֵנוּ וְאַל יִטְּשֵׁנוּ.

(נח) לְהַטּוֹת לְבָבֵנוּ אֵלָיו לָלֶכֶת בְּכָל דְּרָכָיו וְלִשְׁמֹר מִצְוֹתָיו וְחֻקָּיו וּמִשְׁפָּטָיו
אֲשֶׁר צִוָּה אֶת אֲבֹתֵינוּ.

⁵⁴ And so it was, when Solomon had finished praying all this prayer and supplication to the Lord, that he arose from before the altar of the Lord, from kneeling on his knees with his hands spread up to heaven.

⁵⁵ Then he stood and blessed all the assembly of Israel with a loud voice, saying:

⁵⁶ Blessed be the Lord, who has given rest to His people Israel, according to all that He promised. There has not failed one word of all His good promise, which He promised through His servant Moses.

⁵⁷ May the Lord our God be with us, as He was with our fathers. May He not leave us nor forsake us,

⁵⁸ that He may incline our hearts to Himself, to walk in all His ways, and to keep His commandments and His statutes and His judgments, which He commanded our fathers.

Letter to Benjamin Rush (April 21, 1803)

DEAR SIR,

In some of the delightful conversations with you in the evenings of 1798–99, and which served as an anodyne to the afflictions of the crisis through which our country was then laboring, the Christian religion was sometimes our topic; and I then promised you that one day or other I would give you my views of it. They are the result of a life of inquiry and reflection, and very different from that anti-Christian system imputed to me by those who know nothing of my opinions. To the corruptions of Christianity I am indeed opposed, but not to the genuine precepts of Jesus himself. I am a Christian, in the only sense in which he wished anyone to be: sincerely attached to his doctrines in preference to all others, ascribing to himself every *human* excellence, and believing he never claimed any other. At the short interval since these conversations, when I could justifiably abstract my mind from public affairs, the subject has been under my contemplation. But the more I considered it, the more it expanded beyond the measure of either my time or information. In the moment of my late departure from Monticello, I received from Dr. Priestley his little treatise of "Socrates and Jesus Compared." This being a section of the general view I had taken of the field, it became a subject of reflection while on the road and unoccupied otherwise. The result was, to arrange in my mind a syllabus or outline of such an estimate of the comparative merits of Christianity as I wished to see executed by someone of more leisure and information for the task than myself. This I now send you as the only discharge of my promise I can probably ever execute. And in confiding it to you, I know it will not be exposed to the malignant perversions of those who make every word from me a text for new misrepresentations and calumnies. I am moreover averse to the communication of my religious tenets to the public, because it would countenance the presumption of those who have endeavored to draw them before that tribunal, and to seduce public opinion to erect itself into that inquisition over the rights of conscience which the laws have so justly proscribed. It behooves every man who values liberty of conscience for himself, to resist invasions of it in the case of others; or their case may, by change of circumstances, become his own. It behooves him, too, in his own case, to give no example of concession, betraying the common right of independent opinion, by answering questions of faith which the laws have left between God and himself. Accept my affectionate salutations.

Th. Jefferson

Syllabus of an Estimate of the Merit of the Doctrine of Jesus Compared with Those of Others (April 21, 1803)

In a comparative view of the Ethics of the enlightened nations of antiquity, of the Jews and of Jesus, no notice should be taken of the corruptions of reason among the ancients, to wit, the idolatry and superstition of the vulgar, nor of the corruptions of Christianity by the learned among its professors.

Let a just view be taken of the moral principles inculcated by the most esteemed of the sects of ancient philosophy or of their individuals; particularly Pythagoras, Socrates, Epicurus, Cicero, Epictetus, Seneca, Antoninus.

I. Philosophers.
1. Their precepts related chiefly to ourselves, and the government of those passions which, unrestrained, would disturb our tranquillity of mind. In this branch of philosophy they were really great.
2. In developing our duties to others, they were short and defective. They embraced, indeed, the circles of kindred and friends, and inculcated patriotism, or the love of our country in the

aggregate, as a primary obligation: towards our neighbors and countrymen they taught justice, but scarcely viewed them as within the circle of benevolence. Still less have they inculcated peace, charity and love to our fellow men, or embraced with benevolence the whole family of mankind.

II. Jews.

1. Their system was Deism; that is, the belief in one only God. But their ideas of him and of his attributes were degrading and injurious.

2. Their Ethics were not only imperfect, but often irreconcilable with the sound dictates of reason and morality, as they respect intercourse with those around us; and repulsive and anti-social, as respecting other nations. They needed reformation, therefore, in an eminent degree.

III. Jesus.

In this state of things among the Jews, Jesus appeared. His parentage was obscure; his condition poor; his education null; his natural endowments great; his life correct and innocent: he was meek, benevolent, patient, firm, disinterested, and of the sublimest eloquence.

The disadvantages under which his doctrines appear are remarkable.

1. Like Socrates and Epictetus, he wrote nothing himself.

2. But he had not, like them, a Xenophon or an Arrian to write for him. I name not Plato, who only used the name of Socrates to cover the whimsies of his own brain. On the contrary, all the learned of his country, entrenched in its power and riches, were opposed to him, lest his labors should undermine their advantages; and the committing to writing his life and doctrines fell on unlettered and ignorant men, who wrote, too, from memory, and not till long after the transactions had passed.

3. According to the ordinary fate of those who attempt to enlighten and reform mankind, he fell an early victim to the jealousy and combination of the altar and the throne, at about thirty-three years of age, his reason having not yet attained

the *maximum* of its energy, nor the course of his preaching, which was but of three years at most, presented occasions for developing a complete system of morals.

4. Hence the doctrines he really delivered were defective as a whole, and fragments only of what he did deliver have come to us mutilated, misstated, and often unintelligible.

5. They have been still more disfigured by the corruptions of schismatizing followers, who have found an interest in sophisticating and perverting the simple doctrines he taught, by engrafting on them the mysticisms of a Grecian sophist, frittering them into subtleties, and obscuring them with jargon, until they have caused good men to reject the whole in disgust, and to view Jesus himself as an impostor.

Notwithstanding these disadvantages, a system of morals is presented to us which, if filled up in the style and spirit of the rich fragments he left us, would be the most perfect and sublime that has ever been taught by man.

The question of his being a member of the Godhead, or in direct communication with it, claimed for him by some of his followers and denied by others, is foreign to the present view, which is merely an estimate of the intrinsic merits of his doctrines.

1. He corrected the Deism of the Jews, confirming them in their belief of one only God, and giving them juster notions of His attributes and government.

2. His moral doctrines, relating to kindred and friends were more pure and perfect than those of the most correct of the philosophers, and greatly more so than those of the Jews; and they went far beyond both in inculcating universal philanthropy, not only to kindred and friends, to neighbors and countrymen, but to all mankind, gathering all into one family under the bonds of love, charity, peace, common wants and common aids. A development of this head will evince the peculiar superiority of the system of Jesus over all others.

3. The precepts of philosophy, and of the Hebrew code, laid hold of actions only. He pushed his scrutinies into the heart of man; erected his tribunal in the region of his thoughts, and purified the waters at the fountain head.

4. He taught, emphatically, the doctrines of a future state, which was either doubted or disbelieved by the Jews, and wielded it with efficacy as an important incentive, supplementary to the other motives to moral conduct.

JOHN QUINCY ADAMS (1767–1848)

John Quincy Adams was the sixth president of the United States and the eldest son of John Adams. A decade and a half before he was to occupy the presidential office, he penned a series of letters to his son from St. Petersburg, where he was serving as the first US Minister to Russia. This is an excerpt from the second letter.

Letter to His Son (September 15, 1811)

It is the God of the Hebrews alone... who is announced as the Creator of the world. The ideas of God entertained by all the most illustrious and most ingenious nations of antiquity were weak and absurd.... Thus far and no farther could human reason extend. But the first words of the Bible are "In the beginning God created the Heaven and the Earth" [Gen. 1:1]. This blessed and sublime idea of God, the creator the universe... is *revealed* in the first verse of the Book of Genesis.

ABRAHAM LINCOLN (1809–1865)

Abraham Lincoln is one of the beloved figures in American history. Born to a poor family in Kentucky, Lincoln grew up in difficult circumstances. His mother, to whom he was very close, died a slow death from milkweed poisoning when Lincoln was only nine years old. He had a trying relationship with his father, with whom he never reconciled. Lincoln had no formal schooling and was entirely a self-taught man, reading the King James Bible and Euclid on his own. When he was twenty-two years old, Lincoln relocated to New Salem, Illinois, where he was soon elected to the state legislature. The following excerpt is from one of his earliest speeches, a remarkably precocious reflection on the nature of the American political project in self-government, as well as an adept use of the Hebrew Bible.

The Perpetuation of Our Political Institutions: Address before the Young Men's Lyceum of Springfield, Illinois (January 27, 1838)

As a subject for the remarks of the evening, *the perpetuation of our political institutions*, is selected.

In the great journal of things happening under the sun, we, the American People, find our account running, under date of the nineteenth century of the Christian era. We find ourselves in the peaceful possession, of the fairest portion of the earth, as regards extent of territory, fertility of soil, and salubrity of climate. We find ourselves under the government of a system of political institutions, conducing more essentially to the ends of civil and religious liberty, than any of which the history of former times tells us. We, when mounting the stage of existence, found ourselves the legal inheritors of these fundamental blessings. We toiled not in the acquirement or establishment of them – they are a legacy bequeathed us, by a *once* hardy, brave, and patriotic, but *now* lamented and departed race of ancestors. Their's was the task (and nobly they performed it) to possess themselves, and through themselves, us, of this goodly land; and to uprear upon its hills and its valleys, a political edifice of liberty and equal rights; 'tis ours only, to transmit these, the former, unprofaned by the foot of an invader; the latter, undecayed by the lapse of time and untorn by usurpation, to the latest generation that fate shall permit the world to know. This task of gratitude to our fathers, justice to ourselves, duty to posterity, and love for our species in general, all imperatively require us faithfully to perform.

How then shall we perform it? At what point shall we expect the approach of danger? By what means shall we fortify against it? Shall we expect some transatlantic military giant, to step the Ocean, and crush us at a blow? Never! All the armies of Europe, Asia and Africa combined, with all the treasure of the earth (our own excepted) in their military chest; with a Buonaparte for a commander, could not by force, take a drink from the Ohio, or make a track on the Blue Ridge, in a trial of a thousand years.

At what point then is the approach of danger to be expected? I answer, if it ever reach us, it must spring up amongst us. It cannot come from abroad. If destruction be our lot, we must ourselves be its author and finisher. As a nation of freemen, we must live through all time, or die by suicide.

I hope I am over wary; but if I am not, there is, even now, something of ill-omen, amongst us. I mean the increasing disregard for law which pervades the country; the growing disposition to substitute the wild and furious passions, in lieu of the sober judgment of Courts; and the worse than savage mobs, for the executive ministers of justice. This disposition is awfully fearful in any community; and that it now exists in ours, though grating to our feelings to admit, it would be a violation of truth, and an insult to our intelligence, to deny. Accounts of outrages committed by mobs, form the every-day news of the times. They have pervaded the country, from New England to Louisiana; they are neither peculiar to the eternal snows of the former, nor the burning suns of the latter; they are not the creature of climate – neither are they confined to the slave-holding, or the non-slave-holding States. Alike, they spring up among the pleasure hunting masters of Southern slaves, and the order loving citizens of the land of steady habits. Whatever, then, their cause may be, it is common to the whole country....

The question recurs, "how shall we fortify against it?" The answer is simple. Let every American, every lover of liberty, every well wisher to his posterity, swear by the blood of the Revolution, never to violate in the least particular, the laws of the country; and never to tolerate their violation by others. As the patriots of seventy-six did to the support of the Declaration of Independence, so to the support of the Constitution and Laws, let every American pledge his life, his property, and his sacred honor; let every man remember that to violate the law, is to trample on the blood of his father, and to tear the character of his own, and his children's liberty. Let reverence for the laws, be breathed by every American mother, to the lisping babe, that prattles on her lap – let it be taught in schools, in seminaries, and in colleges; let it be written in Primers, spelling books, and in Almanacs; let it be preached from the pulpit, proclaimed in legislative halls, and enforced in courts of justice. And, in short, let it become the *political religion* of the nation; and let the old and the young, the rich and the poor, the grave and the gay, of all sexes and tongues, and colors and conditions, sacrifice unceasingly upon its altars....

Hebraic Source

In his remarks, Lincoln tied political dissolution to disregard for the law. The people must band together and bind themselves to law, for it is the intergenerational covenant of a free nation, much as the law was for the Israelite nation. In a similar vein, the rabbinic tradition recognized that law is essential to liberty.

Exodus 24

(א) וְאֶל מֹשֶׁה אָמַר עֲלֵה אֶל ה' אַתָּה וְאַהֲרֹן נָדָב וַאֲבִיהוּא וְשִׁבְעִים מִזִּקְנֵי יִשְׂרָאֵל וְהִשְׁתַּחֲוִיתֶם מֵרָחֹק.
(ב) וְנִגַּשׁ מֹשֶׁה לְבַדּוֹ אֶל ה' וְהֵם לֹא יִגָּשׁוּ וְהָעָם לֹא יַעֲלוּ עִמּוֹ.
(ג) וַיָּבֹא מֹשֶׁה וַיְסַפֵּר לָעָם אֵת כָּל דִּבְרֵי ה' וְאֵת כָּל הַמִּשְׁפָּטִים וַיַּעַן כָּל הָעָם קוֹל אֶחָד וַיֹּאמְרוּ כָּל הַדְּבָרִים אֲשֶׁר דִּבֶּר ה' נַעֲשֶׂה.
(ד) וַיִּכְתֹּב מֹשֶׁה אֵת כָּל דִּבְרֵי ה' וַיַּשְׁכֵּם בַּבֹּקֶר וַיִּבֶן מִזְבֵּחַ תַּחַת הָהָר וּשְׁתֵּים עֶשְׂרֵה מַצֵּבָה לִשְׁנֵים עָשָׂר שִׁבְטֵי יִשְׂרָאֵל.
(ה) וַיִּשְׁלַח אֶת נַעֲרֵי בְּנֵי יִשְׂרָאֵל וַיַּעֲלוּ עֹלֹת וַיִּזְבְּחוּ זְבָחִים שְׁלָמִים לַה' פָּרִים.
(ו) וַיִּקַּח מֹשֶׁה חֲצִי הַדָּם וַיָּשֶׂם בָּאַגָּנֹת וַחֲצִי הַדָּם זָרַק עַל הַמִּזְבֵּחַ.
(ז) וַיִּקַּח סֵפֶר הַבְּרִית וַיִּקְרָא בְּאָזְנֵי הָעָם וַיֹּאמְרוּ כֹּל אֲשֶׁר דִּבֶּר ה' נַעֲשֶׂה וְנִשְׁמָע.
(ח) וַיִּקַּח מֹשֶׁה אֶת הַדָּם וַיִּזְרֹק עַל הָעָם וַיֹּאמֶר הִנֵּה דַם הַבְּרִית אֲשֶׁר כָּרַת ה' עִמָּכֶם עַל כָּל הַדְּבָרִים הָאֵלֶּה.

[1] And he said unto Moses: Come up unto the Lord, thou, and Aaron, Nadab, and Abihu, and seventy of the elders of Israel; and worship ye afar off.

[2] And Moses alone shall come near the Lord: but they shall not come nigh; neither shall the people go up with him.

[3] And Moses came and told the people all the words of the Lord, and all the judgments: and all the people answered with one voice, and said: All the words which the Lord hath said will we do.

[4] And Moses wrote all the words of the Lord, and rose up early in the morning, and builded an altar under the hill, and twelve pillars, according to the twelve tribes of Israel.

⁵ And he sent young men of the children of Israel, which offered burnt offerings, and sacrificed peace offerings of oxen unto the Lord.

⁶ And Moses took half of the blood, and put it in basins; and half of the blood he sprinkled on the altar.

⁷ And he took the book of the covenant, and read in the audience of the people; and they said: All that the Lord hath said will we do, and be obedient.

⁸ And Moses took the blood, and sprinkled it on the people, and said: Behold the blood of the covenant, which the Lord hath made with you concerning all these words.

Mishna, Avot 6.2

אָמַר רַבִּי יְהוֹשֻׁעַ בֶּן לֵוִי, בְּכָל יוֹם וָיוֹם בַּת קוֹל יוֹצֵאת מֵהַר חוֹרֵב וּמַכְרֶזֶת וְאוֹמֶרֶת, אוֹי לָהֶם לַבְּרִיּוֹת מֵעֶלְבּוֹנָהּ שֶׁל תּוֹרָה. שֶׁכָּל מִי שֶׁאֵינוֹ עוֹסֵק בַּתּוֹרָה נִקְרָא נָזוּף, שֶׁנֶּאֱמַר "נֶזֶם זָהָב בְּאַף חֲזִיר אִשָּׁה יָפָה וְסָרַת טָעַם" (משלי יא:כב). וְאוֹמֵר "וְהַלֻּחֹת מַעֲשֵׂה אֱ-לֹהִים הֵמָּה וְהַמִּכְתָּב מִכְתַּב אֱ-לֹהִים הוּא חָרוּת עַל הַלֻּחֹת" (שמות לב:טז) אַל תִּקְרָא חָרוּת אֶלָּא חֵרוּת, שֶׁאֵין לְךָ בֶן חוֹרִין אֶלָּא מִי שֶׁעוֹסֵק בְּתַלְמוּד תּוֹרָה. וְכָל מִי שֶׁעוֹסֵק בְּתַלְמוּד תּוֹרָה הֲרֵי זֶה מִתְעַלֶּה, שֶׁנֶּאֱמַר "וּמִמַּתָּנָה נַחֲלִיאֵל וּמִנַּחֲלִיאֵל בָּמוֹת" (במדבר כא:יט).

Rabbi Yehoshua ben Levi said: "Each and every day a heavenly echo goes out from Mount Horeb, and announces and says: 'Woe to the creatures for disparaging the Torah,' for anyone who does not involve himself in the Torah is called 'rebuked,' as it is said (Prov. 11:22): 'A ring of gold in a swine's snout is a beautiful woman who turns from discretion,' and it says (Ex. 32:16): 'And the tablets were the work of God, and the writing was the writing of God, graven upon the tablets,' do not read 'graven' (*harut*) but rather 'freedom' (*herut*), for there is no free man except one that involves himself in Torah learning. And anyone who involves himself in Torah learning is elevated, as it is said (Num. 21:19): 'and from Mattanah (a place name that means 'gift,' and so can refer to the gifting of the Torah), Nachaliel; and from Nachaliel, Bamot (a place name that means 'high places').'"

The West

LYMAN BEECHER (1775–1863)

During the period from the Revolutionary to the Civil War, the United States experienced the greatest expansion of evangelical Protestant Christianity in American history. In 1770 there were 2,481 churches in the United States for a population of 2.1 million people; in 1860 there were 52,500 churches for a population of 31 million.[1] While the Second Great Awakening was a broad evangelical movement, there were many fissures over interpretation of free will, atonement, eschatology, and sacraments.[2] Those battles were largely waged within the confines of theological Christianity. Nevertheless, various Hebraic themes such as "chosenness" continued to resonate. The notion of "chosenness" was used to justify Manifest Destiny, as is witnessed by the passages by Lyman Beecher excerpted below.

Lyman Beecher was one of the leaders of the Second Great Awakening. A Protestant and founder of the American Temperance Society, Beecher was president of Lane Theological Seminary near Cincinnati, Ohio, dedicated to training Protestant ministers to evangelize in the West. The following excerpt is taken from an anti-Catholic tract, denouncing Catholicism as false, undemocratic, and anti-American. Beecher's anti-Catholicism struck a note in a diversifying America. He spoke in Boston in 1834 at around the same time that a mob burned a Catholic nunnery in Somerville, Massachusetts, in what

---

1. See Noll, *America's God*, 166.
2. Ibid., 170.

is known as the Ursuline Convent Riots. His evangelization methods were considered unorthodox and he was brought up on charges of heresy, which he eventually overcame. Lyman Beecher was the father of Harriet Beecher Stowe, author of Uncle Tom's Cabin, *one of the most influential books of the nineteenth century.*

A Plea for the West (1835)

Who hath heard such a thing? who hath seen such things? Shall the earth be made to bring forth in one day! or shall a nation be born at once? for as soon as Zion travailed, she brought forth her children.

(ISAIAH lxvi, 8)

EVER since the era of modern missions, sceptical men have ridiculed the efforts of the church to evangelize the world, and predicted their failure. "What," say they, "do these Jews build if a fox do but go up upon the wall, it will fall. The world can never be converted to Christianity by the power of man." And full well do we know it, and most deeply do we feel it, and in all our supplications for aid, most emphatically do we confess our utter impotency; and could no power but the power of man be enlisted, it would be indeed of all experiments the most ridiculous and hopeless. But because man cannot convert the world to Christianity, cannot God do it? Has he not promised to do it, and selected his instruments, and commanded his people to be fellow workers with him. And hath he said, and shall he not do it. Instead of its being a work of difficulty and dilatory movement, when the time to favor Zion comes, it shall outrun all past analogies of moral causes, as if seed-time and harvest should meet on the same field, or a nation should instantly rush up from barbarism to civilization. But as all great eras of prosperity to the church have been aided by the civil condition of the world, and accomplished by the regular operation of moral causes, I consider the text as a prediction of the rapid and universal extension of civil and religious liberty, introductory to the triumphs of universal Christianity. It is certain that the glorious things spoken of the church and of the world, as affected by her prosperity, cannot come to pass under the existing civil organization of the nations. Such a state of society as is predicted to pervade the earth, cannot exist under an arbitrary despotism, and the predominance of feudal institutions and usages.

Of course, it is predicted that revolutions and distress of nations will precede the introduction of the peaceful reign of Jesus Christ on the earth. The mountains shall be cast down, and the valleys shall be exalted and he shall "overturn, and overturn, and overturn, till he whose right it is, shall reign King of nations King of saints" [cf. Ezek. 21:27]. It was the opinion of Edwards, that the millenium would commence in America. When I first encountered this opinion, I thought it chimerical; but all providential developments since, and all the existing signs of the times, lend corroboration to it.

But if it is by the march of revolution and civil liberty, that the way of the Lord is to be prepared, where shall the central energy be found, and from what nation shall the renovating power go forth. What nation is blessed with such experimental knowledge of free institutions, with such facilities and resources of communication, obstructed by so few obstacles, as our own? There is not a nation upon earth which, in fifty years, can by all possible reformation place itself in circumstances so favorable as our own for the free, unembarrassed applications of physical effort and pecuniary and moral power to evangelize the world.

But if this nation is, in the providence of God, destined to lead the way in the moral and political emancipation of the world, it is time she understood her high calling, and were harnessed for the work. For mighty causes, like floods from distant mountains, are rushing with accumulating power, to their consummation of good or evil, and soon our character and destiny will be stereotyped forever. It is equally plain that the religious and political destiny of our nation is to be decided in the West. There is the territory, and there soon will be the population, the wealth, and the political power. The Atlantic commerce and manufactures may confer always some peculiar advantages on the East. But the West is destined to be the great central power of the nation, and under heaven, must affect powerfully the cause of free institutions and the liberty of the world.

The West is a young empire of mind, and power, and wealth, and free institutions, rushing up to a giant manhood, with a rapidity and a power never before witnessed below the sun. And if she carries with her the elements of her preservation, the experiment will be glorious the joy of the nation, the joy of the whole earth, as she rises in the majesty of her intelligence and benevolence, and enterprise, for the emancipation of the world. It is equally clear, that the conflict which is to decide the destiny of the West, will be a conflict of institutions for the education of her sons, for purposes of superstition, or evangelical light; of despotism, or liberty.

Hebraic Sources

Beecher considered Jonathan Edwards's vision of the covenantal possibilities of America to have stood the test of time. Isaiah's Zion, which Beecher identified with the United States, had weathered travails and was flourishing. Like Edwards, Beecher saw the West as the place where a new Zion could be built.

Nehemiah 3

(לג) וַיְהִי כַּאֲשֶׁר שָׁמַע סַנְבַלַּט כִּי אֲנַחְנוּ בוֹנִים אֶת הַחוֹמָה וַיִּחַר לוֹ וַיִּכְעַס הַרְבֵּה וַיַּלְעֵג עַל הַיְּהוּדִים.

(לד) וַיֹּאמֶר לִפְנֵי אֶחָיו וְחֵיל שֹׁמְרוֹן וַיֹּאמֶר מָה הַיְּהוּדִים הָאֲמֵלָלִים עֹשִׂים הֲיַעַזְבוּ לָהֶם הֲיִזְבָּחוּ הַיְכַלּוּ בַיּוֹם הַיְחַיּוּ אֶת הָאֲבָנִים מֵעֲרֵמוֹת הֶעָפָר וְהֵמָּה שְׂרוּפוֹת.

(לה) וְטוֹבִיָּה הָעַמֹּנִי אֶצְלוֹ וַיֹּאמֶר גַּם אֲשֶׁר הֵם בּוֹנִים אִם יַעֲלֶה שׁוּעָל וּפָרַץ חוֹמַת אַבְנֵיהֶם.

[33] But it came to pass, that when Sanballat heard that we builded the wall, he was wroth, and took great indignation, and mocked the Jews.

[34] And he spake before his brethren and the army of Samaria, and said: What do these feeble Jews? Will they fortify themselves? Will they sacrifice? Will they make an end in a day? Will they revive the stones out of the heaps of the rubbish which are burned?

[35] Now Tobiah the Ammonite was by him, and he said: Even that which they build, if a fox go up, he shall break down their stone wall.

Isaiah 66

(ז) בְּטֶרֶם תָּחִיל יָלָדָה בְּטֶרֶם יָבוֹא חֵבֶל לָהּ וְהִמְלִיטָה זָכָר.

(ח) מִי שָׁמַע כָּזֹאת מִי רָאָה כָּאֵלֶּה הֲיוּחַל אֶרֶץ בְּיוֹם אֶחָד אִם יִוָּלֵד גּוֹי פַּעַם אֶחָת כִּי חָלָה גַּם יָלְדָה צִיּוֹן אֶת בָּנֶיהָ.

(ט) הַאֲנִי אַשְׁבִּיר וְלֹא אוֹלִיד יֹאמַר ה' אִם אֲנִי הַמּוֹלִיד וְעָצַרְתִּי אָמַר אֱ־לֹהָיִךְ.

⁷ Before she travailed, she brought forth; before her pain came, she was delivered of a man-child.

⁸ Who hath heard such a thing? Who hath seen such things? Shall the earth be made to bring forth in one day? Or shall a nation be born at once? For as soon as Zion travailed, she brought forth her children.

⁹ Shall I bring to the birth, and not cause to bring forth? saith the Lord; shall I cause to bring forth, and shut the womb? saith thy God.

MORMONISM

Besides Methodism, Mormonism was one of the fastest growing religions in the United States. A distinctly American religion, Mormonism self-consciously traced its roots to the Hebrew Bible.

The Book of Mormon was published in 1830, in the midst of the Second Great Awakening. Joseph Smith claimed to have been visited by the Angel Moroni, who directed him to golden plates buried in a hill in upstate New York. The plates were inscribed in a language he called "reformed Egyptian." The plates could only be read with spectacles, though some accounts claim that Smith read them with seer stones in a top hat that were called Urim *and* Thummim, *also the motto of Yale University. The book recounts the history of Lehi, whom God informed in a dream of the impending destruction of Jerusalem by the Babylonians. Lehi crossed the Arabian Peninsula and fled to America, described as the promised land. In America the descendants of Lehi split into two, the Nephites and Lamanites, and grew into flourishing civilizations. God called prophets among them, and their prophecies are recorded in the Book of Mormon. Hundreds of years after their migration to America, and after his own death, Jesus appeared in America to minister to the descendants of Lehi, after which Christ ascended to heaven. But a few hundred years later (around 350 CE) the tribes fell into war with each other, and the Nephite civilization was destroyed. Before the final destruction, a Nephite prophet named Mormon compiled and abridged all the prophetic writings, which he passed to his son Moroni, who fled and buried them in New York. The Lamanite civilization grew and became the Amerindians (making the Native Americans the descendants of the Israelites). Fourteen hundred years after Moroni buried the plates he appeared to Joseph Smith, in upstate New York, and directed him to them.*

Mormonism attracted both followers and enemies in the 1830s with its message of the later comings of Jesus to the New World. It exerted great appeal

to a segment of the population saturated with language about the impending
rapture. Mormonism did not spring ex nihilo out of American soil but was
in fact part of a fairly long tradition of biblical-style writing that claimed to
be rediscovered lost texts.[3] But many communities were skeptical of Mormonism and often outright hostile to its followers. The hostility they encountered
forced the Mormons to constantly relocate; they became a nomadic people,
moving from Ohio to Missouri, and from thence to Illinois, where Joseph
Smith was killed. His death led to a power vacuum and a fight over control
of the church. It was eventually won by Brigham Young, whose writings are
excerpted below. Young, often called the "American Moses," ultimately established the Mormon community in Utah.

Hebraic Sources
Exodus 28

(ל) וְנָתַתָּ אֶל חֹשֶׁן הַמִּשְׁפָּט אֶת הָאוּרִים וְאֶת הַתֻּמִּים וְהָיוּ עַל לֵב אַהֲרֹן בְּבֹאוֹ
לִפְנֵי ה' וְנָשָׂא אַהֲרֹן אֶת מִשְׁפַּט בְּנֵי יִשְׂרָאֵל עַל לִבּוֹ לִפְנֵי ה' תָּמִיד.

[30] And thou shalt put in the breastplate of judgment the Urim and the Thummim;
and they shall be upon Aaron's heart, when he goeth in before the Lord; and Aaron
shall bear the judgment of the children of Israel upon his heart before the Lord
continually.

Numbers 27

(יח) וַיֹּאמֶר ה' אֶל מֹשֶׁה קַח לְךָ אֶת יְהוֹשֻׁעַ בִּן נוּן אִישׁ אֲשֶׁר רוּחַ בּוֹ וְסָמַכְתָּ
אֶת יָדְךָ עָלָיו.
(יט) וְהַעֲמַדְתָּ אֹתוֹ לִפְנֵי אֶלְעָזָר הַכֹּהֵן וְלִפְנֵי כָּל הָעֵדָה וְצִוִּיתָה אֹתוֹ לְעֵינֵיהֶם.
(כ) וְנָתַתָּה מֵהוֹדְךָ עָלָיו לְמַעַן יִשְׁמְעוּ כָּל עֲדַת בְּנֵי יִשְׂרָאֵל.
(כא) וְלִפְנֵי אֶלְעָזָר הַכֹּהֵן יַעֲמֹד וְשָׁאַל לוֹ בְּמִשְׁפַּט הָאוּרִים לִפְנֵי ה' עַל פִּיו יֵצְאוּ
וְעַל פִּיו יָבֹאוּ הוּא וְכָל בְּנֵי יִשְׂרָאֵל אִתּוֹ וְכָל הָעֵדָה.
(כב) וַיַּעַשׂ מֹשֶׁה כַּאֲשֶׁר צִוָּה ה' אֹתוֹ וַיִּקַּח אֶת יְהוֹשֻׁעַ וַיַּעֲמִדֵהוּ לִפְנֵי אֶלְעָזָר
הַכֹּהֵן וְלִפְנֵי כָּל הָעֵדָה.
(כג) וַיִּסְמֹךְ אֶת יָדָיו עָלָיו וַיְצַוֵּהוּ כַּאֲשֶׁר דִּבֶּר ה' בְּיַד מֹשֶׁה.

---

3. Shalev, 105-8.

¹⁸ And the Lord said unto Moses: Take thee Joshua the son of Nun, a man in whom is the spirit, and lay thine hand upon him;

¹⁹ And set him before Eleazar the priest, and before all the congregation; and give him a charge in their sight.

²⁰ And thou shalt put some of thine honor upon him, that all the congregation of the children of Israel may be obedient.

²¹ And he shall stand before Eleazar the priest, who shall ask counsel for him after the judgment of Urim before the Lord; at his word shall they go out, and at his word they shall come in, both he, and all the children of Israel with him, even all the congregation.

²² And Moses did as the Lord commanded him; and he took Joshua, and set him before Eleazar the priest, and before all the congregation.

²³ And he laid his hands upon him, and gave him a charge, as the Lord commanded by the hand of Moses.

Book of Mormon: Nephi, Chapter 18 (1830)

The following is an excerpt from the first book of Nephi, chapter 18, which recounts the building of the ship that takes Nephi and his family across the Mediterranean and the Atlantic to America, called the promised land, where they arrived in 589 BCE.[4]

1. And it came to pass that they did worship the Lord, and did go forth with me; and we did work timbers of curious workmanship. And the Lord did show me from time to time after what manner I should work the timbers of the ship.

2. Now I, Nephi, did not work the timbers after the manner which was learned by men, neither did I build the ship after the manner of men; but I did build it after the manner which the Lord had shown unto me; wherefore, it was not after the manner of men.

3. And I, Nephi, did go into the mount oft, and I did pray oft unto the Lord; wherefore the Lord showed unto me great things.

4. And it came to pass that after I had finished the ship, according to the word of the Lord, my brethren beheld that it was good, and that the workmanship thereof was exceedingly fine; wherefore, they did humble themselves again before the Lord.

5. And it came to pass that the voice of the Lord came unto my father, that we should arise and go down into the ship.

---

4. https://www.lds.org/scriptures/bofm/1-ne/18?lang=eng.

6. And it came to pass that on the morrow, after we had prepared all things, much fruits and meat from the wilderness, and honey in abundance, and provisions according to that which the Lord had commanded us, we did go down into the ship, with all our loading and our seeds, and whatsoever thing we had brought with us, every one according to his age; wherefore, we did all go down into the ship, with our wives and our children.

7. And now, my father had begat two sons in the wilderness; the elder was called Jacob and the younger Joseph.

8. And it came to pass after we had all gone down into the ship, and had taken with us our provisions and things which had been commanded us, we did put forth into the sea and were driven forth before the wind towards the promised land.

9. And after we had been driven forth before the wind for the space of many days, behold, my brethren and the sons of Ishmael and also their wives began to make themselves merry, insomuch that they began to dance, and to sing, and to speak with much rudeness, yea, even that they did forget by what power they had been brought thither; yea, they were lifted up unto exceeding rudeness.

10. And I, Nephi, began to fear exceedingly lest the Lord should be angry with us, and smite us because of our iniquity, that we should be swallowed up in the depths of the sea; wherefore, I, Nephi, began to speak to them with much soberness; but behold they were angry with me, saying: We will not that our younger brother shall be a ruler over us.

11. And it came to pass that Laman and Lemuel did take me and bind me with cords, and they did treat me with much harshness; nevertheless, the Lord did suffer it that he might show forth his power, unto the fulfilling of his word which he had spoken concerning the wicked.

12. And it came to pass that after they had bound me insomuch that I could not move, the compass, which had been prepared of the Lord, did cease to work.

13. Wherefore, they knew not whither they should steer the ship, insomuch that there arose a great storm, yea, a great and terrible

tempest, and we were driven back upon the waters for the space of three days; and they began to be frightened exceedingly lest they should be drowned in the sea; nevertheless they did not loose me.

14. And on the fourth day, which we had been driven back, the tempest began to be exceedingly sore.

15. And it came to pass that we were about to be swallowed up in the depths of the sea. And after we had been driven back upon the waters for the space of four days, my brethren began to see that the judgments of God were upon them, and that they must perish save that they should repent of their iniquities; wherefore, they came unto me, and loosed the bands which were upon my wrists, and behold they had swollen exceedingly; and also mine ankles were much swollen, and great was the soreness thereof.

16. Nevertheless, I did look unto my God, and I did praise him all the day long; and I did not murmur against the Lord because of mine afflictions.

17. Now my father, Lehi, had said many things unto them, and also unto the sons of Ishmael; but, behold, they did breathe out much threatenings against anyone that should speak for me; and my parents being stricken in years, and having suffered much grief because of their children, they were brought down, yea, even upon their sick-beds.

18. Because of their grief and much sorrow, and the iniquity of my brethren, they were brought near even to be carried out of this time to meet their God; yea, their grey hairs were about to be brought down to lie low in the dust; yea, even they were near to be cast with sorrow into a watery grave.

19. And Jacob and Joseph also, being young, having need of much nourishment, were grieved because of the afflictions of their mother; and also my wife with her tears and prayers, and also my children, did not soften the hearts of my brethren that they would loose me.

20. And there was nothing save it were the power of God, which threatened them with destruction, could soften their hearts;

> wherefore, when they saw that they were about to be swallowed up in the depths of the sea they repented of the thing which they had done, insomuch that they loosed me.
>
> 21. And it came to pass after they had loosed me, behold, I took the compass, and it did work whither I desired it. And it came to pass that I prayed unto the Lord; and after I had prayed the winds did cease, and the storm did cease, and there was a great calm.
>
> 22. And it came to pass that I, Nephi, did guide the ship, that we sailed again towards the promised land.
>
> 23. And it came to pass that after we had sailed for the space of many days we did arrive at the promised land; and we went forth upon the land, and did pitch our tents; and we did call it the promised land.

Hebraic Source

"We will not that our younger brother shall be a ruler over us," calls to mind the biblical Joseph story (particularly, Gen. 37:8), and the entire episode quoted above recalls the book of Jonah.

Jonah 1

(ג) וַיָּקָם יוֹנָה לִבְרֹחַ תַּרְשִׁישָׁה מִלִּפְנֵי ה' וַיֵּרֶד יָפוֹ וַיִּמְצָא אֳנִיָּה בָּאָה תַרְשִׁישׁ וַיִּתֵּן שְׂכָרָהּ וַיֵּרֶד בָּהּ לָבוֹא עִמָּהֶם תַּרְשִׁישָׁה מִלִּפְנֵי ה'.

(ד) וַה' הֵטִיל רוּחַ גְּדוֹלָה אֶל הַיָּם וַיְהִי סַעַר גָּדוֹל בַּיָּם וְהָאֳנִיָּה חִשְּׁבָה לְהִשָּׁבֵר.

(ה) וַיִּירְאוּ הַמַּלָּחִים וַיִּזְעֲקוּ אִישׁ אֶל אֱלֹהָיו וַיָּטִלוּ אֶת הַכֵּלִים אֲשֶׁר בָּאֳנִיָּה אֶל הַיָּם לְהָקֵל מֵעֲלֵיהֶם וְיוֹנָה יָרַד אֶל יַרְכְּתֵי הַסְּפִינָה וַיִּשְׁכַּב וַיֵּרָדַם.

(ו) וַיִּקְרַב אֵלָיו רַב הַחֹבֵל וַיֹּאמֶר לוֹ מַה לְּךָ נִרְדָּם קוּם קְרָא אֶל אֱ-לֹהֶיךָ אוּלַי יִתְעַשֵּׁת הָאֱ-לֹהִים לָנוּ וְלֹא נֹאבֵד.

(ז) וַיֹּאמְרוּ אִישׁ אֶל רֵעֵהוּ לְכוּ וְנַפִּילָה גוֹרָלוֹת וְנֵדְעָה בְּשֶׁלְּמִי הָרָעָה הַזֹּאת לָנוּ וַיַּפִּלוּ גּוֹרָלוֹת וַיִּפֹּל הַגּוֹרָל עַל יוֹנָה.

(ח) וַיֹּאמְרוּ אֵלָיו הַגִּידָה נָּא לָנוּ בַּאֲשֶׁר לְמִי הָרָעָה הַזֹּאת לָנוּ מַה מְּלַאכְתְּךָ וּמֵאַיִן תָּבוֹא מָה אַרְצֶךָ וְאֵי מִזֶּה עַם אָתָּה.

(ט) וַיֹּאמֶר אֲלֵיהֶם עִבְרִי אָנֹכִי וְאֶת ה' אֱ-לֹהֵי הַשָּׁמַיִם אֲנִי יָרֵא אֲשֶׁר עָשָׂה אֶת הַיָּם וְאֶת הַיַּבָּשָׁה.

(י) וַיִּירְאוּ הָאֲנָשִׁים יִרְאָה גְדוֹלָה וַיֹּאמְרוּ אֵלָיו מַה זֹּאת עָשִׂיתָ כִּי יָדְעוּ הָאֲנָשִׁים כִּי מִלִּפְנֵי ה' הוּא בֹרֵחַ כִּי הִגִּיד לָהֶם.

(יא) וַיֹּאמְרוּ אֵלָיו מַה נַּעֲשֶׂה לָּךְ וְיִשְׁתֹּק הַיָּם מֵעָלֵינוּ כִּי הַיָּם הוֹלֵךְ וְסֹעֵר.

(יב) וַיֹּאמֶר אֲלֵיהֶם שָׂאוּנִי וַהֲטִילֻנִי אֶל הַיָּם וְיִשְׁתֹּק הַיָּם מֵעֲלֵיכֶם כִּי יוֹדֵעַ אָנִי כִּי בְשֶׁלִּי הַסַּעַר הַגָּדוֹל הַזֶּה עֲלֵיכֶם.

(יג) וַיַּחְתְּרוּ הָאֲנָשִׁים לְהָשִׁיב אֶל הַיַּבָּשָׁה וְלֹא יָכֹלוּ כִּי הַיָּם הוֹלֵךְ וְסֹעֵר עֲלֵיהֶם.

(יד) וַיִּקְרְאוּ אֶל ה' וַיֹּאמְרוּ אָנָּה ה' אַל נָא נֹאבְדָה בְּנֶפֶשׁ הָאִישׁ הַזֶּה וְאַל תִּתֵּן עָלֵינוּ דָּם נָקִיא כִּי אַתָּה ה' כַּאֲשֶׁר חָפַצְתָּ עָשִׂיתָ.

(טו) וַיִּשְׂאוּ אֶת יוֹנָה וַיְטִלֻהוּ אֶל הַיָּם וַיַּעֲמֹד הַיָּם מִזַּעְפּוֹ.

(טז) וַיִּירְאוּ הָאֲנָשִׁים יִרְאָה גְדוֹלָה אֶת ה' וַיִּזְבְּחוּ זֶבַח לַה' וַיִּדְּרוּ נְדָרִים.

³ But Jonah rose up to flee unto Tarshish from the presence of the Lord, and went down to Jaffa; and he found a ship going to Tarshish; so he paid the fare thereof, and went down into it, to go with them unto Tarshish from the presence of the Lord.

⁴ But the Lord sent out a great wind into the sea, and there was a mighty tempest in the sea, so that the ship was like to be broken.

⁵ Then the mariners were afraid, and cried every man unto his god, and cast forth the wares that were in the ship into the sea, to lighten it of them. But Jonah was gone down into the sides of the ship; and he lay, and was fast asleep.

⁶ So the shipmaster came to him, and said unto him: What meanest thou, O sleeper? arise, call upon thy God, if so be that God will think upon us, that we perish not.

⁷ And they said every one to his fellow: Come, and let us cast lots, that we may know for whose cause this evil is upon us. So they cast lots, and the lot fell upon Jonah.

⁸ Then said they unto him: Tell us, we pray thee, for whose cause this evil is upon us. What is thine occupation? and whence comest thou? what is thy country? and of what people art thou?

⁹ And he said unto them: I am a Hebrew; and I fear the Lord, the God of heaven, which hath made the sea and the dry land.

¹⁰ Then were the men exceedingly afraid, and said unto him: Why hast thou done this? For the men knew that he fled from the presence of the Lord, because he had told them.

¹¹ Then said they unto him: What shall we do unto thee, that the sea may be calm unto us? for the sea wrought, and was tempestuous.

¹² And he said unto them: Take me up, and cast me forth into the sea; so shall the sea be calm unto you: for I know that for my sake this great tempest is upon you.

¹³ Nevertheless the men rowed hard to bring it to the land; but they could not: for the sea wrought, and was tempestuous against them.

¹⁴ Wherefore they cried unto the Lord, and said: We beseech thee, O Lord, we beseech thee, let us not perish for this man's life, and lay not upon us innocent blood: for thou, O Lord, hast done as it pleased thee.

¹⁵ So they took up Jonah, and cast him forth into the sea: and the sea ceased from her raging.

¹⁶ Then the men feared the Lord exceedingly, and offered a sacrifice unto the Lord, and made vows.

Discourses of Brigham Young (1854–1886)

The Land of Zion: This is the land of Zion. West of us is a body of water that we call the Pacific, and to the east there is another large body of water which we call the Atlantic, and to the north is where they have tried to discover a northwest passage; these waters surround the land of Zion. (4:301)

And what is Zion? In one sense Zion is the pure in heart.

But is there a land that ever will be called Zion? Yes, brethren. What land is it? It is the land that the Lord gave to Jacob, who bequeathed it to his son Joseph, and his posterity, and they inhabit it, and that land is North and South America. That is Zion, as to land, as to territory, and location. The children of Zion have not yet much in their possession, but their territory is North and South America to begin with. As to the spirit of Zion, it is in the hearts of the Saints of those who love and serve the Lord with all their might, mind and strength. (2:253)

This American continent will be Zion; for it is so spoken of by the prophets. Jerusalem will be rebuilt and will be the place of gathering, and the tribe of Judah will gather there; but this continent of America is the land of Zion. (5:4)

This is the land of Zion – this is the continent whereon the Lord has commenced his work for the last time, and whereon Jesus will make his appearance the second time, when he comes to gather and save the House of Israel. (8:81–82)

Zion will extend, eventually, all over this earth. There will be no nook or corner upon the earth but what will be in Zion. It will all be Zion. (9:138)

The City of Zion. We look forward to the day when the Lord will prepare for the building of the New Jerusalem, preparatory to the City of Enoch's going to be joined with it when it is built upon this earth. We are anticipating to enjoy that day, whether we sleep in death previous to that, or not. We look forward, with all the anticipation and confidence that children can possess in a parent, that we shall be there when Jesus comes; and if we are not there, we will come with him, in either case we shall be there when becomes. (8:342)

We want all the Latter-day Saints to understand how to build up Zion. The City of Zion, in beauty and magnificence, will outstrip anything that is now known upon the earth. The curse will be taken from the earth and sin and corruption will be swept from its face.

Who will do this great work? Is the Lord going to convince the people that he will redeem the center Stake of Zion, beautify it and then place them there without an exertion on their part? No. He will not come here to build a Temple, a Tabernacle, a Bowery, or to set out fruit trees, make aprons of fig leaves or coats of skins, or work in brass and iron, for we already know how to do these things. He will not come here to teach us how to raise and manufacture cotton, how to make hand cards, how to card, how to make spinning machines, looms, etc., etc.

We have to build up Zion, if we do our duty. (10:172)

I have many times asked the questions, "Where is the man that knows how to lay the first rock for the wall that is to surround the New Jerusalem or the Zion of God on the earth? Where is the man who knows how to construct the first gate of the city? Where is the man who understands how to build up the Kingdom of God in its purity and to prepare for Zion to come down to meet it?" "Well," says one, "I thought the Lord was going to do this." So he is if we will let him. This is what we want. We want the people to be willing for the Lord to do it. But he will do it by means. He will not send his angels to gather up the rock to build up the New Jerusalem. He will not send his angels from the heavens to go to the mountains to cut the timber and make it into lumber to adorn the City of Zion. He has called upon us to do this work; and if we will let him work by, through, and with us, he can accomplish it; otherwise we shall fall short, and shall never have the honor of building up Zion on the earth. (13:313)

The Jews and Jerusalem. Jerusalem is not to be redeemed by our going there and preaching to the inhabitants. It will be redeemed by the high hand of the Almighty. It will be given into the possession of the ancient Israelites by the power of God, and by the pouring out of his judgments. (2:141)

Jerusalem is not to be redeemed by the soft, still voice of the preacher of the Gospel of peace. Why? Because they were once the blessed of the Lord, the chosen of the Lord, the promised seed. They were the people from among whom should spring the Messiah, and salvation could be found only through that people. The Messiah came through them, and they killed him; and they will be the last of all the seed of Abraham to have the privilege of receiving the New and Everlasting Covenant. You may hand out to them gold, you may feed and clothe them, but it is impossible to convert the Jews, until the Lord God Almighty does it (2:142) .... We have a great desire for their welfare, and are looking for the time soon to come when they will gather at Jerusalem, build up the city and the land of Palestine, and prepare for the coming of the Messiah. When he comes again, he will not come as he did when the Jews rejected him, neither will he appear first at Jerusalem when he makes his second appearance on the earth; but he will appear first on the land where he commenced his work in the beginning, and planted the Garden of Eden, and that was done in the land of America (11:279).

Zion will extend, eventually, all over this earth. There will be no nook or corner upon the earth but what will be in Zion. It will all be Zion. (9:138)

Hebraic Sources

The notion that Zion is potentially unlimited, expanding beyond the particular geographic location demarcated in the Hebrew Bible, especially in the end times, finds earlier expression in the rabbinic tradition.

Sifrei, Deuteronomy

פיסקא א'. מניין שעתידה ירושלם להיות מגעת עד דמשק? שנאמר "ודמשק מנוחתו" (זכריה ט:א), ואין מנוחתו אלא ירושלם, שנאמר "זאת מנוחתי עדי עד" (תהלים קלב:יד). אמר לו, מה אתה מקיים "ונבנתה עיר על תלה" (ירמיה ל:יח)? אמר לו, שאין עתידה לזוז ממקומה. אמר לו, מה אני מקיים "ורחבה ונסבה למעלה למעלה לצלעות כי מוסב הבית למעלה למעלה סביב סביב לבית על כן רחב הבית למעלה" (יחזקאל מא:ז)? שעתידה ארץ ישראל להיות מרחבת ועולה מכל צדדיה, כתאנה זו שצרה מלמטה ורחבה מלמעלה, ושערי ירושלם עתידים להיות מגיעים עד דמשק, וכן הוא אומר "אפך כמגדל הלבנון צופה פני דמשק" (שיר השירים ז:ה). וגליות באות וחונות בתוכה, שנאמר "ודמשק מנוחתו" (זכריה ט:א), ואומר "והיה באחרית הימים נכון יהיה הר בית ה' בראש ההרים ונשא מגבעות ונהרו אליו כל הגוים והלכו עמים רבים וגו'" (ישעיה ב:ב-ג).

Sec. 1. From where do we know that in the future Jerusalem will be from Gath to Damascus, as it says, "And Damascus its resting place" (Zech. 9:1), and its resting place is nowhere but Jerusalem, as it says, "This is My resting place forever" (Ps. 132:14). Ask him, what then do you make of the verse, "The city shall be built upon its own mound" (Jer. 30:18)? Say to him that in the future it will not move from its present location. Say to him, what do I make of the verse, "And there was an enlarging, and a winding about still upward to the side chambers: for the winding about of the house went still upward round about the house: therefore the breadth of the house was still upward, and so increased from the lowest chamber to the highest by the midst" (Ezek. 41:7)? That in the future the Land of Israel will be widened from all its sides like a fig that is narrow at the bottom and wide at the top, and the gates of Jerusalem will in the future reach Damascus, and so it says, "Your nose is like the tower of Lebanon which looks toward Damascus" (Songs 7:5). And the exiles will come and camp within her, as it says, "And Damascus, its resting place" (Zech. 9:1), and it says, "Now it shall come to pass in the latter days that the mountain of the Lord's house shall be established on the top of the mountains, and shall be exalted above the hills; and all nations shall flow to it ..." (Is. 2:2–3).

Yalkut Shimoni, Isaiah

רמז תק"ג. כתיב "והיה מדי חדש בחדשו" (ישעיה סו:כג), והיאך אפשר שיבא
כל בשר בירושלים בכל שבת ובכל חדש? אמר רבי לוי: עתידה ירושלים
להיות כארץ ישראל, וארץ ישראל, ככל העולם כלו.

Sec. 503. It is written, "And it shall come to pass that from one New Moon to another..." (Is. 66:23). And how is it possible that all beings will come to Jerusalem every Sabbath and every New Moon? Rabbi Levi said: "In the future Jerusalem will be like the Land of Israel, and the Land of Israel will be like the entire world."

Part Four

Slavery, Abolitionism, and the Civil War

Introduction

Europeans brought the African slave trade with them to the New World. There was slavery throughout almost all of the colonized Americas, from the United States to Brazil. The English colonies contained a relatively small proportion of the overall slave population in the Americas. Most slaves were located in the sugar plantations of the Caribbean and the Spanish and Portuguese empires in Central and South America. In the English North American colonies, the population of slaves was dispersed throughout all states, though localized primarily in the Mid-Atlantic states and the South, with the highest concentrations in South Carolina, eastern Virginia, North Carolina, and along the Mississippi River.

Slavery represented, as Lincoln would say, a powerful interest. Cotton constituted about 50 percent of the nation's exports, giving rise to a continual and high demand for slave labor. But not everyone in the South was a slave owner, in fact far from it. While the center of the South's economy was the plantation, with social rules and habits that modeled themselves on aristocratic fiefdoms, there were in actuality not that many plantations. Only about 5 percent of Southern society owned slaves (400,000 out of a population of 8 million), and of those who owned slaves only 3 percent owned more than twenty. About .001 percent of Southern society owned enough slaves to run a significant plantation. The annual average income in the South was $100 in 1850 and the average cost of a slave was $400.

Slave-ownership was therefore an elite, plutocratic phenomenon. But this minuscule minority dominated the South's politics, economy, and culture. Their views were widely shared and their lifestyle was the object of emulation and ambition. To justify what they called their peculiar institution, the South developed an ideology that slavery was good for both races, that it was ordained by God and justified by science, that it was part of the natural order of things, and that it protected the slave from harsh market conditions that immigrants faced in northern cities.

The life of the slave was grueling. If the slave survived the Middle Passage – in which individuals were treated as cargo, chained body to body below deck in a small ship, lying in their own feces next to the dead and dying – a horrific life awaited him in the New World. Sold at auction block like cattle, with families cruelly separated, individuals were taken to live in small, cramped wooden quarters with little clothing and meager food. The workday was long, from dawn to dusk, with only one day of rest a week. Slave overseers drove them hard, and disobedience met with painful physical repercussions.

The Bible in the era of slavery, abolitionism, and the Civil War played, as we will see below, a decidedly ambivalent role. Lincoln's line in his second inaugural address that "both read the same Bible" was the theme of the age. The Bible was on both sides of the conflict: both abolitionists and supporters of slavery appealed to it. The slave had his Bible, and the master had his; the Bible spoke for the North in their fight for the Union to end slavery, and for the South in their fight for independence and to perpetuate slavery. We saw in the previous chapters that during the Second Great Awakening, the Hebrew Bible was largely displaced in the American imagination by the New Testament. In one respect this trend continued, as the Hebrew Bible, it was thought, supposedly justified slavery, so that the opponents of slavery turned to adages from the New Testament. But in another respect the influence of the Hebrew Bible was gaining strength, both in the culture of the oppressed slave and in the thought of the greatest figure to emerge from the period, Abraham Lincoln.

ABOLITIONISM AND THE HEBREW BIBLE

Abolitionism in the United States arose in three major phases. The first coincided with Revolutionary republican ideas but was localized primarily in the Northern states with smaller slave populations. By 1805 most Northern states had abolished slavery and the new states that came into the Union in the North either banned it from their inception or had minimal slave populations in their southern counties. During the Revolutionary period slavery was considered an affront to republican institutions but a necessary evil; given that a large majority of the southern states were slave-holding, it was thought that forming a union required making compromises with the South. These compromises included counting slaves as three-fifths of a person for purposes of representation, returning escaped slaves to their owners by means of the fugitive slave clause, and allowing the slave trade to continue for twenty years. Many revolutionaries believed that slavery was, in the words of Lincoln, "in the course of ultimate extinction," and that within a few generations it would be gone. They were largely mistaken in that belief.

The second phase of abolitionist sentiment grew with the Second Great Awakening, during which republican ideals of equality combined with Christian moral precepts. Moderates and radicals shared the goal of abolition; their views on the means differed dramatically. Free African Americans agitated for immediate, uncompensated abolition both within and beyond the confines of religious discourse. The first great clarion call from an African American was Richard Allen's *Appeal to the Coloured Citizens of the World* (1829). William Lloyd Garrison (1805–1879), the mouthpiece of what came to be known as the abolitionist movement, also favored immediate emancipation by means of pacifist resistance. He published *The Liberator* in 1831, the views of which were the cornerstone of the American Anti-Slavery Society. Abolitionism was considered a fringe movement until well into the 1850s. It encountered stout and hostile resistance for the better part of two decades, even in the North. Abolitionists who gave speeches often put their lives in danger. Even Garrison was dragged through the streets of Boston itself with a noose around his neck. The mainstream and "respectable" portion of white opinion regarding emancipation in the North favored compensated, gradual emancipation coupled with colonization in Africa or South America. This was the view of the American Colonization Society, which received the support of Daniel Webster, Henry Clay, and later Abraham Lincoln. Both the more radical abolitionists and the American

Colonization Society recognized the sinfulness of slavery, but they differed over the proper remedy.

The second phase of abolitionism was more heated than the first and coincided with a more radical defense of slavery in the South. Famous politicians and national figures like John C. Calhoun (former vice president of the United States) argued that slavery was a positive good. On the Senate floor Calhoun proclaimed that "I hold it to be a good.... Never before has the black race of Central Africa, from the dawn of history to the present day, attained a condition so civilized and improved, not only physically, but morally and intellectually" (Speech on the Reception of Abolition Petitions, 1837). Slavery and the Southern society it supported, he argued against George Fitzhugh, was far more humane than northern individualism, capitalism, and wage labor.

The third phase of abolition came during the Civil War. During the war, Northern opinion shifted dramatically. There was a steady migration of Northern opinion from gradual, compensated emancipation to immediate, uncompensated emancipation. However, emancipation did not mean full equality. While the Civil War, and especially the success of black regiments, changed Northern opinion, blacks were still not seen as fully equal citizens. The story of abolition in the United States is not as simple as a non-racist North and a racist South. Nor is it a simple story of slavery followed by a glorious emancipation. Even in the centers of abolitionist thinking like Boston, there were few citizens who advocated for egalitarian citizenship and equal access. Places of higher learning, public establishments and accommodations, and access to the great opportunities of American life were for the most part closed to African Americans for a long time after the Civil War.

While radical abolitionism often joined hands with some evangelical movements, the relation of the Hebrew Bible to abolitionism, and to slavery more generally, was ambivalent. Henry Adams remarked that "slavery drove the whole Puritan community back on its Puritanism."[1] The language of the abolitionist movement coupled slavery strongly to sin, and urged its eradication as a national purification. They saw themselves as biblical figures and used biblical language to describe their activities,

---

1. Henry Adams, cited in McKenna, 129.

citing Exodus and Isaiah. "Abolitionist iconography was emblazoned with biblical texts: 'I have heard their cry' (Ex. 3:7), 'Let my people go' (Ex. 5:1), 'Liberty proclaimed throughout the land' (Lev. 25:10), 'Break every yoke' (Is. 58:6) and 'Deliverance to the captives' (Luke 4:18)."[2] The abolitionist movement, however, was less focused on the Hebrew Bible than on the New Testament (a strong contrast with the slaves themselves, whose narratives were very much infused with the Hebraic narrative).

The problem with religious denunciations of slavery was that there were also religious defenses of it, many of which had supposedly strong scriptural foundations. Pro-slavery advocates cited Genesis 9:25–27, 14:14–15; Deuteronomy 20:10–11; and Leviticus 25:44–54. Advocates of slavery or racial inequality connected the progeny of Ham, cursed by Noah, with blackness, a theme repeated by the Mormons in the book of Nephi. There seemed to be ample material in the Hebrew Bible to apply to the support of slavery. Many of these readings were not sophisticated or consonant with the Jewish hermeneutic tradition. But to many the Hebrew Bible appeared to sanction slavery. Some therefore turned to the New Testament to defend abolitionism. Others discarded entirely a biblical attack on slavery. Garrison, despite his conversion experience under Lyman Beecher, was largely a secular leader. John Brown, whose famous raid on Harper's Ferry was a catalyst of Northern feeling and Southern fear and resentment, styled himself a new Oliver Cromwell, a prophet of sorts, a leader of a great army. Abolitionism was, like all American movements, diverse.

Hebraic Souces
Anti-Slavery Sources
Exodus 3

(א) וּמֹשֶׁה הָיָה רֹעֶה אֶת צֹאן יִתְרוֹ חֹתְנוֹ כֹּהֵן מִדְיָן וַיִּנְהַג אֶת הַצֹּאן אַחַר הַמִּדְבָּר וַיָּבֹא אֶל הַר הָאֱ-לֹהִים חֹרֵבָה.

(ב) וַיֵּרָא מַלְאַךְ ה' אֵלָיו בְּלַבַּת אֵשׁ מִתּוֹךְ הַסְּנֶה וַיַּרְא וְהִנֵּה הַסְּנֶה בֹּעֵר בָּאֵשׁ וְהַסְּנֶה אֵינֶנּוּ אֻכָּל.

(ג) וַיֹּאמֶר מֹשֶׁה אָסֻרָה נָּא וְאֶרְאֶה אֶת הַמַּרְאֶה הַגָּדֹל הַזֶּה מַדּוּעַ לֹא יִבְעַר הַסְּנֶה.

---

2. See John Coffey, "To Release the Oppressed," *Cambridge Papers* (Dec. 2009), 18:4. Available at http://www.jubilee-centre.org/to-release-the-oppressed-reclaiming-a-biblical-theology-of-liberation-by-john-coffey/.

(ד) וַיַּרְא ה' כִּי סָר לִרְאוֹת וַיִּקְרָא אֵלָיו אֱ-לֹהִים מִתּוֹךְ הַסְּנֶה וַיֹּאמֶר מֹשֶׁה מֹשֶׁה וַיֹּאמֶר הִנֵּנִי.

(ה) וַיֹּאמֶר אַל תִּקְרַב הֲלֹם שַׁל נְעָלֶיךָ מֵעַל רַגְלֶיךָ כִּי הַמָּקוֹם אֲשֶׁר אַתָּה עוֹמֵד עָלָיו אַדְמַת קֹדֶשׁ הוּא.

(ו) וַיֹּאמֶר אָנֹכִי אֱ-לֹהֵי אָבִיךָ אֱ-לֹהֵי אַבְרָהָם אֱ-לֹהֵי יִצְחָק וֵא-לֹהֵי יַעֲקֹב וַיַּסְתֵּר מֹשֶׁה פָּנָיו כִּי יָרֵא מֵהַבִּיט אֶל הָאֱ-לֹהִים.

(ז) וַיֹּאמֶר ה' רָאֹה רָאִיתִי אֶת עֳנִי עַמִּי אֲשֶׁר בְּמִצְרָיִם וְאֶת צַעֲקָתָם שָׁמַעְתִּי מִפְּנֵי נֹגְשָׂיו כִּי יָדַעְתִּי אֶת מַכְאֹבָיו.

(ח) וָאֵרֵד לְהַצִּילוֹ מִיַּד מִצְרַיִם וּלְהַעֲלֹתוֹ מִן הָאָרֶץ הַהִוא אֶל אֶרֶץ טוֹבָה וּרְחָבָה אֶל אֶרֶץ זָבַת חָלָב וּדְבָשׁ אֶל מְקוֹם הַכְּנַעֲנִי וְהַחִתִּי וְהָאֱמֹרִי וְהַפְּרִזִּי וְהַחִוִּי וְהַיְבוּסִי.

(ט) וְעַתָּה הִנֵּה צַעֲקַת בְּנֵי יִשְׂרָאֵל בָּאָה אֵלָי וְגַם רָאִיתִי אֶת הַלַּחַץ אֲשֶׁר מִצְרַיִם לֹחֲצִים אֹתָם.

(י) וְעַתָּה לְכָה וְאֶשְׁלָחֲךָ אֶל פַּרְעֹה וְהוֹצֵא אֶת עַמִּי בְנֵי יִשְׂרָאֵל מִמִּצְרָיִם.

[1] Now Moses kept the flock of Jethro his father in law, the priest of Midian: and he led the flock to the backside of the desert, and came to the mountain of God, even to Horeb.
[2] And the angel of the Lord appeared unto him in a flame of fire out of the midst of a bush: and he looked, and, behold, the bush burned with fire, and the bush was not consumed.
[3] And Moses said, I will now turn aside, and see this great sight, why the bush is not burnt.
[4] And when the Lord saw that he turned aside to see, God called unto him out of the midst of the bush, and said, Moses, Moses. And he said, Here am I.
[5] And he said, Draw not nigh hither: put off thy shoes from off thy feet, for the place whereon thou standest is holy ground.
[6] Moreover he said, I am the God of thy father, the God of Abraham, the God of Isaac, and the God of Jacob. And Moses hid his face; for he was afraid to look upon God.
[7] And the Lord said, I have surely seen the affliction of my people which are in Egypt, and have heard their cry by reason of their taskmasters; for I know their sorrows;
[8] And I am come down to deliver them out of the hand of the Egyptians, and to bring them up out of that land unto a good land and a large, unto a land flowing with milk and honey; unto the place of the Canaanites, and the Hittites, and the Amorites, and the Perizzites, and the Hivites, and the Jebusites.
[9] Now therefore, behold, the cry of the children of Israel is come unto me: and I have also seen the oppression wherewith the Egyptians oppress them.
[10] Come now therefore, and I will send thee unto Pharaoh, that thou mayest bring forth my people the children of Israel out of Egypt.

Exodus 5

(א) וְאַחַר בָּאוּ מֹשֶׁה וְאַהֲרֹן וַיֹּאמְרוּ אֶל פַּרְעֹה כֹּה אָמַר ה' אֱ־לֹהֵי יִשְׂרָאֵל שַׁלַּח אֶת עַמִּי וְיָחֹגּוּ לִי בַּמִּדְבָּר.

(ב) וַיֹּאמֶר פַּרְעֹה מִי ה' אֲשֶׁר אֶשְׁמַע בְּקֹלוֹ לְשַׁלַּח אֶת יִשְׂרָאֵל לֹא יָדַעְתִּי אֶת ה' וְגַם אֶת יִשְׂרָאֵל לֹא אֲשַׁלֵּחַ.

(ג) וַיֹּאמְרוּ אֱ־לֹהֵי הָעִבְרִים נִקְרָא עָלֵינוּ נֵלֲכָה נָּא דֶּרֶךְ שְׁלֹשֶׁת יָמִים בַּמִּדְבָּר וְנִזְבְּחָה לַה' אֱ־לֹהֵינוּ פֶּן יִפְגָּעֵנוּ בַּדֶּבֶר אוֹ בֶחָרֶב.

(ד) וַיֹּאמֶר אֲלֵהֶם מֶלֶךְ מִצְרַיִם לָמָּה מֹשֶׁה וְאַהֲרֹן תַּפְרִיעוּ אֶת הָעָם מִמַּעֲשָׂיו לְכוּ לְסִבְלֹתֵיכֶם.

(ה) וַיֹּאמֶר פַּרְעֹה הֵן רַבִּים עַתָּה עַם הָאָרֶץ וְהִשְׁבַּתֶּם אֹתָם מִסִּבְלֹתָם.

[1] And afterward Moses and Aaron went in, and told Pharaoh, Thus saith the Lord God of Israel, Let my people go, that they may hold a feast unto me in the wilderness.

[2] And Pharaoh said, Who is the Lord, that I should obey his voice to let Israel go? I know not the Lord, neither will I let Israel go.

[3] And they said, The God of the Hebrews hath met with us: let us go, we pray thee, three days' journey into the desert, and sacrifice unto the Lord our God; lest he fall upon us with pestilence, or with the sword.

[4] And the king of Egypt said unto them, Wherefore do ye, Moses and Aaron, let the people from their works? get you unto your burdens.

[5] And Pharaoh said, Behold, the people of the land now are many, and ye make them rest from their burdens.

Leviticus 25

(ח) וְסָפַרְתָּ לְךָ שֶׁבַע שַׁבְּתֹת שָׁנִים שֶׁבַע שָׁנִים שֶׁבַע פְּעָמִים וְהָיוּ לְךָ יְמֵי שֶׁבַע שַׁבְּתֹת הַשָּׁנִים תֵּשַׁע וְאַרְבָּעִים שָׁנָה.

(ט) וְהַעֲבַרְתָּ שׁוֹפַר תְּרוּעָה בַּחֹדֶשׁ הַשְּׁבִעִי בֶּעָשׂוֹר לַחֹדֶשׁ בְּיוֹם הַכִּפֻּרִים תַּעֲבִירוּ שׁוֹפָר בְּכָל אַרְצְכֶם.

(י) וְקִדַּשְׁתֶּם אֵת שְׁנַת הַחֲמִשִּׁים שָׁנָה וּקְרָאתֶם דְּרוֹר בָּאָרֶץ לְכָל יֹשְׁבֶיהָ יוֹבֵל הִוא תִּהְיֶה לָכֶם וְשַׁבְתֶּם אִישׁ אֶל אֲחֻזָּתוֹ וְאִישׁ אֶל מִשְׁפַּחְתּוֹ תָּשֻׁבוּ.

[8] And thou shalt number seven sabbaths of years unto thee, seven times seven years; and the space of the seven sabbaths of years shall be unto thee forty and nine years.

[9] Then shalt thou cause the trumpet of the jubile to sound on the tenth day of the seventh month, in the day of atonement shall ye make the trumpet sound throughout all your land.

[10] And ye shall hallow the fiftieth year, and proclaim liberty throughout all the land unto all the inhabitants thereof: it shall be a jubile unto you; and ye shall return every man unto his possession, and ye shall return every man unto his family.

Isaiah 58

(א) קְרָא בְגָרוֹן אַל תַּחְשֹׂךְ כַּשּׁוֹפָר הָרֵם קוֹלֶךָ וְהַגֵּד לְעַמִּי פִּשְׁעָם וּלְבֵית יַעֲקֹב חַטֹּאתָם.

(ב) וְאוֹתִי יוֹם יוֹם יִדְרֹשׁוּן וְדַעַת דְּרָכַי יֶחְפָּצוּן כְּגוֹי אֲשֶׁר צְדָקָה עָשָׂה וּמִשְׁפַּט אֱלֹהָיו לֹא עָזָב יִשְׁאָלוּנִי מִשְׁפְּטֵי צֶדֶק קִרְבַת אֱלֹהִים יֶחְפָּצוּן.

(ג) לָמָּה צַּמְנוּ וְלֹא רָאִיתָ עִנִּינוּ נַפְשֵׁנוּ וְלֹא תֵדָע הֵן בְּיוֹם צֹמְכֶם תִּמְצְאוּ חֵפֶץ וְכָל עַצְּבֵיכֶם תִּנְגֹּשׂוּ.

(ד) הֵן לְרִיב וּמַצָּה תָּצוּמוּ וּלְהַכּוֹת בְּאֶגְרֹף רֶשַׁע לֹא תָצוּמוּ כַיּוֹם לְהַשְׁמִיעַ בַּמָּרוֹם קוֹלְכֶם.

(ה) הֲכָזֶה יִהְיֶה צוֹם אֶבְחָרֵהוּ יוֹם עַנּוֹת אָדָם נַפְשׁוֹ הֲלָכֹף כְּאַגְמֹן רֹאשׁוֹ וְשַׂק וָאֵפֶר יַצִּיעַ הֲלָזֶה תִּקְרָא צוֹם וְיוֹם רָצוֹן לַה'.

(ו) הֲלוֹא זֶה צוֹם אֶבְחָרֵהוּ פַּתֵּחַ חַרְצֻבּוֹת רֶשַׁע הַתֵּר אֲגֻדּוֹת מוֹטָה וְשַׁלַּח רְצוּצִים חָפְשִׁים וְכָל מוֹטָה תְּנַתֵּקוּ.

(ז) הֲלוֹא פָרֹס לָרָעֵב לַחְמֶךָ וַעֲנִיִּים מְרוּדִים תָּבִיא בָיִת כִּי תִרְאֶה עָרֹם וְכִסִּיתוֹ וּמִבְּשָׂרְךָ לֹא תִתְעַלָּם.

(ח) אָז יִבָּקַע כַּשַּׁחַר אוֹרֶךָ וַאֲרֻכָתְךָ מְהֵרָה תִצְמָח וְהָלַךְ לְפָנֶיךָ צִדְקֶךָ כְּבוֹד ה' יַאַסְפֶךָ.

(ט) אָז תִּקְרָא וַה' יַעֲנֶה תְּשַׁוַּע וְיֹאמַר הִנֵּנִי אִם תָּסִיר מִתּוֹכְךָ מוֹטָה שְׁלַח אֶצְבַּע וְדַבֶּר אָוֶן.

[1] Cry aloud, spare not, lift up thy voice like a trumpet, and shew my people their transgression, and the house of Jacob their sins.
[2] Yet they seek me daily, and delight to know my ways, as a nation that did righteousness, and forsook not the ordinance of their God: they ask of me the ordinances of justice; they take delight in approaching to God.
[3] Wherefore have we fasted, say they, and thou seest not? wherefore have we afflicted our soul, and thou takest no knowledge? Behold, in the day of your fast ye find pleasure, and exact all your labours.
[4] Behold, ye fast for strife and debate, and to smite with the fist of wickedness: ye shall not fast as ye do this day, to make your voice to be heard on high.
[5] Is it such a fast that I have chosen? a day for a man to afflict his soul? is it to bow down his head as a bulrush, and to spread sackcloth and ashes under him? wilt thou call this a fast, and an acceptable day to the Lord?
[6] Is not this the fast that I have chosen? to loose the bands of wickedness, to undo the heavy burdens, and to let the oppressed go free, and that ye break every yoke?
[7] Is it not to deal thy bread to the hungry, and that thou bring the poor that are cast out to thy house? when thou seest the naked, that thou cover him; and that thou hide not thyself from thine own flesh?

[8] Then shall thy light break forth as the morning, and thine health shall spring forth speedily: and thy righteousness shall go before thee; the glory of the Lord shall be thy rereward.

[9] Then shalt thou call, and the Lord shall answer; thou shalt cry, and he shall say, Here I am. If thou take away from the midst of thee the yoke, the putting forth of the finger, and speaking vanity;

Pro-Slavery Sources
Genesis 9

(כ) וַיָּחֶל נֹחַ אִישׁ הָאֲדָמָה וַיִּטַּע כָּרֶם.

(כא) וַיֵּשְׁתְּ מִן הַיַּיִן וַיִּשְׁכָּר וַיִּתְגַּל בְּתוֹךְ אָהֳלֹה.

(כב) וַיַּרְא חָם אֲבִי כְנַעַן אֵת עֶרְוַת אָבִיו וַיַּגֵּד לִשְׁנֵי אֶחָיו בַּחוּץ.

(כג) וַיִּקַּח שֵׁם וָיֶפֶת אֶת הַשִּׂמְלָה וַיָּשִׂימוּ עַל שְׁכֶם שְׁנֵיהֶם וַיֵּלְכוּ אֲחֹרַנִּית וַיְכַסּוּ אֵת עֶרְוַת אֲבִיהֶם וּפְנֵיהֶם אֲחֹרַנִּית וְעֶרְוַת אֲבִיהֶם לֹא רָאוּ.

(כד) וַיִּיקֶץ נֹחַ מִיֵּינוֹ וַיֵּדַע אֵת אֲשֶׁר עָשָׂה לוֹ בְּנוֹ הַקָּטָן.

(כה) וַיֹּאמֶר אָרוּר כְּנָעַן עֶבֶד עֲבָדִים יִהְיֶה לְאֶחָיו.

(כו) וַיֹּאמֶר בָּרוּךְ ה' אֱ-לֹהֵי שֵׁם וִיהִי כְנַעַן עֶבֶד לָמוֹ.

(כז) יַפְתְּ אֱ-לֹהִים לְיֶפֶת וְיִשְׁכֹּן בְּאָהֳלֵי שֵׁם וִיהִי כְנַעַן עֶבֶד לָמוֹ.

[20] And Noah began to be an husbandman, and he planted a vineyard:

[21] And he drank of the wine, and was drunken; and he was uncovered within his tent.

[22] And Ham, the father of Canaan, saw the nakedness of his father, and told his two brethren without.

[23] And Shem and Japheth took a garment, and laid it upon both their shoulders, and went backward, and covered the nakedness of their father; and their faces were backward, and they saw not their father's nakedness.

[24] And Noah awoke from his wine, and knew what his younger son had done unto him.

[25] And he said, Cursed be Canaan; a servant of servants shall he be unto his brethren.

[26] And he said, Blessed be the Lord God of Shem; and Canaan shall be his servant.

[27] God shall enlarge Japheth, and he shall dwell in the tents of Shem; and Canaan shall be his servant.

Genesis 14

(א) וַיְהִי בִּימֵי אַמְרָפֶל מֶלֶךְ שִׁנְעָר אַרְיוֹךְ מֶלֶךְ אֶלָּסָר כְּדָרְלָעֹמֶר מֶלֶךְ עֵילָם וְתִדְעָל מֶלֶךְ גּוֹיִם.

(ב) עָשׂוּ מִלְחָמָה אֶת בֶּרַע מֶלֶךְ סְדֹם וְאֶת בִּרְשַׁע מֶלֶךְ עֲמֹרָה שִׁנְאָב מֶלֶךְ אַדְמָה וְשֶׁמְאֵבֶר מֶלֶךְ צְבֹיִים וּמֶלֶךְ בֶּלַע הִיא צֹעַר.

(י) וְעֵמֶק הַשִּׂדִּים בֶּאֱרֹת בֶּאֱרֹת חֵמָר וַיָּנֻסוּ מֶלֶךְ סְדֹם וַעֲמֹרָה וַיִּפְּלוּ שָׁמָּה וְהַנִּשְׁאָרִים הֶרָה נָּסוּ.

(יא) וַיִּקְחוּ אֶת כָּל רְכֻשׁ סְדֹם וַעֲמֹרָה וְאֶת כָּל אָכְלָם וַיֵּלֵכוּ.

(יב) וַיִּקְחוּ אֶת לוֹט וְאֶת רְכֻשׁוֹ בֶּן אֲחִי אַבְרָם וַיֵּלֵכוּ וְהוּא יֹשֵׁב בִּסְדֹם.

(יג) וַיָּבֹא הַפָּלִיט וַיַּגֵּד לְאַבְרָם הָעִבְרִי וְהוּא שֹׁכֵן בְּאֵלֹנֵי מַמְרֵא הָאֱמֹרִי אֲחִי אֶשְׁכֹּל וַאֲחִי עָנֵר וְהֵם בַּעֲלֵי בְרִית אַבְרָם.

(יד) וַיִּשְׁמַע אַבְרָם כִּי נִשְׁבָּה אָחִיו וַיָּרֶק אֶת חֲנִיכָיו יְלִידֵי בֵיתוֹ שְׁמֹנָה עָשָׂר וּשְׁלֹשׁ מֵאוֹת וַיִּרְדֹּף עַד דָּן.

(טו) וַיֵּחָלֵק עֲלֵיהֶם לַיְלָה הוּא וַעֲבָדָיו וַיַּכֵּם וַיִּרְדְּפֵם עַד חוֹבָה אֲשֶׁר מִשְּׂמֹאל לְדַמָּשֶׂק.

[1] And it came to pass in the days of Amraphel king of Shinar, Arioch king of Ellasar, Chedorlaomer king of Elam, and Tidal king of nations;

[2] That these made war with Bera king of Sodom, and with Birsha king of Gomorrah, Shinab king of Admah, and Shemeber king of Zeboiim, and the king of Bela, which is Zoar.

[10] And the vale of Siddim was full of slimepits; and the kings of Sodom and Gomorrah fled, and fell there; and they that remained fled to the mountain.

[11] And they took all the goods of Sodom and Gomorrah, and all their victuals, and went their way.

[12] And they took Lot, Abram's brother's son, who dwelt in Sodom, and his goods, and departed.

[13] And there came one that had escaped, and told Abram the Hebrew; for he dwelt in the plain of Mamre the Amorite, brother of Eshcol, and brother of Aner: and these were confederate with Abram.

[14] And when Abram heard that his brother was taken captive, he armed his trained servants, born in his own house, three hundred and eighteen, and pursued them unto Dan.

[15] And he divided himself against them, he and his servants, by night, and smote them, and pursued them unto Hobah, which is on the left hand of Damascus.

Deuteronomy 20

(י) כִּי תִקְרַב אֶל עִיר לְהִלָּחֵם עָלֶיהָ וְקָרָאתָ אֵלֶיהָ לְשָׁלוֹם.

(יא) וְהָיָה אִם שָׁלוֹם תַּעַנְךָ וּפָתְחָה לָךְ וְהָיָה כָּל הָעָם הַנִּמְצָא בָהּ יִהְיוּ לְךָ לָמַס וַעֲבָדוּךָ.

(יב) וְאִם לֹא תַשְׁלִים עִמָּךְ וְעָשְׂתָה עִמְּךָ מִלְחָמָה וְצַרְתָּ עָלֶיהָ.

(יג) וּנְתָנָהּ ה' אֱ־לֹהֶיךָ בְּיָדֶךָ וְהִכִּיתָ אֶת כָּל זְכוּרָהּ לְפִי חָרֶב.

(יד) רַק הַנָּשִׁים וְהַטַּף וְהַבְּהֵמָה וְכֹל אֲשֶׁר יִהְיֶה בָעִיר כָּל שְׁלָלָהּ תָּבֹז לָךְ וְאָכַלְתָּ אֶת שְׁלַל אֹיְבֶיךָ אֲשֶׁר נָתַן ה' אֱ־לֹהֶיךָ לָךְ.

(טו) כֵּן תַּעֲשֶׂה לְכָל הֶעָרִים הָרְחֹקֹת מִמְּךָ מְאֹד אֲשֶׁר לֹא מֵעָרֵי הַגּוֹיִם הָאֵלֶּה הֵנָּה.

[10] When thou comest nigh unto a city to fight against it, then proclaim peace unto it.

¹¹ And it shall be, if it make thee answer of peace, and open unto thee, then it shall be, that all the people that is found therein shall be tributaries unto thee, and they shall serve thee.

¹² And if it will make no peace with thee, but will make war against thee, then thou shalt besiege it:

¹³ And when the Lord thy God hath delivered it into thine hands, thou shalt smite every male thereof with the edge of the sword:

¹⁴ But the women, and the little ones, and the cattle, and all that is in the city, even all the spoil thereof, shalt thou take unto thyself; and thou shalt eat the spoil of thine enemies, which the Lord thy God hath given thee.

¹⁵ Thus shalt thou do unto all the cities which are very far off from thee, which are not of the cities of these nations.

Leviticus 25

(מד) וְעַבְדְּךָ וַאֲמָתְךָ אֲשֶׁר יִהְיוּ לָךְ מֵאֵת הַגּוֹיִם אֲשֶׁר סְבִיבֹתֵיכֶם מֵהֶם תִּקְנוּ עֶבֶד וְאָמָה.

(מה) וְגַם מִבְּנֵי הַתּוֹשָׁבִים הַגָּרִים עִמָּכֶם מֵהֶם תִּקְנוּ וּמִמִּשְׁפַּחְתָּם אֲשֶׁר עִמָּכֶם אֲשֶׁר הוֹלִידוּ בְּאַרְצְכֶם וְהָיוּ לָכֶם לַאֲחֻזָּה.

(מו) וְהִתְנַחַלְתֶּם אֹתָם לִבְנֵיכֶם אַחֲרֵיכֶם לָרֶשֶׁת אֲחֻזָּה לְעֹלָם בָּהֶם תַּעֲבֹדוּ וּבְאַחֵיכֶם בְּנֵי יִשְׂרָאֵל אִישׁ בְּאָחִיו לֹא תִרְדֶּה בוֹ בְּפָרֶךְ.

(מז) וְכִי תַשִּׂיג יַד גֵּר וְתוֹשָׁב עִמָּךְ וּמָךְ אָחִיךָ עִמּוֹ וְנִמְכַּר לְגֵר תּוֹשָׁב עִמָּךְ אוֹ לְעֵקֶר מִשְׁפַּחַת גֵּר.

(מח) אַחֲרֵי נִמְכַּר גְּאֻלָּה תִּהְיֶה לּוֹ אֶחָד מֵאֶחָיו יִגְאָלֶנּוּ.

(מט) אוֹ דֹדוֹ אוֹ בֶן דֹּדוֹ יִגְאָלֶנּוּ אוֹ מִשְּׁאֵר בְּשָׂרוֹ מִמִּשְׁפַּחְתּוֹ יִגְאָלֶנּוּ אוֹ הִשִּׂיגָה יָדוֹ וְנִגְאָל.

(נ) וְחִשַּׁב עִם קֹנֵהוּ מִשְּׁנַת הִמָּכְרוֹ לוֹ עַד שְׁנַת הַיֹּבֵל וְהָיָה כֶּסֶף מִמְכָּרוֹ בְּמִסְפַּר שָׁנִים כִּימֵי שָׂכִיר יִהְיֶה עִמּוֹ.

(נא) אִם עוֹד רַבּוֹת בַּשָּׁנִים לְפִיהֶן יָשִׁיב גְּאֻלָּתוֹ מִכֶּסֶף מִקְנָתוֹ.

(נב) וְאִם מְעַט נִשְׁאַר בַּשָּׁנִים עַד שְׁנַת הַיֹּבֵל וְחִשַּׁב לוֹ כְּפִי שָׁנָיו יָשִׁיב אֶת גְּאֻלָּתוֹ.

(נג) כִּשְׂכִיר שָׁנָה בְּשָׁנָה יִהְיֶה עִמּוֹ לֹא יִרְדֶּנּוּ בְּפֶרֶךְ לְעֵינֶיךָ.

(נד) וְאִם לֹא יִגָּאֵל בְּאֵלֶּה וְיָצָא בִּשְׁנַת הַיֹּבֵל הוּא וּבָנָיו עִמּוֹ.

(נה) כִּי לִי בְנֵי יִשְׂרָאֵל עֲבָדִים עֲבָדַי הֵם אֲשֶׁר הוֹצֵאתִי אוֹתָם מֵאֶרֶץ מִצְרָיִם אֲנִי ה' אֱ־לֹהֵיכֶם.

⁴⁴ Both thy bondmen, and thy bondmaids, which thou shalt have, shall be of the heathen that are round about you; of them shall ye buy bondmen and bondmaids.

⁴⁵ Moreover of the children of the strangers that do sojourn among you, of them shall ye buy, and of their families that are with you, which they begat in your land: and they shall be your possession.

⁴⁶ And ye shall take them as an inheritance for your children after you, to inherit them for a possession; they shall be your bondmen for ever: but over your brethren the children of Israel, ye shall not rule one over another with rigour.

⁴⁷ And if a sojourner or stranger wax rich by thee, and thy brother that dwelleth by him wax poor, and sell himself unto the stranger or sojourner by thee, or to the stock of the stranger's family:

⁴⁸ After that he is sold he may be redeemed again; one of his brethren may redeem him: ⁴⁹ Either his uncle, or his uncle's son, may redeem him, or any that is nigh of kin unto him of his family may redeem him; or if he be able, he may redeem himself.

⁵⁰ And he shall reckon with him that bought him from the year that he was sold to him unto the year of jubile: and the price of his sale shall be according unto the number of years, according to the time of an hired servant shall it be with him.

⁵¹ If there be yet many years behind, according unto them he shall give again the price of his redemption out of the money that he was bought for.

⁵² And if there remain but few years unto the year of jubile, then he shall count with him, and according unto his years shall he give him again the price of his redemption.

⁵³ And as a yearly hired servant shall he be with him: and the other shall not rule with rigour over him in thy sight.

⁵⁴ And if he be not redeemed in these years, then he shall go out in the year of jubile, both he, and his children with him.

⁵⁵ For unto me the children of Israel are servants; they are my servants whom I brought forth out of the land of Egypt: I am the Lord your God.

The Debate over Slavery

Benjamin Rush, "An Address to the Inhabitants of the British Settlements in America upon Slave Keeping" (1773)

Benjamin Rush was an early abolitionist. In the following excerpt, Dr. Rush argues that slavery is immoral, uneconomical, and imprudent, and that it goes against Christianity.

But there are some who have gone so far as to say that Slavery is not repugnant to the Genius of Christianity, and that it is not forbidden in any part of the Scripture. Natural and Revealed Religion always speak the same things, although the latter delivers its precepts with a louder and more distinct voice than the former. If it could be proved that no testimony was to be found in the Bible against a practice so pregnant with evils of the most destructive tendency to society, it would be sufficient to overthrow its divine Original. We read it is true of Abraham's having slaves born in his house; and we have reason to believe, that part of the riches of the patriarchs consisted in them; but we can no more infer the lawfulness of the practice, from the short account which the Jewish historian gives us of these facts, than we can vindicate telling a lie, because Rahab is not condemned for it in the account which is given of her deceiving the king of Jericho.

  We read that some of the same men indulged themselves in a plurality of wives, without any strictures being made upon their conduct for it; and yet no one will pretend to say, that this is not forbidden in many parts of the Old Testament. But we are told the Jews kept the Heathens in perpetual bondage. The Design of providence in permitting this evil, was probably to prevent the Jews from marrying amongst strangers, to which their intercourse with them upon any other footing than that of slaves, would naturally have inclined them. Had this taken place – their national religion would have been corrupted – they would have contracted all their vices, and the intention of Providence in keeping them a distant people, in order to accomplish the promise made to Abraham, that "in his seed all the nations of the earth should be blessed," would have been defeated; so that the descent of the Messiah from Abraham, could not have been traced, and the divine commission of the Son of God, would have wanted one of its most powerful arguments to support it. But with regard to their own countrymen, it is plain, perpetual slavery was not tolerated. Hence, at the end of seven years or in the year of the jubilee, all the Hebrew slaves were set at liberty, and it was held unlawful to detain them in servitude longer than that time, except by their own Consent. But if, in the partial Revelation which God made, of his will to the Jews, we find such testimonies against slavery, what may we not expect from the Gospel, the Design of which was to abolish all distinctions of name and country. While the Jews thought they complied with the precepts of the law, in confining the love of their neighbour "to the children of their own people," Christ commands us to look upon all mankind even our Enemies as our neighbours and brethren, and "in all things, to do unto them whatever we would wish they should do unto us." He tells us further that his "Kingdom is not of this World," and therefore constantly avoids saying any thing that might interfere directly with the Roman or Jewish Governments: and although he does not call upon masters to emancipate their slaves, or slaves to assert that Liberty wherewith God and Nature had made them free, yet there is scarcely a parable or a sermon in the whole history of his life, but what contains the strongest arguments against Slavery. Every prohibition of Covetousness – Intemperance – Pride – Uncleanness – Theft – and Murder, which he delivered, every lesson of meekness, humility, forbearance, Charity, Self-denial, and brotherly-love, which he taught, are levelled against this evil; for Slavery, while it includes all the former Vices, necessarily excludes the practice of all the latter Virtues, both from the Master and the Slave. Let such, therefore, who vindicate the traffic of buying and selling Souls, seek some modern System of Religion to support it, and not presume to sanctify their crimes by attempting to reconcile it to the sublime and perfect Religion of the Great Author of Christianity.

There are some amongst us who cannot help allowing the force of our last argument, but plead as a motive for importing and keeping slaves, that they become acquainted with the principles of the religion of our country. This is like justifying a highway robbery because part of the money acquired in this manner was appropriated to some religious use. Christianity will never be propagated by any other methods than those employed by Christ and his Apostles. Slavery is an engine as little fitted for that purpose as Fire or the Sword. A Christian Slave is a contradiction in terms. But if we enquire into the methods employed for converting the Negroes to Christianity, we shall find the means suited to the end proposed. In many places Sunday is appropriated to work for themselves, reading and writing are discouraged among them. A belief is even inculcated amongst some, that they have no Souls. In a word, every attempt to instruct or convert them, has been constantly opposed by their masters. Nor has the example of their christian masters any tendency to prejudice them in favor of our religion. How often do they betray, in their sudden transports of anger and resentment (against which there is no restraint provided towards their Negroes) the most violent degrees of passion and fury! What luxury – what ingratitude to the supreme being – what impiety in their ordinary conversation do some of them discover in the presence of their slaves! I say nothing of the dissolution of marriage vows, or the entire abolition of matrimony, which the frequent sale of them introduces, and which are directly contrary to the laws of nature and the principles of christianity. Would to Heaven I could here conceal the shocking violations of chastity, which some of them are obliged to undergo without daring to complain. Husbands have been forced to prostitute their wives, and mothers their daughters to gratify the brutal lust of a master. This – all – this is practised – Blush – ye impure and hardened wretches, while I repeat it – by men who call themselves christians!

Hebraic Sources

Dr. Rush argued that slave-holding in the Hebrew Bible was for specific limited purposes, including preventing mixing with other nations, which no longer had any validity with the advent of Christianity.

Genesis 12

(טז) וּלְאַבְרָם הֵיטִיב בַּעֲבוּרָהּ וַיְהִי לוֹ צֹאן וּבָקָר וַחֲמֹרִים וַעֲבָדִים וּשְׁפָחֹת וַאֲתֹנֹת וּגְמַלִּים.

[16] And he entreated Abram well for her sake: and he had sheep, and oxen, and he asses, and menservants, and maidservants, and she asses, and camels.

Genesis 14

(יד) וַיִּשְׁמַע אַבְרָם כִּי נִשְׁבָּה אָחִיו וַיָּרֶק אֶת חֲנִיכָיו יְלִידֵי בֵיתוֹ שְׁמֹנָה עָשָׂר וּשְׁלֹשׁ מֵאוֹת וַיִּרְדֹּף עַד דָּן.

[14] And when Abram heard that his brother was taken captive, he armed his trained servants, born in his own house, three hundred and eighteen, and pursued them unto Dan.

Genesis 17

(כג) וַיִּקַּח אַבְרָהָם אֶת יִשְׁמָעֵאל בְּנוֹ וְאֵת כָּל יְלִידֵי בֵיתוֹ וְאֵת כָּל מִקְנַת כַּסְפּוֹ כָּל זָכָר בְּאַנְשֵׁי בֵּית אַבְרָהָם וַיָּמָל אֶת בְּשַׂר עָרְלָתָם בְּעֶצֶם הַיּוֹם הַזֶּה כַּאֲשֶׁר דִּבֶּר אִתּוֹ אֱ־לֹהִים.

[23] And Abraham took Ishmael his son, and all that were born in his house, and all that were bought with his money, every male among the men of Abraham's house; and circumcised the flesh of their foreskin in the selfsame day, as God had said unto him.

Leviticus 25

(מד) וְעַבְדְּךָ וַאֲמָתְךָ אֲשֶׁר יִהְיוּ לָךְ מֵאֵת הַגּוֹיִם אֲשֶׁר סְבִיבֹתֵיכֶם מֵהֶם תִּקְנוּ עֶבֶד וְאָמָה.
(מה) וְגַם מִבְּנֵי הַתּוֹשָׁבִים הַגָּרִים עִמָּכֶם מֵהֶם תִּקְנוּ וּמִמִּשְׁפַּחְתָּם אֲשֶׁר עִמָּכֶם אֲשֶׁר הוֹלִידוּ בְּאַרְצְכֶם וְהָיוּ לָכֶם לַאֲחֻזָּה.
(מו) וְהִתְנַחַלְתֶּם אֹתָם לִבְנֵיכֶם אַחֲרֵיכֶם לָרֶשֶׁת אֲחֻזָּה לְעֹלָם בָּהֶם תַּעֲבֹדוּ וּבְאַחֵיכֶם בְּנֵי יִשְׂרָאֵל אִישׁ בְּאָחִיו לֹא תִרְדֶּה בוֹ בְּפָרֶךְ.

44 Both thy bondmen, and thy bondmaids, which thou shalt have, shall be of the heathen that are round about you; of them shall ye buy bondmen and bondmaids.

45 Moreover of the children of the strangers that do sojourn among you, of them shall ye buy, and of their families that are with you, which they begat in your land: and they shall be your possession.

46 And ye shall take them as an inheritance for your children after you, to inherit them for a possession; they shall be your bondmen for ever: but over your brethren the children of Israel, ye shall not rule one over another with rigour.

Exodus 34

(י) וַיֹּאמֶר הִנֵּה אָנֹכִי כֹּרֵת בְּרִית נֶגֶד כָּל עַמְּךָ אֶעֱשֶׂה נִפְלָאֹת אֲשֶׁר לֹא נִבְרְאוּ בְכָל הָאָרֶץ וּבְכָל הַגּוֹיִם וְרָאָה כָל הָעָם אֲשֶׁר אַתָּה בְקִרְבּוֹ אֶת מַעֲשֵׂה ה' כִּי נוֹרָא הוּא אֲשֶׁר אֲנִי עֹשֶׂה עִמָּךְ.

(יא) שְׁמָר לְךָ אֵת אֲשֶׁר אָנֹכִי מְצַוְּךָ הַיּוֹם הִנְנִי גֹרֵשׁ מִפָּנֶיךָ אֶת הָאֱמֹרִי וְהַכְּנַעֲנִי וְהַחִתִּי וְהַפְּרִזִּי וְהַחִוִּי וְהַיְבוּסִי.

(יב) הִשָּׁמֶר לְךָ פֶּן תִּכְרֹת בְּרִית לְיוֹשֵׁב הָאָרֶץ אֲשֶׁר אַתָּה בָּא עָלֶיהָ פֶּן יִהְיֶה לְמוֹקֵשׁ בְּקִרְבֶּךָ.

(יג) כִּי אֶת מִזְבְּחֹתָם תִּתֹּצוּן וְאֶת מַצֵּבֹתָם תְּשַׁבֵּרוּן וְאֶת אֲשֵׁרָיו תִּכְרֹתוּן.

(יד) כִּי לֹא תִשְׁתַּחֲוֶה לְאֵל אַחֵר כִּי ה' קַנָּא שְׁמוֹ אֵ-ל קַנָּא הוּא.

(טו) פֶּן תִּכְרֹת בְּרִית לְיוֹשֵׁב הָאָרֶץ וְזָנוּ אַחֲרֵי אֱלֹהֵיהֶם וְזָבְחוּ לֵאלֹהֵיהֶם וְקָרָא לְךָ וְאָכַלְתָּ מִזִּבְחוֹ.

(טז) וְלָקַחְתָּ מִבְּנֹתָיו לְבָנֶיךָ וְזָנוּ בְנֹתָיו אַחֲרֵי אֱלֹהֵיהֶן וְהִזְנוּ אֶת בָּנֶיךָ אַחֲרֵי אֱלֹהֵיהֶן.

10 And he said, Behold, I make a covenant: before all thy people I will do marvels, such as have not been done in all the earth, nor in any nation: and all the people among which thou art shall see the work of the Lord: for it is a terrible thing that I will do with thee.

11 Observe thou that which I command thee this day: behold, I drive out before thee the Amorite, and the Canaanite, and the Hittite, and the Perizzite, and the Hivite, and the Jebusite.

12 Take heed to thyself, lest thou make a covenant with the inhabitants of the land whither thou goest, lest it be for a snare in the midst of thee:

13 But ye shall destroy their altars, break their images, and cut down their groves:

14 For thou shalt worship no other god: for the Lord, whose name is Jealous, is a jealous God:

15 Lest thou make a covenant with the inhabitants of the land, and they go a whoring after their gods, and do sacrifice unto their gods, and one call thee, and thou eat of his sacrifice;

16 And thou take of their daughters unto thy sons, and their daughters go a whoring after their gods, and make thy sons go a whoring after their gods.

Exodus 21

(ב) כִּי תִקְנֶה עֶבֶד עִבְרִי שֵׁשׁ שָׁנִים יַעֲבֹד וּבַשְּׁבִעת יֵצֵא לַחָפְשִׁי חִנָּם.
(ג) אִם בְּגַפּוֹ יָבֹא בְּגַפּוֹ יֵצֵא אִם בַּעַל אִשָּׁה הוּא וְיָצְאָה אִשְׁתּוֹ עִמּוֹ.
(ד) אִם אֲדֹנָיו יִתֶּן לוֹ אִשָּׁה וְיָלְדָה לוֹ בָנִים אוֹ בָנוֹת הָאִשָּׁה וִילָדֶיהָ תִּהְיֶה לַאדֹנֶיהָ וְהוּא יֵצֵא בְגַפּוֹ.
(ה) וְאִם אָמֹר יֹאמַר הָעֶבֶד אָהַבְתִּי אֶת אֲדֹנִי אֶת אִשְׁתִּי וְאֶת בָּנָי לֹא אֵצֵא חָפְשִׁי.
(ו) וְהִגִּישׁוֹ אֲדֹנָיו אֶל הָאֱלֹהִים וְהִגִּישׁוֹ אֶל הַדֶּלֶת אוֹ אֶל הַמְּזוּזָה וְרָצַע אֲדֹנָיו אֶת אָזְנוֹ בַּמַּרְצֵעַ וַעֲבָדוֹ לְעֹלָם.

[2] If thou buy a Hebrew servant, six years he shall serve; and in the seventh he shall go out free for nothing.
[3] If he came in by himself, he shall go out by himself; if he were married, then his wife shall go out with him.
[4] If his master has given him a wife, and she has born him sons or daughters; the wife and her children shall be her master's, and he shall go out by himself.
[5] And if the servant shall plainly say: I love my master, my wife, and my children; I will not go out free;
[6] Then his master shall bring him unto the judges; he shall also bring him to the door, or unto the door post; and his master shall bore his ear through with an awl; and he shall serve him for ever.

Thomas Paine, "African Slavery in America" (1775)

Some of the most enlightened men of the Revolutionary era held slaves, including Jefferson and Washington. Those who supported abolition did not also necessarily support full egalitarian citizenship and what was then called the "mixing of the races." Ahead of his time, Thomas Paine denounced slavery in the United States. In the following excerpt, he argued against those who declared that the Bible supports slavery.

Most shocking of all is alleging the sacred scriptures to favour this wicked practice. One would have thought none but infidel cavillers would endeavour to make them appear contrary to the plain dictates of natural light, and the conscience, in a matter of common Justice and Humanity; which they cannot be. Such worthy men, as referred to before, judged otherways; Mr. Baxter declared, the Slave-Traders should be called Devils, rather than Christians; and that it is a heinous crime to buy them. But some say, "the practice was permitted to the Jews." To which may be replied,

1. The example of the Jews, in many things, may not be imitated by us; they had not only orders to cut off several nations altogether, but if they were obliged to war with others, and conquered them, to cut off every male; they were suffered to use polygamy and divorces, and other things utterly unlawful to us under clearer light.
2. The plea is, in a great measure, false; they had no permission to catch and enslave people who never injured them.
3. Such arguments ill become us, since the time of reformation came, under Gospel light. All distinctions of nations and privileges of one above others, are ceased; Christians are taught to account all men their neighbours; and love their neighbours as themselves; and do to all men as they would be done by; to do good to all men; and Man-stealing is ranked with enormous crimes. Is the barbarous enslaving our inoffensive neighbours, and treating them like wild beasts subdued by force, reconcilable with the Divine precepts! Is this doing to them as we would desire they should do to us? If they could carry off and enslave some thousands of us, would we think it just? – One would almost wish they could for once; it might convince more than reason, or the Bible.

As much in vain, perhaps, will they search ancient history for examples of the modern Slave-Trade. Too many nations enslaved the prisoners they took in war. But to go to nations with whom there is no war, who have no way provoked, without farther design of conquest, purely to catch inoffensive people, like wild beasts, for slaves, is an height of outrage against humanity and justice, that seems left by heathen nations to be practised by pretended Christian. How shameful are all attempts to colour and excuse it!

William Lloyd Garrison, *The Liberator* (December 15, 1837)

William Lloyd Garrison was one of the most well-known abolitionists in Antebellum America. He founded the American Anti-Slavery Society and was a founder and contributing author to The Liberator, *an anti-slavery newspaper.*

In entering upon our eighth volume, the abolition of slavery will still be the grand object of our labors, though not, perhaps, so exclusively as heretofore. There are other topics, which, in our opinion, are intimately connected with the great doctrine of inalienable human rights; and which, while they conflict with no religious sect, or political party, as such, are pregnant with momentous consequences to the freedom, equality, and happiness of mankind. These we shall discuss as time and opportunity may permit.

The motto upon our banner has been, from the commencement of our moral warfare, "OUR COUNTRY IS THE WORLD – OUR COUNTRYMEN ARE ALL MANKIND." We trust that it will be our only epitaph. Another motto we have chosen is, UNIVERSAL EMANCIPATION. Up to this time we have limited its application to those who are held in this country, by Southern taskmasters, as marketable commodities, goods and chattels, and implements of husbandry. Henceforth we shall use it in its widest latitude: the emancipation of our whole race from the dominion of man, from the thralldom of self, from the government of brute force, from the bondage of sin – and bringing them under the dominion of God, the control of an inward spirit, the government of the law of love, and into the obedience and liberty of Christ, who is "*the same*, yesterday, TODAY, and forever."

It has never been our design, in conducting the *Liberator*, to require of the friends of emancipation any political or sectarian shibboleth [specific creed]; though, in consequence of the general corruption of all political parties and religious sects, and of the obstacles which they have thrown into the path of emancipation, we have been necessitated to reprove them all. Nor have we any intention, – at least, not while ours professes to be an anti-slavery publication, distinctively and eminently, – to assail or give the preference to any sect or party. We are bound by no denominational trammels; we are not political partisans; we have taken upon our lips no human creed: we are guided by no human authority; we cannot consent to wear the livery of any fallible body. The abolition of American slavery we hold to be COMMON GROUND, upon which men of all creeds, complexions and parties, if they have true humanity in their hearts, may meet on amicable and equal terms to effect a common object. But whoever marches on to that ground, loving his creed, or sect, or party, or any worldly interest, or personal reputation or property, or friends, or wife, or children, or life itself, more than the cause of bleeding humanity, – or expecting to promote his political designs, or to enforce his sectarian dogmas, or to drive others from the ranks on account of their modes of faith, – will assuredly prove himself to be unworthy of his abolition profession, and his real character will be made manifest to all, for severe and unerring tests will be applied frequently: it will not be possible for him to make those sacrifices, or to endure those trials, which unbending integrity to the cause will require. For ourselves, we care not who is found upon this broad platform of our common nature: if he will join hands with us, in good faith, to undo the heavy burdens and break the yokes of our enslaved countrymen, we shall not stop to inquire whether he is a Trinitarian or Unitarian, Baptist or Methodist, Catholic or Covenanter, Presbyterian or Quaker, Swedenborgian or Perfectionist. However widely we may differ in our views on other subjects, we shall not refuse to labor with him against slavery, in the same phalanx, if he refuse not to labor with us. Certainly no man can truly affirm that we have sought to bring any other religious or political tests into this philanthropic enterprise than these: "Thou shalt love thy neighbor as thyself" [Lev. 19:18] – "Whatsoever ye would that men should do to you, do ye even so to them" – "Remember those in bonds as bound with them."

Next to the overthrow of slavery, the cause of PEACE will command our attention. The doctrine of non-resistance as commonly received and practiced by Friends, or Quakers, and certain members of other religious denominations, we conceive to be utterly indefensible in its application to national wars: not that it "goes too far," but that it does not go far enough. If a nation may not redress its wrongs by physical force – if it may not repel or punish a foreign enemy who comes to plunder, enslave or murder its inhabitants – then it may not resort to arms to quell an insurrection, or send to prison or suspend upon a gibbet any transgressors upon its soil. If the slaves of the South have not an undoubted right to resist their masters in the last resort, then no man, or body of men, may appeal to the law of violence in self-defense – for none have ever suffered, or can suffer, more than they. If, when men are robbed of their earnings, their liberties, their personal ownership, their wives and children, they may not resist, in no case can physical resistance be allowable, either in an individual or collective capacity.

Now the doctrine we shall endeavor to inculcate is, that the kingdoms of this world are to become the kingdoms of our Lord and of his Christ; consequently, that they are all to be supplanted, whether they are called despotic, monarchical, or republican, and he only who is King of kings, and Lord of lords, is to rule in righteousness. The kingdom of God is to be established IN ALL THE EARTH, and it shall never be destroyed, but it shall "BREAK IN PIECES AND CONSUME ALL OTHERS" [cf. Dan. 2:44]: its elements are righteousness and peace, and joy in the Holy Ghost; without are dogs, and sorcerers, and whoremongers, and murderers, and idolaters, and whatsoever loveth and maketh a lie. Its government is one of love, not of military coercion or physical restraint: its laws are not written upon parchment, but upon the hearts of its subjects – they are not conceived in the wisdom of man, but framed by the Spirit of God: its weapons are not carnal, but spiritual. Its soldiers are clad in the whole armor of God, having their loins girt about with truth, and having on the breastplate of righteousness; their feet are shod with the preparation of the gospel of peace; with the shield of faith they are able to quench all the fiery darts of the wicked, and they wear the helmet of salvation, and wield the sword of the spirit, which is the word of God. Hence, when smitten on the one cheek, they turn the other also; being defamed, they entreat; being deviled, they bless; being persecuted, they suffer it; they take joyfully the spoiling of their goods; they rejoice, inasmuch as they are partakers of Christ's sufferings; they are sheep in the midst of wolves; in no Extremity whatever, even if their enemies are determined to nail them to the cross with Jesus, and if they, like him, could summon legions of angels to their rescue, will they resort to the law of violence.

As to the governments of this world, whatever their titles or forms, we shall endeavor to prove that, in their essential elements, and as at present administered, they are all Anti-Christ; that they can never, by human wisdom, be brought into conformity to the will of God; that they cannot be maintained except by naval and military power; that all their penal enactments, being a dead letter without an army to carry them into effect, are virtually written in human blood; and that the followers of Jesus should instinctively shun their stations of honor, power, and emolument – at the same time "submitting to every ordinance of man, for the Lord's sake," and offering no physical resistance to any of their mandates, however unjust or tyrannical. The language of Jesus is, "My kingdom is not of this world, else would my servants fight." Calling his disciples to him, he said to them, "Ye know that they which are accustomed to rule over the Gentiles, exercise lordship Over them; and their great ones exercise authority upon them. *But so it* SHALL NOT *be* among You; but whosoever will be great among you, shall be your minister; and whosoever of you will be the chiefest, shall be servant of all. For even the Son of man came not to be ministered unto, but to minister, and to give his life a ransom for many."

Human governments are to be viewed as judicial punishments. If a people turn the grace of God into lasciviousness, or make their liberty, an occasion for anarchy, or if they refuse to belong to the "one fold and one Shepherd," – they shall be scourged by governments of their own choosing, and burdened with taxation, and subjected to physical control, and torn by factions, and made to eat the fruit of their evil doings, until they are prepared to receive the liberty and the rest which remain, on earth as well as in heaven, for THE PEOPLE OF GOD. This is in strict accordance with the arrangement of Divine Providence.

So long as men contemn the perfect government of the Most High, persons, just so long will they desire to usurp authority over each other – just so long will they pertinaciously cling to human governments, *fashioned in the likeness and* administered *in the spirit of their own disobedience*. Now, if the prayer of our Lord be not a mockery; if the Kingdom of God is to come universally, and his will to be alone ON EARTH AS IT IS IN HEAVEN; and if, in that kingdom, no carnal weapon can be wielded, and swords are beaten into ploughshares, and spears into pruning-hooks, and there is none to molest or make afraid, and no statute-book but the Bible, and no judge but Christ; then why are not Christians obligated to come out NOW, and be separate from "the kingdoms of this world," which are all based upon THE PRINCIPLE OF VIOLENCE, and which require their officers and servants to govern and be governed by that principle?

Hebraic Source

Garrison mostly drew from the New Testament for his abolitionism, although he referenced Daniel's interpretation of the dream of the four beasts and kingdoms and the ultimate establishment of the kingdom of heaven, which in Garrison's view could not arrive without abolition.

Daniel 2

(לא) אנתה [אַנְתְּ] מַלְכָּא חָזֵה הֲוַיְתָ וַאֲלוּ צְלֵם חַד שַׂגִּיא צַלְמָא דִכֵּן רַב וְזִיוֵהּ יַתִּיר קָאֵם לְקָבְלָךְ וְרֵוֵהּ דְּחִיל.

(לב) הוּא צַלְמָא רֵאשֵׁהּ דִּי דְהַב טָב חֲדוֹהִי וּדְרָעוֹהִי דִּי כְסַף מְעוֹהִי וְיַרְכָתֵהּ דִּי נְחָשׁ.

(לג) שָׁקוֹהִי דִּי פַרְזֶל רַגְלוֹהִי מנהון [מִנְּהֵן] די פַרְזֶל ומנהון [וּמִנְּהֵן] דִּי חֲסַף.

(לד) חָזֵה הֲוַיְתָ עַד דִּי הִתְגְּזֶרֶת אֶבֶן דִּי לָא בִידַיִן וּמְחָת לְצַלְמָא עַל רַגְלוֹהִי דִּי פַרְזְלָא וְחַסְפָּא וְהַדֵּקֶת הִמּוֹן.

(לה) בֵּאדַיִן דָּקוּ כַחֲדָה פַּרְזְלָא חַסְפָּא נְחָשָׁא כַּסְפָּא וְדַהֲבָא וַהֲווֹ כְּעוּר מִן אִדְּרֵי קַיִט וּנְשָׂא הִמּוֹן רוּחָא וְכָל אֲתַר לָא הִשְׁתְּכַח לְהוֹן וְאַבְנָא דִּי מְחָת לְצַלְמָא הֲוָת לְטוּר רַב וּמְלָאת כָּל אַרְעָא.

(לו) דְּנָה חֶלְמָא וּפִשְׁרֵהּ נֵאמַר קֳדָם מַלְכָּא.

(לז) אנתה [אַנְתְּ] מַלְכָּא מֶלֶךְ מַלְכַיָּא דִּי אֱלָהּ שְׁמַיָּא מַלְכוּתָא חִסְנָא וְתָקְפָּא וִיקָרָא יְהַב לָךְ.

(לח) וּבְכָל דִּי דארין [דָאֲרִין] בְּנֵי אֲנָשָׁא חֵיוַת בָּרָא וְעוֹף שְׁמַיָּא יְהַב בִּידָךְ וְהַשְׁלְטָךְ בְּכָלְּהוֹן אנתה [אַנְתְּ] הוּא רֵאשָׁה דִּי דַהֲבָא.

(לט) וּבָתְרָךְ תְּקוּם מַלְכוּ אָחֳרִי ארעא [אֲרַע] מִנָּךְ וּמַלְכוּ תליתיא [תְלִיתָאָה] אָחֳרִי דִּי נְחָשָׁא דִּי תִשְׁלַט בְּכָל אַרְעָא.

(מ) וּמַלְכוּ רביעיה [וּרְבִיעָאָה] תֶּהֱוֵא תַקִּיפָה כְּפַרְזְלָא כָּל קֳבֵל דִּי פַרְזְלָא מְהַדֵּק וְחָשֵׁל כֹּלָּא וּכְפַרְזְלָא דִּי מְרָעַע כָּל אִלֵּן תַּדִּק וְתֵרֹעַ.

(מא) וְדִי חֲזַיְתָה רַגְלַיָּא וְאֶצְבְּעָתָא מנהון [מִנְּהֵן] חֲסַף דִּי פֶחָר ומנהון [וּמִנְּהֵן] פַּרְזֶל מַלְכוּ פְלִיגָה תֶּהֱוֵה וּמִן נִצְבְּתָא דִּי פַרְזְלָא לֶהֱוֵא בַהּ כָּל קֳבֵל דִּי חֲזַיְתָה פַּרְזְלָא מְעָרַב בַּחֲסַף טִינָא.

(מב) וְאֶצְבְּעָת רַגְלַיָּא מנהון [מִנְּהֵן] פַּרְזֶל ומנהון [וּמִנְּהֵן] חֲסַף מִן קְצָת מַלְכוּתָא תֶּהֱוֵה תַקִּיפָה וּמִנַּהּ תֶּהֱוֵה תְבִירָה.

(מג) די [וְדִי] חֲזַיְתָ פַּרְזְלָא מְעָרַב בַּחֲסַף טִינָא מִתְעָרְבִין לֶהֱוֹן בִּזְרַע אֲנָשָׁא וְלָא לֶהֱוֹן דָּבְקִין דְּנָה עִם דְּנָה הֵא כְדִי פַרְזְלָא לָא מִתְעָרַב עִם חַסְפָּא.

(מד) וּבְיוֹמֵיהוֹן דִּי מַלְכַיָּא אִנּוּן יְקִים אֱלָהּ שְׁמַיָּא מַלְכוּ דִּי לְעָלְמִין לָא תִתְחַבַּל וּמַלְכוּתָה לְעַם אָחֳרָן לָא תִשְׁתְּבִק תַּדִּק וְתָסֵיף כָּל אִלֵּין מַלְכְוָתָא וְהִיא תְּקוּם לְעָלְמַיָּא.

[31] Thou, O king, sawest, and behold a great image. This great image, whose brightness was excellent, stood before thee; and the form thereof was terrible.

[32] This image's head was of fine gold, his breast and his arms of silver, his belly and his thighs of brass,

[33] His legs of iron, his feet part of iron and part of clay.

[34] Thou sawest till that a stone was cut out without hands, which smote the image upon his feet that were of iron and clay, and brake them to pieces.

[35] Then was the iron, the clay, the brass, the silver, and the gold, broken to pieces together, and became like the chaff of the summer threshingfloors; and the wind carried them away, that no place was found for them: and the stone that smote the image became a great mountain, and filled the whole earth.

[36] This is the dream; and we will tell the interpretation thereof before the king.

[37] Thou, O king, art a king of kings: for the God of heaven hath given thee a kingdom, power, and strength, and glory.

[38] And wheresoever the children of men dwell, the beasts of the field and the fowls of the heaven hath he given into thine hand, and hath made thee ruler over them all. Thou art this head of gold.

[39] And after thee shall arise another kingdom inferior to thee, and another third kingdom of brass, which shall bear rule over all the earth.

[40] And the fourth kingdom shall be strong as iron: forasmuch as iron breaketh in pieces and subdueth all things: and as iron that breaketh all these, shall it break in pieces and bruise.

[41] And whereas thou sawest the feet and toes, part of potters' clay, and part of iron, the kingdom shall be divided; but there shall be in it of the strength of the iron, forasmuch as thou sawest the iron mixed with miry clay.

[42] And as the toes of the feet were part of iron, and part of clay, so the kingdom shall be partly strong, and partly broken.

[43] And whereas thou sawest iron mixed with miry clay, they shall mingle themselves with the seed of men: but they shall not cleave one to another, even as iron is not mixed with clay.

[44] And in the days of these kings shall the God of heaven set up a kingdom, which shall never be destroyed: and the kingdom shall not be left to other people, but it shall break in pieces and consume all these kingdoms, and it shall stand for ever.

William Channing, *Slavery* (1835)

Congregationalist minister William Channing (1780–1842) worked on a Virginia plantation for two years before leaning towards abolitionism. Like many Northern abolitionists, he mixed Lockean natural rights theory with theological principles. Here is an excerpt from his book Slavery.

I come now to what is to my own mind the great argument against seizing and using a man as property. He cannot be property in the sight of God and justice, because he is a Rational, Moral, Immortal Being; because created in God's image, and therefore in the highest sense his child; because created to unfold godlike faculties, and to govern himself by a Divine Law written on his heart, and republished in God's Word. His whole nature forbids that he should be seized as property. From his very nature it follows, that so to seize him is to offer an insult to his Maker, and to inflict aggravated social wrong. Into every human being God has breathed an immortal spirit, more precious than the whole outward creation. No earthly or celestial language can exaggerate the worth of a human being. No matter how obscure his condition. Thought, Reason, Conscience, the capacity of Virtue, the capacity of Christian Love, an immortal Destiny, an intimate moral connection with God, – here are attributes of our common humanity which reduce to insignificance all outward distinctions, and make every human being unspeakably dear to his Maker. No matter how ignorant he may be. The capacity of Improvement allies him to the more instructed of his race, and places within his reach the knowledge and happiness of higher worlds. Every human being has in him the germ of the greatest idea in the universe, the idea of God; and to unfold this is the end of his existence. Every human being has in his breast the elements of that Divine Everlasting Law, which the highest orders of the creation obey. He has the idea of Duty, and to unfold, revere, obey this, is the very purpose for which life was given. Every human being has the idea of what is meant by that word, Truth; that is, he sees, however dimly, the great object of Divine and created intelligence, and is capable of ever-enlarging perceptions of truth. Every human being has affections, which may be purified and expanded into a Sublime Love. He has, too, the idea of Happiness, and a thirst for it which cannot be appeased. Such is our nature. Wherever we see a man, we see the possessor of these great capacities. Did God make such a being to be owned as a tree or a brute? How plainly was he made to exercise, unfold, improve his highest powers, made for a moral, spiritual good! and how is he wronged, and his Creator opposed, when he is forced and broken into a tool to another's physical enjoyment!

Such a being was plainly made for an End in Himself. He is a Person, not a Thing. He is an End, not a mere Instrument or Means. He was made for his own virtue and happiness. Is this end reconcilable with his being held and used as a chattel? The sacrifice of such a being to another's will, to another's present, outward, ill-comprehended good, is the greatest violence which can be offered to any creature of God. It is to degrade him from his rank in the universe, to make him a means, not an end, to cast him out from God's spiritual family into the brutal herd.

Hebraic Sources

Channing argued that to treat a man as property was a violation against human nature, an idea which certainly finds resonance in the Hebrew Bible and the rabbinic tradition.

Deuteronomy 24

(ז) כִּי יִמָּצֵא אִישׁ גֹּנֵב נֶפֶשׁ מֵאֶחָיו מִבְּנֵי יִשְׂרָאֵל וְהִתְעַמֶּר בּוֹ וּמְכָרוֹ וּמֵת הַגַּנָּב הַהוּא וּבִעַרְתָּ הָרָע מִקִּרְבֶּךָ.

[7] If a man be found stealing any of his brethren of the children of Israel, and maketh merchandise of him, or selleth him; then that thief shall die; and thou shalt put evil away from among you.

Mishna, Avot 3.14

הוּא הָיָה אוֹמֵר, חָבִיב אָדָם שֶׁנִּבְרָא בְצֶלֶם. חִבָּה יְתֵרָה נוֹדַעַת לוֹ שֶׁנִּבְרָא בְצֶלֶם, שֶׁנֶּאֱמַר "כִּי בְּצֶלֶם אֱ-לֹהִים עָשָׂה אֶת הָאָדָם" (בראשית ט:ו). חֲבִיבִין יִשְׂרָאֵל שֶׁנִּקְרְאוּ בָנִים לַמָּקוֹם. חִבָּה יְתֵרָה נוֹדַעַת לָהֶם שֶׁנִּקְרְאוּ בָנִים לַמָּקוֹם, שֶׁנֶּאֱמַר "בָּנִים אַתֶּם לַה' אֱ-לֹהֵיכֶם" (דברים יד:א). חֲבִיבִין יִשְׂרָאֵל שֶׁנִּתַּן לָהֶם כְּלִי חֶמְדָּה. חִבָּה יְתֵרָה נוֹדַעַת לָהֶם שֶׁנִּתַּן לָהֶם כְּלִי חֶמְדָּה שֶׁבּוֹ נִבְרָא הָעוֹלָם, שֶׁנֶּאֱמַר "כִּי לֶקַח טוֹב נָתַתִּי לָכֶם, תּוֹרָתִי אַל תַּעֲזֹבוּ" (משלי ד:ב).

He used to say: "Beloved is man who was created in the image [of God]. [It was a mark of] superabundant love that it was made known to him that he had been created in the image [of God], as it is said, 'For in the image of God he made man' (Gen. 9:6). Beloved are [the people of] Israel who were called children of the Omnipresent. [It was a mark of] superabundant love that it was made known to them that they were called children of the Omnipresent, as it is said, 'You are children of the Lord your God' (Deut. 14:1). Beloved are [the people of Israel] for a precious object was given to them. [It was a mark of] superabundant love that it was made known to them that the precious object, through which the world had been created, was given to them, as it is said, 'For I give you good instruction; do not forsake my teaching' (Prov. 4:2)."

Babylonian Talmud, Sanhedrin 74a

רוֹצֵחַ גּוּפֵיהּ מְנָא לָן? סְבָרָא הוּא, דְּהַהוּא דַּאֲתָא לְקַמֵּיהּ דְּרַבָּה, וַאֲמַר לֵיהּ:
"אֲמַר לִי מָרֵי דוּרָאי: 'זִיל קַטְלֵיהּ לִפְלָנְיָא, וְאִי לָא, קָטְלִינָא לָךְ'". אֲמַר לֵיהּ:
"לִקְטְלוּךְ, וְלָא תִּיקְטוֹל. מִי יֵימַר דְּדָמָא דִּידָךְ סוּמָק טְפֵי? דִּילְמָא דָּמָא דְהוּא
גַּבְרָא סוּמָק טְפֵי!"

And how do we know this of murder itself? It is common sense, as we see with the person who came before Rabba and said to him, "The governor of my town has ordered me, 'Go and kill so and so; if not, I will kill you.'" He responded, "Let him kill you rather than you kill; who is to say that your blood is redder? Perhaps the blood of that person [the potential victim] is redder!"

David Walker, *Appeal to the Colored Citizens of the World* (1829)
David Walker's father was a slave but his mother was free. In this important early book about the horrors of slavery, Walker (1796–1830) roused Northern opinion against slavery and contributed to the spread and radicalization of abolitionist sentiment in the North.

My beloved brethren: The Indians of North and of South America – the Greeks – the Irish, subjected under the king of Great Britain – the Jews, that ancient people of the Lord – the inhabitants of the islands of the sea – in fine, all the inhabitants of the earth (except however, the sons of Africa) are called men, and of course are, and ought to be free. But we (coloured people) and our children are brutes!! and of course are, and ought to be slaves to the American people and their children forever!! to dig their mines and work their farms; and thus go on enriching them, from one generation to another with our blood and our tears!!!!

I promised in a preceding page to demonstrate to the satisfaction of the most incredulous, that we (coloured people of these United States of America) are the *most wretched, degraded* and *abject* set of beings that *ever lived* since the world began, and that the white Americans having reduced us to the wretched state of *slavery*, treat us in that condition *more cruel* (they being an enlightened and Christian people) than any heathen nation did any people whom it had reduced to our condition. These affirmations are so well confirmed in the minds of all unprejudiced men, who have taken the trouble to read histories, that they need no elucidation from me. But to put them beyond all doubt, I refer you in the first place to the children of Jacob, or of Israel in Egypt, under Pharaoh and his people. Some of my brethren do not know who Pharaoh and the Egyptians were – I know it to be a fact, that some of them take the Egyptians to have been a gang of *devils*, not knowing any better, and that they (Egyptians) having got possession of the Lord's people, treated them *nearly* as cruel as *Christian Americans* do us, at the present day. For the information of such, I would only mention that the Egyptians, were Africans or coloured people, such as we are – some of them yellow and others dark – a mixture of Ethiopians and the natives of Egypt – about the same as you see the coloured people of the United States at the present day. I say, I call your attention then, to the children of Jacob, while I point out particularly to you his son, among the rest, in Egypt.

"And Pharaoh, said unto Joseph, thou shalt be over my house, and according unto thy word shall all my people be ruled: only in the throne will I be greater than thou.

"And Pharaoh said unto Joseph, see, I have set thee over all the land of Egypt."

"And Pharaoh said unto Joseph, I am Pharaoh, and without thee shall no man lift up his hand or foot in all the land of Egypt" [Gen. 41:39-41,44].

Now I appeal to heaven and to earth, and particularly to the American people themselves, who cease not to declare that our condition is not *hard*, and that we are comparatively satisfied to rest in wretchedness and misery, under them and their children. Not, indeed, to show me a coloured President, a Governor, a Legislator, a Senator, a Mayor, or an Attorney at the Bar. But to show me a man of colour, who holds the low office of Constable, or one who sits in a Juror Box, even on a case of one of his wretched brethren, throughout this great Republic!! But let us pass Joseph the son of Israel a little farther in review, as he existed with that heathen nation.

"And Pharaoh called Joseph's name Zaphnath-paaneah; and he gave him to wife Asenath the daughter of Potipherah priest of On. And Joseph went out over all the land of Egypt" [Gen. 41:45].

Compare the above, with the American institutions. Do they not institute laws to prohibit us from marrying among the whites? I would wish, candidly, however, before the Lord, to be understood, that I would not give a *pinch of snuff* to be married to any white person I ever saw in all the days of my life. And I do say it, that the black man, or man of colour, who will leave his own colour (provided he can get one, who is good for any thing) and marry a white woman, to be a double slave to her, just because she is *white*, ought to be treated by her as he surely will be, viz: as a NIGGER!!!! It is not, indeed, what I care about inter-marriages with the whites, which induced me to pass this subject in review; for the Lord knows, that there is a day coming when they will be glad enough to get into the company of the blacks, notwithstanding, we are, in this generation, levelled by them, almost on a level with the brute creation: and some of us they treat even worse than they do the brutes that perish. I only made this extract to show how much lower we are held, and how much more cruel we are treated by the Americans, than were the children of Jacob, by the Egyptians. We will notice the sufferings of Israel some further, under *heathen Pharaoh*, compared with ours under the *enlightened Christians of America*.

"And Pharaoh spoke unto Joseph, saying, thy father and thy brethren are come unto thee:

"The land of Egypt is before thee: in the best of the land make thy father and brethren to dwell; in the land of Goshen let them dwell: and if thou knowest any men of activity among them, then make them rulers over my cattle" [Gen. 47:5-6].

I ask those people who treat us so *well*, Oh! I ask them, where is the most barren spot of land which they have given unto us? Israel had the most fertile land in all Egypt. Need I mention the very notorious fact, that I have known a poor man of colour, who laboured night and day, to acquire a little money, and having acquired it, he vested it in a small piece of land, and got him a house erected thereon, and having paid for the whole, he moved his family into it, where he was suffered to remain but nine months, when he was cheated out of his property by a white man, and driven out of door! And is not this the case generally? Can a man of colour buy a piece of land and keep it peaceably? Will not some white man try to get it from him, even if it is in a *mud hole*? I need not comment any farther on a subject, which all both black and white, will readily admit. But I must, really, observe that in this very city, when a man of colour dies, if he owned any real estate it most generally falls into the hands of some white person. The wife and children of the deceased may weep and lament if they please, but the estate will be kept snug enough by its white possessor.

But to prove farther that the condition of the Israelites was better under the Egyptians than ours is under the whites. I call upon the professing Christians, I call upon the philanthropist, I call upon the very tyrant himself, to show me a page of history, either sacred or profane, on which a verse can be found, which maintains, that the Egyptians heaped the *insupportable insult* upon the children of Israel, by telling them that they were not of the *human family*. Can the whites deny this charge? Have they not, after having reduced us to the deplorable condition of slaves under their feet, held us up as descending originally from the tribes of *Monkeys* or *Orang-Outangs*? O! my God! I appeal to every man of feeling – is not this insupportable? Is it not heaping the most gross insult upon our miseries, because they have got us under their feet and we cannot help ourselves? Oh! pity us we pray thee, Lord Jesus, Master. Has Mr. Jefferson declared to the world, that we are inferior to the whites, both in the endowments of our bodies and our minds? It is indeed surprising, that a man of such great learning, combined with such excellent natural parts, should speak so of a set of men in chains. I do not know what to compare it to, unless, like putting one wild deer in an iron cage, where it will be secured, and hold another by the side of the same, then let it go, and expect the one in the cage to run as fast as the one at liberty. So far, my brethren, were the Egyptians from heaping these insults upon their slaves, that Pharaoh's daughter took Moses, a son of Israel for her own, as will appear by the following.

"And Pharaoh's daughter said unto her [Moses' mother], take this child away, and nurse it for me, and I will pay thee thy wages. And the woman took the child [Moses] and nursed it."

"And the child grew, and she brought him unto Pharaoh's daughter and he became her son. And she called his name Moses: and she said because I drew him out of the water" [Ex. 2:9-10].

In all probability, Moses would have become Prince Regent to the throne, and no doubt, in process of time but he would have been seated on the throne of Egypt. But he had rather suffer shame, with the people of God, than to enjoy pleasures with that wicked people for a season. O! that the coloured people were long since of Moses' excellent disposition, instead of courting favour with, and telling news and lies to our *natural enemies*, against each other – aiding them to keep their hellish chains of slavery upon us. Would we not long before this time, have been respectable men, instead of such wretched victims of oppression as we are? Would they be able to drag our mothers, our fathers, our wives, our children and ourselves, around the world in chains and handcuffs as they do, to dig up gold and silver for them and theirs? This question, my brethren, I leave for you to digest: and may God Almighty force it home to your hearts. Remember that unless you are united, keeping your tongues within your teeth, you will be afraid to trust your secrets to each other, and thus perpetuate our miseries under the *Christians!!!!!*

Richard Fuller, *Domestic Slavery Considered as a Scriptural Institution* (1845)

Richard Fuller (1804–1876) was a Southern Baptist pastor. He debated the scriptural foundations of slavery in letters with another pastor, Francis Wayland, president of Brown University. They published their correspondence in book form under the title Domestic Slavery Considered as a Scriptural Institution.

The first thing I am to prove is, that God did sanction slavery in the Old Testament; and here can any prolonged examination be required? First, you admit that the patriarchs, whose piety is held up in the Bible for our admiration, were masters of slaves. Of all these holy men, Abraham was the most eminent. He was "the friend of God" [cf. Is. 41:8], and walked with God in the closest and most endearing intercourse; nor can any thing be more exquisitely touching than those words, "Shall I hide from Abraham that thing which I do?" [Gen. 18:17]. It is the language of a friend, who feels that concealment would wrong the confidential intimacy existing. The love of this venerable servant of God in his promptness to immolate his son, has been the theme of apostles and preachers for ages: and such was his faith, that all who believe are called "the children of faithful Abraham." This Abraham, you admit, held slaves. Who is surprised that Whitefield, with this single fact before him, could not believe slavery to be a sin? Yet if your definition of slavery be correct, holy Abraham lived all his life in the commission of one of the most aggravated crimes against God and man which can be conceived. His life was spent in outraging the rights of hundreds of human beings, as moral, intellectual, immortal, fallen creatures; and in violating their relations as parents and children and husbands and wives. And God not only connived at this appalling iniquity, but, in the covenant of circumcision made with Abraham, expressly mentions it, and confirms the patriarch in it; speaking of those "bought with his money" [Gen. 17:23], and requiring him to circumcise them. Why, at the very first blush, every Christian will cry out against this statement. To this, however, you must come, or yield your position; and this is only the first utterly incredible and monstrous corollary involved in the assertion that slavery is essentially and always "a sin of appalling magnitude."

The natural descendants of Abraham were holders of slaves, and God took them into special relation to himself. "He made known his ways unto Moses, his acts unto the children of Israel" [Ps. 103:7]; and he instituted regulations for their government, into which he expressly incorporated a permission to buy and hold slaves. These institutes not only recognise slavery as lawful, but contain very minute directions. It is not necessary for me to argue this point, as it is conceded by you. Slaves were held by the priests. "A sojourner of a priest, or an hired servant, shall not eat of the holy thing. But if the priest buy any soul with his money, he shall eat of it, and he that is born in his house, they shall eat of it." (Lev. xxii. 10, 11.) They might be bought of the Canaanites around, or of strangers living among the Hebrews. "Both thy bondmen, and thy bondmaids, which thou shalt have, shall be of the heathen that are round about you; of them shall ye buy bondmen and bondmaids. Moreover, of the children of the strangers that do sojourn among you, of them shall ye buy, and of their families that are with you, which they begat in your land; and they shall be your possession." (Lev. xxii. 44, 45.) They were regarded as property; and were called "money," "possession:" "If a man smite his servant or his maid, with a rod, and he die under his hand; he shall be surely punished. Notwithstanding, if he continue a day or two, he shall not be punished: for he is his money." (Exod. xxi. 20, 21.) They might be sold. This is implied in the term "money;" but it is plainly taken for granted: "Thou shalt not make merchandise of her, because thou hast humbled her." (Deut. xxi. 14.) See also Exod. xxi. 7, 8. "And if a man sell his daughter to be a maidservant, she shall not go out as the menservants do. If she please not her master, who hath betrothed her to himself, then shall he let her be redeemed: to sell her to a strange nation he shall have no power, seeing he hath dealt deceitfully with her." The slavery thus expressly sanctioned was hereditary and perpetual: "Ye shall take them as an inheritance for your children after you, to inherit them for a possession. They shall be your bondmen forever." (Lev. xxv. 46.) Lastly, Hebrews, if bought, were to be treated, not as slaves, but as hired servants, and to go free at the year of jubilee. "If thy brother that dwelleth by thee be waxen poor, and be sold unto thee, thou shalt not compel him to serve as a bond servant; but as an hired servant and as a sojourner shall he be with thee, and shall serve thee unto the year of jubilee: and then shall he depart from thee, both he and his children with him, and shall return unto his own family, and unto the possession of his father shall he return." (Lev. xxv. 39–41.) If during the Hebrew's time of service he married a slave, and had children, the wife and children were not set at liberty with him. If he consented, he might become a slave for life: "If thou buy a Hebrew servant, six years shall he serve: and in the seventh he shall go out free for nothing. If he came in by himself, he shall go out by himself: if he were married, then his wife shall go out with him. If his master have given him a wife, and she have borne him sons or daughters, the wife and her children shall be her master's, and he shall go out by himself. And if the servant shall plainly say, I love my master, my wife, and my children; I will not go out free. Then his master shall bring him unto the judges: he shall also bring him to the door, or unto the door-post; and his master shall bore his ear through with an awl; and he shall serve him forever." (Exod. xxi. 2–6.)

Such are some parts of the Mosaic institution. Let me add, also, that the decalogue twice recognises slavery, and forbids one Israelite to covet the man-servant or maid-servant of another. And, now, how does all this appear if your assumption be for a moment tenable, that slavery is as great a crime as can be committed? Suppose these regulations had thus sanctioned piracy, or idolatry, would they ever have commanded the faith of the world as divine? How conclusive this that slavery is not among crimes in the estimation of mankind, and according to the immutable and eternal principles of morality!

Hebraic Sources

Fuller relied on the special and intimate relationship Abraham had with God as an authorization for slave holding. These passages, however, should be contrasted with Abraham's ability to question whether God is acting justly in the context of Sodom's destruction.

Isaiah 41:8

(ח) וְאַתָּה יִשְׂרָאֵל עַבְדִּי יַעֲקֹב אֲשֶׁר בְּחַרְתִּיךָ זֶרַע אַבְרָהָם אֹהֲבִי.

[8] But thou, Israel, art my servant, Jacob whom I have chosen, the seed of Abraham my friend.

Genesis 18

(טז) וַיָּקֻמוּ מִשָּׁם הָאֲנָשִׁים וַיַּשְׁקִפוּ עַל פְּנֵי סְדֹם וְאַבְרָהָם הֹלֵךְ עִמָּם לְשַׁלְּחָם.
(יז) וַה' אָמָר הַמְכַסֶּה אֲנִי מֵאַבְרָהָם אֲשֶׁר אֲנִי עֹשֶׂה.
(יח) וְאַבְרָהָם הָיוֹ יִהְיֶה לְגוֹי גָּדוֹל וְעָצוּם וְנִבְרְכוּ בוֹ כֹּל גּוֹיֵי הָאָרֶץ.
(יט) כִּי יְדַעְתִּיו לְמַעַן אֲשֶׁר יְצַוֶּה אֶת בָּנָיו וְאֶת בֵּיתוֹ אַחֲרָיו וְשָׁמְרוּ דֶּרֶךְ ה' לַעֲשׂוֹת צְדָקָה וּמִשְׁפָּט לְמַעַן הָבִיא ה' עַל אַבְרָהָם אֵת אֲשֶׁר דִּבֶּר עָלָיו.
(כ) וַיֹּאמֶר ה' זַעֲקַת סְדֹם וַעֲמֹרָה כִּי רָבָּה וְחַטָּאתָם כִּי כָבְדָה מְאֹד.
(כא) אֵרְדָה נָּא וְאֶרְאֶה הַכְּצַעֲקָתָהּ הַבָּאָה אֵלַי עָשׂוּ כָּלָה וְאִם לֹא אֵדָעָה.

(כב) וַיִּפְנוּ מִשָּׁם הָאֲנָשִׁים וַיֵּלְכוּ סְדֹמָה וְאַבְרָהָם עוֹדֶנּוּ עֹמֵד לִפְנֵי ה'.
(כג) וַיִּגַּשׁ אַבְרָהָם וַיֹּאמַר הַאַף תִּסְפֶּה צַדִּיק עִם רָשָׁע.
(כד) אוּלַי יֵשׁ חֲמִשִּׁים צַדִּיקִם בְּתוֹךְ הָעִיר הַאַף תִּסְפֶּה וְלֹא תִשָּׂא לַמָּקוֹם לְמַעַן חֲמִשִּׁים הַצַּדִּיקִם אֲשֶׁר בְּקִרְבָּהּ.
(כה) חָלִלָה לְּךָ מֵעֲשֹׂת כַּדָּבָר הַזֶּה לְהָמִית צַדִּיק עִם רָשָׁע וְהָיָה כַצַּדִּיק כָּרָשָׁע חָלִלָה לָּךְ הֲשֹׁפֵט כָּל הָאָרֶץ לֹא יַעֲשֶׂה מִשְׁפָּט.

[16] And the men rose up from thence, and looked toward Sodom: and Abraham went with them to bring them on the way.

[17] And the Lord said, Shall I hide from Abraham that thing which I do;

[18] Seeing that Abraham shall surely become a great and mighty nation, and all the nations of the earth shall be blessed in him?

[19] For I know him, that he will command his children and his household after him, and they shall keep the way of the Lord, to do justice and judgment; that the Lord may bring upon Abraham that which he hath spoken of him.

[20] And the Lord said, Because the cry of Sodom and Gomorrah is great, and because their sin is very grievous;

[21] I will go down now, and see whether they have done altogether according to the cry of it, which is come unto me; and if not, I will know.

[22] And the men turned their faces from thence, and went toward Sodom: but Abraham stood yet before the Lord.

[23] And Abraham drew near, and said, Wilt thou also destroy the righteous with the wicked?

[24] Peradventure there be fifty righteous within the city: wilt thou also destroy and not spare the place for the fifty righteous that are therein?

[25] That be far from thee to do after this manner, to slay the righteous with the wicked: and that the righteous should be as the wicked, that be far from thee: Shall not the Judge of all the earth do right?

J. W. Tucker, *Sermon*, Fayetteville, North Carolina (May 1862)

Both the North and the South invoked God for their cause during the Civil War. The following sermon is representative of the patriotic sermons of the South that linked the cause of the Southern states with God's own purposes and defended the righteousness and sanctity of the Southern soldier.

We should pray to God to give success to our cause, and triumph to our arms. God will defend the right. We may approach him then in full assurance of faith; with strong confidence that he will hear and answer and bless us. Prayer touches the nerve of omnipotence; prayer moves the hand that moves the world....

Our cause is sacred. It should ever be so in the eyes of all true men in the South. How can we doubt it, when we know it has been consecrated by a holy baptism of fire and blood. It has been rendered glorious by the martyr-like devotion of Johnson, McCulloch, Garnett, Bartow, Fisher, McKinney, and hundreds of others who have offered their lives as a sacrifice on the altar of their country's freedom.

Soldiers of the South, be firm, be courageous, be brave; be faithful to your God, your country and yourselves, and you shall be invincible. Never forget that the patriot, like the Christian, is immortal till his work is finished.

You are fighting for everything that is near and dear, and sacred to you as men, as Christians and as patriots; for country, for home, for property, for the honor of mothers, daughters, wives, sisters, and loved ones. Your cause is the cause of God, of Christ, of humanity. It is a conflict of truth with error – of the Bible with Northern infidelity – of a pure Christianity with Northern fanaticism – of liberty with despotism – of right with might.

In such a cause victory is not with the greatest number, nor the heaviest artillery, but with the good, the pure, the true, the noble, the brave. We are proud of you, and grateful to you for the victories of the past. We look to your valor and prowess, under the blessing of God, for the triumphs of the future.

Dr. M. J. Raphall, "The Bible View of Slavery" (1861)

An erudite polyglot born in Sweden and educated in England, Morris Jacob Raphall (1798–1868) became rabbi of Congregation B'nai Jeshurun in New York, where he served until 1866. He gave this sermon on slavery to his congregation on January 15, 1861. This was during the period in between Lincoln's election and the official start of the Civil War, when the fate of the nation hung in the balance.

"The people of Nineveh believed in God, proclaimed a fast, and put on sackcloth from the greatest of them even to the least of them. For the matter reached the King of Nineveh, and he arose from his throne, laid aside his robe, covered himself with sackcloth, and seated himself in ashes. And he caused it to be proclaimed and published through Nineveh, by decree of the King and his magnates, saying; 'Let neither man nor beast, herd nor flock, taste anything; let them not feed nor drink any water. But let man and beast be covered with sackcloth, and cry with all their strength unto God; and let them turn every individual from his evil way and from the violence that is in their hands. Who knoweth but God may turn and relent; yea, turn away from his fierce anger, that we perish not.' And God saw their works, that they turned from their evil way: and God relented of the evil which he had said that he would inflict upon them; and he did it not." – Jonah iii. 5–10.

My friends, we meet here this day under circumstances not unlike those described in my text. Not many weeks ago, on the invitation of the Governor of this State, we joined in thanksgiving for the manifold mercies the L-rd had vouchsafed to bestow upon us during the past year. But "coming events cast their shadows before," and our thanks were tinctured by the foreboding of danger impending over our country. The evil we then dreaded has now come home to us. As the cry of the prophet, "Yet forty days and Nineveh shall be overthrown" [Jonah 3:4], alarmed that people, so the proclamation, "the Union is dissolved," has startled the inhabitants of the United States. The President – the chief officer placed at the helm to guide the vessel of the commonwealth on its course – stands aghast at the signs of the times. He sees the black clouds gathering overhead, he hears the fierce howl of the tornado, and the hoarse roar of the breakers all around him. An aged man, his great experience has taught him that "man's extremity is God's opportunity;" and conscious of his own inability to weather the storm without help from on high, he calls upon every individual "to feel a personal responsibility towards God," even as the King of Nineveh desired all persons "to cry unto God with all their strength" – and it is in compliance with this call of the Chief Magistrate of these United States that we, like the many millions of our fellow-citizens, devote this day to public prayer and humiliation. The President, more polished, though less plain-spoken than the King of Nineveh, does not in direct terms require every one to turn from his "evil way, and from the violence that is in their hands." But to me these two expressions seem in a most signal manner to describe our difficulty, and to apply to the actual condition of things both North and South. The "violence in their hands" is the great reproach we must address to the sturdy fire-eater who in the hearing of an indignant world proclaims "Cotton is King." King indeed, and a most righteous and merciful one, no doubt, in his own conceit; since he only tars and feathers the wretches who fall in his power, and whom he suspects of not being sufficiently loyal and obedient to his sovereignty. And the "evil of his ways" is the reproach we must address to the sleek rhetorician who in the hearing of a God fearing world declared "Thought is King." King indeed, and a most mighty and magnanimous one – no doubt – in his own conceit; all-powerful to foment and augment the strife, though powerless to allay it. Of all the fallacies coined in the north, the arrogant assertion that "Thought is King" is the very last with which, at this present crisis, the patience of a reflecting people should have been abused. For in fact, the material greatness of the United States seems to have completely outgrown the grasp of our most gifted minds; so that urgent as is our need, pressing as is the occasion, no man or set of men have yet come forward capable of rising above the narrow horizon of sectional influences and prejudices, and with views enlightened, just, and beneficent, to embrace the entirety of the Union and to secure its prosperity and preservation. No, my friends, "Cotton" is not King, and "Human thought" is not King. *Hashem melech*! Hashem alone is King! *Umalkuso bakol mashalah*, and His royalty reigneth over all. This very day of humiliation and of prayer – what is it but the recognition of His supremacy, the confession of His power and of our own weakness, the supplications which our distress addresses to His mercy? But in order that these supplications may be graciously received, that His supreme protection may be vouchsafed unto our Country, it is necessary that we should begin as the people of Nineveh did; we must "believe in God." – And when I say "We," I do not mean merely us handful of peaceable Union-loving Hebrews, but I mean the whole of the people throughout the United States: the President and his Cabinet, the President elect and his advisers, the leaders of public opinion, North and South. If they truly and honestly desire to save our country, let them believe in God and in His Holy Word; and then when the authority of the Constitution is to be set aside for a higher Law, they will be able to appeal to the highest Law of all, the revealed Law and Word of God, which affords its supreme sanction to the Constitution. There can be no doubt, my friends, that however much of personal ambition, selfishness, pride, and obstinacy, there may enter into the present unhappy quarrel between the two great sections of the Commonwealth – I say it is certain that the origin of the quarrel itself is the difference of opinion respecting slave-holding, which the one section denounces as sinful – aye, as the most heinous of sins – while the other section upholds it as perfectly lawful. It is the province of statesmen to examine the circumstances under which the Constitution of the United States recognizes the legality of slave-holding; and under what circumstances, if any, it becomes a crime against the law of the land. *But the question whether slave-holding is a sin before God, is one that belongs to the theologian. I have been requested by prominent citizens of other denominations, that I should on this day examine the Bible view of slavery, as the religious mind of the country requires to be enlightened on the subject.*

In compliance with that request, and after humbly praying that the Father of Truth and of Mercy may enlighten my mind, and direct my words for good, I am about to solicit your earnest attention, my friends, to this serious subject. My discourse will, I fear, take up more of your time than I am in the habit of exacting from you; but this is a day of penitence, and the having to listen to a long and sober discourse must be accounted as a penitential infliction.

> The subject of my investigation falls into three parts: –
> First, How far back can we trace the existence of slavery?
> Secondly, Is slaveholding condemned as a sin in sacred Scripture?
> Thirdly, What was the condition of the slave in Biblical times, and among the Hebrews; and saying with our Father Jacob, "for Thy help, I hope, O L-rd!" [Gen. 49:18] I proceed to examine the question, how far back can we trace the existence of slavery?

I. It is generally admitted, that slavery had its origin in war, public or private. The victor having it in his power to take the life of his vanquished enemy, prefers to let him live, and reduces him to bondage. The life he has spared, the body he might have mutilated or destroyed, become his absolute property. He may dispose of it in any way he pleases. Such was, and through a great part of the world still is, the brutal law of force. When this state of things first began, it is next to impossible to decide. If we consult Sacred Scripture, the oldest and most truthful collection of records now or at any time in existence, we find the word *evved* "slave" which the English version renders "servant," first used by Noah, who, in Genesis ix. 25, curses the descendants of his son Ham, by saying they should be *Evved Avadim*, the "meanest of slaves," or as the English version has it "servant of servants." The question naturally arises how came Noah to use the expression? How came he to know anything of slavery? There existed not at that time any human being on earth except Noah and his family of three sons, apparently by one mother, born free and equal, with their wives and children. Noah had no slaves. From the time that he quitted the ark he could have none. It therefore becomes evident that Noah's acquaintance with the word slave and the nature of slavery must date from before the Flood, and existed in his memory only until the crime of Ham called it forth. You and I may regret that in his anger Noah should from beneath the waters of wrath again have fished up the idea and practice of slavery; but that he did so is a fact which rests on the authority of Scripture. I am therefore justified when tracing slavery as far back as it can be traced, I arrive at the conclusion, that next to the domestic relations of husband and wife, parents and children, the oldest relation of society with which we are acquainted is that of master and slave.

Let us for an instant stop at this curse by Noah with which slavery after the Flood is recalled into existence. Among the many prophecies contained in the Bible and having reference to particular times, persons, and events, there are three singular predictions referring to three distinct races or peoples, which seem to be intended for all times, and accordingly remain in full force to this day. The first of these is the doom of Ham's descendants, the African race, pronounced upwards of 4,000 years ago. The second is the character of the descendants of Ishmael, the Arabs, pronounced nearly 4,000 years ago; and the third and last is the promise of continued and indestructible nationality promised to us, Israelites, full 2,500 years ago. It has been said that the knowledge that a particular prophecy exists, helped to work out its fulfillment, and I am quite willing to allow that with us, Israelites, such is the fact. The knowledge we have of God's gracious promises renders us imperishable, even though the greatest and most powerful nations of the olden time have utterly perished. It may be doubted whether the fanatic Arab of the desert ever heard of the prophecy that he is to be a "wild man, his hand against every man, and every man's hand against him" [Gen. 16:12]. But you and I, and all men of ordinary education, know that this prediction at all times has been, and is now, literally fulfilled, and that it has never been interrupted. Not even when the followers of Mahomet rushed forth to spread his doctrines, the Koran in one hand and the sword in the other, and when Arab conquest rendered the fairest portion of the Old World subject to the empire of their Caliph, did the descendants of Ishmael renounce their characteristics. Even the boasted civilization of the present century, and frequent intercourse with Western travellers, still leave the Arab a wild man, "his hand against everybody, and every man's hand against him," a most convincing and durable proof that the Word of God is true, and that the prophecies of the Bible were dictated by the Spirit of the Most High. But though, in the case of the Arab, it is barely possible that he may be acquainted with the prediction made to Hagar, yet we may be sure that the fetish-serving benighted African has no knowledge of Noah's prediction; which, however, is nowhere more fully or more atrociously carried out than in the native home of the African. Witness the horrid fact, that the King of Dahomey is, at this very time, filling a large and deep trench with human blood, sufficient to float a good-sized boat; that the victims are innocent men, murdered to satisfy some freak of what he calls his religion; and that this monstrous and most fiendish act has met with no opposition, either from the pious indignation of Great Britain, or from the zealous humanity of our country.

No, I am well aware that the Biblical critics called Rationalists, who deny the possibility of prophecy, have taken upon themselves to assert, that the prediction of which I have spoken was never uttered by Noah, but was made up many centuries after him by the Hebrew writer of the Bible, in order to smoothe over the extermination of the Canaanites, whose land was conquered by the Israelites. With superhuman knowledge like that of the Rationalists, who claim to sit in judgement on the Word of God, I do not think it worth while to argue. But I would ask you how it is that a prediction, manufactured for a purpose – a fraud in short, and that a most base and unholy one, should nevertheless continue in force, and be carried out during four, or three, or even two thousand years; for a thousand years more or less can here make no difference. Noah, on the occasion in question, bestows on his son Shem a spiritual blessing: "Blessed be the L-rd, the God of Shem" [Gen. 9:26] and to this day it remains a fact which cannot be denied, that whatever knowledge of God and of religious truth is possessed by the human race, has been promulgated by the descendants of Shem. Noah bestows on his son Japheth a blessing, chiefly temporal, but partaking also of spiritual good. "May God enlarge Japheth, and may he dwell in the tents of Shem" [Gen. 9:27], and to this day it remains a fact which cannot be denied, that the descendants of Japheth (Europeans and their offspring) have been enlarged so that they possess dominion in every part of the earth; while, at the same time, they share in that knowledge of religious truth which the descendants of Shem were the first to promulgate. Noah did not bestow any blessing on his son Ham, but uttered a bitter curse against his descendants, and to this day it remains a fact which cannot be gainsaid that in his own native home, and generally throughout the world, the unfortunate negro is indeed the meanest of slaves. Much has been said respecting the inferiority of his intellectual powers, and that no man of his race has ever inscribed his name on the Pantheon of human excellence, either mental or moral. But this is a subject I will not discuss. I do not attempt to build up a theory, not yet to defend the moral government of Providence. I state facts; and having done so, I remind you that our own fathers were slaves in Egypt, and afflicted four hundred years; and then I bid you reflect on the words of inspired Isaiah (lv. 8.), "My thoughts are not your thoughts, neither are your ways my ways, saith the L-rd."

II. Having thus, on the authority of the sacred Scripture, traced slavery back to the remotest period, I next request your attention to the question, "Is slaveholding condemned as a sin in sacred Scripture?" How this question can at all arise in the mind of any man that has received a religious education, and is acquainted with the history of the Bible, is a phenomenon I cannot explain to myself, and which fifty years ago no man dreamed of. But we live in times when we must not be surprised at anything. Last Sunday an eminent preacher is reported to have declared from the pulpit, "The Old Testament requirements served their purpose during the physical and social development of mankind, and were rendered no longer necessary now when we were to be guided by the superior doctrines of the New in the moral instruction of the race." I had always thought that in the "moral instruction of the race," the requirements of Jewish Scriptures and Christian Scriptures were identically the same; that to abstain from murder, theft, adultery, that "to do justice, to love mercy, and to walk humbly with God" [Mic. 6:8], were "requirements" equally imperative in the one course of instruction as in the other. But it appears I was mistaken. "We have altered all that now," says this eminent divine, in happy imitation of Molière's physician, whose new theory removed the heart from the left side of the human body to the right. But when I remember that the "now" refers to a period of which you all, though no very aged men, witnessed the rise; when, moreover, I remember that the "WE" the reverend preacher speaks of, is limited to a few impulsive declaimers, gifted with great zeal, but little knowledge; more eloquent than learned; better able to excite our passions than to satisfy our reason; and when, lastly, I remember the scorn with which sacred Scripture (Deut. xxxii. 18) speaks of "newfangled notions, lately sprung up, which your fathers esteemed not;" when I consider all this, I think you and I had rather continue to take our "requirements for moral instruction" from Moses and the Prophets than from the eloquent preacher of Brooklyn [Henry Ward Beecher]. But as that reverend gentleman takes a lead among those who most loudly and most vehemently denounce slaveholding as a sin, I wished to convince myself whether he had any Scripture warranty for so doing; and whether such denunciation was one of those "requirements for moral instruction" advanced by the New Testament. I have accordingly examined the various books of Christian Scripture, and find that they afford the reverend gentleman and his compeers no authority whatever for his and their declamations. The New Testament nowhere, directly or indirectly, condemns slaveholding, which, indeed, is proved by the universal practice of all Christian nations during many centuries. Receiving slavery as one of the conditions of society, the New Testament nowhere interferes with or contradicts the slave code of Moses; it even preserves a letter written by one of the most eminent Christian teachers to a slaveowner

on sending back to him his runaway slave. And when we next refer to
the history and "requirements" of our own sacred Scriptures, we find
that on the most solemn occasion therein recorded, when God gave
the Ten Commandments on Mount Sinai –

> There where His finger scorched, the tablet shone;
> There where His shadow on his people shone His glory,
> shrouded in its garb of fire,
> Himself no eye might see and not expire.

Even on that most solemn and most holy occasion, slaveholding is not
only recognized and sanctioned as an integral part of the social structure, when it is commanded that the Sabbath of the L-rd is to bring
rest to *Avdecha ve'Amasecha*, "Thy male slave and thy female slave"
(Exod. xx. 10; Deut. v. 14). But the property in slaves is placed under
the same protection as any other species of lawful property, when
it is said, "Thou shalt not covet thy neighbor's house, or his field, or
his male slave, or his female slave, or his ox, or his ass, or aught that
belongeth to thy neighbor" (Ibid. xx. 17; v.21). That the male slave and
the female slave here spoken of do not designate the Hebrew bondman, but the heathen slave, I shall presently show you. That the Ten
Commandments are the word of God, and as such, of the very highest
authority, is acknowledged by Christians as well as by Jews. I would
therefore ask the reverend gentleman of Brooklyn and his compeers
– How dare you, in the face of the sanction and protection afforded to
slave property in the Ten Commandments – how dare you denounce
slaveholding as a sin? When you remember that Abraham, Isaac, Jacob,
Job – the men with whom the Almighty conversed, with whose names
he emphatically connects his own most holy name, and to whom He
vouchsafed to give the character of "perfect, upright, fearing God
and eschewing evil" (Job i. 8) – that all these men were slaveholders,
does it not strike you that you are guilty of something very little short
of blasphemy? And if you answer me, "Oh, in their time slaveholding was lawful, but now it has become a sin," I in my turn ask you,
"When and by what authority you draw the line? Tell us the precise
time when slaveholding ceased to be permitted, and became sinful?"

When we remember the mischief which this inventing a new sin, not known in the Bible, is causing; how it has exasperated the feelings of the South, and alarmed the conscience of the North, to a degree that men who should be brothers are on the point of embruing their hands in each other's blood, are we not entitled to ask the reverend preacher of Brooklyn, "What right have you to insult and exasperate thousands of God-fearing, law-abiding citizens, whose moral worth and patriotism, whose purity of conscience and of life, are fully equal to your own? What right have you to place yonder grey-headed philanthropist on a level with a murderer, or yonder mother of a family on a line with an adulteress, or yonder honorable and honest man in one rank with a thief, and all this solely because they exercise a right which your own fathers and progenitors, during many generations, held and exercised without reproach or compunction. You profess to frame your "moral instruction of the race" according to the "requirements" of the New Testament – but tell us where and by whom it was said, "Whosoever shall say to his neighbor, *rakah* (worthless sinner), shall be in danger of the council; but whosoever shall say, thou fool, shall be in danger of the judgment." My friends, I find, and I am sorry to find, that I am delivering a pro-slavery discourse. I am no friend to slavery in the abstract, and still less friendly to the practical working of slavery. But I stand here as a teacher in Israel; not to place before you my own feelings and opinions, but to propound to you the word of God, the Bible view of slavery. With a due sense of my responsibility, I must state to you the truth and nothing but the truth, however unpalatable or unpopular that truth may be.

III. It remains for me now to examine what was the condition of the slave in Biblical times and among the Hebrews. And here at once we must distinguish between the Hebrew bondman and the heathen slave. The former could only be reduced to bondage from two causes. If he had committed theft and had not wherewithal to make full restitution, he was "sold for his theft." (Exod. xxii. 3.) Or if he became so miserably poor that he could not sustain life except by begging, he had permission to "sell" or bind himself in servitude. (Levit. xxv. 39 *et seq.*) But in either case his servitude was limited in duration and character. "Six years shall he serve, and in the seventh he shall go out free for nothing" (Exod. xxi. 2). And if even the bondman preferred bondage to freedom, he could not, under any circumstances, be held to servitude longer than the jubilee then next coming. At that period the estate which had originally belonged to his father, or remoter ancestor, reverted to his possession, so that he went forth at once a freeman and a landed proprietor. As his privilege of Hebrew citizen was thus only suspended, and the law, in permitting him to be sold, contemplated his restoration to his full rights, it took care that during his servitude his mind should not be crushed to the abject and cringing condition of a slave. "Ye shall not rule over one another with rigor," is the provision of the law. (Lev. xxv. 46.) Thus he is fenced round with protection against any abuse of power on the part of his employer; and tradition so strictly interpreted the letter of the law in his favor, that it was a common saying of Biblical times and homes, which Maimonides has preserved to us, that "he who buys an Hebrew bondman gets himself a master." Though in servitude, this Hebrew was in nowise exempt from his religious duties. Therefore it is not for him or his that the Ten Commandments stipulated for rest on the Sabbath of the L-rd; for his employer could not compel him to work on that day; and if he did work of his own accord, he became guilty of death, like any other Sabbath-breaker. Neither does the prohibition, "thou shalt not covet the property of thy neighbor," apply to him, for he was not the property of his employer. In fact, between the Hebrew bondman and the Southern slave there is no point of resemblance. There were, however, slaves among the Hebrews, whose general condition was analogous to that of their Southern fellow sufferers. That was the heathen slave, who was to be bought "from the heathens that were round about the land of Israel, or from the heathen strangers that sojourned in the land; they should be a possession, to be bequeathed as an inheritance to the owner's children, after his death, for ever." (Levit. xxv. 44–46.) Over these heathen slaves the owner's property was absolute; he could put them to hard labor, to the utmost extent of their physical strength; he could inflict on them any degree of chastisement short of injury to life and limb. If his heathen slave ran away or strayed from home, every Israelite was bound to bring or send him back, as he would have to do with any other portion of his neighbor's property that had been lost or strayed. (Deut. xxii. 3.)

Now, you may, perhaps, ask me how I can reconcile this statement with the text of Scripture so frequently quoted against the Fugitive Slave Law, "Thou shalt not surrender unto his master the slave who has escaped from his master unto thee." (Deut. xxiii. 16.) I answer you that, according to all legists, this text applies to a heathen slave, who, from any foreign country escapes from his master, even though that master be an Hebrew, residing out of the land of Israel. Such a slave – but such a slave only – is to find a permanent asylum in any part of the country he may choose. This interpretation is fully borne out by the words of the precept. The pronoun "thou," is not here used in the same sense as in the Ten Commandments. There it designates every soul in Israel individually; since every one has it in his power, and is in duty bound to obey the commandments. But as the security and protection to be bestowed on the runaway slaves are beyond the power of any individual, and require the consent and concurrence of the whole community, the pronoun "thou" here means the whole of the people, and not one portion in opposition to any other portion of the people. And as the expression remains the same throughout the precept, "With thee he shall dwell, even among ye, in the place he shall choose in one of thy gates where it liketh him best" [Deut. 23:17], it plainly shows that the whole of the land was open to him, and the whole of the people were to protect the fugitive, which could not have been carried out if it had applied to the slave who escaped from one tribe into the territory of another. Had the precept been expounded in any other than its strictly literal sense, it would have caused great confusion, since it would have nullified two other precepts of God's law; that which directs that "slaves, like lands and houses, were to be inherited for ever," and that which commands "property, lost or strayed, to be restored to the owner." Any other interpretation would, moreover, have caused heartburning and strife between the tribes, for men were as tenacious of their rights and property in those days as they are now. But no second opinion was ever entertained; the slave who ran away from Dan to Beersheba had to be given up, even as the runaway from South Carolina has to be given up by Massachusetts; whilst the runaway from Edom, or from Syria, found an asylum in the land of Israel, as the runaway slave from Cuba or Brazil would find in New York. Accordingly, Shimei reclaimed and recovered his runaway slaves from Achish, king of Gath, at that time a vassal of Israel (Kings ii. 39, 40). And Saul of Tarsus sent back the runaway slave, Onesimus, unto his owner Philemon. But to surrender to a ruthless, lawless heathen, the wretched slave who had escaped from his cruelty, would have been to give up the fugitive to certain death, or at least to tortures repugnant to the spirit of God's law, the tender care of which protected the bird in its nest, the beast at the plough, and the slave in his degradation. Accordingly, the extradition was not permitted in Palestine any more than it is in Canada. While thus the owner possessed full right over and security for his property, the exercise of that power was confined within certain limits which he could not outstep. His female slave was not to be the tool or castaway toy of his sensuality, nor could he sell her, but was bound to "let her go free," "because he had humbled her" (Deut. xxi. 14). His male slave was protected against excessive punishment; for if the master in any way mutilated his slave, even to knock a single tooth out of his head, the slave became free (Exod. xxi. 26, 27). And while thus two of the worst passions of human nature, lust and cruelty, were kept under due restraint, the third bad passion, cupidity, was not permitted free scope; for the law of God secured to the slave his Sabbaths and days of rest; while public opinion, which in a country so densely peopled as Palestine must have been all-powerful, would not allow any slave-owner to impose heavier tasks on his slaves, or to feed them worse than his neighbors did. This, indeed, is the great distinction which the Bible view of slavery derives from its divine source. The slave is a *person* in whom the dignity of human nature is to be respected; *he has rights.* Whereas, the heathen view of slavery which prevailed at Rome, and which, I am sorry to say, is adopted in the South, reduces the slave to a *thing*, and a thing can have no rights. The result to which the Bible view of slavery leads us, is – 1st. That slavery has existed since the earliest time; 2d. That slaveholding is no sin, and that slave property is expressly placed under the protection of the Ten Commandments; 3d. That the slave is a person, and has rights not conflicting with the lawful exercise of the rights of his owner. If our Northern fellow-citizens, content with following the word of God, would not insist on being "righteous overmuch," or denouncing "sin" which the Bible knows not, but which is plainly taught by the precepts of men – they would entertain more equity and less ill feeling towards their Southern brethren. And if our Southern fellow-citizens would adopt the Bible view of slavery, and discard the heathen slave code, which permits a few bad men to indulge in an abuse of power that throws a stigma and disgrace on the whole body of slaveholders – if both North and South would do what is right, then "God would see their works and that they turned from the evil of their ways;" and in their case, as in that of the people of Nineveh, would mercifully avert the impending evil, for with Him alone is the power to do so. Therefore let us pray.

Almighty and merciful God, we approach Thee this day, our hearts heavy with the weight of our sins, our looks downcast under the sense of our ingratitude, national and individual. Thou, Father all-bounteous, hast in Thine abundant goodness plentifully bestowed upon us every good and every blessing, spiritual, mental, temporal, that in the present state of the world men can desire. But we have perverted and abused Thy gifts; in our arrogance and selfishness we have contrived to extract poison from Thy most precious boons; the spiritual have degenerated into unloving self-righteousness; the mental have rendered us vainglorious and conceited; and the temporal have degraded us into Mammon-worshipping slaves of avarice. Intoxicated with our prosperity, we have forgotten Thee; drunken with pride, we reel on towards the precipice of disunion and ruin. What hand can stay us if it be not Thine, O God! Thou who art long-suffering as Thou art almighty, to Thee we turn in the hour of our utmost need. Hear us, Father, for on Thee our hopes are fixed. Help us, Father, for thou alone canst do it. Punish us not according to our arrogance; afflict us not according to our deserts. Remove from our breasts the heart of stone, and from our minds the obstinacy of self-willed pride. Extend thy grace unto us, that we may acknowledge our own transgressions. Open our eyes that we may behold and renounce the wrong we inflict on our neighbors. God of justice and of mercy, suffer not despots to rejoice at our dissensions, nor tyrants to triumph over our fall. Let them not point at us the finger of scorn, or say, "Look there at the

fruits of freedom and self-government – of equal rights and popular sovereignty – strife without any real cause – destruction without
any sufficient motive." Oh, let not them who trust in Thee be put to
shame, or those who seek Thee be disgraced. Almighty God, extend
thy gracious protection to the United States. Pour out over the citizens thereof, and those whom they have elected to be their rulers, the
spirit of grace and of supplication, the spirit of wisdom and brotherly
love, so that henceforth, even as hitherto, they may know that union is
strength, and that it is good and pleasant for brethren to dwell together
in unity. And above all things, L-rd merciful and gracious, avert the
calamity of civil war from our midst. If in Thy supreme wisdom Thou
hast decreed that this vast commonwealth, which has risen under Thy
blessing, shall now be separated, then we beseech Thee let that separation be peaceable; that no human blood may be shed, but that the
canopy of Thy peace may still remain spread over all the land. May
we address our prayers to Thee, O L-rd, at an acceptable time; mayest Thou, O God, in Thy abundant mercy, answer us with the truth
of Thy salvation. Amen.

Hebraic Sources

R. Dr. Raphall traced the institution of slavery throughout the Hebrew Bible,
including discussions of both the narrative and legal sections therein.

Genesis 9

(כ) וַיָּחֶל נֹחַ אִישׁ הָאֲדָמָה וַיִּטַּע כָּרֶם.

(כא) וַיֵּשְׁתְּ מִן הַיַּיִן וַיִּשְׁכָּר וַיִּתְגַּל בְּתוֹךְ אָהֳלֹה.

(כב) וַיַּרְא חָם אֲבִי כְנַעַן אֵת עֶרְוַת אָבִיו וַיַּגֵּד לִשְׁנֵי אֶחָיו בַּחוּץ.

(כג) וַיִּקַּח שֵׁם וָיֶפֶת אֶת הַשִּׂמְלָה וַיָּשִׂימוּ עַל שְׁכֶם שְׁנֵיהֶם וַיֵּלְכוּ אֲחֹרַנִּית וַיְכַסּוּ
אֵת עֶרְוַת אֲבִיהֶם וּפְנֵיהֶם אֲחֹרַנִּית וְעֶרְוַת אֲבִיהֶם לֹא רָאוּ.

(כד) וַיִּיקֶץ נֹחַ מִיֵּינוֹ וַיֵּדַע אֵת אֲשֶׁר עָשָׂה לוֹ בְּנוֹ הַקָּטָן.

(כה) וַיֹּאמֶר אָרוּר כְּנָעַן עֶבֶד עֲבָדִים יִהְיֶה לְאֶחָיו.

(כו) וַיֹּאמֶר בָּרוּךְ ה' אֱ־לֹהֵי שֵׁם וִיהִי כְנַעַן עֶבֶד לָמוֹ.

(כז) יַפְתְּ אֱ־לֹהִים לְיֶפֶת וְיִשְׁכֹּן בְּאָהֳלֵי שֵׁם וִיהִי כְנַעַן עֶבֶד לָמוֹ.

²⁰ And Noah began to be an husbandman, and he planted a vineyard:

²¹ And he drank of the wine, and was drunken; and he was uncovered within his tent.

²² And Ham, the father of Canaan, saw the nakedness of his father, and told his two brethren without.

²³ And Shem and Japheth took a garment, and laid it upon both their shoulders, and went backward, and covered the nakedness of their father; and their faces were backward, and they saw not their father's nakedness.

²⁴ And Noah awoke from his wine, and knew what his younger son had done unto him.

²⁵ And he said, Cursed be Canaan; a servant of servants shall he be unto his brethren.

²⁶ And he said, Blessed be the Lord God of Shem; and Canaan shall be his servant.

²⁷ God shall enlarge Japheth, and he shall dwell in the tents of Shem; and Canaan shall be his servant.

Genesis 16

(א) וְשָׂרַי אֵשֶׁת אַבְרָם לֹא יָלְדָה לוֹ וְלָהּ שִׁפְחָה מִצְרִית וּשְׁמָהּ הָגָר.

(ב) וַתֹּאמֶר שָׂרַי אֶל אַבְרָם הִנֵּה נָא עֲצָרַנִי ה' מִלֶּדֶת בֹּא נָא אֶל שִׁפְחָתִי אוּלַי אִבָּנֶה מִמֶּנָּה וַיִּשְׁמַע אַבְרָם לְקוֹל שָׂרָי.

(ג) וַתִּקַּח שָׂרַי אֵשֶׁת אַבְרָם אֶת הָגָר הַמִּצְרִית שִׁפְחָתָהּ מִקֵּץ עֶשֶׂר שָׁנִים לְשֶׁבֶת אַבְרָם בְּאֶרֶץ כְּנָעַן וַתִּתֵּן אֹתָהּ לְאַבְרָם אִישָׁהּ לוֹ לְאִשָּׁה.

(ד) וַיָּבֹא אֶל הָגָר וַתַּהַר וַתֵּרֶא כִּי הָרָתָה וַתֵּקַל גְּבִרְתָּהּ בְּעֵינֶיהָ.

(ה) וַתֹּאמֶר שָׂרַי אֶל אַבְרָם חֲמָסִי עָלֶיךָ אָנֹכִי נָתַתִּי שִׁפְחָתִי בְּחֵיקֶךָ וַתֵּרֶא כִּי הָרָתָה וָאֵקַל בְּעֵינֶיהָ יִשְׁפֹּט ה' בֵּינִי וּבֵינֶיךָ.

(ו) וַיֹּאמֶר אַבְרָם אֶל שָׂרַי הִנֵּה שִׁפְחָתֵךְ בְּיָדֵךְ עֲשִׂי לָהּ הַטּוֹב בְּעֵינָיִךְ וַתְּעַנֶּהָ שָׂרַי וַתִּבְרַח מִפָּנֶיהָ.

(ז) וַיִּמְצָאָהּ מַלְאַךְ ה' עַל עֵין הַמַּיִם בַּמִּדְבָּר עַל הָעַיִן בְּדֶרֶךְ שׁוּר.

(ח) וַיֹּאמַר הָגָר שִׁפְחַת שָׂרַי אֵי מִזֶּה בָאת וְאָנָה תֵלֵכִי וַתֹּאמֶר מִפְּנֵי שָׂרַי גְּבִרְתִּי אָנֹכִי בֹּרַחַת.

(ט) וַיֹּאמֶר לָהּ מַלְאַךְ ה' שׁוּבִי אֶל גְּבִרְתֵּךְ וְהִתְעַנִּי תַּחַת יָדֶיהָ.

(י) וַיֹּאמֶר לָהּ מַלְאַךְ ה' הַרְבָּה אַרְבֶּה אֶת זַרְעֵךְ וְלֹא יִסָּפֵר מֵרֹב.

(יא) וַיֹּאמֶר לָהּ מַלְאַךְ ה' הִנָּךְ הָרָה וְיֹלַדְתְּ בֵּן וְקָרָאת שְׁמוֹ יִשְׁמָעֵאל כִּי שָׁמַע ה' אֶל עָנְיֵךְ.

(יב) וְהוּא יִהְיֶה פֶּרֶא אָדָם יָדוֹ בַכֹּל וְיַד כֹּל בּוֹ וְעַל פְּנֵי כָל אֶחָיו יִשְׁכֹּן.

(יג) וַתִּקְרָא שֵׁם ה' הַדֹּבֵר אֵלֶיהָ אַתָּה אֵ־ל רֳאִי כִּי אָמְרָה הֲגַם הֲלֹם רָאִיתִי אַחֲרֵי רֹאִי.

(יד) עַל כֵּן קָרָא לַבְּאֵר בְּאֵר לַחַי רֹאִי הִנֵּה בֵין קָדֵשׁ וּבֵין בָּרֶד.

(טו) וַתֵּלֶד הָגָר לְאַבְרָם בֵּן וַיִּקְרָא אַבְרָם שֵׁם בְּנוֹ אֲשֶׁר יָלְדָה הָגָר יִשְׁמָעֵאל.

(טז) וְאַבְרָם בֶּן שְׁמֹנִים שָׁנָה וְשֵׁשׁ שָׁנִים בְּלֶדֶת הָגָר אֶת יִשְׁמָעֵאל לְאַבְרָם.

¹ Now Sarai Abram's wife bare him no children: and she had an handmaid, an Egyptian, whose name was Hagar.

² And Sarai said unto Abram, Behold now, the Lord hath restrained me from bearing: I pray thee, go in unto my maid; it may be that I may obtain children by her. And Abram hearkened to the voice of Sarai.

³ And Sarai Abram's wife took Hagar her maid the Egyptian, after Abram had dwelt ten years in the land of Canaan, and gave her to her husband Abram to be his wife.

⁴ And he went in unto Hagar, and she conceived: and when she saw that she had conceived, her mistress was despised in her eyes.

⁵ And Sarai said unto Abram, My wrong be upon thee: I have given my maid into thy bosom; and when she saw that she had conceived, I was despised in her eyes: the Lord judge between me and thee.

⁶ But Abram said unto Sarai, Behold, thy maid is in thy hand; do to her as it pleaseth thee. And when Sarai dealt hardly with her, she fled from her face.

⁷ And the angel of the Lord found her by a fountain of water in the wilderness, by the fountain in the way to Shur.

⁸ And he said, Hagar, Sarai's maid, whence camest thou? and whither wilt thou go? And she said, I flee from the face of my mistress Sarai.

⁹ And the angel of the Lord said unto her, Return to thy mistress, and submit thyself under her hands.

¹⁰ And the angel of the Lord said unto her, I will multiply thy seed exceedingly, that it shall not be numbered for multitude.

¹¹ And the angel of the Lord said unto her, Behold, thou art with child, and shalt bear a son, and shalt call his name Ishmael; because the Lord hath heard thy affliction.

¹² And he will be a wild man; his hand will be against every man, and every man's hand against him; and he shall dwell in the presence of all his brethren.

¹³ And she called the name of the Lord that spake unto her, Thou God seest me: for she said, Have I also here looked after him that seeth me?

¹⁴ Wherefore the well was called Beerlahairoi; behold, it is between Kadesh and Bered.

¹⁵ And Hagar bare Abram a son: and Abram called his son's name, which Hagar bare, Ishmael.

¹⁶ And Abram was fourscore and six years old, when Hagar bare Ishmael to Abram.

Exodus 20

(א) וַיְדַבֵּר אֱ-לֹהִים אֵת כָּל הַדְּבָרִים הָאֵלֶּה לֵאמֹר.

(ב) אָנֹכִי ה' אֱ-לֹהֶיךָ אֲשֶׁר הוֹצֵאתִיךָ מֵאֶרֶץ מִצְרַיִם מִבֵּית עֲבָדִים לֹא יִהְיֶה לְךָ אֱלֹהִים אֲחֵרִים עַל פָּנָי.

(ג) לֹא תַעֲשֶׂה לְךָ פֶסֶל וְכָל תְּמוּנָה אֲשֶׁר בַּשָּׁמַיִם מִמַּעַל וַאֲשֶׁר בָּאָרֶץ מִתָּחַת וַאֲשֶׁר בַּמַּיִם מִתַּחַת לָאָרֶץ.

(ד) לֹא תִשְׁתַּחֲוֶה לָהֶם וְלֹא תָעָבְדֵם כִּי אָנֹכִי ה' אֱ-לֹהֶיךָ אֵ-ל קַנָּא פֹּקֵד עֲוֹן אָבֹת עַל בָּנִים עַל שִׁלֵּשִׁים וְעַל רִבֵּעִים לְשֹׂנְאָי.

(ה) וְעֹשֶׂה חֶסֶד לַאֲלָפִים לְאֹהֲבַי וּלְשֹׁמְרֵי מִצְוֹתָי.

(ו) לֹא תִשָּׂא אֶת שֵׁם ה' אֱ-לֹהֶיךָ לַשָּׁוְא כִּי לֹא יְנַקֶּה ה' אֵת אֲשֶׁר יִשָּׂא אֶת שְׁמוֹ לַשָּׁוְא.

(ז) זָכוֹר אֶת יוֹם הַשַּׁבָּת לְקַדְּשׁוֹ.

(ח) שֵׁשֶׁת יָמִים תַּעֲבֹד וְעָשִׂיתָ כָּל מְלַאכְתֶּךָ.

(ט) וְיוֹם הַשְּׁבִיעִי שַׁבָּת לַה' אֱ-לֹהֶיךָ לֹא תַעֲשֶׂה כָל מְלָאכָה אַתָּה וּבִנְךָ וּבִתֶּךָ עַבְדְּךָ וַאֲמָתְךָ וּבְהֶמְתֶּךָ וְגֵרְךָ אֲשֶׁר בִּשְׁעָרֶיךָ.

(י) כִּי שֵׁשֶׁת יָמִים עָשָׂה ה' אֶת הַשָּׁמַיִם וְאֶת הָאָרֶץ אֶת הַיָּם וְאֶת כָּל אֲשֶׁר בָּם וַיָּנַח בַּיּוֹם הַשְּׁבִיעִי עַל כֵּן בֵּרַךְ ה' אֶת יוֹם הַשַּׁבָּת וַיְקַדְּשֵׁהוּ.

(יא) כַּבֵּד אֶת אָבִיךָ וְאֶת אִמֶּךָ לְמַעַן יַאֲרִכוּן יָמֶיךָ עַל הָאֲדָמָה אֲשֶׁר ה' אֱ-לֹהֶיךָ נֹתֵן לָךְ.

(יב) לֹא תִרְצָח לֹא תִנְאָף לֹא תִגְנֹב לֹא תַעֲנֶה בְרֵעֲךָ עֵד שָׁקֶר.

(יג) לֹא תַחְמֹד בֵּית רֵעֶךָ לֹא תַחְמֹד אֵשֶׁת רֵעֶךָ וְעַבְדּוֹ וַאֲמָתוֹ וְשׁוֹרוֹ וַחֲמֹרוֹ וְכֹל אֲשֶׁר לְרֵעֶךָ.

[1] And God spake all these words, saying,

[2] [2] I am the Lord thy God, which have brought thee out of the land of Egypt, out of the house of bondage.

[3] Thou shalt have no other gods before me.

[4] [3] Thou shalt not make unto thee any graven image, or any likeness of any thing that is in heaven above, or that is in the earth beneath, or that is in the water under the earth:

[5] [4] Thou shalt not bow down thyself to them, nor serve them: for I the Lord thy God am a jealous God, visiting the iniquity of the fathers upon the children unto the third and fourth generation of them that hate me;

[6] [5] And shewing mercy unto thousands of them that love me, and keep my commandments.

[7] [6] Thou shalt not take the name of the Lord thy God in vain; for the Lord will not hold him guiltless that taketh his name in vain.

[8] [7] Remember the sabbath day, to keep it holy.

[9] [8] Six days shalt thou labour, and do all thy work:

[10] [9] But the seventh day is the sabbath of the Lord thy God: in it thou shalt not do any work, thou, nor thy son, nor thy daughter, thy manservant, nor thy maidservant, nor thy cattle, nor thy stranger that is within thy gates:

[11] [10] For in six days the Lord made heaven and earth, the sea, and all that in them is, and rested the seventh day: wherefore the Lord blessed the sabbath day, and hallowed it.

[12] [11] Honour thy father and thy mother: that thy days may be long upon the land which the Lord thy God giveth thee.

[13] [12] Thou shalt not kill.

[14] Thou shalt not commit adultery.

[15] Thou shalt not steal.

[16] Thou shalt not bear false witness against thy neighbour.

¹⁷ [¹³] Thou shalt not covet thy neighbour's house, thou shalt not covet thy neighbour's wife, nor his manservant, nor his maidservant, nor his ox, nor his ass, nor any thing that is thy neighbour's.

Deuteronomy 5

(ו) אָנֹכִי ה' אֱ־לֹהֶיךָ אֲשֶׁר הוֹצֵאתִיךָ מֵאֶרֶץ מִצְרַיִם מִבֵּית עֲבָדִים לֹא יִהְיֶה לְךָ אֱלֹהִים אֲחֵרִים עַל פָּנָי.

(ז) לֹא תַעֲשֶׂה לְךָ פֶסֶל כָּל תְּמוּנָה אֲשֶׁר בַּשָּׁמַיִם מִמַּעַל וַאֲשֶׁר בָּאָרֶץ מִתַּחַת וַאֲשֶׁר בַּמַּיִם מִתַּחַת לָאָרֶץ.

(ח) לֹא תִשְׁתַּחֲוֶה לָהֶם וְלֹא תָעָבְדֵם כִּי אָנֹכִי ה' אֱ־לֹהֶיךָ אֵ־ל קַנָּא פֹּקֵד עֲוֹן אָבוֹת עַל בָּנִים וְעַל שִׁלֵּשִׁים וְעַל רִבֵּעִים לְשֹׂנְאָי.

(ט) וְעֹשֶׂה חֶסֶד לַאֲלָפִים לְאֹהֲבַי וּלְשֹׁמְרֵי מצותו [מִצְוֹתָי].

(י) לֹא תִשָּׂא אֶת שֵׁם ה' אֱ־לֹהֶיךָ לַשָּׁוְא כִּי לֹא יְנַקֶּה ה' אֵת אֲשֶׁר יִשָּׂא אֶת שְׁמוֹ לַשָּׁוְא.

(יא) שָׁמוֹר אֶת יוֹם הַשַּׁבָּת לְקַדְּשׁוֹ כַּאֲשֶׁר צִוְּךָ ה' אֱ־לֹהֶיךָ.

(יב) שֵׁשֶׁת יָמִים תַּעֲבֹד וְעָשִׂיתָ כָּל מְלַאכְתֶּךָ.

(יג) וְיוֹם הַשְּׁבִיעִי שַׁבָּת לַה' אֱ־לֹהֶיךָ לֹא תַעֲשֶׂה כָל מְלָאכָה אַתָּה וּבִנְךָ וּבִתֶּךָ וְעַבְדְּךָ וַאֲמָתֶךָ וְשׁוֹרְךָ וַחֲמֹרְךָ וְכָל בְּהֶמְתֶּךָ וְגֵרְךָ אֲשֶׁר בִּשְׁעָרֶיךָ לְמַעַן יָנוּחַ עַבְדְּךָ וַאֲמָתְךָ כָּמוֹךָ.

(יד) וְזָכַרְתָּ כִּי עֶבֶד הָיִיתָ בְּאֶרֶץ מִצְרַיִם וַיֹּצִאֲךָ ה' אֱ־לֹהֶיךָ מִשָּׁם בְּיָד חֲזָקָה וּבִזְרֹעַ נְטוּיָה עַל כֵּן צִוְּךָ ה' אֱ־לֹהֶיךָ לַעֲשׂוֹת אֶת יוֹם הַשַּׁבָּת.

(טו) כַּבֵּד אֶת אָבִיךָ וְאֶת אִמֶּךָ כַּאֲשֶׁר צִוְּךָ ה' אֱ־לֹהֶיךָ לְמַעַן יַאֲרִיכֻן יָמֶיךָ וּלְמַעַן יִיטַב לָךְ עַל הָאֲדָמָה אֲשֶׁר ה' אֱ־לֹהֶיךָ נֹתֵן לָךְ.

(טז) לֹא תִרְצָח וְלֹא תִנְאָף וְלֹא תִגְנֹב וְלֹא תַעֲנֶה בְרֵעֲךָ עֵד שָׁוְא.

(יז) וְלֹא תַחְמֹד אֵשֶׁת רֵעֶךָ וְלֹא תִתְאַוֶּה בֵּית רֵעֶךָ שָׂדֵהוּ וְעַבְדּוֹ וַאֲמָתוֹ שׁוֹרוֹ וַחֲמֹרוֹ וְכֹל אֲשֶׁר לְרֵעֶךָ.

⁶ [⁶] I am the Lord thy God, which brought thee out of the land of Egypt, from the house of bondage.

⁷ Thou shalt have none other gods before me.

⁸ [⁷] Thou shalt not make thee any graven image, or any likeness of any thing that is in heaven above, or that is in the earth beneath, or that is in the waters beneath the earth:

⁹ [⁸] Thou shalt not bow down thyself unto them, nor serve them: for I the Lord thy God am a jealous God, visiting the iniquity of the fathers upon the children unto the third and fourth generation of them that hate me,

¹⁰ [⁹] And shewing mercy unto thousands of them that love me and keep my commandments.

^{11 [10]} Thou shalt not take the name of the Lord thy God in vain: for the Lord will not hold him guiltless that taketh his name in vain.

^{12 [11]} Keep the sabbath day to sanctify it, as the Lord thy God hath commanded thee.

^{13 [12]} Six days thou shalt labour, and do all thy work:

^{14 [13]} But the seventh day is the sabbath of the Lord thy God: in it thou shalt not do any work, thou, nor thy son, nor thy daughter, nor thy manservant, nor thy maidservant, nor thine ox, nor thine ass, nor any of thy cattle, nor thy stranger that is within thy gates; that thy manservant and thy maidservant may rest as well as thou.

^{15 [14]} And remember that thou wast a servant in the land of Egypt, and that the Lord thy God brought thee out thence through a mighty hand and by a stretched out arm: therefore the Lord thy God commanded thee to keep the sabbath day.

^{16 [15]} Honour thy father and thy mother, as the Lord thy God hath commanded thee; that thy days may be prolonged, and that it may go well with thee, in the land which the Lord thy God giveth thee.

^{17 [16]} Thou shalt not kill.

¹⁸ Neither shalt thou commit adultery.

¹⁹ Neither shalt thou steal.

²⁰ Neither shalt thou bear false witness against thy neighbour.

^{21 [17]} Neither shalt thou desire thy neighbour's wife, neither shalt thou covet thy neighbour's house, his field, or his manservant, or his maidservant, his ox, or his ass, or any thing that is thy neighbour's.

Exodus 22

(לז) כִּי יִגְנֹב אִישׁ שׁוֹר אוֹ שֶׂה וּטְבָחוֹ אוֹ מְכָרוֹ חֲמִשָּׁה בָקָר יְשַׁלֵּם תַּחַת הַשּׁוֹר וְאַרְבַּע צֹאן תַּחַת הַשֶּׂה.

(א) אִם בַּמַּחְתֶּרֶת יִמָּצֵא הַגַּנָּב וְהֻכָּה וָמֵת אֵין לוֹ דָּמִים.

(ב) אִם זָרְחָה הַשֶּׁמֶשׁ עָלָיו דָּמִים לוֹ שַׁלֵּם יְשַׁלֵּם אִם אֵין לוֹ וְנִמְכַּר בִּגְנֵבָתוֹ.

^{1 [21:37]} If a man shall steal an ox, or a sheep, and kill it, or sell it; he shall restore five oxen for an ox, and four sheep for a sheep.

^{2 [22:1]} If a thief be found breaking up, and be smitten that he die, there shall no blood be shed for him.

^{3 [22:2]} If the sun be risen upon him, there shall be blood shed for him; for he should make full restitution; if he have nothing, then he shall be sold for his theft.

Exodus 21

(כו) וְכִי יַכֶּה אִישׁ אֶת עֵין עַבְדּוֹ אוֹ אֶת עֵין אֲמָתוֹ וְשִׁחֲתָהּ לַחָפְשִׁי יְשַׁלְּחֶנּוּ תַּחַת עֵינוֹ.

(כז) וְאִם שֵׁן עַבְדּוֹ אוֹ שֵׁן אֲמָתוֹ יַפִּיל לַחָפְשִׁי יְשַׁלְּחֶנּוּ תַּחַת שִׁנּוֹ.

[26] And if a man smite the eye of his servant, or the eye of his maid, that it perish; he shall let him go free for his eye's sake.

[27] And if he smite out his manservant's tooth, or his maidservant's tooth; he shall let him go free for his tooth's sake.

Leviticus 25

(לט) וְכִי יָמוּךְ אָחִיךָ עִמָּךְ וְנִמְכַּר לָךְ לֹא תַעֲבֹד בּוֹ עֲבֹדַת עָבֶד.

(מ) כְּשָׂכִיר כְּתוֹשָׁב יִהְיֶה עִמָּךְ עַד שְׁנַת הַיֹּבֵל יַעֲבֹד עִמָּךְ.

(מא) וְיָצָא מֵעִמָּךְ הוּא וּבָנָיו עִמּוֹ וְשָׁב אֶל מִשְׁפַּחְתּוֹ וְאֶל אֲחֻזַּת אֲבֹתָיו יָשׁוּב.

(מב) כִּי עֲבָדַי הֵם אֲשֶׁר הוֹצֵאתִי אֹתָם מֵאֶרֶץ מִצְרָיִם לֹא יִמָּכְרוּ מִמְכֶּרֶת עָבֶד.

(מג) לֹא תִרְדֶּה בוֹ בְּפָרֶךְ וְיָרֵאתָ מֵאֱ-לֹהֶיךָ.

(מד) וְעַבְדְּךָ וַאֲמָתְךָ אֲשֶׁר יִהְיוּ לָךְ מֵאֵת הַגּוֹיִם אֲשֶׁר סְבִיבֹתֵיכֶם מֵהֶם תִּקְנוּ עֶבֶד וְאָמָה.

(מה) וְגַם מִבְּנֵי הַתּוֹשָׁבִים הַגָּרִים עִמָּכֶם מֵהֶם תִּקְנוּ וּמִמִּשְׁפַּחְתָּם אֲשֶׁר עִמָּכֶם אֲשֶׁר הוֹלִידוּ בְּאַרְצְכֶם וְהָיוּ לָכֶם לַאֲחֻזָּה.

(מו) וְהִתְנַחַלְתֶּם אֹתָם לִבְנֵיכֶם אַחֲרֵיכֶם לָרֶשֶׁת אֲחֻזָּה לְעֹלָם בָּהֶם תַּעֲבֹדוּ וּבְאַחֵיכֶם בְּנֵי יִשְׂרָאֵל אִישׁ בְּאָחִיו לֹא תִרְדֶּה בוֹ בְּפָרֶךְ.

(מז) וְכִי תַשִּׂיג יַד גֵּר וְתוֹשָׁב עִמָּךְ וּמָךְ אָחִיךָ עִמּוֹ וְנִמְכַּר לְגֵר תּוֹשָׁב עִמָּךְ אוֹ לְעֵקֶר מִשְׁפַּחַת גֵּר.

(מח) אַחֲרֵי נִמְכַּר גְּאֻלָּה תִּהְיֶה לּוֹ אֶחָד מֵאֶחָיו יִגְאָלֶנּוּ.

(מט) אוֹ דֹדוֹ אוֹ בֶן דֹּדוֹ יִגְאָלֶנּוּ אוֹ מִשְּׁאֵר בְּשָׂרוֹ מִמִּשְׁפַּחְתּוֹ יִגְאָלֶנּוּ אוֹ הִשִּׂיגָה יָדוֹ וְנִגְאָל.

(נ) וְחִשַּׁב עִם קֹנֵהוּ מִשְּׁנַת הִמָּכְרוֹ לוֹ עַד שְׁנַת הַיֹּבֵל וְהָיָה כֶּסֶף מִמְכָּרוֹ בְּמִסְפַּר שָׁנִים כִּימֵי שָׂכִיר יִהְיֶה עִמּוֹ.

(נא) אִם עוֹד רַבּוֹת בַּשָּׁנִים לְפִיהֶן יָשִׁיב גְּאֻלָּתוֹ מִכֶּסֶף מִקְנָתוֹ.

(נב) וְאִם מְעַט נִשְׁאַר בַּשָּׁנִים עַד שְׁנַת הַיֹּבֵל וְחִשַּׁב לוֹ כְּפִי שָׁנָיו יָשִׁיב אֶת גְּאֻלָּתוֹ.

(נג) כִּשְׂכִיר שָׁנָה בְּשָׁנָה יִהְיֶה עִמּוֹ לֹא יִרְדֶּנּוּ בְּפֶרֶךְ לְעֵינֶיךָ.

(נד) וְאִם לֹא יִגָּאֵל בְּאֵלֶּה וְיָצָא בִּשְׁנַת הַיֹּבֵל הוּא וּבָנָיו עִמּוֹ.

(נה) כִּי לִי בְנֵי יִשְׂרָאֵל עֲבָדִים עֲבָדַי הֵם אֲשֶׁר הוֹצֵאתִי אוֹתָם מֵאֶרֶץ מִצְרָיִם אֲנִי ה' אֱ-לֹהֵיכֶם.

[39] And if thy brother that dwelleth by thee be waxen poor, and be sold unto thee; thou shalt not compel him to serve as a bondservant:

[40] But as an hired servant, and as a sojourner, he shall be with thee, and shall serve thee unto the year of jubile:

[41] And then shall he depart from thee, both he and his children with him, and shall return unto his own family, and unto the possession of his fathers shall he return.

⁴² For they are my servants, which I brought forth out of the land of Egypt: they shall not be sold as bondmen.

⁴³ Thou shalt not rule over him with rigour; but shalt fear thy God.

⁴⁴ Both thy bondmen, and thy bondmaids, which thou shalt have, shall be of the heathen that are round about you; of them shall ye buy bondmen and bondmaids.

⁴⁵ Moreover of the children of the strangers that do sojourn among you, of them shall ye buy, and of their families that are with you, which they begat in your land: and they shall be your possession.

⁴⁶ And ye shall take them as an inheritance for your children after you, to inherit them for a possession; they shall be your bondmen for ever: but over your brethren the children of Israel, ye shall not rule one over another with rigour.

⁴⁷ And if a sojourner or stranger wax rich by thee, and thy brother that dwelleth by him wax poor, and sell himself unto the stranger or sojourner by thee, or to the stock of the stranger's family:

⁴⁸ After that he is sold he may be redeemed again; one of his brethren may redeem him:

⁴⁹ Either his uncle, or his uncle's son, may redeem him, or any that is nigh of kin unto him of his family may redeem him; or if he be able, he may redeem himself.

⁵⁰ And he shall reckon with him that bought him from the year that he was sold to him unto the year of jubile: and the price of his sale shall be according unto the number of years, according to the time of an hired servant shall it be with him.

⁵¹ If there be yet many years behind, according unto them he shall give again the price of his redemption out of the money that he was bought for.

⁵² And if there remain but few years unto the year of jubile, then he shall count with him, and according unto his years shall he give him again the price of his redemption.

⁵³ And as a yearly hired servant shall he be with him: and the other shall not rule with rigour over him in thy sight.

⁵⁴ And if he be not redeemed in these years, then he shall go out in the year of jubile, both he, and his children with him.

⁵⁵ For unto me the children of Israel are servants; they are my servants whom I brought forth out of the land of Egypt: I am the Lord your God.

Deuteronomy 21

(י) כִּי־תֵצֵא לַמִּלְחָמָה עַל־אֹיְבֶיךָ וּנְתָנוֹ ה' אֱ-לֹהֶיךָ בְּיָדֶךָ וְשָׁבִיתָ שִׁבְיוֹ.

(יא) וְרָאִיתָ בַּשִּׁבְיָה אֵשֶׁת יְפַת תֹּאַר וְחָשַׁקְתָּ בָהּ וְלָקַחְתָּ לְךָ לְאִשָּׁה.

(יב) וַהֲבֵאתָהּ אֶל־תּוֹךְ בֵּיתֶךָ וְגִלְּחָה אֶת־רֹאשָׁהּ וְעָשְׂתָה אֶת־צִפָּרְנֶיהָ.

(יג) וְהֵסִירָה אֶת־שִׂמְלַת שִׁבְיָהּ מֵעָלֶיהָ וְיָשְׁבָה בְּבֵיתֶךָ וּבָכְתָה אֶת־אָבִיהָ וְאֶת־אִמָּהּ יֶרַח יָמִים וְאַחַר כֵּן תָּבוֹא אֵלֶיהָ וּבְעַלְתָּהּ וְהָיְתָה לְךָ לְאִשָּׁה.

(יד) וְהָיָה אִם־לֹא חָפַצְתָּ בָּהּ וְשִׁלַּחְתָּהּ לְנַפְשָׁהּ וּמָכֹר לֹא־תִמְכְּרֶנָּה בַּכָּסֶף לֹא־תִתְעַמֵּר בָּהּ תַּחַת אֲשֶׁר עִנִּיתָהּ.

¹⁰ When thou goest forth to war against thine enemies, and the Lord thy God hath delivered them into thine hands, and thou hast taken them captive,

¹¹ And seest among the captives a beautiful woman, and hast a desire unto her, that thou wouldest have her to thy wife;

¹² Then thou shalt bring her home to thine house; and she shall shave her head, and pare her nails;

¹³ And she shall put the raiment of her captivity from off her, and shall remain in thine house, and bewail her father and her mother a full month: and after that thou shalt go in unto her, and be her husband, and she shall be thy wife.

¹⁴ And it shall be, if thou have no delight in her, then thou shalt let her go whither she will; but thou shalt not sell her at all for money, thou shalt not make merchandise of her, because thou hast humbled her.

Deuteronomy 22

(א) לֹא תִרְאֶה אֶת שׁוֹר אָחִיךָ אוֹ אֶת שֵׂיוֹ נִדָּחִים וְהִתְעַלַּמְתָּ מֵהֶם הָשֵׁב תְּשִׁיבֵם לְאָחִיךָ.

(ב) וְאִם לֹא קָרוֹב אָחִיךָ אֵלֶיךָ וְלֹא יְדַעְתּוֹ וַאֲסַפְתּוֹ אֶל תּוֹךְ בֵּיתֶךָ וְהָיָה עִמְּךָ עַד דְּרֹשׁ אָחִיךָ אֹתוֹ וַהֲשֵׁבֹתוֹ לוֹ.

(ג) וְכֵן תַּעֲשֶׂה לַחֲמֹרוֹ וְכֵן תַּעֲשֶׂה לְשִׂמְלָתוֹ וְכֵן תַּעֲשֶׂה לְכָל אֲבֵדַת אָחִיךָ אֲשֶׁר תֹּאבַד מִמֶּנּוּ וּמְצָאתָהּ לֹא תוּכַל לְהִתְעַלֵּם.

¹ Thou shalt not see thy brother's ox or his sheep go astray, and hide thyself from them: thou shalt in any case bring them again unto thy brother.

² And if thy brother be not nigh unto thee, or if thou know him not, then thou shalt bring it unto thine own house, and it shall be with thee until thy brother seek after it, and thou shalt restore it to him again.

³ In like manner shalt thou do with his ass; and so shalt thou do with his raiment; and with all lost thing of thy brother's, which he hath lost, and thou hast found, shalt thou do likewise: thou mayest not hide thyself.

Deuteronomy 23

(טז) לֹא תַסְגִּיר עֶבֶד אֶל אֲדֹנָיו אֲשֶׁר יִנָּצֵל אֵלֶיךָ מֵעִם אֲדֹנָיו.

(יז) עִמְּךָ יֵשֵׁב בְּקִרְבְּךָ בַּמָּקוֹם אֲשֶׁר יִבְחַר בְּאַחַד שְׁעָרֶיךָ בַּטּוֹב לוֹ לֹא תּוֹנֶנּוּ.

¹⁶ Thou shalt not deliver unto his master the servant which is escaped from his master unto thee.

¹⁷ He shall dwell with thee, even among you, in that place which he shall choose in one of thy gates, where it liketh him best; thou shalt not oppress him.

I Kings 2

(לט) וַיְהִי מִקֵּץ שָׁלֹשׁ שָׁנִים וַיִּבְרְחוּ שְׁנֵי עֲבָדִים לְשִׁמְעִי אֶל אָכִישׁ בֶּן מַעֲכָה מֶלֶךְ גַּת וַיַּגִּידוּ לְשִׁמְעִי לֵאמֹר הִנֵּה עֲבָדֶיךָ בְּגַת. (מ) וַיָּקָם שִׁמְעִי וַיַּחֲבֹשׁ אֶת חֲמֹרוֹ וַיֵּלֶךְ גַּתָה אֶל אָכִישׁ לְבַקֵּשׁ אֶת עֲבָדָיו וַיֵּלֶךְ שִׁמְעִי וַיָּבֵא אֶת עֲבָדָיו מִגַּת.

[39] And it came to pass at the end of three years, that two of the servants of Shimei ran away unto Achish son of Maachah king of Gath. And they told Shimei, saying, Behold, thy servants be in Gath.
[40] And Shimei arose, and saddled his ass, and went to Gath to Achish to seek his servants: and Shimei went, and brought his servants from Gath.

Frederick Douglass, "An Appeal to the British People" (1846)

One of the most learned and eloquent men of his generation, Frederick Douglass (1818–1895) was born into slavery. He escaped and settled in New York, where he was cast into the national spotlight when he went on speaking tours to promote abolitionism by recounting his life as a slave. He became friends with Abraham Lincoln and published his autobiography, Narrative of the Life of Frederick Douglass, An American Slave, *in 1845. When he gained national prominence, his friends in the abolitionist movement feared that he would be captured and sent back into slavery. He then traveled to Ireland and England, where he delivered a number of anti-slavery speeches. Douglass is widely agreed to have been among the nation's most prominent spokesmen for African American rights and the American ideals of liberty and human equality. The following excerpt is taken from a speech delivered at Finsbury Chapel, Moorfields, England, in 1846.*

But you will ask me, can these things be possible in a land professing Christianity? Yes, they are so; and this is not the worst. No; a darker feature is yet to be presented than the mere existence of these facts. I have to inform you that the religion of the southern states, at this time, is the great supporter, the great sanctioner of the bloody atrocities to which I have referred. While America is printing tracts and bibles; sending missionaries abroad to convert the heathen; expending her money in various ways for the promotion of the gospel in foreign lands – the slave not only lies forgotten, uncared for, but is trampled under foot by the very churches of the land. What have we in America? Why, we have slavery made part of the religion of the land. Yes, the pulpit there stands up as the great defender of this cursed institution, as it is called. Ministers of religion come forward and torture the hallowed pages of inspired wisdom to sanction the bloody deed. They stand forth as the foremost, the strongest defenders of this "institution." As a proof of this, I need not do more than state the general fact, that slavery has existed under the droppings of the sanctuary of the south for the last two hundred years, and there has not been any war between the religion and the slavery of the south. Whips, chains, gags, and thumb-screws have all lain under the droppings of the sanctuary, and instead of rusting from off the limbs of the bondman, those droppings have served to preserve them in all their strength. Instead of preaching the gospel against this tyranny, rebuke, and wrong, ministers of religion have sought, by all and every means, to throw in the back-ground whatever in the bible could be construed into opposition to slavery, and to bring forward that which they could torture into its support. This I conceive to be the darkest feature of slavery, and the most dif-ficult to attack, because it is identified with religion, and exposes those who denounce it to the charge of infidelity. Yes, those with whom I have been laboring, namely, the old organization anti-slavery society of America, have been again and again stigmatized as infidels, and for what reason? Why, solely in consequence of the faithfulness of their attacks upon the slaveholding religion of the southern states, and the northern religion that sympathizes with it. I have found it difficult to speak on this matter without persons coming forward and saying, "Douglass, are you not afraid of injuring the cause of Christ? You do not desire to do so, we know; but are you not undermining religion?" This has been said to me again and again, even since I came to this country, but I cannot be induced to leave off these exposures.

I love the religion of our blessed Saviour, I love that religion that comes from above, in the "wisdom of God, which is first pure, then peaceable, gentle, and easy to be entreated, full of mercy and good fruits, without partiality and without hypocrisy." I love that religion that sends its votaries to bind up the wounds of him that has fallen among thieves. I love that religion that makes it the duty of its disciples to visit the fatherless and widow in their affliction. I love that religion that is based upon the glorious principle, of love to God and love to man; which makes its followers do unto others as they themselves would be done by. If you demand liberty to yourself, it says, grant it to your neighbours. If you claim a right to think for yourselves, it says, allow your neighbours the same right. If you claim to act for yourselves, it says, allow your neighbours the same right. It is because I love this religion that I hate the slave-holding, the woman-whipping, the mind-darkening, the soul-destroying religion that exists in the southern states of America. It is because I regard the one as good, and pure, and holy, that I cannot but regard the other as bad, corrupt, and wicked. Loving the one I must hate the other, holding to the one I must reject the other, and I, therefore, proclaim myself an infidel to the slave-holding religion of America.

Why, as I said in another place, to a smaller audience the other day, in answer to the question, "Mr. Douglass, are there not Methodist churches, Baptist churches, Congregational churches, Episcopal churches, Roman Catholic churches, Presbyterian churches in the United States, and in the southern states of America, and do they not have revivals of religion, accessions to their ranks from day to day, and will you tell me that these men are not followers of the meek and lowly Saviour?" Most unhesitatingly I do. Revivals in religion, and revivals in the slave trade, go hand in hand together. The church and the slave prison stand next to each other; the groans and cries of the heartbroken slave are often drowned in the pious devotions of his religious master. The church-going bell and the auctioneer's bell chime in with each other; the pulpit and the auctioneer's block stand in the same neighbourhood; while the blood-stained gold goes to support the pulpit, the pulpit covers the infernal business with the garb of Christianity. We have men sold to build churches, women sold to support missionaries, and babies sold to buy Bibles and communion services for the churches.

Abraham Lincoln, Speech on the Dred Scott Decision (June 1857)

In 1836, a man named Emerson moved to the Wisconsin Territory with his slave Dred Scott, where he rented him out for labor. The Northwest Ordinance and the

Missouri Compromise prohibited slavery, and Scott argued that since he spent extended periods of time in a free state where slavery was prohibited, he became free. The Supreme Court disagreed with him. Chief Justice of the Supreme Court Roger B. Taney, wishing to settle the slavery question in the United States once and for all, ruled that slaves were not citizens of the United States and therefore Scott could not bring suit, and that the Missouri Compromise was unconstitutional because the federal government had no power to ban slavery in the territory of the Louisiana Purchase. The Dred Scott decision marked only the second overturning of a federal law as unconstitutional since Marbury v. Madison, which established the principle of judicial review. The decision was reviled in the North, raising fear that all states would soon be slave states.

Abraham Lincoln was elected to one term in Congress in 1846 but based on an agreement with the local Whig Party he did not run for reelection. Thinking his political career had come to an end, Lincoln went into law and prospered. He reentered politics in 1854 after the passage of the Kansas-Nebraska Act, which repealed the Missouri Compromise that kept slavery out of the northern territories in the West. Lincoln gave a number of speeches against the act, fearing that the nation was drifting away from the spirit of freedom that animated the founding generation. The following is an excerpt from one of those speeches. Notice how Lincoln defends his idea that all men are free and equal.

There is a natural disgust in the minds of nearly all white people, to the idea of an indiscriminate amalgamation of the white and black races; and Judge Douglas evidently is basing his chief hope, upon the chances of being able to appropriate the benefit of this disgust to himself. If he can, by much drumming and repeating, fasten the odium of that idea upon his adversaries, he thinks he can struggle through the storm. He therefore clings to this hope, as a drowning man to the last plank. He makes an occasion for lugging it in from the opposition to the Dred Scott decision. He finds the Republicans insisting that the Declaration of Independence includes ALL men, black as well as white; and forth-with he boldly denies that it includes negroes at all, and proceeds to argue gravely that all who contend it does, do so only because they want to vote, and eat, and sleep, and marry with negroes! He will have it that they cannot be consistent else. Now I protest against that counterfeit logic which concludes that, because I do not want a black woman for a slave I must necessarily want her for a wife. I need not have her for either, I can just leave her alone. In some respects she certainly is not my equal; but in her natural right to eat the bread she earns with her own hands without asking leave of any one else, she is my equal, and the equal of all others.

Hebraic Source

Lincoln here cited the Hebrew Bible for the proposition that every person has the right to the fruit of his or her labors.

Genesis 3

(יז) וּלְאָדָם אָמַר כִּי שָׁמַעְתָּ לְקוֹל אִשְׁתֶּךָ וַתֹּאכַל מִן הָעֵץ אֲשֶׁר צִוִּיתִיךָ לֵאמֹר לֹא תֹאכַל מִמֶּנּוּ אֲרוּרָה הָאֲדָמָה בַּעֲבוּרֶךָ בְּעִצָּבוֹן תֹּאכֲלֶנָּה כֹּל יְמֵי חַיֶּיךָ. (יח) וְקוֹץ וְדַרְדַּר תַּצְמִיחַ לָךְ וְאָכַלְתָּ אֶת עֵשֶׂב הַשָּׂדֶה. (יט) בְּזֵעַת אַפֶּיךָ תֹּאכַל לֶחֶם עַד שׁוּבְךָ אֶל הָאֲדָמָה כִּי מִמֶּנָּה לֻקָּחְתָּ כִּי עָפָר אַתָּה וְאֶל עָפָר תָּשׁוּב.

[17] And unto Adam he said: Because thou hast hearkened unto the voice of thy wife, and hast eaten of the tree, of which I commanded thee, saying, Thou shalt not eat of it: cursed is the ground for thy sake; in sorrow shalt thou eat of it all the days of thy life;
[18] Thorns also and thistles shall it bring forth to thee; and thou shalt eat the herb of the field;
[19] In the sweat of thy face shalt thou eat bread, till thou return unto the ground; for out of it wast thou taken: for dust thou art, and unto dust shalt thou return.

Slave Spirituals and African American Culture

INTRODUCTION

There is no group in American history who interpreted their collective experience in the New World as closely along Hebraic lines as the African Americans.[1] With their collective story of forced enslavement in a foreign land, the yearning for liberation and freedom, hoping for a place they could call home, they identified strongly with the story of Exodus. A Union Army commander said of his black soldiers: "There is no part of the Bible with which they are so familiar as the story of the deliverance of Israel. Moses is their *ideal* of all that is high, noble, and perfect in man. I think they have been accustomed to regard Christ not so much in the light of a *spiritual* deliverer, as that of a second Moses who would eventually lead them out of their prison-house of bondage."[2] The African American experience is, like the Hebraic, one of exile, bondage, yearning, and deliverance. When Lincoln entered war-torn Richmond after its fall, the only people that came out into the streets were former slaves.

---

1. Two overall helpful works that do not appear in the notes below are Albert J. Raboteau's *Slave Religion* (Oxford: Oxford University Press, 1978) and Eugene D. Genovese, *Roll, Jordan, Roll: The World the Slaves Made* (New York: Vintage Books, 1972).
2. Allen Dwight Callahan, *The Talking book: African Americans and the Hebrew Bible* (New Haven: Yale University Press, 2008), 94.

All around, the word that was in everyone's mouth was that they had seen Father Abraham, and they called him Moses. Such was the power of the image of Moses in their mind.

Unlike the Puritans, African Americans did not identify America with the chosen land or themselves with the chosen people. It was the North that was seen as the promised land, the place yearned for. Frederick Douglass himself said that "a keen observer might have detected in our repeated singing of 'O Canaan, sweet Canaan, I am bound for the land of Canaan,' something more than a hope of reaching haven. We meant to reach the *North*, and the North was our Canaan."

The African American experience with the Bible was, if not unique in the American experience, quite different from that of white Americans. Their native, ancestral beliefs from West Africa, which included voodoo and shamanism, mingled with Christianity, which came to them largely beginning with the First Great Awakening. Biblical stories were appropriated into a preexisting religious framework to create an eclectic spirituality. Take, for example, the biblical scene where Moses's staff turns into a snake and consumes the snakes of Pharaoh's court magicians. The snake is a subject of fear and veneration in West African religions, and this story resonated strongly with a culture in which powerful magic is best countered by more powerful magic.[3] In addition to being eclectic, slave Christianity was an oral tradition.[4] Among the oppressive techniques of the slave system was the law forbidding anyone from teaching slaves to read or write, thereby forcing the slaves to be illiterate. After the foiled slave revolt of Denmark Vesey in 1822, meetings of slaves for religious worship were closely monitored. For the slaves, the Bible thus became a tradition of oral stories, something heard and recited but to which the vast majority of slaves did not have first-hand access. The biblical stories they transmitted were ornamented with details derived from contemporary life. For instance, they told the story of Cain, a gambler and a shooter, who fought Abel because of a dispute over a watermelon patch.

---

3. Callahan, 92.
4. Ralph Ellison, the great African American writer of the twentieth century said, "we are by no means, as it is said of the Jews, 'people of the book.' Our expression has been oral as against literary" (cited in Callahan, 19).

Christianity for the slave was further complicated and tarnished because the preacher's gospel was one that commanded obedience to slave masters, citing biblical passages that command subservience. Frederick Douglass remarked that "I have met many religious colored people, at the South, who are under the delusion that God requires them to submit to slavery and to wear chains with meekness and humanity."[5] There were therefore multiple Christianities in the South in the nineteenth century, among them that of the slave and that of the master. That of the master was a hypocritical justification of his vile and hard oppression, which maintained the slave in a state of abject subservience; that of the slave was a non-textual, syncretic spirituality of hope and deliverance, with the expectation that his oppressors would meet with retribution in the world to come.

Hebraic influence is most visible in the spiritual liturgy of the oppressed. The oral tradition of biblical transmission combined with the slaves' West African heritage produced a style of religious worship, replete with song and dance, which must be considered one of the great contributions to American culture, with later reverberations in gospel, jazz, blues, rap, poetry, and the American novel. Moses and other biblical prophets figure prominently in the spirituals, along with other Hebraic ideas such as the year of the jubilee (see for instance Lev. 25:39–40). Jubilee in the slave communities was associated with liberation and freedom, and the celebration of freedom came to be known as jubilee songs.[6] The great beauty of the music is in the singing, and the songs are done an injustice if their lyrics are only read. But we have included many of them below to provide a sense of the numerous Hebraic themes that permeated slave culture.

Hebraic Source
Leviticus 25

(לט) וְכִי יָמוּךְ אָחִיךָ עִמָּךְ וְנִמְכַּר לָךְ לֹא תַעֲבֹד בּוֹ עֲבֹדַת עָבֶד.

(מ) כְּשָׂכִיר כְּתוֹשָׁב יִהְיֶה עִמָּךְ עַד שְׁנַת הַיֹּבֵל יַעֲבֹד עִמָּךְ.

(מא) וְיָצָא מֵעִמָּךְ הוּא וּבָנָיו עִמּוֹ וְשָׁב אֶל מִשְׁפַּחְתּוֹ וְאֶל אֲחֻזַּת אֲבֹתָיו יָשׁוּב.

(מב) כִּי עֲבָדַי הֵם אֲשֶׁר הוֹצֵאתִי אֹתָם מֵאֶרֶץ מִצְרָיִם לֹא יִמָּכְרוּ מִמְכֶּרֶת עָבֶד.

---

5. Frederick Douglass, *My Bondage and My Freedom* (New York: Miller, Orton and Mulligan, 1855), 159.

6. Callahan, 84.

(מג) לֹא תִרְדֶּה בוֹ בְּפָרֶךְ וְיָרֵאתָ מֵאֱלֹהֶיךָ.

(מד) וְעַבְדְּךָ וַאֲמָתְךָ אֲשֶׁר יִהְיוּ לָךְ מֵאֵת הַגּוֹיִם אֲשֶׁר סְבִיבֹתֵיכֶם מֵהֶם תִּקְנוּ עֶבֶד וְאָמָה.

(מה) וְגַם מִבְּנֵי הַתּוֹשָׁבִים הַגָּרִים עִמָּכֶם מֵהֶם תִּקְנוּ וּמִמִּשְׁפַּחְתָּם אֲשֶׁר עִמָּכֶם אֲשֶׁר הוֹלִידוּ בְּאַרְצְכֶם וְהָיוּ לָכֶם לַאֲחֻזָּה.

(מו) וְהִתְנַחַלְתֶּם אֹתָם לִבְנֵיכֶם אַחֲרֵיכֶם לָרֶשֶׁת אֲחֻזָּה לְעֹלָם בָּהֶם תַּעֲבֹדוּ וּבְאַחֵיכֶם בְּנֵי יִשְׂרָאֵל אִישׁ בְּאָחִיו לֹא תִרְדֶּה בוֹ בְּפָרֶךְ.

³⁹ And if thy brother that dwelleth by thee be waxen poor, and be sold unto thee; thou shalt not compel him to serve as a bondservant:

⁴⁰ But as an hired servant, and as a sojourner, he shall be with thee, and shall serve thee unto the year of jubile:

⁴¹ And then shall he depart from thee, both he and his children with him, and shall return unto his own family, and unto the possession of his fathers shall he return.

⁴² For they are my servants, which I brought forth out of the land of Egypt: they shall not be sold as bondmen.

⁴³ Thou shalt not rule over him with rigour; but shalt fear thy God.

⁴⁴ Both thy bondmen, and thy bondmaids, which thou shalt have, shall be of the heathen that are round about you; of them shall ye buy bondmen and bondmaids.

⁴⁵ Moreover of the children of the strangers that do sojourn among you, of them shall ye buy, and of their families that are with you, which they begat in your land: and they shall be your possession.

⁴⁶ And ye shall take them as an inheritance for your children after you, to inherit them for a possession; they shall be your bondmen for ever: but over your brethren the children of Israel, ye shall not rule one over another with rigour.

"Joshua Fit the Battle of Jericho"

Joshua fit the battle of Jericho
Jericho, Jericho,
Joshua fit the battle of Jericho
And the walls came tumbling down.

You may talk about your man of Gideon
You may talk about your man of Saul
There's none like good old Joshua
At the battle of Jericho.

Hebraic Source
Joshua 6

(ב) וַיֹּאמֶר ה' אֶל יְהוֹשֻׁעַ רְאֵה נָתַתִּי בְיָדְךָ אֶת יְרִיחוֹ וְאֶת מַלְכָּהּ גִּבּוֹרֵי הֶחָיִל.

(ג) וְסַבֹּתֶם אֶת הָעִיר כֹּל אַנְשֵׁי הַמִּלְחָמָה הַקֵּיף אֶת הָעִיר פַּעַם אֶחָת כֹּה תַעֲשֶׂה שֵׁשֶׁת יָמִים.

(ד) וְשִׁבְעָה כֹהֲנִים יִשְׂאוּ שִׁבְעָה שׁוֹפָרוֹת הַיּוֹבְלִים לִפְנֵי הָאָרוֹן וּבַיּוֹם הַשְּׁבִיעִי תָּסֹבּוּ אֶת הָעִיר שֶׁבַע פְּעָמִים וְהַכֹּהֲנִים יִתְקְעוּ בַּשּׁוֹפָרוֹת.

(ה) וְהָיָה בִּמְשֹׁךְ בְּקֶרֶן הַיּוֹבֵל בשמעכם [כְּשָׁמְעֲכֶם] אֶת קוֹל הַשּׁוֹפָר יָרִיעוּ כָל הָעָם תְּרוּעָה גְדוֹלָה וְנָפְלָה חוֹמַת הָעִיר תַּחְתֶּיהָ וְעָלוּ הָעָם אִישׁ נֶגְדּוֹ.

(טו) וַיְהִי בַּיּוֹם הַשְּׁבִיעִי וַיַּשְׁכִּמוּ כַּעֲלוֹת הַשַּׁחַר וַיָּסֹבּוּ אֶת הָעִיר כַּמִּשְׁפָּט הַזֶּה שֶׁבַע פְּעָמִים רַק בַּיּוֹם הַהוּא סָבְבוּ אֶת הָעִיר שֶׁבַע פְּעָמִים.

(טז) וַיְהִי בַּפַּעַם הַשְּׁבִיעִית תָּקְעוּ הַכֹּהֲנִים בַּשּׁוֹפָרוֹת וַיֹּאמֶר יְהוֹשֻׁעַ אֶל הָעָם הָרִיעוּ כִּי נָתַן ה' לָכֶם אֶת הָעִיר.

(כ) וַיָּרַע הָעָם וַיִּתְקְעוּ בַּשֹּׁפָרוֹת וַיְהִי כִשְׁמֹעַ הָעָם אֶת קוֹל הַשּׁוֹפָר וַיָּרִיעוּ הָעָם תְּרוּעָה גְדוֹלָה וַתִּפֹּל הַחוֹמָה תַּחְתֶּיהָ וַיַּעַל הָעָם הָעִירָה אִישׁ נֶגְדּוֹ וַיִּלְכְּדוּ אֶת הָעִיר.

[2] And the Lord said unto Joshua: See, I have given into thine hand Jericho, and the king thereof, and the mighty men of valour.

[3] And ye shall compass the city, all ye men of war, and go round about the city once. Thus shalt thou do six days.

[4] And seven priests shall bear before the ark seven trumpets of rams' horns: and the seventh day ye shall compass the city seven times, and the priests shall blow with the trumpets.

[5] And it shall come to pass, that when they make a long blast with the ram's horn, and when ye hear the sound of the trumpet, all the people shall shout with a great shout; and the wall of the city shall fall down flat, and the people shall ascend up every man straight before him.

[15] And it came to pass on the seventh day, that they rose early about the dawning of the day, and compassed the city after the same manner seven times: only on that day they compassed the city seven times.

[16] And it came to pass at the seventh time, when the priests blew with the trumpets, Joshua said unto the people: Shout; for the Lord hath given you the city.

[20] So the people shouted when the priests blew with the trumpets: and it came to pass, when the people heard the sound of the trumpet, and the people shouted with a great shout, that the wall fell down flat, so that the people went up into the city, every man straight before him, and they took the city.

"Go Down Moses"

When Israel was in Egypt's land,
Let my people go.
Oppressed so hard they could not stand,
Let my people go.

Go down, Moses, way down in Egypt land.
Tell old Pharaoh: "Let my people go."

"Thus spoke the Lord," bold Moses said,
Let my people go.
"If not I'll strike your firstborn dead,"
Let my people go.

Go down, Moses, way down in Egypt land.
Tell old Pharaoh: "Let my people go."

"No more shall they in bondage toil,"
Let my people go.
"Let them come out with Egypt's spoil,"
Let my people go.

Go down, Moses, way down in Egypt land.
Tell old Pharaoh: "Let my people go."

Hebraic Sources
Exodus 5

(א) וְאַחַר בָּאוּ מֹשֶׁה וְאַהֲרֹן וַיֹּאמְרוּ אֶל פַּרְעֹה כֹּה אָמַר ה' אֱ־לֹהֵי יִשְׂרָאֵל שַׁלַּח אֶת עַמִּי וְיָחֹגּוּ לִי בַּמִּדְבָּר.

(ב) וַיֹּאמֶר פַּרְעֹה מִי ה' אֲשֶׁר אֶשְׁמַע בְּקֹלוֹ לְשַׁלַּח אֶת יִשְׂרָאֵל לֹא יָדַעְתִּי אֶת ה' וְגַם אֶת יִשְׂרָאֵל לֹא אֲשַׁלֵּחַ.

(ג) וַיֹּאמְרוּ אֱ־לֹהֵי הָעִבְרִים נִקְרָא עָלֵינוּ נֵלְכָה נָּא דֶּרֶךְ שְׁלֹשֶׁת יָמִים בַּמִּדְבָּר וְנִזְבְּחָה לַה' אֱ־לֹהֵינוּ פֶּן יִפְגָּעֵנוּ בַּדֶּבֶר אוֹ בֶחָרֶב.

¹ And afterward Moses and Aaron went in, and told Pharaoh: Thus saith the Lord God of Israel, Let My people go, that they may hold a feast unto Me in the wilderness.
² And Pharaoh said: Who is the Lord, that I should obey his voice to let Israel go? I know not the Lord, neither will I let Israel go.
³ And they said: The God of the Hebrews hath met with us. Let us go, we pray thee, three days' journey into the desert, and sacrifice unto the Lord our God; lest He fall upon us with pestilence, or with the sword.

Exodus 4

(כא) וַיֹּאמֶר ה' אֶל מֹשֶׁה בְּלֶכְתְּךָ לָשׁוּב מִצְרַיְמָה רְאֵה כָּל הַמֹּפְתִים אֲשֶׁר שַׂמְתִּי בְיָדֶךָ וַעֲשִׂיתָם לִפְנֵי פַרְעֹה וַאֲנִי אֲחַזֵּק אֶת לִבּוֹ וְלֹא יְשַׁלַּח אֶת הָעָם.
(כב) וְאָמַרְתָּ אֶל פַּרְעֹה כֹּה אָמַר ה' בְּנִי בְכֹרִי יִשְׂרָאֵל.
(כג) וָאֹמַר אֵלֶיךָ שַׁלַּח אֶת בְּנִי וְיַעַבְדֵנִי וַתְּמָאֵן לְשַׁלְּחוֹ הִנֵּה אָנֹכִי הֹרֵג אֶת בִּנְךָ בְּכֹרֶךָ.

²¹ And the Lord said unto Moses, When thou goest to return into Egypt, see that thou do all those wonders before Pharaoh, which I have put in thine hand: but I will harden his heart, that he shall not let the people go.
²² And thou shalt say unto Pharaoh, Thus saith the Lord, Israel is my son, even my firstborn:
²³ And I say unto thee, Let my son go, that he may serve me: and if thou refuse to let him go, behold, I will slay thy son, even thy firstborn.

Exodus 11

(א) וַיֹּאמֶר ה' אֶל מֹשֶׁה עוֹד נֶגַע אֶחָד אָבִיא עַל פַּרְעֹה וְעַל מִצְרַיִם אַחֲרֵי כֵן יְשַׁלַּח אֶתְכֶם מִזֶּה כְּשַׁלְּחוֹ כָּלָה גָּרֵשׁ יְגָרֵשׁ אֶתְכֶם מִזֶּה.
(ב) דַּבֶּר נָא בְּאָזְנֵי הָעָם וְיִשְׁאֲלוּ אִישׁ מֵאֵת רֵעֵהוּ וְאִשָּׁה מֵאֵת רְעוּתָהּ כְּלֵי כֶסֶף וּכְלֵי זָהָב.
(ג) וַיִּתֵּן ה' אֶת חֵן הָעָם בְּעֵינֵי מִצְרָיִם גַּם הָאִישׁ מֹשֶׁה גָּדוֹל מְאֹד בְּאֶרֶץ מִצְרַיִם בְּעֵינֵי עַבְדֵי פַרְעֹה וּבְעֵינֵי הָעָם.
(ד) וַיֹּאמֶר מֹשֶׁה כֹּה אָמַר ה' כַּחֲצֹת הַלַּיְלָה אֲנִי יוֹצֵא בְּתוֹךְ מִצְרָיִם.
(ה) וּמֵת כָּל בְּכוֹר בְּאֶרֶץ מִצְרַיִם מִבְּכוֹר פַּרְעֹה הַיֹּשֵׁב עַל כִּסְאוֹ עַד בְּכוֹר הַשִּׁפְחָה אֲשֶׁר אַחַר הָרֵחָיִם וְכֹל בְּכוֹר בְּהֵמָה.
(ו) וְהָיְתָה צְעָקָה גְדֹלָה בְּכָל אֶרֶץ מִצְרָיִם אֲשֶׁר כָּמֹהוּ לֹא נִהְיָתָה וְכָמֹהוּ לֹא תֹסִף.
(ז) וּלְכֹל בְּנֵי יִשְׂרָאֵל לֹא יֶחֱרַץ כֶּלֶב לְשֹׁנוֹ לְמֵאִישׁ וְעַד בְּהֵמָה לְמַעַן תֵּדְעוּן אֲשֶׁר יַפְלֶה ה' בֵּין מִצְרַיִם וּבֵין יִשְׂרָאֵל.
(ח) וְיָרְדוּ כָל עֲבָדֶיךָ אֵלֶּה אֵלַי וְהִשְׁתַּחֲווּ לִי לֵאמֹר צֵא אַתָּה וְכָל הָעָם אֲשֶׁר בְּרַגְלֶיךָ וְאַחֲרֵי כֵן אֵצֵא וַיֵּצֵא מֵעִם פַּרְעֹה בָּחֳרִי אָף.

¹ And the Lord said unto Moses, Yet will I bring one plague more upon Pharaoh, and upon Egypt; afterwards he will let you go hence: when he shall let you go, he shall surely thrust you out hence altogether.

² Speak now in the ears of the people, and let every man borrow of his neighbour, and every woman of her neighbour, jewels of silver, and jewels of gold.

³ And the Lord gave the people favour in the sight of the Egyptians. Moreover the man Moses was very great in the land of Egypt, in the sight of Pharaoh's servants, and in the sight of the people.

⁴ And Moses said, Thus saith the Lord, About midnight will I go out into the midst of Egypt:

⁵ And all the firstborn in the land of Egypt shall die, from the firstborn of Pharaoh that sitteth upon his throne, even unto the firstborn of the maidservant that is behind the mill; and all the firstborn of beasts.

⁶ And there shall be a great cry throughout all the land of Egypt, such as there was none like it, nor shall be like it any more.

⁷ But against any of the children of Israel shall not a dog move his tongue, against man or beast: that ye may know how that the Lord doth put a difference between the Egyptians and Israel.

⁸ And all these thy servants shall come down unto me, and bow down themselves unto me, saying, Get thee out, and all the people that follow thee: and after that I will go out. And he went out from Pharaoh in a great anger.

"Canaan Is the Land for Me"

Canaan land is the land for me,
And let God's saints come in.

There was a wicked man,
He kept them children in Egypt land.

Canaan land is the land for me,
And let God's saints come in.

God did say to Moses one day,
Say, Moses, go to Egypt land,
And tell him to let my people go.

Canaan land is the land for me,
And let God's saints come in.

Hebraic Source
Deuteronomy 7

(א) כִּי יְבִיאֲךָ ה' אֱ-לֹהֶיךָ אֶל הָאָרֶץ אֲשֶׁר אַתָּה בָא שָׁמָּה לְרִשְׁתָּהּ וְנָשַׁל גּוֹיִם רַבִּים מִפָּנֶיךָ הַחִתִּי וְהַגִּרְגָּשִׁי וְהָאֱמֹרִי וְהַכְּנַעֲנִי וְהַפְּרִזִּי וְהַחִוִּי וְהַיְבוּסִי שִׁבְעָה גוֹיִם רַבִּים וַעֲצוּמִים מִמֶּךָּ.

(ב) וּנְתָנָם ה' אֱ-לֹהֶיךָ לְפָנֶיךָ וְהִכִּיתָם הַחֲרֵם תַּחֲרִים אֹתָם לֹא תִכְרֹת לָהֶם בְּרִית וְלֹא תְחָנֵּם.

(ג) וְלֹא תִתְחַתֵּן בָּם בִּתְּךָ לֹא תִתֵּן לִבְנוֹ וּבִתּוֹ לֹא תִקַּח לִבְנֶךָ.

(ד) כִּי יָסִיר אֶת בִּנְךָ מֵאַחֲרַי וְעָבְדוּ אֱלֹהִים אֲחֵרִים וְחָרָה אַף ה' בָּכֶם וְהִשְׁמִידְךָ מַהֵר.

(ה) כִּי אִם כֹּה תַעֲשׂוּ לָהֶם מִזְבְּחֹתֵיהֶם תִּתֹּצוּ וּמַצֵּבֹתָם תְּשַׁבֵּרוּ וַאֲשֵׁירֵהֶם תְּגַדֵּעוּן וּפְסִילֵיהֶם תִּשְׂרְפוּן בָּאֵשׁ.

(ו) כִּי עַם קָדוֹשׁ אַתָּה לַה' אֱ-לֹהֶיךָ בְּךָ בָּחַר ה' אֱ-לֹהֶיךָ לִהְיוֹת לוֹ לְעַם סְגֻלָּה מִכֹּל הָעַמִּים אֲשֶׁר עַל פְּנֵי הָאֲדָמָה.

(ז) לֹא מֵרֻבְּכֶם מִכָּל הָעַמִּים חָשַׁק ה' בָּכֶם וַיִּבְחַר בָּכֶם כִּי אַתֶּם הַמְעַט מִכָּל הָעַמִּים.

(ח) כִּי מֵאַהֲבַת ה' אֶתְכֶם וּמִשָּׁמְרוֹ אֶת הַשְּׁבֻעָה אֲשֶׁר נִשְׁבַּע לַאֲבֹתֵיכֶם הוֹצִיא ה' אֶתְכֶם בְּיָד חֲזָקָה וַיִּפְדְּךָ מִבֵּית עֲבָדִים מִיַּד פַּרְעֹה מֶלֶךְ מִצְרָיִם.

[1] When the Lord thy God shall bring thee into the land whither thou goest to possess it, and hath cast out many nations before thee, the Hittites, and the Girgashites, and the Amorites, and the Canaanites, and the Perizzites, and the Hivites, and the Jebusites, seven nations greater and mightier than thou;

[2] And when the Lord thy God shall deliver them before thee; thou shalt smite them, and utterly destroy them; thou shalt make no covenant with them, nor shew mercy unto them:

[3] Neither shalt thou make marriages with them; thy daughter thou shalt not give unto his son, nor his daughter shalt thou take unto thy son.

[4] For they will turn away thy son from following me, that they may serve other gods: so will the anger of the Lord be kindled against you, and destroy thee suddenly.

[5] But thus shall ye deal with them; ye shall destroy their altars, and break down their images, and cut down their groves, and burn their graven images with fire.

[6] For thou art an holy people unto the Lord thy God: the Lord thy God hath chosen thee to be a special people unto himself, above all people that are upon the face of the earth.

[7] The Lord did not set his love upon you, nor choose you, because ye were more in number than any people; for ye were the fewest of all people:

[8] But because the Lord loved you, and because he would keep the oath which he had sworn unto your fathers, hath the Lord brought you out with a mighty hand, and redeemed you out of the house of bondmen, from the hand of Pharaoh king of Egypt.

"There Is a Balm in Gilead"

There is a balm in Gilead
To make the wounded whole.
There is a balm in Gilead
To heal the sin-sick soul.

Hebraic Source
Jeremiah 8

(יח) מַבְלִיגִיתִי עֲלֵי יָגוֹן עָלַי לִבִּי דַוָּי.
(יט) הִנֵּה קוֹל שַׁוְעַת בַּת עַמִּי מֵאֶרֶץ מַרְחַקִּים הַה׳ אֵין בְּצִיּוֹן אִם מַלְכָּהּ אֵין בָּהּ מַדּוּעַ הִכְעִסוּנִי בִּפְסִלֵיהֶם בְּהַבְלֵי נֵכָר.
(כ) עָבַר קָצִיר כָּלָה קָיִץ וַאֲנַחְנוּ לוֹא נוֹשָׁעְנוּ.
(כא) עַל שֶׁבֶר בַּת עַמִּי הָשְׁבָּרְתִּי קָדַרְתִּי שַׁמָּה הֶחֱזִקָתְנִי.
(כב) הַצֳרִי אֵין בְּגִלְעָד אִם רֹפֵא אֵין שָׁם כִּי מַדּוּעַ לֹא עָלְתָה אֲרֻכַת בַּת עַמִּי.

[18] When I would comfort myself against sorrow, my heart is faint in me.
[19] Behold the voice of the cry of the daughter of my people because of them that dwell in a far country: Is not the Lord in Zion? Is not her king in her? Why have they provoked me to anger with their graven images, and with strange vanities?
[20] The harvest is past, the summer is ended, and we are not saved.
[21] For the hurt of the daughter of my people am I hurt; I am black; astonishment hath taken hold on me.
[22] Is there no balm in Gilead; is there no physician there? Why then is not the health of the daughter of my people recovered?

"Didn't Ol' Pharaoh Get Lost?"

Didn't ol' Pharaoh get lost,
Get lost, get lost,
In the Red Sea, true believer,
O, Didn't ol' Pharaoh get lost,
Get lost, get lost,
In the Red Sea.

Hebraic Source
Exodus 13–14

(יז) וַיְהִי בְּשַׁלַּח פַּרְעֹה אֶת הָעָם וְלֹא נָחָם אֱ־לֹהִים דֶּרֶךְ אֶרֶץ פְּלִשְׁתִּים כִּי קָרוֹב
הוּא כִּי אָמַר אֱ־לֹהִים פֶּן יִנָּחֵם הָעָם בִּרְאֹתָם מִלְחָמָה וְשָׁבוּ מִצְרָיְמָה.

(יח) וַיַּסֵּב אֱ־לֹהִים אֶת הָעָם דֶּרֶךְ הַמִּדְבָּר יַם סוּף וַחֲמֻשִׁים עָלוּ בְנֵי יִשְׂרָאֵל
מֵאֶרֶץ מִצְרָיִם.

(יט) וַיִּקַּח מֹשֶׁה אֶת עַצְמוֹת יוֹסֵף עִמּוֹ כִּי הַשְׁבֵּעַ הִשְׁבִּיעַ אֶת בְּנֵי יִשְׂרָאֵל לֵאמֹר
פָּקֹד יִפְקֹד אֱ־לֹהִים אֶתְכֶם וְהַעֲלִיתֶם אֶת עַצְמֹתַי מִזֶּה אִתְּכֶם.

(כ) וַיִּסְעוּ מִסֻּכֹּת וַיַּחֲנוּ בְאֵתָם בִּקְצֵה הַמִּדְבָּר.

(כא) וַה' הֹלֵךְ לִפְנֵיהֶם יוֹמָם בְּעַמּוּד עָנָן לַנְחֹתָם הַדֶּרֶךְ וְלַיְלָה בְּעַמּוּד אֵשׁ לְהָאִיר
לָהֶם לָלֶכֶת יוֹמָם וָלָיְלָה.

(כב) לֹא יָמִישׁ עַמּוּד הֶעָנָן יוֹמָם וְעַמּוּד הָאֵשׁ לָיְלָה לִפְנֵי הָעָם.

(א) וַיְדַבֵּר ה' אֶל מֹשֶׁה לֵּאמֹר.

(ב) דַּבֵּר אֶל בְּנֵי יִשְׂרָאֵל וְיָשֻׁבוּ וְיַחֲנוּ לִפְנֵי פִּי הַחִירֹת בֵּין מִגְדֹּל וּבֵין הַיָּם לִפְנֵי
בַּעַל צְפֹן נִכְחוֹ תַחֲנוּ עַל הַיָּם.

(ג) וְאָמַר פַּרְעֹה לִבְנֵי יִשְׂרָאֵל נְבֻכִים הֵם בָּאָרֶץ סָגַר עֲלֵיהֶם הַמִּדְבָּר.

(ד) וְחִזַּקְתִּי אֶת לֵב פַּרְעֹה וְרָדַף אַחֲרֵיהֶם וְאִכָּבְדָה בְּפַרְעֹה וּבְכָל חֵילוֹ וְיָדְעוּ
מִצְרַיִם כִּי אֲנִי ה' וַיַּעֲשׂוּ כֵן.

(ה) וַיֻּגַּד לְמֶלֶךְ מִצְרַיִם כִּי בָרַח הָעָם וַיֵּהָפֵךְ לְבַב פַּרְעֹה וַעֲבָדָיו אֶל הָעָם וַיֹּאמְרוּ
מַה זֹּאת עָשִׂינוּ כִּי שִׁלַּחְנוּ אֶת יִשְׂרָאֵל מֵעָבְדֵנוּ.

(ו) וַיֶּאְסֹר אֶת רִכְבּוֹ וְאֶת עַמּוֹ לָקַח עִמּוֹ.

(ז) וַיִּקַּח שֵׁשׁ מֵאוֹת רֶכֶב בָּחוּר וְכֹל רֶכֶב מִצְרָיִם וְשָׁלִשִׁם עַל כֻּלּוֹ.

[17] And it came to pass, when Pharaoh had let the people go, that God led them not by the way of the land of the Philistines, although that was near; for God said: Lest peradventure the people repent when they see war, and they return to Egypt.

[18] But God led the people about, by the way of the wilderness by the Red Sea; and the children of Israel went up armed out of the land of Egypt.

[19] And Moses took the bones of Joseph with him; for he had straitly sworn the children of Israel, saying: God will surely remember you; and ye shall carry up my bones away hence with you.

[20] And they took their journey from Succoth, and encamped in Etham, in the edge of the wilderness.

[21] And the Lord went before them by day in a pillar of cloud, to lead them the way; and by night in a pillar of fire, to give them light; that they might go by day and by night:

[22] The pillar of cloud by day, and the pillar of fire by night, departed not from before the people.

[1] And the Lord spoke unto Moses, saying:

² Speak unto the children of Israel, that they turn back and encamp before Pi-hahiroth, between Migdol and the sea, before Baal-zephon, over against it shall ye encamp by the sea.
³ And Pharaoh will say of the children of Israel: They are entangled in the land, the wilderness hath shut them in.
⁴ And I will harden Pharaoh's heart, and he shall follow after them; and I will get Me honour upon Pharaoh, and upon all his host; and the Egyptians shall know that I am the Lord. And they did so.
⁵ And it was told the king of Egypt that the people were fled; and the heart of Pharaoh and of his servants was turned towards the people, and they said: What is this we have done, that we have let Israel go from serving us?
⁶ And he made ready his chariots, and took his people with him.
⁷ And he took six hundred chosen chariots, and all the chariots of Egypt, and captains over all of them.

"He's Jus' de Same Today"

When Moses and his soldiers from Egypt's land did flee,
His enemies were in behind him, and in front of him the sea.
God raised the water like a wall, and opened up the way,
And the God that lived in Moses' time is just the same today.

He's jus' de same today,
Jus' de same today,

And the God that lived in Moses' time is just the same today.
When Daniel, faithful to his God, would not bow down to men,
And by God's enemy he was hurled into the lion's den,
God locked the lion's jaw, we read, and robbed him of his prey,
And the God that lived in Daniel's time is just the same today.

Hebraic Sources
Exodus 14

(ח) וַיְחַזֵּק ה' אֶת לֵב פַּרְעֹה מֶלֶךְ מִצְרַיִם וַיִּרְדֹּף אַחֲרֵי בְּנֵי יִשְׂרָאֵל וּבְנֵי יִשְׂרָאֵל יֹצְאִים בְּיָד רָמָה.

(ט) וַיִּרְדְּפוּ מִצְרַיִם אַחֲרֵיהֶם וַיַּשִּׂיגוּ אוֹתָם חֹנִים עַל הַיָּם כָּל סוּס רֶכֶב פַּרְעֹה וּפָרָשָׁיו וְחֵילוֹ עַל פִּי הַחִירֹת לִפְנֵי בַּעַל צְפֹן.

(י) וּפַרְעֹה הִקְרִיב וַיִּשְׂאוּ בְנֵי יִשְׂרָאֵל אֶת עֵינֵיהֶם וְהִנֵּה מִצְרַיִם נֹסֵעַ אַחֲרֵיהֶם וַיִּירְאוּ מְאֹד וַיִּצְעֲקוּ בְנֵי יִשְׂרָאֵל אֶל ה'.

(יא) וַיֹּאמְרוּ אֶל מֹשֶׁה הֲמִבְּלִי אֵין קְבָרִים בְּמִצְרַיִם לְקַחְתָּנוּ לָמוּת בַּמִּדְבָּר מַה זֹּאת עָשִׂיתָ לָּנוּ לְהוֹצִיאָנוּ מִמִּצְרָיִם.

(יב) הֲלֹא זֶה הַדָּבָר אֲשֶׁר דִּבַּרְנוּ אֵלֶיךָ בְמִצְרַיִם לֵאמֹר חֲדַל מִמֶּנּוּ וְנַעַבְדָה אֶת מִצְרָיִם כִּי טוֹב לָנוּ עֲבֹד אֶת מִצְרַיִם מִמֻּתֵנוּ בַּמִּדְבָּר.

(יג) וַיֹּאמֶר מֹשֶׁה אֶל הָעָם אַל תִּירָאוּ הִתְיַצְּבוּ וּרְאוּ אֶת יְשׁוּעַת ה' אֲשֶׁר יַעֲשֶׂה לָכֶם הַיּוֹם כִּי אֲשֶׁר רְאִיתֶם אֶת מִצְרַיִם הַיּוֹם לֹא תֹסִיפוּ לִרְאֹתָם עוֹד עַד עוֹלָם.

(יד) ה' יִלָּחֵם לָכֶם וְאַתֶּם תַּחֲרִישׁוּן.

(טו) וַיֹּאמֶר ה' אֶל מֹשֶׁה מַה תִּצְעַק אֵלָי דַּבֵּר אֶל בְּנֵי יִשְׂרָאֵל וְיִסָּעוּ.

(טז) וְאַתָּה הָרֵם אֶת מַטְּךָ וּנְטֵה אֶת יָדְךָ עַל הַיָּם וּבְקָעֵהוּ וְיָבֹאוּ בְנֵי יִשְׂרָאֵל בְּתוֹךְ הַיָּם בַּיַּבָּשָׁה.

(יז) וַאֲנִי הִנְנִי מְחַזֵּק אֶת לֵב מִצְרַיִם וְיָבֹאוּ אַחֲרֵיהֶם וְאִכָּבְדָה בְּפַרְעֹה וּבְכָל חֵילוֹ בְּרִכְבּוֹ וּבְפָרָשָׁיו.

(יח) וְיָדְעוּ מִצְרַיִם כִּי אֲנִי ה' בְּהִכָּבְדִי בְּפַרְעֹה בְּרִכְבּוֹ וּבְפָרָשָׁיו.

(יט) וַיִּסַּע מַלְאַךְ הָאֱ-לֹהִים הַהֹלֵךְ לִפְנֵי מַחֲנֵה יִשְׂרָאֵל וַיֵּלֶךְ מֵאַחֲרֵיהֶם וַיִּסַּע עַמּוּד הֶעָנָן מִפְּנֵיהֶם וַיַּעֲמֹד מֵאַחֲרֵיהֶם.

(כ) וַיָּבֹא בֵּין מַחֲנֵה מִצְרַיִם וּבֵין מַחֲנֵה יִשְׂרָאֵל וַיְהִי הֶעָנָן וְהַחֹשֶׁךְ וַיָּאֶר אֶת הַלָּיְלָה וְלֹא קָרַב זֶה אֶל זֶה כָּל הַלָּיְלָה.

(כא) וַיֵּט מֹשֶׁה אֶת יָדוֹ עַל הַיָּם וַיּוֹלֶךְ ה' אֶת הַיָּם בְּרוּחַ קָדִים עַזָּה כָּל הַלַּיְלָה וַיָּשֶׂם אֶת הַיָּם לֶחָרָבָה וַיִּבָּקְעוּ הַמָּיִם.

(כב) וַיָּבֹאוּ בְנֵי יִשְׂרָאֵל בְּתוֹךְ הַיָּם בַּיַּבָּשָׁה וְהַמַּיִם לָהֶם חוֹמָה מִימִינָם וּמִשְּׂמֹאלָם.

(כג) וַיִּרְדְּפוּ מִצְרַיִם וַיָּבֹאוּ אַחֲרֵיהֶם כֹּל סוּס פַּרְעֹה רִכְבּוֹ וּפָרָשָׁיו אֶל תּוֹךְ הַיָּם.

(כד) וַיְהִי בְּאַשְׁמֹרֶת הַבֹּקֶר וַיַּשְׁקֵף ה' אֶל מַחֲנֵה מִצְרַיִם בְּעַמּוּד אֵשׁ וְעָנָן וַיָּהָם אֵת מַחֲנֵה מִצְרָיִם.

(כה) וַיָּסַר אֵת אֹפַן מַרְכְּבֹתָיו וַיְנַהֲגֵהוּ בִּכְבֵדֻת וַיֹּאמֶר מִצְרַיִם אָנוּסָה מִפְּנֵי יִשְׂרָאֵל כִּי ה' נִלְחָם לָהֶם בְּמִצְרָיִם.

(כו) וַיֹּאמֶר ה' אֶל מֹשֶׁה נְטֵה אֶת יָדְךָ עַל הַיָּם וְיָשֻׁבוּ הַמַּיִם עַל מִצְרַיִם עַל רִכְבּוֹ וְעַל פָּרָשָׁיו.

(כז) וַיֵּט מֹשֶׁה אֶת יָדוֹ עַל הַיָּם וַיָּשָׁב הַיָּם לִפְנוֹת בֹּקֶר לְאֵיתָנוֹ וּמִצְרַיִם נָסִים לִקְרָאתוֹ וַיְנַעֵר ה' אֶת מִצְרַיִם בְּתוֹךְ הַיָּם.

(כח) וַיָּשֻׁבוּ הַמַּיִם וַיְכַסּוּ אֶת הָרֶכֶב וְאֶת הַפָּרָשִׁים לְכֹל חֵיל פַּרְעֹה הַבָּאִים אַחֲרֵיהֶם בַּיָּם לֹא נִשְׁאַר בָּהֶם עַד אֶחָד.

(כט) וּבְנֵי יִשְׂרָאֵל הָלְכוּ בַיַּבָּשָׁה בְּתוֹךְ הַיָּם וְהַמַּיִם לָהֶם חֹמָה מִימִינָם וּמִשְּׂמֹאלָם.

(ל) וַיּוֹשַׁע ה' בַּיּוֹם הַהוּא אֶת יִשְׂרָאֵל מִיַּד מִצְרָיִם וַיַּרְא יִשְׂרָאֵל אֶת מִצְרַיִם מֵת עַל שְׂפַת הַיָּם.

(לא) וַיַּרְא יִשְׂרָאֵל אֶת הַיָּד הַגְּדֹלָה אֲשֶׁר עָשָׂה ה' בְּמִצְרַיִם וַיִּירְאוּ הָעָם אֶת ה' וַיַּאֲמִינוּ בַּה' וּבְמֹשֶׁה עַבְדּוֹ.

⁸ And the Lord hardened the heart of Pharaoh king of Egypt, and he pursued after the children of Israel and the children of Israel went out with an high hand.

⁹ But the Egyptians pursued after them, all the horses and chariots of Pharaoh, and his horsemen, and his army, and overtook them encamping by the sea, beside Pihahiroth, before Baalzephon.

¹⁰ And when Pharaoh drew nigh, the children of Israel lifted up their eyes, and, behold, the Egyptians marched after them; and they were sore afraid: and the children of Israel cried out unto the Lord.

¹¹ And they said unto Moses: Because there were no graves in Egypt, hast thou taken us away to die in the wilderness? Wherefore hast thou dealt thus with us, to carry us forth out of Egypt?

¹² Is not this the word that we did tell thee in Egypt, saying: Let us alone, that we may serve the Egyptians? For it had been better for us to serve the Egyptians, than that we should die in the wilderness.

¹³ And Moses said unto the people: Fear ye not, stand still, and see the salvation of the Lord, which He will show to you to day: for the Egyptians whom ye have seen to day, ye shall see them again no more for ever.

¹⁴ The Lord shall fight for you, and ye shall hold your peace.

¹⁵ And the Lord said unto Moses: Wherefore criest thou unto me? Speak unto the children of Israel, that they go forward.

¹⁶ But lift thou up thy rod, and stretch out thine hand over the sea, and divide it; and the children of Israel shall go on dry ground through the midst of the sea.

¹⁷ And I, behold, I will harden the hearts of the Egyptians, and they shall follow them; and I will get me honour upon Pharaoh, and upon all his host, upon his chariots, and upon his horsemen.

¹⁸ And the Egyptians shall know that I am the Lord, when I have gotten me honour upon Pharaoh, upon his chariots, and upon his horsemen.

¹⁹ And the angel of God, which went before the camp of Israel, removed and went behind them; and the pillar of the cloud went from before their face, and stood behind them.

²⁰ And it came between the camp of the Egyptians and the camp of Israel; and it was a cloud and darkness to them, but it gave light by night to these; so that the one came not near the other all the night.

²¹ And Moses stretched out his hand over the sea; and the Lord caused the sea to go back by a strong east wind all that night, and made the sea dry land, and the waters were divided.

²² And the children of Israel went into the midst of the sea upon the dry ground; and the waters were a wall unto them on their right hand, and on their left.

²³ And the Egyptians pursued, and went in after them to the midst of the sea, even all Pharaoh's horses, his chariots, and his horsemen.

²⁴ And it came to pass, that in the morning watch the Lord looked unto the host of the Egyptians through the pillar of fire and of the cloud, and troubled the host of the Egyptians,

²⁵ And took off their chariot wheels, that they drave them heavily; so that the Egyptians said: Let us flee from the face of Israel; for the Lord fighteth for them against the Egyptians.

²⁶ And the Lord said unto Moses: Stretch out thine hand over the sea, that the waters may come again upon the Egyptians, upon their chariots, and upon their horsemen.

²⁷ And Moses stretched forth his hand over the sea, and the sea returned to its strength when the morning appeared; and the Egyptians fled against it; and the Lord overthrew the Egyptians in the midst of the sea.

²⁸ And the waters returned, and covered the chariots, and the horsemen, and all the host of Pharaoh that came into the sea after them; there remained not so much as one of them.

²⁹ But the children of Israel walked upon dry land in the midst of the sea; and the waters were a wall unto them on their right hand, and on their left.

³⁰ Thus the Lord saved Israel that day out of the hand of the Egyptians; and Israel saw the Egyptians dead upon the sea shore.

³¹ And Israel saw that great work which the Lord did upon the Egyptians: and the people feared the Lord, and believed in the Lord, and his servant Moses.

Daniel 5-6

(א) וְדָרְיָוֶשׁ מדיא [מָדָאָה] קַבֵּל מַלְכוּתָא כְּבַר שְׁנִין שִׁתִּין וְתַרְתֵּין.

(ב) שְׁפַר קֳדָם דָּרְיָוֶשׁ וַהֲקִים עַל מַלְכוּתָא לַאֲחַשְׁדַּרְפְּנַיָּא מְאָה וְעֶשְׂרִין דִּי לֶהֱוֹן בְּכָל מַלְכוּתָא.

(ג) וְעֵלָּא מִנְּהוֹן סָרְכִין תְּלָתָא דִּי דָנִיֵּאל חַד מִנְּהוֹן דִּי לֶהֱוֹן אֲחַשְׁדַּרְפְּנַיָּא אִלֵּין יָהֲבִין לְהוֹן טַעְמָא וּמַלְכָּא לָא לֶהֱוֵא נָזִק.

(ד) אֱדַיִן דָּנִיֵּאל דְּנָה הֲוָא מִתְנַצַּח עַל סָרְכַיָּא וַאֲחַשְׁדַּרְפְּנַיָּא כָּל קֳבֵל דִּי רוּחַ יַתִּירָא בֵּהּ וּמַלְכָּא עֲשִׁית לַהֲקָמוּתֵהּ עַל כָּל מַלְכוּתָא.

(ה) אֱדַיִן סָרְכַיָּא וַאֲחַשְׁדַּרְפְּנַיָּא הֲווֹ בָעַיִן עִלָּה לְהַשְׁכָּחָה לְדָנִיֵּאל מִצַּד מַלְכוּתָא וְכָל עִלָּה וּשְׁחִיתָה לָא יָכְלִין לְהַשְׁכָּחָה כָּל קֳבֵל דִּי מְהֵימַן הוּא וְכָל שָׁלוּ וּשְׁחִיתָה לָא הִשְׁתְּכַחַת עֲלוֹהִי.

(ו) אֱדַיִן גֻּבְרַיָּא אִלֵּךְ אָמְרִין דִּי לָא נְהַשְׁכַּח לְדָנִיֵּאל דְּנָה כָּל עִלָּא לָהֵן הַשְׁכַּחְנָה עֲלוֹהִי בְּדָת אֱ-לָהֵהּ.

(ז) אֱדַיִן סָרְכַיָּא וַאֲחַשְׁדַּרְפְּנַיָּא אִלֵּן הַרְגִּשׁוּ עַל מַלְכָּא וְכֵן אָמְרִין לֵהּ דָּרְיָוֶשׁ מַלְכָּא לְעָלְמִין חֱיִי.

(ח) אִתְיָעַטוּ כֹּל סָרְכֵי מַלְכוּתָא סִגְנַיָּא וַאֲחַשְׁדַּרְפְּנַיָּא הַדָּבְרַיָּא וּפַחֲוָתָא לְקַיָּמָה קְיָם מַלְכָּא וּלְתַקָּפָה אֱסָר דִּי כָל דִּי יִבְעֵה בָעוּ מִן כָּל אֱלָהּ וֶאֱנָשׁ עַד יוֹמִין תְּלָתִין לָהֵן מִנָּךְ מַלְכָּא יִתְרְמֵא לְגֹב אַרְיָוָתָא.

(ט) כְּעַן מַלְכָּא תְּקִים אֱסָרָא וְתִרְשֻׁם כְּתָבָא דִּי לָא לְהַשְׁנָיָה כְּדָת מָדַי וּפָרַס דִּי לָא תֶעְדֵּא.

(י) כָּל קֳבֵל דְּנָה מַלְכָּא דָּרְיָוֶשׁ רְשַׁם כְּתָבָא וֶאֱסָרָא.

(יא) וְדָנִיֵּאל כְּדִי יְדַע דִּי רְשִׁים כְּתָבָא עַל לְבַיְתֵהּ וְכַוִּין פְּתִיחָן לֵהּ בְּעִלִּיתֵהּ נֶגֶד יְרוּשְׁלֶם וְזִמְנִין תְּלָתָה בְּיוֹמָא הוּא בָּרֵךְ עַל בִּרְכוֹהִי וּמְצַלֵּא וּמוֹדֵא קֳדָם אֱ-לָהֵהּ כָּל קֳבֵל דִּי הֲוָא עָבֵד מִן קַדְמַת דְּנָה.

(יב) אֱדַיִן גֻּבְרַיָּא אִלֵּךְ הַרְגִּשׁוּ וְהַשְׁכַּחוּ לְדָנִיֵּאל בָּעֵא וּמִתְחַנַּן קֳדָם אֱ־לָהֵהּ.

(יג) בֵּאדַיִן קְרִיבוּ וְאָמְרִין קֳדָם מַלְכָּא עַל אֱסָר מַלְכָּא הֲלָא אֱסָר רְשַׁמְתָּ דִּי כָל אֱנָשׁ דִּי יִבְעֵה מִן כָּל אֱלָהּ וֶאֱנָשׁ עַד יוֹמִין תְּלָתִין לָהֵן מִנָּךְ מַלְכָּא יִתְרְמֵא לְגוֹב אַרְיָוָתָא עָנֵה מַלְכָּא וְאָמַר יַצִּיבָא מִלְּתָא כְּדָת מָדַי וּפָרַס דִּי לָא תֶעְדֵּא.

(יד) בֵּאדַיִן עֲנוֹ וְאָמְרִין קֳדָם מַלְכָּא דִּי דָנִיֵּאל דִּי מִן בְּנֵי גָלוּתָא דִּי יְהוּד לָא שָׂם עֲלֵיךְ [עֲלָךְ] מַלְכָּא טְעֵם וְעַל אֱסָרָא דִּי רְשַׁמְתָּ וְזִמְנִין תְּלָתָה בְּיוֹמָא בָּעֵא בָּעוּתֵהּ.

(טו) אֱדַיִן מַלְכָּא כְּדִי מִלְּתָא שְׁמַע שַׂגִּיא בְּאֵשׁ עֲלוֹהִי וְעַל דָּנִיֵּאל שָׂם בָּל לְשֵׁיזָבוּתֵהּ וְעַד מֶעָלֵי שִׁמְשָׁא הֲוָא מִשְׁתַּדַּר לְהַצָּלוּתֵהּ.

(טז) בֵּאדַיִן גֻּבְרַיָּא אִלֵּךְ הַרְגִּשׁוּ עַל מַלְכָּא וְאָמְרִין לְמַלְכָּא דַּע מַלְכָּא דִּי דָת לְמָדַי וּפָרַס דִּי כָל אֱסָר וּקְיָם דִּי מַלְכָּא יְהָקֵים לָא לְהַשְׁנָיָה.

(יז) בֵּאדַיִן מַלְכָּא אֲמַר וְהַיְתִיו לְדָנִיֵּאל וּרְמוֹ לְגֻבָּא דִּי אַרְיָוָתָא עָנֵה מַלְכָּא וְאָמַר לְדָנִיֵּאל אֱ־לָהָךְ דִּי אנתה [אַנְתְּ] פָּלַח לֵהּ בִּתְדִירָא הוּא יְשֵׁיזְבִנָּךְ.

(יח) וְהֵיתָיִת אֶבֶן חֲדָה וְשֻׂמַת עַל פֻּם גֻּבָּא וְחַתְמַהּ מַלְכָּא בְּעִזְקְתֵהּ וּבְעִזְקָת רַבְרְבָנוֹהִי דִּי לָא תִשְׁנֵא צְבוּ בְּדָנִיֵּאל.

(יט) אֱדַיִן אֲזַל מַלְכָּא לְהֵיכְלֵהּ וּבָת טְוָת וְדַחֲוָן לָא הַנְעֵל קָדָמוֹהִי וְשִׁנְתֵהּ נַדַּת עֲלוֹהִי.

(כ) בֵּאדַיִן מַלְכָּא בִּשְׁפַּרְפָּרָא יְקוּם בְּנָגְהָא וּבְהִתְבְּהָלָה לְגֻבָּא דִּי אַרְיָוָתָא אֲזַל.

(כא) וּכְמִקְרְבֵהּ לְגֻבָּא לְדָנִיֵּאל בְּקָל עֲצִיב זְעִק עָנֵה מַלְכָּא וְאָמַר לְדָנִיֵּאל עֲבֵד אֱ־לָהָא חַיָּא אֱ־לָהָךְ דִּי אנתה [אַנְתְּ] פָּלַח לֵהּ בִּתְדִירָא הַיְכִל לְשֵׁיזָבוּתָךְ מִן אַרְיָוָתָא.

(כב) אֱדַיִן דָּנִיֵּאל עִם מַלְכָּא מַלִּל מַלְכָּא לְעָלְמִין חֱיִי.

(כג) אֱ־לָהִי שְׁלַח מַלְאֲכֵהּ וּסֲגַר פֻּם אַרְיָוָתָא וְלָא חַבְּלוּנִי כָּל קֳבֵל דִּי קָדָמוֹהִי זָכוּ הִשְׁתְּכַחַת לִי וְאַף קָדָמָיִךְ [קָדָמָךְ] מַלְכָּא חֲבוּלָה לָא עַבְדֵת.

(כד) בֵּאדַיִן מַלְכָּא שַׂגִּיא טְאֵב עֲלוֹהִי וּלְדָנִיֵּאל אֲמַר לְהַנְסָקָה מִן גֻּבָּא וְהֻסַּק דָּנִיֵּאל מִן גֻּבָּא וְכָל חֲבָל לָא הִשְׁתְּכַח בֵּהּ דִּי הֵימִן בֵּא־לָהֵהּ.

(כה) וַאֲמַר מַלְכָּא וְהַיְתִיו וְהַיְתִיו גֻּבְרַיָּא אִלֵּךְ דִּי אֲכַלוּ קַרְצוֹהִי דִּי דָנִיֵּאל וּלְגֹב אַרְיָוָתָא רְמוֹ אִנּוּן בְּנֵיהוֹן וּנְשֵׁיהוֹן וְלָא מְטוֹ לְאַרְעִית גֻּבָּא עַד דִּי שְׁלִטוּ בְהוֹן אַרְיָוָתָא וְכָל גַּרְמֵיהוֹן הַדִּקוּ.

(כו) בֵּאדַיִן דָּרְיָוֶשׁ מַלְכָּא כְּתַב לְכָל עַמְמַיָּא אֻמַּיָּא וְלִשָּׁנַיָּא דִּי דארין [דָּיְרִין] בְּכָל אַרְעָא שְׁלָמְכוֹן יִשְׂגֵּא.

(כז) מִן קֳדָמַי שִׂים טְעֵם דִּי בְכָל שָׁלְטָן מַלְכוּתִי לֶהֱוֹן זאעין [זָיְעִין] וְדָחֲלִין מִן קֳדָם אֱ־לָהֵהּ דִּי דָנִיֵּאל דִּי הוּא אֱ־לָהָא חַיָּא וְקַיָּם לְעָלְמִין וּמַלְכוּתֵהּ דִּי לָא תִתְחַבַּל וְשָׁלְטָנֵהּ עַד סוֹפָא.

(כח) מְשֵׁיזִב וּמַצִּל וְעָבֵד אָתִין וְתִמְהִין בִּשְׁמַיָּא וּבְאַרְעָא דִּי שֵׁיזִיב לְדָנִיֵּאל מִן יַד אַרְיָוָתָא.

(כט) וְדָנִיֵּאל דְּנָה הַצְלַח בְּמַלְכוּת דָּרְיָוֶשׁ וּבְמַלְכוּת כּוֹרֶשׁ פרסיא [פָּרְסָאָה].

5:31 [6:1] And Darius the Median took the kingdom, being about threescore and two years old.

1 [2] It pleased Darius to set over the kingdom a hundred and twenty princes, which should be over the whole kingdom.

2 [3] And over these, three presidents, of whom Daniel was first; that the princes might give accounts unto them, and the king should have no damage.

3 [4] Then this Daniel was preferred above the presidents and princes, because an excellent spirit was in him; and the king thought to set him over the whole realm.

4 [5] Then the presidents and princes sought to find occasion against Daniel concerning the kingdom; but they could find none occasion nor fault; forasmuch as he was faithful, neither was there any error or fault found in him.

5 [6] Then said these men: We shall not find any occasion against this Daniel, except we find it against him concerning the law of his God.

6 [7] Then these presidents and princes assembled together to the king, and said thus unto him, King Darius, live for ever.

7 [8] All the presidents of the kingdom, the governors, and the princes, the counsellors, and the captains, have consulted together to establish a royal statute, and to make a firm decree, that whosoever shall ask a petition of any God or man for thirty days, save of thee, O king, he shall be cast into the den of lions.

8 [9] Now, O king, establish the decree, and sign the writing, that it be not changed, according to the law of the Medes and Persians, which altereth not.

9 [10] Wherefore King Darius signed the writing and the decree.

10 [11] Now when Daniel knew that the writing was signed, he went into his house; and his windows being open in his chamber toward Jerusalem, he kneeled upon his knees three times a day, and prayed, and gave thanks before his God, as he did aforetime.

11 [12] Then these men assembled, and found Daniel praying and making supplication before his God.

12 [13] Then they came near, and spake before the king concerning the king's decree: Hast thou not signed a decree, that every man that shall ask a petition of any God or man within thirty days, save of thee, O king, shall be cast into the den of lions? The king answered and said: The thing is true, according to the law of the Medes and Persians, which altereth not.

13 [14] Then answered they and said before the king: That Daniel, which is of the children of the captivity of Judah, regardeth not thee, O king, nor the decree that thou hast signed, but maketh his petition three times a day.

14 [15] Then the king, when he heard these words, was sore displeased with himself, and set his heart on Daniel to deliver him; and he laboured till the going down of the sun to deliver him.

15 [16] Then these men assembled unto the king, and said unto the king: Know, O king, that the law of the Medes and Persians is, that no decree nor statute which the king establisheth may be changed.

16 [17] Then the king commanded, and they brought Daniel, and cast him into the den of lions. Now the king spake and said unto Daniel: Thy God whom thou servest continually, he will deliver thee.

¹⁷ [¹⁸] And a stone was brought, and laid upon the mouth of the den; and the king sealed it with his own signet, and with the signet of his lords; that the purpose might not be changed concerning Daniel.

¹⁸ [¹⁹] Then the king went to his palace, and passed the night fasting: neither were instruments of music brought before him: and his sleep went from him.

¹⁹ [²⁰] Then the king arose very early in the morning, and went in haste unto the den of lions.

²⁰ [²¹] And when he came to the den, he cried with a lamentable voice unto Daniel; and the king spake and said to Daniel: O Daniel, servant of the living God, is thy God, whom thou servest continually, able to deliver thee from the lions?

²¹ [²²] Then said Daniel unto the king: O king, live for ever.

²² [²³] My God hath sent his angel, and hath shut the lions' mouths, that they have not hurt me: forasmuch as before him innocency was found in me; and also before thee, O king, have I done no hurt.

²³ [²⁴] Then was the king exceedingly glad for him, and commanded that they should take Daniel up out of the den. So Daniel was taken up out of the den, and no manner of hurt was found upon him, because he believed in his God.

²⁴ [²⁵] And the king commanded, and they brought those men which had accused Daniel, and they cast them into the den of lions, them, their children, and their wives; and the lions had the mastery of them, and brake all their bones in pieces or ever they came at the bottom of the den.

²⁵ [²⁶] Then king Darius wrote unto all people, nations, and languages, that dwell in all the earth: Peace be multiplied unto you.

²⁶ [²⁷] I make a decree, that in every dominion of my kingdom men tremble and fear before the God of Daniel: for he is the living God, and stedfast for ever, and his kingdom that which shall not be destroyed, and his dominion shall be even unto the end.

²⁷ [²⁸] He delivereth and rescueth, and he worketh signs and wonders in heaven and in earth, who hath delivered Daniel from the power of the lions.

²⁸ [²⁹] So this Daniel prospered in the reign of Darius, and in the reign of Cyrus the Persian.

PSALM 137

"Babel's Streams"

By Babylon's streams we sat and wept,
While Zion we thought upon;
Amidst thereof we hung our harps,
The willow trees upon.
With all the pow'r of skill I have,
I'll gently touch each string;
If I can teach the charming sound,
I'll tune my harp again.

314

Hebraic Source
Psalm 137

(א) עַל נַהֲרוֹת בָּבֶל שָׁם יָשַׁבְנוּ גַּם בָּכִינוּ בְּזָכְרֵנוּ אֶת צִיּוֹן.

(ב) עַל עֲרָבִים בְּתוֹכָהּ תָּלִינוּ כִּנֹּרוֹתֵינוּ.

(ג) כִּי שָׁם שְׁאֵלוּנוּ שׁוֹבֵינוּ דִּבְרֵי שִׁיר וְתוֹלָלֵינוּ שִׂמְחָה שִׁירוּ לָנוּ מִשִּׁיר צִיּוֹן.

(ד) אֵיךְ נָשִׁיר אֶת שִׁיר ה' עַל אַדְמַת נֵכָר.

(ה) אִם אֶשְׁכָּחֵךְ יְרוּשָׁלָם תִּשְׁכַּח יְמִינִי.

(ו) תִּדְבַּק לְשׁוֹנִי לְחִכִּי אִם לֹא אֶזְכְּרֵכִי אִם לֹא אַעֲלֶה אֶת יְרוּשָׁלַם עַל רֹאשׁ שִׂמְחָתִי.

(ז) זְכֹר ה' לִבְנֵי אֱדוֹם אֵת יוֹם יְרוּשָׁלָם הָאֹמְרִים עָרוּ עָרוּ עַד הַיְסוֹד בָּהּ.

(ח) בַּת בָּבֶל הַשְּׁדוּדָה אַשְׁרֵי שֶׁיְשַׁלֶּם לָךְ אֶת גְּמוּלֵךְ שֶׁגָּמַלְתְּ לָנוּ.

(ט) אַשְׁרֵי שֶׁיֹּאחֵז וְנִפֵּץ אֶת עֹלָלַיִךְ אֶל הַסָּלַע.

[1] By the rivers of Babylon, there we sat down, yea, we wept, when we remembered Zion.
[2] We hanged our harps upon the willows in the midst thereof.
[3] For there they that carried us away captive required of us a song; and they that wasted us required of us mirth, saying: Sing us one of the songs of Zion.
[4] How shall we sing the Lord's song in a strange land?
[5] If I forget thee, O Jerusalem, let my right hand forget her cunning.
[6] If I do not remember thee, let my tongue cleave to the roof of my mouth; if I prefer not Jerusalem above my chief joy.
[7] Remember, O Lord, the children of Edom in the day of Jerusalem; who said: Rase it, rase it, even to the foundation thereof.
[8] O daughter of Babylon, who art to be destroyed; happy shall he be, that rewardeth thee as thou hast served us.
[9] Happy shall he be, that taketh and dasheth thy little ones against the stones.

Psalm 137: Lincoln and Douglass

A remark by Abraham Lincoln refers to the same biblical passage and provides an interesting and instructive juxtaposition to the slave spiritual. In speaking to the mayor and citizens of Philadelphia, Lincoln said about the Declaration and Independence Hall, where it was signed: "All my political warfare has been in favor of the teachings coming forth from that sacred hall. May my right hand forget its cunning and my tongue cleave to the roof of my mouth, if ever I prove false to those teachings."[7]

---

7.   Roy P. Basler, *Collected Works of Abraham Lincoln*, vol. 4 (New Brunswick: Rutgers University Press, 1953), 238-239.

The psalm was also used by Frederick Douglass in his celebrated speech, "The Meaning of July Fourth for the Negro":

I say it with a sad sense of the disparity between us. I am not included within the pale of this glorious anniversary! Your high independence only reveals the immeasurable distance between us. The blessings in which you, this day, rejoice, are not enjoyed in common. The rich inheritance of justice, liberty, prosperity and independence, bequeathed by your fathers, is shared by you, not by me. The sunlight that brought light and healing to you, has brought stripes and death to me. This Fourth of July is yours, not mine. You may rejoice, I must mourn. To drag a man in fetters into the grand illuminated temple of liberty, and call upon him to join you in joyous anthems, were inhuman mockery and sacrilegious irony. Do you mean, citizens, to mock me, by asking me to speak to-day? If so, there is a parallel to your conduct. And let me warn you that it is dangerous to copy the example of a nation whose crimes, towering up to heaven, were thrown down by the breath of the Almighty, burying that nation in irrevocable ruin! I can to-day take up the plaintive lament of a peeled and woe-smitten people!

By the rivers of Babylon, there we sat down. Yea! we wept when we remembered Zion. We hanged our harps upon the willows in the midst thereof. For there, they that carried us away captive, required of us a song; and they who wasted us required of us mirth, saying, Sing us one of the songs of Zion. How can we sing the Lord's song in a strange land? If I forget thee, O Jerusalem, let my right hand forget her cunning. If I do not remember thee, let my tongue cleave to the roof of my mouth.

Fellow-citizens; above your national, tumultuous joy, I hear the mournful wail of millions! whose chains, heavy and grievous yesterday, are, to-day, rendered more intolerable by the jubilee shouts that reach them. If I do forget, if I do not faithfully remember those bleeding children of sorrow this day, "may my right hand forget her cunning, and may my tongue cleave to the roof of my mouth!" To forget them, to pass lightly over their wrongs, and to chime in with the popular theme, would be treason most scandalous and shocking, and would make me a reproach before God and the world.

EZEKIEL 37

"Dem Bones, Dem Dry Bones"

Chorus
Dem bones, dem bones, dem dry bones.
Dem bones, dem bones, dem dry bones.
Dem bones, dem bones, dem dry bones.
Now hear the word of the Lord.

Verses
Toe bone connected to the foot bone
Foot bone connected to the leg bone
Leg bone connected to the knee bone…etc.

Hebraic Source
Ezekiel 37

(א) הָיְתָה עָלַי יַד ה' וַיּוֹצִאֵנִי בְרוּחַ ה' וַיְנִיחֵנִי בְּתוֹךְ הַבִּקְעָה וְהִיא מְלֵאָה עֲצָמוֹת.

(ב) וְהֶעֱבִירַנִי עֲלֵיהֶם סָבִיב סָבִיב וְהִנֵּה רַבּוֹת מְאֹד עַל פְּנֵי הַבִּקְעָה וְהִנֵּה יְבֵשׁוֹת מְאֹד.

(ג) וַיֹּאמֶר אֵלַי בֶּן אָדָם הֲתִחְיֶינָה הָעֲצָמוֹת הָאֵלֶּה וָאֹמַר אֲדֹנָי ה' אַתָּה יָדָעְתָּ.

(ד) וַיֹּאמֶר אֵלַי הִנָּבֵא עַל הָעֲצָמוֹת הָאֵלֶּה וְאָמַרְתָּ אֲלֵיהֶם הָעֲצָמוֹת הַיְבֵשׁוֹת שִׁמְעוּ דְּבַר ה'.

(ה) כֹּה אָמַר אֲדֹנָי ה' לָעֲצָמוֹת הָאֵלֶּה הִנֵּה אֲנִי מֵבִיא בָכֶם רוּחַ וִחְיִיתֶם.

(ו) וְנָתַתִּי עֲלֵיכֶם גִּדִים וְהַעֲלֵתִי עֲלֵיכֶם בָּשָׂר וְקָרַמְתִּי עֲלֵיכֶם עוֹר וְנָתַתִּי בָכֶם רוּחַ וִחְיִיתֶם וִידַעְתֶּם כִּי אֲנִי ה'.

(ז) וְנִבֵּאתִי כַּאֲשֶׁר צֻוֵּיתִי וַיְהִי קוֹל כְּהִנָּבְאִי וְהִנֵּה רַעַשׁ וַתִּקְרְבוּ עֲצָמוֹת עֶצֶם אֶל עַצְמוֹ.

(ח) וְרָאִיתִי וְהִנֵּה עֲלֵיהֶם גִּדִים וּבָשָׂר עָלָה וַיִּקְרַם עֲלֵיהֶם עוֹר מִלְמָעְלָה וְרוּחַ אֵין בָּהֶם.

(ט) וַיֹּאמֶר אֵלַי הִנָּבֵא אֶל הָרוּחַ הִנָּבֵא בֶן אָדָם וְאָמַרְתָּ אֶל הָרוּחַ כֹּה אָמַר אֲדֹנָי ה' מֵאַרְבַּע רוּחוֹת בֹּאִי הָרוּחַ וּפְחִי בַּהֲרוּגִים הָאֵלֶּה וְיִחְיוּ.

(י) וְהִנַּבֵּאתִי כַּאֲשֶׁר צִוָּנִי וַתָּבוֹא בָהֶם הָרוּחַ וַיִּחְיוּ וַיַּעַמְדוּ עַל רַגְלֵיהֶם חַיִל גָּדוֹל מְאֹד מְאֹד.

(יא) וַיֹּאמֶר אֵלַי בֶּן אָדָם הָעֲצָמוֹת הָאֵלֶּה כָּל בֵּית יִשְׂרָאֵל הֵמָּה הִנֵּה אֹמְרִים יָבְשׁוּ עַצְמוֹתֵינוּ וְאָבְדָה תִקְוָתֵנוּ נִגְזַרְנוּ לָנוּ.

(יב) לָכֵן הִנָּבֵא וְאָמַרְתָּ אֲלֵיהֶם כֹּה אָמַר אֲדֹנָי ה' הִנֵּה אֲנִי פֹתֵחַ אֶת קִבְרוֹתֵיכֶם
וְהַעֲלֵיתִי אֶתְכֶם מִקִּבְרוֹתֵיכֶם עַמִּי וְהֵבֵאתִי אֶתְכֶם אֶל אַדְמַת יִשְׂרָאֵל.
(יג) וִידַעְתֶּם כִּי אֲנִי ה' בְּפִתְחִי אֶת קִבְרוֹתֵיכֶם וּבְהַעֲלוֹתִי אֶתְכֶם מִקִּבְרוֹתֵיכֶם עַמִּי.
(יד) וְנָתַתִּי רוּחִי בָכֶם וִחְיִיתֶם וְהִנַּחְתִּי אֶתְכֶם עַל אַדְמַתְכֶם וִידַעְתֶּם כִּי אֲנִי ה'
דִּבַּרְתִּי וְעָשִׂיתִי נְאֻם ה'.

[1] The hand of the Lord was upon me, and carried me out in the spirit of the Lord, and set me down in the midst of the valley which was full of bones;

[2] And caused me to pass by them round about: and, behold, there were very many in the open valley; and, lo, they were very dry.

[3] And he said unto me: Son of man, can these bones live? And I answered, O Lord God, Thou knowest.

[4] Again he said unto me: Prophesy upon these bones, and say unto them: O ye dry bones, hear the word of the Lord.

[5] Thus saith the Lord God unto these bones: Behold, I will cause breath to enter into you, and ye shall live:

[6] And I will lay sinews upon you, and will bring up flesh upon you, and cover you with skin, and put breath in you, and ye shall live; and ye shall know that I am the Lord.

[7] So I prophesied as I was commanded; and as I prophesied, there was a noise, and behold a shaking, and the bones came together, bone to his bone.

[8] And when I beheld, lo, the sinews and the flesh came up upon them, and the skin covered them above: but there was no breath in them.

[9] Then said he unto me: Prophesy unto the wind, prophesy, son of man, and say to the wind: Thus saith the Lord God: Come from the four winds, O breath, and breathe upon these slain, that they may live.

[10] So I prophesied as he commanded me, and the breath came into them, and they lived, and stood up upon their feet, an exceeding great army.

[11] Then he said unto me: Son of man, these bones are the whole house of Israel; behold, they say: Our bones are dried, and our hope is lost; we are cut off for our parts.

[12] Therefore prophesy and say unto them: Thus saith the Lord God: Behold, O my people, I will open your graves, and cause you to come up out of your graves, and bring you into the land of Israel.

[13] And ye shall know that I am the Lord, when I have opened your graves, O My people, and brought you up out of your graves,

[14] And shall put my spirit in you, and ye shall live, and I shall place you in your own land: then shall ye know that I the Lord have spoken it, and performed it, saith the Lord.

Lincoln's Use of Ezekiel 37

Abraham Lincoln, in an 1842 address to a temperance society, also cited this passage from Ezekiel.

In my judgment, such of us as have never fallen victims, have been spared more by the absence of appetite, than from any mental or moral superiority over those who have. Indeed, I believe, if we take habitual drunkards as a class, their heads and their hearts will bear an advantageous comparison with those of any other class. There seems ever to have been a proneness in the brilliant, and warm-blooded, to fall into this vice. The demon of intemperance ever seems to have delighted in sucking the blood of genius and of generosity. What one of us but can call to mind some dear relative, more promising in youth than all his fellows, who has fallen a sacrifice to his rapacity? He ever seems to have gone forth, like the Egyptian angel of death, commissioned to slay if not the first, the fairest born of every family. Shall he now be arrested in his desolating career? In that arrest, all can give aid that will; and who shall be excused that *can*, and will not? Far around as human breath has ever blown, he keeps our fathers, our brothers, our sons, and our friends, prostrate in the chains of moral death. To all the living every where we cry, "come sound the moral resurrection trump, that these may rise and stand up, an exceeding great army" – "Come from the four winds, O breath! and breathe upon these slain, that they may live."

If the relative grandeur of revolutions shall be estimated by the great amount of human misery they alleviate, and the small amount they inflict, then, indeed, will this be the grandest the world shall ever have seen. Of our political revolution of '76, we all are justly proud. It has given us a degree of political freedom, far exceeding that of any other nation of the earth. In it the world has found a solution of the long mooted problem, as to the capability of man to govern himself. In it was the germ which has vegetated, and still is to grow and expand into the universal liberty of mankind.

But with all these glorious results, past, present, and to come, it had its evils too. It breathed forth famine, swam in blood and rode in fire; and long, long after, the orphan's cry, and the widow's wail, continued to break the sad silence that ensued. These were the price, the inevitable price, paid for the blessings it bought.

Turn now, to the temperance revolution. In *it*, we shall find a stronger bondage broken; a viler slavery, manumitted; a greater tyrant deposed. In *it*, more of want supplied, more disease healed, more sorrow assuaged. By *it* no orphans starving, no widows weeping. By *it*, none wounded in feeling, none injured in interest. Even the dram-maker, and dram seller, will have glided into other occupations *so* gradually, as never to have felt the change; and will stand ready to join all others in the universal song of gladness.

And what a noble ally this, to the cause of political freedom. With such an aid, its march cannot fail to be on and on, till every son of earth shall drink in rich fruition, the sorrow quenching draughts of perfect liberty. Happy day, when, all appetites controlled, all poisons subdued, all matter subjected, *mind*, all conquering *mind*, shall live and move the monarch of the world. Glorious consummation! Hail fall of Fury! Reign of Reason, all hail!

And when the victory shall be complete – when there shall be neither a slave nor a drunkard on the earth – how proud the title of that *Land*, which may truly claim to be the birth-place and the cradle of both those revolutions, that shall have ended in that victory. How nobly distinguished that People, who shall have planted, and nurtured to maturity, both the political and moral freedom of their species.

This is the one hundred and tenth anniversary of the birth-day of Washington. We are met to celebrate this day. Washington is the mightiest name of earth – *long since* mightiest in the cause of civil liberty; *still* mightiest in moral reformation. On that name, an eulogy is expected. It cannot be. To add brightness to the sun, or glory to the name of Washington, is alike impossible. Let none attempt it. In solemn awe pronounce the name, and in its naked deathless splendor, leave it shining on.

Slave Revolt of Denmark Vesey

In 1822, Denmark Vesey, a charismatic former slave, planned a revolt to free hundreds of slaves in South Carolina, and then take Charleston. After a time, they would commandeer a boat and sail for Haiti. Betrayed by two people who heard of the plot, he was captured and hanged, along with thirty-five others, for plotting a slave revolt. He became a personal hero of Frederick Douglass.

After Vesey's plot was uncovered, new laws were enacted that restricted the reading, writing, and assembling of slaves.

One of the informants gave this report of Vesey's meeting with the co-conspirators:

That night at Vesey's we determined to have arms made, and each man put in 12.5 cents toward that purpose. Though Vesey's room was full I did not know an individual there. At this meeting Vesey said we were to take the Guard-House Magazine to get arms; that we ought to rise up and fight against the white for our liberties; he was the first to rise up and speak, and he read to us from the Bible, how the Children of Israel were delivered out of Egypt from bondage. He said that the rising would take place, last Sunday night week ....

The Civil War

INTRODUCTION

The election of Abraham Lincoln was the catalyst that began secession. By the time Lincoln assumed office in March 1861, South Carolina, Georgia, Alabama, Florida, Texas, Mississippi, and Louisiana had
already seceded. After the fall of Fort Sumter in April, Virginia, Tennessee, North Carolina, and Arkansas joined them. The Civil War's initial
aim was to maintain the Union, and that was the stance Lincoln maintained throughout most of 1861, when the war began, and into the early
part of 1862. In his famous letter to Horace Greeley, editor of the *New
York Tribune*, Lincoln said: "I would save the Union. I would save it the
shortest way under the Constitution.... If there be those who would
not save the Union unless they could at the same time save Slavery, I do
not agree with them. If there be those who would not save the Union
unless they could at the same time destroy Slavery, I do not agree with
them. My paramount object in this struggle is to save the Union, and is
not either to save or destroy Slavery. If I could save the Union without
freeing any slave, I would do it, and if I could save it by freeing all the
slaves, I would do it, and if I could save it by freeing some and leaving
others alone, I would also do that."[1]

Lincoln was concerned that if the war's aim was to end slavery,
Kentucky, Maryland, and Missouri would go to the South. Lincoln was

---

1.   Letter to Horace Greeley, August 24, 1862.

a moderate when it came to abolition; he was at first for gradual, compensated emancipation, and only later supported immediate emancipation without compensation. Lincoln's early position was too slow for the radical republicans and too fast for the conservative ones. In July 1862, after slightly more than a year in office, Lincoln discussed the Emancipation Proclamation with his cabinet. He issued a preliminary proclamation in late September, after the victory at Antietam, and the full proclamation went into effect on January 1, 1863. The Proclamation was issued under the president's war powers and applied only to those areas of states that were in rebellion, and thus where the Union forces were largely incapable of enforcing it. (The original draft did not include a reference to God, but it was suggested to Lincoln by William Seward, his secretary of state.) The Emancipation Proclamation thus had little immediate effect. It was, however, broadly representative of a shift of war aims. By the time of Lincoln's second inaugural address in March 1865, as the war was nearing its conclusion, Lincoln was able to claim that everyone knew that slavery caused the war. That was not something he would have said publicly in 1862. The war changed America.

In any great struggle each side thinks they have the blessing of a higher power. In the South preachers argued that slavery was a God-given right, part of the natural order of things. The Civil War renewed in the North the evangelical Protestantism of the Second Great Awakening. Preachers and laymen in the North thought that theirs was the holy cause, and that their sword was the expression of God's wrath and vengeance on a sinful South. There is no better expression of that Northern sentiment than the "Battle Hymn of the Republic," in which God's truth is advanced by burnished rows of steel. Lincoln's reflections on God stood apart from the mainstream of Northern opinion. He was very reluctant to collapse God's purpose into the war aims of either the North or the South. The tragedy of the war, and the death of his son Willie, increasingly convinced him that God's ways were mysterious, and that though the South would make war to keep slavery, both North and South were complicit in national sin and neither received God's full backing. In fact, for Lincoln, the war was God's punishment for American transgression. This was most beautifully expressed in his second inaugural address, excerpted below. Frederick Douglass called it a "sacred effort," for it was a speech more fitting for a pastor than a president. It remains, perhaps, the single greatest speech in American history.

HENRY WARD BEECHER, "THE BATTLE SET IN ARRAY" (1861)

Henry Ward Beecher (1813–1887), son of Lyman Beecher, was one of the most famous preachers of his generation. After a brief stint in Indianapolis, he became preacher at Plymouth Church in Brooklyn. He gave this sermon during the battle for Fort Sumter. He begins with a discussion of a Hebraic example, and then turns to why the war is just and secession is wrong.

"And the Lord said unto Moses, Wherefore criest thou unto me? speak unto the children of Israel, that they go forward."
– Exod. xiv. 15.

MOSES was raised up to be the emancipator of three millions of people. At the age of forty, having, through a singular providence, been reared in the midst of luxury, in the proudest, most intelligent, and most civilized court on the globe, with a heart uncorrupt, with a genuine love of his own race and people, he began to act as their emancipator. He boldly slew one of their oppressors. And, seeing dissension among his brethren, he sought to bring them to peace. He was rejected, reproved, and reproached; and finding himself discovered, he fled, and, for the sake of liberty, became a fugitive and a martyr. For forty years, uncomplaining, he dwelt apart with his father-in-law, Jethro, in the wilderness, in the peaceful pursuits of a herdsman.

At eighty – the time when most men lay down the burden of life, or have long laid it down – he began his life work. He was called back by the voice of God; and now, accompanied with companions, he returned, confronted the king, and, moved by Divine inspiration, demanded, repeatedly, the release of his people. The first demand was sanctioned by a terrific plague; the second, by a second terrible judgment; the third, by a third frightful devastation; the fourth, by a fourth dreadful blow; the fifth, by a fifth desolating, sweeping mischief. A sixth, a seventh, an eighth, and a ninth time, he demanded their release. And when was there ever, on the face of the earth, a man that, once having power, would let it go till life itself went with it? Pharaoh, who is the grand type of oppressors, held on in spite of the Divine command and of the Divine punishment. Then God let fly the last terrific judgment, and smote the first-born of Egypt; and there was wailing in every house of the midnight land. And then, in the midst of the first gush of grief and anguish, the tyrant said, "Let them go! let them go!" And he did let them go; he shoved them out; and they went pell-mell in great confusion on their way, taking up their line of march, and escaped from Egypt. But as soon as the first effects of the grief and anguish had passed away, Pharaoh came back to his old nature – just as many men whose hearts are softened, and whose lives are made better by affliction, come back to the old way of feeling and living, as soon as they have ceased to experience the first effects of the affliction – and he followed on after the people. As they lay encamped – these three millions of people, men, women, and children – just apart from the land of bondage, near the fork and head of the Red Sea, with great hills on either side of them, and the sea before them, someone brought panic into the camp, saying, "I see the signs of an advancing host! The air far on the horizon is filled with rising clouds!" Presently, through these clouds, began to be seen glancing spears, mounted horsemen, and a great swelling army. Such, to these lately enslaved, but just emancipated people, was the first token of the coming adversary. Surely, they were unable to cope with the disciplined cohorts of this Egyptian king. They, that were unused to war, that had never been allowed to hold weapons in their hands, that were a poor, despoiled people not only, but that had been subjected to the blighting touch of slavery, had lost courage. They did not dare to be free. And there is no wonder, therefore, that they reproached Moses, and said, "Because there were no graves in Egypt, hast thou taken us away to die in the wilderness?" [Ex. 14:11]. I have no doubt that, if Pharaoh's courtiers had heard that, they would have said, "Ah! they do not want to be free. They do not believe in freedom." "Because there were no graves in Egypt, hast thou taken us away to die in the wilderness? Wherefore hast thou dealt thus with us, to carry us forth out of Egypt?" Were these people miserable specimens of humanity? They were just what slavery makes everybody to be. "Is not this the word that we did tell thee in Egypt, saying, Let us alone, that we may serve the Egyptians?" [Ex. 14:12]. They would rather have had peace with servitude, than liberty with the manly daring required to obtain it. "For it had been better for us to serve the Egyptians, than that we should die in the wilderness."

That is just the difference between a man and a slave. They would rather have lived slaves, and eaten their pottage, than to suffer for the sake of liberty; a man would rather die in his tracks, than live in ease as a slave. These, then, were the people that Moses undertook to emancipate, and this was the beginning of Moses's life-work. "And Moses said unto the people, Fear ye not, stand still – " That was wrong, but he did not know any better. "Fear ye not, stand still, and see the salvation of the Lord, which he will show you to-day: for the Egyptians, whom ye have seen to-day, ye shall see them again no more forever. The Lord shall fight for you, and ye shall hold your peace" [Ex. 14:13-14]. He was a little too fast. He was right in respect to the result, but wrong in respect to the means. "And the Lord said unto Moses, Wherefore criest thou unto me? Speak unto the children of Israel, that they go forward" [Ex. 14:15]. They were, after all, to do something and dare something for their liberty. No standing still, but going forward! "Lift up thy rod, and stretch out thine hand over the sea, and divide it; and the children of Israel shall go on dry ground through the midst of the sea" [Ex. 14:16]. You recollect the rest. They walked through the sea that stood up as a wall on either side for them. They reached the other side. They were divided from the camp of the Egyptians by a fiery cloud, and the Egyptians could not touch them. And what was the fate of the Egyptians? They attempted to follow the children of Israel through the sea, when the waters closed together, and their host was destroyed. God has raised up many men, at different periods of the world, to bring his cause forth from its various exigencies.

Wherever a man is called to defend a truth or a principle, a church or a people, a nation or an age, he may be said to be, like Moses, the leader of God's people. And in every period of the world God has shut up his people, at one time or another, to himself. He has brought their enemies behind them, as he brought the Egyptians behind the children of Israel: He has hedged them in on either hand.

He has spread out the unfordable sea before them. He has so beset them with difficulties, when they were attempting to live for right, for duty, and for liberty, that they have been like Israel.

When men stand for a moral principle, their troubles are not a presumption that they are in the wrong. Since the world began, men that have stood for the right have had to stand for it, as Christ stood for the world, suffering for victory.

In the history which belongs peculiarly to us, over and over again the same thing has occurred. In that grand beginning struggle in which Luther figured so prominently, he stood in a doubtful conflict. He was in the minority; he was vehemently pressed with enemies on every side; nine times out of ten during his whole life the odds were against him. And yet he died victorious, and we reap the fruit of his victory. In one of the consequences of that noble struggle, the assertion in the Netherlands of civil liberty and religious toleration, the same thing took place. Almost the entire globe was against this amphibious republic, until England cared for them; and England cared for them but very doubtfully and very imperfectly. All the reigning influences, all the noblest of the commanding men of the Continent, were against them. The conflict was a long and dubious one, in which they suffered extremely, and conquered through their suffering. In the resulting struggle in England, which was borrowed largely from the Continent – the Puritan uprising, the Puritan struggle – the same thing occurred. The Puritans were enveloped in darkness. Their enemies were more than their friends. The issue was exceedingly doubtful. Their very victory began in apparent defeat. For when at last, wearied and discouraged, they could no longer abide the restriction of their liberty in England, they fled away to plant colonies upon these shores. On the sea did they venture, but the ocean, black and wild, before they left it was covered with winter. In every one of these instances darkness and the flood lay before the champions of truth and rectitude. God in his providence said to them, though they were without apparent instrumentalities, "Go forward! Venture everything! Endure everything! Yield the precious truths never! Live forever by them! Die with them, if you die at all." The whole lesson of the past, then, is that safety and honor come by holding fast to one's principles; by pressing them with courage; by going into darkness and defeat cheerfully for them.

And now our turn has come. Right before us lies the Red Sea of war. It is red indeed. There is blood in it. We have come to the very edge of it, and the Word of God to us to-day is, "Speak unto this people that they go forward!" It is not of our procuring. It is not of our wishing. It is not our hand that has stricken the first stroke, nor drawn the first blood. We have prayed against it. We have struggled against it. Ten thousand times we have said, "Let this cup pass from us." It has been overruled. We have yielded everything but manhood, and principle, and truth, and honor, and we have heard the voice of God saying, "Yield these never!" And these not being yielded, war has been let loose upon this land....

When the trumpet of God has sounded, and that grand procession is forming; as Italy has risen, and is wheeling into the ranks; as Hungary, though mute, is beginning to beat time, and make ready for the march; as Poland, having long slept, has dreamt of liberty again, and is waking; as the thirty million serfs are hearing the roll of the drum, and are going forward toward citizenship – let it not be your miserable fate, nor mine, to live in a nation that shall be seen reeling and staggering and wallowing in the orgies of despotism! We, too, have a right to march in this grand procession of liberty. By the memory of the fathers; by the sufferings of the Puritan ancestry; by the teaching of our national history; by our faith and hope of religion; by every line of the Declaration of Independence, and every article of our Constitution; by what we are and what our progenitors were – we have a right to walk foremost in this procession of nations toward the bright millennial future!

Julia Ward Howe (1819–1910) was both a woman of letters and a woman of action, advocating for abolitionism and women's suffrage. She is best known for writing "The Battle Hymn of the Republic" at the end of 1861, following a meeting with President Lincoln, which quickly became one of the most popular Union songs during the Civil War. It encapsulates the North's self-image of doing God's work.

JULIA W. HOWE, "BATTLE HYMN OF THE REPUBLIC" (1861)

Mine eyes have seen the glory of the coming of the Lord;
He is trampling out the vintage where the grapes of wrath are
stored;
He hath loosed the fateful lightning of His terrible swift sword:
His truth is marching on.

Chorus
Glory, glory, hallelujah!
Glory, glory, hallelujah!
Glory, glory, hallelujah!
His truth is marching on.

I have seen Him in the watch-fires of a hundred circling camps,
They have builded Him an altar in the evening dews and damps;
I can read His righteous sentence by the dim and flaring lamps:
His day is marching on.

I have read a fiery gospel writ in burnished rows of steel:
"As ye deal with my contemners, so with you my grace shall deal";
Let the Hero, born of woman, crush the serpent with his heel,
Since God is marching on.

He has sounded forth the trumpet that shall never call retreat;
He is sifting out the hearts of men before His judgment-seat:
Oh, be swift, my soul, to answer Him! be jubilant, my feet!
Our God is marching on.

In the beauty of the lilies Christ was born across the sea,
With a glory in His bosom that transfigures you and me.
As He died to make men holy, let us die to make men free,
While God is marching on.

He is coming like the glory of the morning on the wave,
He is Wisdom to the mighty, He is Succour to the brave,

So the world shall be His footstool, and the soul of Time His slave,
Our God is marching on.

OLIVER WENDELL HOLMES, JR., "TO CANAAN" (1862)

Oliver Wendell Holmes, Jr., (1841–1935) was one of the most famous justices of the United States Supreme Court. In his senior year in college at Harvard, at the beginning of the Civil War, Holmes joined the Union army. He fought for three years and was wounded on multiple occasions. The following is a poem written by Holmes during the beginning of his service.

WHERE are you going, soldiers,
With banner, gun, and sword?
We're marching South to Canaan
To battle for the Lord
What Captain leads your armies
Along the rebel coasts?
The Mighty One of Israel,
His name is Lord of Hosts!
To Canaan, to Canaan
The Lord has led us forth,
To blow before the heathen walls
The trumpets of the North!

What flag is this you carry
Along the sea and shore?
The same our grandsires lifted up,-
The same our fathers bore
In many a battle's tempest
It shed the crimson rain,-
What God has woven in his loom
Let no man rend in twain!
To Canaan, to Canaan
The Lord has led us forth,
To plant upon the rebel towers

What troop is this that follows,
All armed with picks and spades?
These are the swarthy bondsmen,-
The iron-skin brigades!
They'll pile up Freedom's breastwork,
They'll scoop out rebels' graves;
Who then will be their owner
And march them off for slaves?
To Canaan, to Canaan
The Lord has led us forth,
To strike upon the captive's chain
The hammers of the North!

What song is this you're singing?
The same that Israel sung
When Moses led the mighty choir,
And Miriam's timbrel rung!
To Canaan! To Canaan!
The priests and maidens cried:
To Canaan! To Canaan!
The people's voice replied.
To Canaan, to Canaan
The Lord has led us forth,
To thunder through its adder dens
The anthems of the North.

When Canaan's hosts are scattered,
And all her walls lie flat,
What follows next in order?
The Lord will see to that
We'll break the tyrant's sceptre,-
We'll build the people's throne,-
When half the world is Freedom's,
Then all the world's our own
To Canaan, to Canaan
The Lord has led us forth,

To sweep the rebel threshing-floors,
A whirlwind from the North.

ABRAHAM LINCOLN

Meditation on the Divine Will (1862)

The will of God prevails. In great contests each party claims to act in accordance with the will of God. Both *may* be, and one *must* be, wrong. God cannot be *for* and *against* the same thing at the same time. In the present civil war it is quite possible that God's purpose is something different from the purpose of either party – and yet the human instrumentalities, working just as they do, are of the best adaptation to effect His purpose. I am almost ready to say that this is probably true – that God wills this contest, and wills that it shall not end yet. By his mere great power, on the minds of the now contestants, He could have either *saved* or *destroyed* the Union without a human contest. Yet the contest began. And, having begun He could give the final victory to either side any day. Yet the contest proceeds.

Gettysburg Address (1863)

Four score and seven years ago our fathers brought forth on this continent, a new nation, conceived in Liberty, and dedicated to the proposition that all men are created equal.

Now we are engaged in a great civil war, testing whether that nation, or any nation so conceived and so dedicated, can long endure. We are met on a great battle-field of that war. We have come to dedicate a portion of that field, as a final resting place for those who here gave their lives that that nation might live. It is altogether fitting and proper that we should do this.

But, in a larger sense, we can not dedicate – we can not consecrate – we can not hallow – this ground. The brave men, living and dead, who struggled here, have consecrated it, far above our poor power to add or detract. The world will little note, nor long remember what we say here, but it can never forget what they did here. It is for us the living, rather, to be dedicated here to the unfinished work which they who fought here have thus far so nobly advanced. It is rather for us to be here dedicated to the great task remaining before us – that from these honored dead we take increased devotion to that cause for which they gave the last full measure of devotion – that we here highly resolve that these dead shall not have died in vain – that this nation, under God, shall have a new birth of freedom – and that government of the people, by the people, for the people, shall not perish from the earth.

Second Inaugural Address (March 4, 1865)

Fellow-Countrymen:

At this second appearing to take the oath of the Presidential office there is less occasion for an extended address than there was at the first. Then a statement somewhat in detail of a course to be pursued seemed fitting and proper. Now, at the expiration of four years, during which public declarations have been constantly called forth on every point and phase of the great contest which still absorbs the attention and engrosses the energies of the nation, little that is new could be presented. The progress of our arms, upon which all else chiefly depends, is as well known to the public as to myself, and it is, I trust, reasonably satisfactory and encouraging to all. With high hope for the future, no prediction in regard to it is ventured.

On the occasion corresponding to this four years ago all thoughts were anxiously directed to an impending civil war. All dreaded it, all sought to avert it. While the inaugural address was being delivered from this place, devoted altogether to saving the Union without war, insurgent agents were in the city seeking to destroy it without war – seeking to dissolve the Union and divide effects by negotiation. Both parties deprecated war, but one of them would *make* war rather than let the nation survive, and the other would accept war rather than let it perish, and the war came.

One-eighth of the whole population were colored slaves, not distributed generally over the Union, but localized in the southern part of it. These slaves constituted a peculiar and powerful interest. All knew that this interest was somehow the cause of the war. To strengthen, perpetuate, and extend this interest was the object for which the insurgents would rend the Union even by war, while the Government claimed no right to do more than to restrict the territorial enlargement of it. Neither party expected for the war the magnitude or the duration which it has already attained. Neither anticipated that the cause of the conflict might cease with or even before the conflict itself should cease. Each looked for an easier triumph, and a result less fundamental and astounding. Both read the same Bible and pray to the same God, and each invokes His aid against the other. It may seem strange that any men should dare to ask a just God's assistance in wringing their bread from the sweat of other men's faces, but let us judge not, that we be not judged. The prayers of both could not be answered. That of neither has been answered fully. The Almighty has His own purposes. "Woe unto the world because of offenses; for it must needs be that offenses come, but woe to that man by whom the offense cometh." If we shall suppose that American slavery is one of those offenses which, in the providence of God, must needs come, but which, having continued through His appointed time, He now wills to remove, and that He gives to both North and South this terrible war as the woe due to those by whom the offense came, shall we discern therein any departure from those divine attributes which the believers in a living God always ascribe to Him? Fondly do we hope, fervently do we pray, that this mighty scourge of war may speedily pass away. Yet, if God wills that it continue until all the wealth piled by the bondsman's two hundred and fifty years of unrequited toil shall be sunk, and until every drop of blood drawn with the lash shall be paid by another drawn with the sword, as was said three thousand years ago, so still it must be said "the judgments of the Lord are true and righteous altogether" [Ps. 19:10].

With malice toward none, with charity for all, with firmness in the right as God gives us to see the right, let us strive on to finish the work we are in, to bind up the nation's wounds, to care for him who shall have borne the battle and for his widow and his orphan, to do all which may achieve and cherish a just and lasting peace among ourselves and with all nations.

Hebraic Source
Psalm 19

(י) יִרְאַת ה' טְהוֹרָה עוֹמֶדֶת לָעַד מִשְׁפְּטֵי ה' אֱמֶת צָדְקוּ יַחְדָּו.

[10] The fear of the Lord is clean, enduring for ever; the ordinances of the Lord are true, they are righteous altogether.

Postscript

The Hebrew Bible and the Civil Rights Movement

W e have elected to end the source volume at the end of the Civil War. We very well could have continued to trace the Hebraic echoes in American public life into Reconstruction, Progressivism, debates surrounding American imperialism, the transformation of the United States through the New Deal, and the 1960s. We could have brought those sources up until today, since the Hebrew Bible has continued to resonate as a source of inspiration and a focal point of cultural heritage.

But that resonance grew weaker after the Civil War. Late nineteenth- and early twentieth-century American Protestantism departed from the distinctly Hebraic qualities that characterized the Puritans and the founders. Social and cultural movements such as Progressivism and the Social Gospel movements sought more inspiration from the figure of Jesus as a reformer than from the Hebraic themes of covenant or chosenness. In other aspects of American life, the continued resonance of Hebraic ideas was still audible, but in softer and more muted tones. For instance, as Americans expanded westward, they did continue to see themselves as members of a chosen nation with a specific and manifest destiny. As we have tried to demonstrate, that destiny is a reflection of, and is culturally embedded in, Hebraic sources. The nineteenth-century American debate about the scope and meaning of the American destiny was conducted by men like Albert Beveridge (US Senator and historian), William Sumner (a well-known professor at Yale), and Woodrow Wilson. There are undeniably religious overtones to the speeches and writings of these men, but they are more ecumenical and less deeply Hebraic.

In the twentieth century, and through the Roosevelt and Eisenhower administrations, the United States developed a sense of itself as a Judeo-Christian nation. The various branches of American religions, it was thought, shared the same moral roots that brought Jew and Christian together in a happy moral consensus. President Harry Truman captured this spirit well in his 1948 State of the Union Address: "The basic source of our strength is spiritual. For we are a people with a faith. We believe in the dignity of man. We believe that he was created in the image of the Father of us all." This ecumenical spirit, seen from the perspective of the historically fraught relationship between Judaism and Christianity, and indeed between Christian sects in America, was in an important way a most welcome development. It remains to be seen whether, balanced against the unmistakable social benefits that came from the unity of a Judeo-Christian nation, other unforeseen consequences of the abstracted notion of a suprareligious sensibility have arisen that have tended to hollow religious commitment, decrease religious observance, arrest attendance at houses of worship, vacate the public square from religious language and symbols, and generally undermine the particular demands of a particular faith that alone can command our allegiance and conscience. Because the Hebraic elements of American public life exercised such formative influence in the beginning, they are part of the American story and they remain present with us. But they are harder to perceive as time goes on, as America and Americans change.

One of the most impressive and thoroughgoing flowerings of American Hebraism continued to blossom after the Civil War. The Hebraic themes we trace in this source volume remained lodestars of the African American experience throughout the twentieth century. African

Americans, shut out of the emerging American consensus in the 1950s, still longed for the liberation that had always been more a promise than a reality. Though the Civil War had done much to release African Americans from bondage, the unfulfilled aspirations for liberty and equality of the Civil War seemed a vague and distant memory when juxtaposed with the cold realities of life in the Jim Crow South. The great African American writer and social activist W. E. B. Dubois (1868–1963) put it well when he said in his masterpiece *The Souls of Black Folk* (1903) that

> way back in the days of bondage they thought to see in one divine event the end of all doubt and disappointment; few men ever worshipped Freedom with half such unquestioning faith as did the American Negro for two centuries. To him, so far as he thought and dreamed, slavery was indeed the sum of all villainies, the cause of all sorrow, the root of all prejudice; Emancipation was the key to a promised land of sweeter beauty than ever stretched before the eyes of wearied Israelites.... The Nation has not yet found peace from its sins; the freedman has not yet found in freedom his promised land.[1]

There is perhaps no community in American life after the founding generation that so deeply embodied the Hebraic spirit as the African American community. From Rastafarianism to the Civil Rights movement, African American political movements have traditionally been infused with a longing to escape the bondage of Egypt and return to the promised land of freedom. African American public leaders taught their audiences to see themselves as participating in a great historical drama, directed by God's hand. In Martin Luther King Jr., the country as a whole saw American politics and the Hebraic imagination fused together with biblical potency.

The Hebraicism of the African American community was an integral part of American culture, stretching back to the haunting spirituals that longed for liberation. Progress on civil rights for African Americans

---

1. *The Souls of Black Folk*, "Of Our Spiritual Strivings" (Chicago: A. C. McClurg & Co., 1903). Available at https://www.bartleby.com/114/1.html.

was slow in the United States. In the early twentieth century, dispirited with the state of conditions in the South, African Americans began a journey north, a new Exodus. In what came to be called the Great Migration, African Americans moved in large numbers into the urban North, settling in Detroit, Cincinnati, Baltimore, and New York. As earlier generations of African American artists had done, the authors of the Great Migration's poetry and prose drew on Hebraic tropes depicting the North as "freedom land" and the migration as a journey home, harkening back to the cultural power of the Exodus narrative and of the movement from slavery toward Zion. Capturing this energy, and symbolic of it, Zora Neale Hurston wrote a novel entitled *Moses, Man of the Mountain* (1939), in which the Hebraic Moses is blended with the Moses of the African American oral and folkloric tradition to tell an American story of struggle and liberation.

One of the fruits of the Great Migration was the artistic and cultural epicenter that was Harlem. Throughout the early years of the twentieth century, this district in northern Manhattan saw an efflorescence of literature, poetry, and music, in what is now known as the Harlem Renaissance. Intellectuals and artists associated with this cultural movement include Alain Locke, Langston Hughes, Louis Armstrong, Mahalia Jackson, and Marion Anderson. While recognizing that Christianity and the Church were central cultural elements of the African American experience, and even though mass migrations north swelled church numbers, some artists and writers of the Harlem Renaissance saw themselves as modernists in an avant-garde that leaned secular; freedom for these artists required them to disburden themselves from the religious ideas that, for them, represented the old order of corruption and moral stain. But other African American poets in New York still saw in the Hebraic legacy a promise of freedom. James Weldon Johnson, the first black professor at New York University, wrote a number of religious poems, several of which are published in *God's Trombones: Seven Negro Sermons in Verse* (1927). He retells the stories of creation, the prodigal son, Noah's Ark, the crucifixion, and judgment day. "Let My People Go," the story of Moses, has a beautiful refrain reminiscent of slave spirituals: "Therefore, Moses, go down, / Go down into Egypt, / And tell Old Pharaoh, / To let my people go."

Progress for African Americans, while painfully slow, accelerated after World War II. President Truman desegregated the military in 1948, a year after baseball was officially desegregated. In 1954 the Supreme Court handed down *Brown v. Board of Education*, which mandated the desegregation of the nation's schools and was a moral blow to Jim Crow. The most significant movement for civil rights was initiated by African Americans themselves in the South, led by such large figures as Ralph Abernathy and Martin Luther King Jr. The Civil Rights movement organized boycotts and sit-ins across the South, and was met with fierce and strong resistance by local and state governments. Much of civil rights agitation in the South centered around churches, which were places of both political and spiritual congregation. The famous 1955 Montgomery Bus Boycott prompted the formation of the Southern Christian Leadership Conference, an umbrella organization for Southern churches, led by one of America's most ardent and skillful Hebraic minds, Martin Luther King Jr.

King promoted a method of peaceful, non-violent resistance, inspired by the teachings of Christ and the Hebrew Bible. He thought America was infused with a moral promise of equality and dignity that was deeply rooted in biblical morality. To be great, he preached, a nation must be dedicated to high ideals. King was the most biblical American leader of the twentieth century, a poignant expression of the enduring power of religious tropes and narratives in American political thought.

Peaceful and nonviolent resistance was not the only option available to the oppressed African Americans at the time. Malcolm X, a convert to Islam – who later repudiated the Nation of Islam and was killed by them – was a charismatic, handsome, and uproarious leader of a more militant resistance to oppression and racism. In his early life, he advocated violent resistance to the white power structure, the separation of the races, emigration to Africa, and pan-Africanism that saw Africans beyond Africa as a diaspora seeking to return to their homeland. (He later renounced these earlier positions.) In his promotion of emigration to Africa and pan-Africanism, Malcolm X followed in the footsteps of Marcus Garvey, a Jamaican political leader who advocated return to Africa. Speaking in Toronto on August 29, 1937, Garvey said: "The Negroes of the United States and Canada may not go to Africa in this lifetime, but one day the call will come for us to return as the Jews are now returning to Palestine."[2] Garvey was influential on the Nation of Islam and Rastafarianism, the movement known for its iconic music deeply infused with Hebraic themes of diaspora, exodus, and return, as in the Melodians' song based on Psalm 127, with its refrain: "By the rivers of Babylon, there we sat down, Ye-eah we wept, when we remembered Zion." Malcolm X however did not ultimately choose to side with the Christian and Hebraic legacy in the United States. He rejected that tradition as complicit with oppression of the black community and looked for an alternative in the Nation of Islam, which, while it had broad appeal in the African American community, had no purchase on the broader American community.

But the religious sentiment of the country was not fully on the side of civil rights. Martin Luther King Jr. lamented in his famous "Letter from a Birmingham Jail" that

> when I was suddenly catapulted into the leadership of the bus protest in Montgomery, Alabama, a few years ago, I felt we would be supported by the white church. I felt that the white ministers, priests and rabbis of the South would be among our strongest allies. Instead, some have been outright opponents, refusing to understand the freedom movement and misrepresenting its leaders; all too many others have been more cautious than courageous and have remained silent behind the anesthetizing security of stained glass windows.

King weaved together like no other the Hebraic and the American. In his great "I Have a Dream" speech given in a civil rights march on Washington, he said:

> "When will you be satisfied?" We can never be satisfied as long as the Negro is the victim of the unspeakable horrors of police

---

2. Nathaniel Samuel Murrell and Lewin Williams, "The Black Biblical Hermeneutics of Rastafari," in *Chanting Down Babylon: The Rastafari Reader*, eds. Nathaniel Samuel Murrell, William David Spencer, and Adrian Anthony McFarlane (Philadelphia: Temple Press, 1998), 328. See also "Babylon In Rastafarian Discourse: Garvey, Rastafari, And Marley" available at https://www.sbl-site.org/publications/article.aspx?articleId=496.

brutality. We can never be satisfied, as long as our bodies, heavy with the fatigue of travel, cannot gain lodging in the motels of the highways and the hotels of the cities. We cannot be satisfied as long as the Negro's basic mobility is from a smaller ghetto to a larger one. We can never be satisfied as long as our children are stripped of their selfhood and robbed of their dignity by signs stating "For Whites Only." We cannot be satisfied as long as a Negro in Mississippi cannot vote and a Negro in New York believes he has nothing for which to vote. No, no, we are not satisfied, and we will not be satisfied until justice rolls down like waters and righteousness like a mighty stream.

This last sentence references Amos 5:24: "But let justice well up as waters, and righteousness as a mighty stream."

Like Isaiah, from whom he also quoted so often, Martin Luther King Jr. spoke like a prophet to the people. He chastised them for their failings, placing them in the biblical context of sin and redemption.

He reminded them of their covenant and their moral destiny. In his last speech on April 6, 1968, before he was assassinated, he echoed Moses. We read in Deuteronomy 24:1–5:

Moses went up from the plains of Moab unto the mountain of Nebo, to the top of Pisgah, that is over against Jericho. And the Lord showed him all the land of Gilead, unto Dan; and all Naphtali, and the land of Ephraim, and Manasseh, and all the land of Judah, unto the utmost sea; and the south, and the plain of the valley of Jericho, the city of palm trees, unto Zoar. And the Lord said unto him: This is the land which I swore unto Abraham, unto Isaac, and unto Jacob, saying, I will give it unto thy seed: I have caused thee to see it with thine eyes, but thou shalt not go over thither. So Moses the servant of the Lord died there in the land of Moab, according to the word of the Lord.

Martin Luther King Jr. ended his last speech in Memphis, Tennessee, on a similar note. With death threats in the air, he said with staunch defiance:

Well, I don't know what will happen now. We've got some difficult days ahead. But it really doesn't matter with me now, because I've been to the mountaintop. And I don't mind. Like anybody, I would like to live a long life. Longevity has its place. But I'm not concerned about that now. I just want to do God's will. And He's allowed me to go up to the mountain. And I've looked over. And I've seen the Promised Land. I may not get there with you. But I want you to know tonight, that we, as a people, will get to the Promised Land! And so I'm happy tonight; I'm not worried about anything; I'm not fearing any man. Mine eyes have seen the glory of the coming of the Lord.

The United States has changed a lot since the constitutional crisis of the nineteenth century drove us to civil war. In significant ways, our public life is less laden with Hebraic symbols than it once was. But we believe that one cannot understand this country – its institutions, its culture, its way of balancing order and freedom, liberty and equality, centralized and federated power – without reference to the Hebraic sources that inspired its architects, founders, and public leaders. Although this source reader focuses on an earlier period of American history, some of the greatest figures of the twentieth and twenty-first centuries – including every American president up to this day – have relied on Hebrew Scripture to evoke the Hebraic mentality of American life. More often than Greek and Latin literature of classical antiquity, more often than modern political thinkers and legal theories, the Hebrew Bible and the tradition it engendered unites Americans across generations.

About the Editors

Rabbi Dr. Meir Y. Soloveichik is Director of the Zahava and Moshael Straus Center for Torah and Western Thought of Yeshiva University and Rabbi at Congregation Shearith Israel in Manhattan. He graduated summa cum laude from Yeshiva College, received his semikha from RIETS, and was a member of its Beren Kollel Elyon. In 2010, he received his doctorate in religion from Princeton University. Rabbi Soloveichik has lectured throughout the United States, in Europe, and in Israel to both Jewish and non-Jewish audiences on topics relating to Jewish theology, bioethics, wartime ethics, and Jewish-Christian relations. His essays on these subjects have appeared in the *Wall Street Journal, Commentary, First Things, Azure, Tradition,* and the *Torah U-Madda Journal.*

Dr. Matthew Holbreich is the Resident Scholar at the Zahava and Moshael Straus Center for Torah and Western Thought of Yeshiva University, where he teaches classes in the history of political thought, American political thought, and literature. He has published on Abraham Lincoln and the Hebrew Bible in *History of Political Thought,* and writes for the *Jewish Review of Books.* He received his PhD from University of Notre Dame, where he wrote on the perpetuation of democratic life in French political thought.

Dr. Jonathan Silver is a Senior Director at the Tikvah Fund, and Executive Director of its Jewish Leadership Conference. He was educated at Tufts University and the Hebrew University of Jerusalem, and holds a PhD from the Department of Government at Georgetown University.

Rabbi Dr. Stuart W. Halpern is Senior Advisor to the Provost of Yeshiva University and Senior Program Officer of the Zahava and Moshael Straus Center for Torah and Western Thought, and is responsible for developing and executing interdisciplinary educational and communal initiatives. During his thirteen years at Yeshiva University, Dr. Halpern has served in various capacities, including Chief of Staff to the President and as an Instructor in Bible. He has edited or co-edited sixteen books, including *Gleanings: Reflections on Ruth* and *Books of the People: Revisiting Classic Works of Jewish Thought* (both with Maggid Books and Yeshiva University Press), and has lectured in synagogues, Hillels, and adult Jewish educational settings across the US.